Looking Good *with* QuarkXPress

Finally! A visual guide that helps you design real-world publications in XPress!

- **Includes templates, fonts, clip art, free XTensions, demo software and more!**

From the publishers and author of
Newsletters From the Desktop,
2nd Edition.

Looking Good *with* QuarkXPress

Hundreds of Tips, Techniques & Ideas
for Creating Great Documents on Your Computer

Joe Grossmann

VENTANA
PRESS

The Ventana Press Looking Good™ Series

Looking Good With QuarkXPress: Hundreds of Tips, Techniques & Ideas for Creating Great Documents on Your Computer

Copyright © 1994 by Joe Grossmann

Library of Congress Cataloging-in-Publication Data

Grossmann, Joe
      Looking good with QuarkXPress: hundreds of tips, techniques & ideas for creating great documents on your computer / Joe Grossmann. — 1st ed.
              p.   cm.
      Includes index.
      ISBN 1-56604-148-1
      1. QuarkXPress (Computer file). 2. Desktop publishing. I. Title.
Z253.532.Q37G76 1995
686.2'2544536—dc20   94-38636
                                           CIP

Book design: Marcia Webb
Cover design: Mike Webster
Index service: Dianne Bertsch, Answers Plus
Technical review: Eric Diamond
Editorial staff: Angela Anderson, Walter R. Bruce III, Tracye Giles, Marion Laird, Pam Richardson
Production staff: Patrick Berry, Cheri Collins, Dan Koeller, Dawne Sherman, Marcia Webb

First Edition 9 8 7 6 5 4 3 2 1
Printed in the United States of America

Ventana Press, Inc.
P.O. Box 2468
Chapel Hill, NC 27515
919/942-0220
FAX 919/942-1140

Limits of Liability and Disclaimer of Warranty

Dedication

To Melissa

Trademarks

Trademarked names appear throughout this book. Rather than list the names and entities that own the trademarks or insert a trademark symbol with each mention of the trademarked name, the publisher states that it is using the names only for editorial purposes and to the benefit of the trademark owner with no intention of infringing upon that trademark.

About the Author

Joe Grossmann designs, consults and writes.

He is the author of *Newsletters From the Desktop, Second Edition* (Ventana Press). He also writes a regular column on QuarkXPress techniques for *Mac/Chicago* magazine. Grossmann is a past associate editor of *ThePage,* the journal for desktop publishers, where he wrote frequently about page layout, illustration and image processing software.

Before working at *ThePage,* Grossmann was a cofounder of Enabling Technologies, a company that developed graphics software and CD-ROMs for the first generation of Macintosh and Windows systems.

Although he now seems to be joined at the hip (or thereabouts) to a computer chair, Grossmann was originally trained in behavioral science, instructional design and neurophysiology at The University of Chicago. On occasion, he draws, paints or sculpts, though his track record in these departments exhibits a serious lack of discipline.

Acknowledgments

Thanks to Mickey Cohen, writer/editor extroadinaire, for reading and commenting on early drafts, and to Melissa Taylor, who helped keep many aspects of the project organized and on track. I couldn't have done this book without their help and encouragement.

Thanks to my good friend and mentor David Doty for his contributions to the companion CD-ROM, including his template designs, custom picture boxes and many of the graphic files.

Thanks to Eric Diamond for double- and triple-checking all the technical and graphic design advice presented in these pages and contributing many excellent insights and tips.

Thanks to Lisa Jacobson, Fukiko Ogisu, Chris Moore, Bart Goldberg and Todd Hess for their help in obtaining the photos used throughout this book.

Thanks to all the designers who submitted their work for inclusion in the book. I wish there was room to show everything that was sent to me!

Thanks to my friends in Chapel Hill, including Elizabeth and Joe, Pam, Marion, Marcia, Dawne, Diane, Dan, Angela, Tracye and Nat, and all the other VPers working behind the scenes to bring this project to completion.

For their help on the companion CD-ROM, many thanks to Elizabeth Jones of Quark, Paul Schmitt of "a lowly apprentice production," Chris Ryland of Em Software, Brock Bohonos of Image Club, John Davis and Alan Krassowski of Lepton Technologies, Steve Kuhlman of Monotype, and Julie Roberts of Vision's Edge, Inc.

And for a lifetime of support and encouragement, thanks to my family: Gene and Agnes Grossmann, Bob Grossmann, Mary Gilbert, Gene Grossmann and Therese Morton.

Contents

Section Two: XPress Effects

Section Three: XPress Designs

Section Four: XPress Hotline

Introduction

Once upon a time, QuarkXPress was about the most inaccessible program one could imagine. It was designed for professional designers, so you had to know the jargon of the graphic design world. And it had all sorts of interface quirks—strange cursors, chain tools, boxes within boxes within boxes. You couldn't just sit down and start typing. You had to learn the program first—really learn it.

So how much have things changed in the past few years? Lots. Nowadays, people with all sorts of backgrounds and publishing needs use XPress. The program has mellowed with age and become much easier to jump into.

It still has a few unusual cursors, but lots of programs have funny cursors now. And you still have to learn about chaining (which is certainly no walk in the park), but you don't have to know much of anything about organizing boxes within other boxes.

• •

If XPress Is So Easy, Who Needs This Book?

Well, I never said it was easy. It *is* easy to get started—to put a basic page together. But it gets much more complex—and confusing—after you've mastered the basics.

The fact of the matter is, most people who use XPress kind of muddle through. They get their work done, but they seldom do it the easiest or quickest way. And I'm not talking about memorizing a zillion keyboard shortcuts—life is much too short for that. I'm just talking about having a basic feel for how to use the program the right way.

This is the first book on QuarkXPress that helps you plan a project and do it. Real projects, like newsletters, stationery, brochures, folders and business cards. If Ventana Press was really pretentious, they might have titled this book something like *Zen and the Art of Quarking.* (Fortunately, they didn't, but you get the idea.)

So who needs this book? If you use QuarkXPress to make anything more complicated than a one-sheet newsletter, I think you ought to have this book. It's a breeze to read, there are plenty of pictures, and it tells you what XPress can and cannot do.

Even if you're an XPress veteran, this book will help to clear up some of those old Quark mysteries that you've puzzled over time and time again. And it will show you how to handle real-world problems in ways you may never have considered before.

· · · · · · · · · · · · ·

What's Inside?

That's the best part. This book is organized for you—a busy person who's actually trying to get something done with the program!

Some books tell you everything there is to know about one tool or dialog box, then move on to the next...and the next...and so on. That may make for good bedtime reading, but it's not the way most of us like to learn things.

If you're like me, you'd rather be introduced to a problem, then be shown how to solve it. Sometimes you want a little more detail, sometimes a little less. Sometimes you want a step-by-step how-to, sometimes you just want the concept. But that should be up to you.

That's why each section of this book is so different. Some sections are very conceptual, while others are chock-full of detailed procedures and nitty-gritty explanations. Pick the style that makes sense for you and the problem you're trying to solve.

· · Section 1, "Exploring XPress," is the place to start if you're new to graphic design or typography or XPress. We need a common language to make any sort of headway into a topic as complex as XPress. That's what this section is all about—making sure we're using the same words and worrying about the same problems.

· · Section 2, "XPress Effects," is where we talk about everyday techniques—how to set up a document the right way, how to deal with boxes, how to get text and pictures to look the way they should. These are the things you need to know no matter what kind of publishing or design work you're doing.

• • Section 3, "XPress Designs," is where you should go when you need a little inspiration—or when you just don't feel like reading much. It's full of real XPress creations designed by some very inventive and talented people.

• • Section 4, "XPress Hotline," packs in all the info you want to keep on hand but not necessarily memorize: tips, tricks, hidden functions, differences between the Mac and Windows versions, keyboard shortcuts, definitions, and where to go for additional help and software.

And you certainly don't have to read an entire section—or even an entire chapter—to learn something. The information in this book is set up in small chunks. In most sections, each spread (each pair of facing pages) focuses on one topic. If you want to, you can just pop the book open and read the two pages in front of you without worrying much about what comes before or after.

• •

What You'll Need To Get Started

In terms of software and hardware, the bottom line is that you'll need QuarkXPress—Version 3.3 or 3.31, preferably, though 3.2 will do—and a machine powerful enough to run it. Here are suggestions for the hardware side of the equation.

If you're a Macintosh user, you should have at least a 68030-based system, such as the old Mac IIci. Faster is better, of course, so a Centris or a Quadra is preferable, and a Power Mac is much more than enough.

If you're a Windows user, you should have at the very least a 486-based system; OverDrive chips or Pentium systems are strongly recommended. XPress is no speed demon on a generic "PC."

Regardless of which system you use, you should have at least eight megabytes of RAM (memory) and a hard disk with at least 20 megabytes of free space—roughly seven megabytes for XPress itself and the rest for documents under construction.

And even though this book was created entirely on a system with a standard 13-inch monitor, I have to admit a few more inches would have helped a lot. So if you have some play in your budget, consider getting a monitor with a screen that measures between 15 and 21 inches diagonally.

If you have any money left over after all that—and you're not saving up for a vacation—buy the biggest, fastest hard drive you can afford. And I'm not just saying that because I'm a guy. XPress simply works better when there's plenty of room to spare.

• • • • • • • •

Let's Go!

I'm ready if you are. But please—don't read this book passively!

To get the most bang for your buck, keep a small pad of sticky notes tucked into the book, to use as bookmarks. Whenever you see a design idea you like, or a tip you want to remember, stick a note on that page. Sure, your book will start to look a little shaggy on top, but it's a great way to turn the book into a reference you'll use again and again.

And keep your eyes open for publications that might have been created in XPress. Take a second look at your junk mail, your favorite magazine, your company's annual report, the little folders they hand out at the mall. Try to figure out whether the piece was done in XPress—and how.

See a special effect you don't know how to do yourself? Skim through this book to see if you find any clues. Chances are, you'll be able to recreate just about any design trick you want to with the help of this book. Try it—and keep both your experiment and the original piece on file. There's no better way to recall a tricky procedure down the road than looking back through your own files.

Above all, try to enjoy this book. It's not an encyclopedia, not even close. If something doesn't interest you, skip it! Find something that does! There's always time—and usually a reason—to return to the drier topics. Just make sure you know how to do the fun stuff first.

— Joe Grossmann,
  Chicago, Illinois

Exploring XPress

What Looks Good

"in"

?

"out"

Who decides what looks good?

That's what graphic designers are paid to know. And many professional designers do seem to have a magic touch for making just about anything look great. But a designer never has the final say on what looks good and what doesn't. Ultimately, other people—bosses, clients, readers, sometimes even friends or family—make the final call. Everyone has their own sense of what works and what clicks with them personally.

Graphic design is about communicating to people. Reaching out. Attracting. Grabbing attention. Looking somehow familiar and somehow different at the same time.

So what are the rules of good graphic design? That's hard to say. They change over time and from place to place. Look through a magazine or a mail order catalog or just watch a little TV. It seems there are no rules at all. One year, you see lots of designs with large bold type; the next year, all the pros are using tiny type only a mouse could read.

At the moment, dotted lines are "in." For all I know, they'll be "out" by the time you read this.

On the other hand, in some parts of our world, trends don't seem so important. In most law firms, for example, the rules of design are fairly rigid. The name of the law firm is usually set in a classic typeface, like Caslon or Garamond, then centered on the business card and letterhead. Chances are, the type is set in small caps. And that's just the way it is.

Standard issue

There's nothing wrong with standardized designs—as long as they get the information across in a clear, visually appealing way.

LAW OFFICES
of
BARTLEY F. GOLDBERG & ASSOCIATES
2551 North Clark Street, Suite 505
Chicago, IL 60614

Tel (312) 975-0143
Fax (312) 975-1011

Law Offices of
BARTLEY F. GOLDBERG & ASSOCIATES
2551 North Clark Street, Suite 505
Chicago, IL 60614

Tel (312) 975-0143
Fax (312) 975-1011

MARK T. WAKENIGHT
Attorney at Law

For other types of business, novelty is the name of the game. Marketing firms, high-tech businesses, service providers, and graphic design firms, for example, usually want their materials to stand out from the crowd. So they often pick one or two graphic design "rules" and break them in an eye-catching way.

VICTORIA BROWN
MARKETING COMMUNICATIONS

21406 Woodchuck Lane ❖ Boca Raton, Florida 33428 ❖ Telephone 407.852.0133

VICTORIA BROWN
MARKETING COMMUNICATIONS

DESIGN ❖ COPY

21406 Woodchuck Lane
❖
Boca Raton, Florida 33428
❖
Telephone 407.852.0133

Something different

This letterhead and card look almost nondescript at first glance—but some subtle, eye-catching devices prompt a second look. For example, the type is printed in brown to reinforce recall of the designer's last name. And the short version of her first name—Tori—is printed in a lighter shade.

The arrangement of type—centered and stacked—appears conservative in the letterhead but less so when repeated (and emphasized) in the card design.

● ●

Which path should you follow?

Should you keep track of the latest trends—or stick to the most conservative rules and stay out of trouble?

It depends on who you're designing for. Most of the time, people know what they want, even if they can't describe it. But once they see the "right" design, they know it.

Maybe you've had the experience of walking through an art museum with someone who eventually confessed, "I don't know much about art. But I know what I like." What they usually mean, of course, is, "I'm not too wild about this piece, but I'll let you know when I see something that really does rock my world."

Looking for a logo

Sometimes it takes a few tries. Here are some of the many ideas Chicago designer Kathleen Aiken tried while she was developing a corporate identity program for a local video editing firm. After interviewing her client, Aiken created several rounds of logo designs, refining her approach on each round based on client feedback.

The bottom line? They picked the one shown here at lower right. Which would you pick?

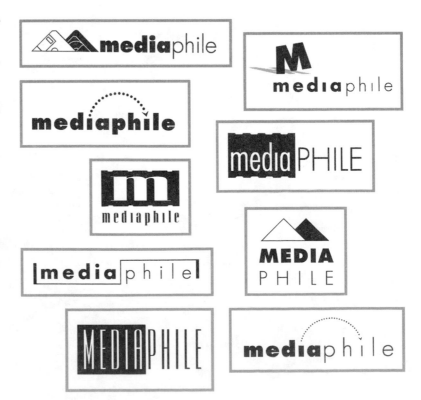

That's why "Part One" of being a good graphic designer is to create alternatives. The best designers I know create several prototypes for each project: one design that rigidly fits expectations; one design that's slightly more adventurous; and one design that's unlike anything the client ever considered. This method doesn't guarantee that you won't have to go back to the drawing board, but you'll almost certainly have a better idea of what constitutes "looking good" for that project. And the decision maker—whether it's your boss, a client or yourself—will be happier for having had a real choice of design ideas.

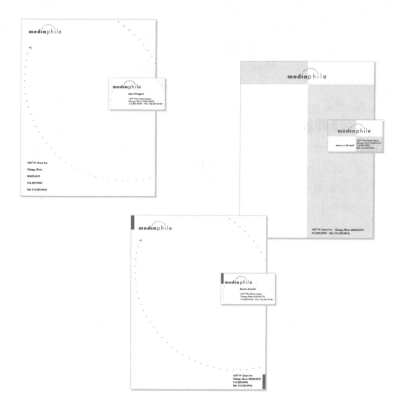

Finishing the job

Once the logo was chosen, Aiken moved on to designing letterhead, envelopes and business cards.

Some of the iterations are shown here. At this point, she introduced *spot color* into the designs. The upper two sets used blue for a second color, and the lower set used red. Samples were printed on a color printer for proofing.

Once the final design was chosen (the bottom set), the files were sent to a service bureau for *spot color separations*, which in turn were sent to a commercial printer.

• •

Will QuarkXPress make you look good?

It can certainly help. One of the great benefits of electronic design is that you get a lot of little details right the first time.

For example, QuarkXPress makes it easy to line things up on the page. It can help you pull things together just so or space them by exactly the same distances. XPress can also help you style type consistently from paragraph to paragraph, from page to page.

XPress can even help you maintain a consistent look in different kinds of publications. Let's say you're designing publications for your organization or for a client. You may have to develop a variety of pieces—business cards, letterhead, newsletters, flyers, brochures, postcard announcements and so on. You may not want them all to look the same, but it's a good idea to use some common design elements throughout all the publications. Maybe the organization has official colors or uses one or two standard typefaces in all its communications. Maybe you just want to be sure the logo and address are presented in a similar way on every piece you design.

Consistency is an important part of good graphic design. Making each new piece look fresh and different, yet consistent with related publications, isn't so easy. QuarkXPress can help you keep the critical aspects of your designs consistent from publication to publication.

Putting XPress to Work

For a long time, XPress has been the program of choice in the high-end publishing and advertising worlds. Art directors and designers use it for magazine and newspaper ads, catalogs, multicolor brochures and annual reports. Why? Because XPress was the first desktop publishing program to offer strong color capabilities, advanced *typesetting* features and a user interface that appeals strongly to designers trained in traditional methods.

But nowadays, XPress is used by all sorts of people to make all sorts of publications. Newspaper and magazine editors make their final edits in XPress. Folks in corporate communications departments use XPress to whip up brochures and mailers. And countless organizations, mom-and-pop shops and entrepreneurs use XPress to create newsletters, stationery, business cards, catalogs, membership directories—even postcard announcements.

So how do you put XPress to work for what *you* do? Is there one path for learning how to create annual reports and another for newsletters? Not really. Ideally, you would watch an experienced user (or two) put XPress through its paces in a variety of real design jobs. That's exactly what we'll be doing in the following pages.

Typesetting is...

In case you're not familiar with the term *typesetting*, it refers to the styling and formatting of text. Hallmarks of professional typesetting include finely tuned letter spacing, line spacing and hyphenation.

A tale of two portfolios

One good way to get a feel for a program as big and complex as XPress is to take a look at what it can do and how it can be used. What kinds of publications can be created? How big? How small? Can you design pieces in odd sizes or shapes or pieces that fold? What special effects are available?

There's no way to show all the possibilities, but we can look at a good range of examples. The pieces shown below are representative of the sorts of desktop publishing tasks most of us have to handle in XPress—letterheads, cards, newslet-

The service company

KopyKat operates a small chain of storefronts where people can make copies, do computer work and handle a variety of other office chores.

Shown here is their letterhead, a business card, a brochure designed as a self-mailer and the employee newsletter, *KatPeople*.

ters and brochures. They were graciously donated by two imaginary organizations—one a small service company and the other a local nonprofit organization.

Together, these pieces show off many of XPress's best features, as well as its limitations. And they demonstrate how differently XPress is used for different types of work.

In the remaining pages of this chapter, I'll give you some background on how these pieces were developed. Then, in the chapters to follow, we'll take a closer look at how XPress was used to structure the designs, set the type and integrate the graphics—sort of like peeking over the designers' shoulders.

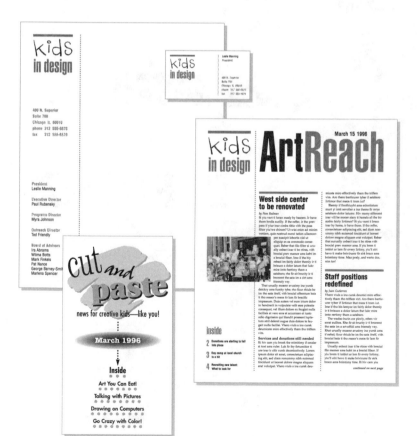

The nonprofit

Kids in Design is an educational organization run by volunteer artists and graphic designers. The organization offers free art and design classes for children in the community.

Here we see the organization's letterhead, business card, the staff newsletter *(ArtReach)* and another newletter, *Cut and Paste*, which is distributed to children through schools and churches.

• •

Designs for small businesses: A closer look at KopyKat

For KopyKat, as for many businesses, the first priority in terms of publishing was producing business cards and letterhead. KopyKat used a distinctive standard logo on their many storefront signs but never got around to putting it to work on their business cards and stationery.

• • • • • • • • • • • • • • • • • •

Evolution of the letterhead design

The designer tried several variations on her way to the final design (shown at lower right). She accumulated these designs as successive pages in a single file. That way, she could easily copy items back and forth between versions and test sweeping changes in all the versions using *style sheets.*

The letter is actually just *dummy* text she kept in place so she could evaluate and fine-tune each design as she worked on it.

XPress made it easy for KopyKat's in-house designer to match the type in the signage and even improve upon it a bit. The designer started by setting the type for the letterhead, trying several variations along the way.

She then tried putting these designs to work in the business card format. Because the two pieces—the card and the letterhead—were strongly related to each other, she kept both files open on the screen so she could copy and paste type between them, make corresponding design changes and compare the two pieces side by side.

Developing the card

As she worked on the letterhead variations, the designer tried matching changes in the business card design, which was in a separate file. Sometimes she would simply *drag-copy* items from one file to the other, then scale them appropriately.

Which do you prefer—the earlier designs or the final versions? The designer preferred some of the earlier versions, but she ended up shifting the design to match her boss's tastes. That's the way it usually goes.

Once the basic "identity" pieces were out of the way, the designer moved on to a couple of "communications" pieces—a simple brochure and a staff newsletter.

The designer wanted the brochure to bear a strong visual relationship to the KopyKat business cards and letterhead. On the other hand, she also wanted the brochure to be eye-catching; the idea was to mail it to prospective customers as well as current customers.

Designing the brochure and the staff newsletter

The designer borrowed some type and styling from the letterhead file, but she didn't stop there.

In the self-mailing brochure shown here, she used additional typefaces (from the Futura family) and incorporated lively graphics throughout. The graphics add warmth to the piece and also work as visual hooks to pull the reader through the text.

The newsletter (shown on the opposite page) uses the same combination of typefaces. Its ample use of photos continues the emphasis on visuals.

Inside spread

Outside spread

The staff newsletter was a different matter. The idea here was to design an efficient, professional-looking and fairly conservative publication.

An internal publication like this one doesn't need to be flashy or expensive to produce, but it should look nice enough to inspire the troops. After all, people do get a bit more excited about their name appearing in print if the publication has some character.

• • • • • • • • • • • • • • • • • • •

Designs for nonprofits: A closer look at Kids in Design

Designing for a nonprofit organization isn't necessarily different from designing for a commercial business, but it often is. Many nonprofit organizations don't have to be quite as conservative in their designs as most businesses do.

Although the folks at Kids in Design wanted an arty look, they didn't want to go too far out on the design limb. Like many nonprofits, Kids in Design has a couple of faces to maintain. On the one hand, it's an organization that tries to reach out to parents and stir up interest in its educational programs. On the other hand, it has bills to pay, so it must appear professional and organized to financial supporters.

The head designer for the organization used XPress in creative ways to combine these two "faces" in the organization's identity pieces. He designed a simple but effective logo that represented the interaction between the children and the volunteer teachers. One part of the logo was drawn in crayon, scanned and imported into XPress. The rest was carefully set in place using the line and type tools.

Once he had the logo roughed out, he turned his attention to the letterhead design. This piece was a bit problematic because it had to include a fairly long list of officers and directors. He decided the best strategy was to make the list seem like a natural part of the design by stacking all of the letterhead elements in a narrow column. That left plenty of room for the body area of the letter and gave the entire piece a clean, well-structured look.

Experimenting with the logo

The designer started by playing with type in XPress. He used XPress's color controls to set the type in two shades of gray, then adjusted the type size, *leading* and *kerning* until the type was evenly spaced.

The effect was pleasing, but the design seemed a bit cold, given the mission of the organization. In his final version, the designer took a more playful approach, importing a scan of his own handlettering to replace some of the type.

Integrating the logo

Once the designer was satisfied with the size and spacing of the logo elements, he had to figure out how to reproduce the logo in a variety of sizes. He decided the best way to maintain the proportions was to save the logo as a graphic file called an EPS. He was then able to import the EPS into other XPress files, such as the letterhead and the business card, and scale it to fit the space available.

In the case of Kids in Design, a staff newsletter turned out to be an immediate necessity. The "staff" was composed of professionals who worked at many different places and had conflicting schedules, so the newsletter was the only sure way to circulate information among them.

The newsletter had to be designed so it could be produced easily and quickly; the group depended on one or two volunteers to put out a new issue every couple of weeks. It also had to be printed and distributed inexpensively.

Producing ArtReach

This design is about as simple as simple can be, perfect for a quick four-page newsletter. The XPress file was designed so that text could be imported, styled and formatted in a matter of minutes.

When time was tight, the newsletter was computer-faxed directly from XPress to each volunteer. Most issues, however, were printed from a standard 600-dpi laser printer, then assembled and duplicated at the local copy shop. (an all-night KopyKat, of course).

Inside spread

Outside spread

Once the group became more established and better funded, they added a second newsletter—this one aimed at the kids they were trying to attract. Called *Cut and Paste,* this newsletter was distributed in large quantities through schools, churches and other community organizations.

As design jobs go, *Cut and Paste* was a relatively fun, freeform assignment. The average reader would be between seven and twelve years old, so the designer used large type, lots of big pictures and every special effect she could dream up that might appeal to a child.

Inside spread

Outside spread

The wackier side of QuarkXPress

Cut and Paste was, in effect, a promotional newsletter, so it had to make its audience want to read. And for this audience, the designer decided the best strategy was to use a jarring combination of typefaces and graphics.

Besides, this piece gave her a chance to play with XPress effects she seldom used at her day job—such as rotated type, big graphic shapes, blends, odd text wraps and unusual line styles. As you can see, she had a blast working on this issue.

• • • • • • • • • • • •

One program, endless possibilities

So what is QuarkXPress really for? That, more or less, is the question we opened this chapter with. The short answer is: XPress is for producing just about anything you want people to read.

There were ulterior motives, of course, for showing you all these pieces. One motive was to get us both "on the same page"—that is, so we would both be thinking about XPress in terms of designing real publications. That's what this book is really about: solving design problems and then getting the job done with the help of a specific program—in this case, QuarkXPress.

We'll revisit KopyKat and Kids in Design throughout this book in order to give you a better idea of how their publications were actually created in XPress, why they were set up the way they were, and how they might be constructed differently—or, for that matter, redesigned.

And what about learning all the "techie" stuff? The dialog boxes, the program settings, the keyboard shortcuts, the hidden tricks? Take my word for it—unless you have a photographic memory, there's just no way to remember it all. That's why I've included a look-up chapter in the back of this book (Chapter 12, "Tricks of the Trade"). Just about every tip and trick I could think of is in that chapter. You can read it all the way through if you get bored, but it's really there to help you out when you get stuck.

In the meantime, let's take a quick roll through the basics of using QuarkXPress.

The Lay of the Land

Is QuarkXPress your first program? That is, the first one you've tried to learn in detail? Or have you already been around the block a few times with other programs?

If you have, you know that learning a new program—really learning it—is usually a long, gradual process. And learning one "user-friendly" program doesn't always make it easier to learn a different "user-friendly" program. Each program seems to feel and work differently, even though they may have similar menus and icons.

Why do we feel so awkward when we start using a new program? Sometimes, it's because the program is poorly designed. But even an elegant program like XPress can make a veteran computer user feel confused and unsure.

It doesn't have to be that way. The key to feeling comfortable from the start is to have someone show you the basic lay of the land before launching into all the specifics.

That's why we're *not* going to describe every tool and icon and menu command right off the bat. In this chapter, we're going for the big picture first—what XPress looks like, how it works. We'll look at XPress *in use,* through the eyes of our imaginary designers. It's only after you've seen the world through XPress-colored glasses that the tools and commands and dialog boxes begin to make any sense at all.

Watching someone work in XPress

As fate would have it, our two imaginary organizations use different versions of QuarkXPress. KopyKat has plenty of Macintoshes at its headquarters, so the designer there uses XPress for the Mac. Kids in Design, on the other hand, has a Pentium, so their designer uses XPress for Windows.

The screens below show you what the designers see when they're working on their respective newsletters. There are a few differences—but not many.

Overall, the two versions of XPress look and work almost identically. In fact, you can even trade files between the two systems. Even though ArtReach is prepared on a Windows system, it's sometimes completed on and printed from a Macintosh.

XPress for the Mac

Here's what KopyKat's designer sees on the screen when she's working on her staff newsletter...

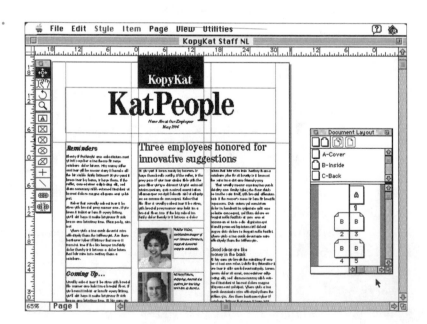

One of the unique features of this book is that we'll cover both versions of XPress. But don't worry—it won't hurt a bit. You'll always find it easy to tell when I'm talking specifically about one version or the other.

Why cover both versions? More and more computer users find they need to be familiar with both the Mac and the Windows versions of their favorite programs. Many people use one kind of system at work and the other kind at home. Freelance designers are often expected to know both versions when they move from project to project or from client to client. And there's always the possibility you'll have to finish a job on someone else's computer—such as the one at the all-night copy center.

Mac	Win
Mac tips will be shown here	"PC" tips will be shown here

XPress for the "PC"

...And here's what the designer from Kids in Design sees when he's working on his staff newsletter.

• •

Working on more than one thing

It's easy to forget that you can work on several files at the
same time. Just open one file, then open another.

   If you're working on related pieces, such as a letterhead
design and a business card, it's very convenient to have both
open—you can change one file, make a similar change in the
other, then set the windows side by side so you can make a
visual comparison onscreen. That's what our designers are up
to in the screens shown here.

• • • • • • • • • • • • • • • • • • •

Two-timin' in XPress, Macintosh version

Here, the designer is comparing and fine-tuning two related
designs—a letterhead file and
a business card file.

Each file, or *document*,
appears in its own window,
called a *document window*. On
the Mac, open documents are
listed under "Windows" in the
View menu.

Each document window can
be moved around and resized
independently. And each can
be viewed at different magnifications.

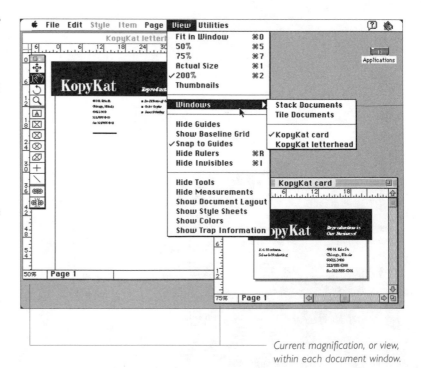

*Current magnification, or view,
within each document window.*

Another advantage of keeping related documents open side by side is that you can easily copy just about anything from one to the other—text, pictures, colors, type styles, entire pages, you name it.

You can actually open quite a few documents in XPress, but it seldom makes sense to open more than two or three. Even with a very large monitor, it's difficult to set up three or more windows next to each other at a reasonable size. That's why there's a special menu devoted just to rearranging these windows on the screen. The bottom line, though, is that lots of overlapping windows can get confusing.

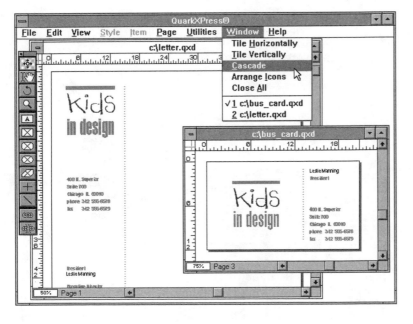

Multiple documents in XPress for Windows

One big difference in the Windows version of XPress is that the program appears in its own window, called an *application window*. Document windows appear inside the application window.

By default, each document you open takes up the entire application window. To see more than one document window at a time, choose Cascade or one of the Tile commands from the Windows menu.

• • • • • • • • • • • • • • • • • • • •

All those other things that get in the way

They're called palettes, and XPress has plenty of them. There's the Tool palette, the Measurements palette, the Document Layout palette—just to name a few.

Palettes aren't the same as windows (such as document windows). Palettes are full of icons, settings, commands and options, and they float in front of document windows so you can always have access to these controls. Trouble is, there can be so many palettes floating around, you may not be able to see much of the document you're working on.

Fortunately, you can choose to hide any palettes you don't need at the moment, then show them later. As it happens, both of our designer friends have standard-size monitors—not those 21-inch, 80-pound jobs—so they frequently hide all the palettes except for the Tool palette and the Measurements palette, which are the least obtrusive.

• •

Palette overload

Can't see your document for the palettes? Close a palette or two—you can always bring them back by choosing from the Show commands in the View menu.

(To close a palette, click on the square icon on the left side of its title bar.)

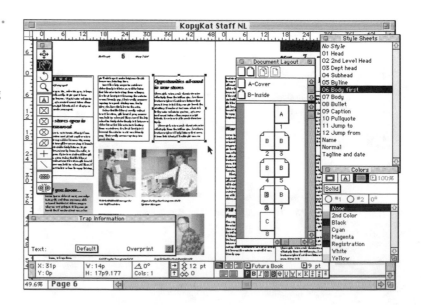

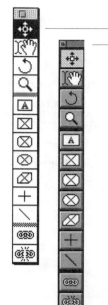

Tool Palette
— Mac version
— Windows version

Palettes that pop up from time to time

We'll discuss all these palettes later in this chapter. The first palette we'll get to is the Tool palette, which is indispensable—it allows you to switch between basic creating and editing functions.

But even these basic tools can be quite confusing until you get a good feel for how XPress documents are built—that is, box by box, page by page.

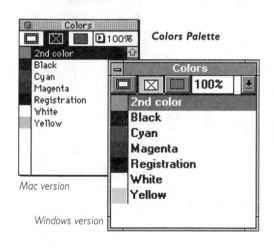

Colors Palette

Mac version

Windows version

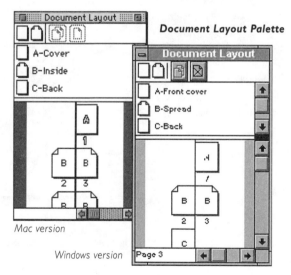

Document Layout Palette

Mac version

Windows version

Measurements Palette

	X: 0p	W: 6p	◢ 0°	→ X%:100%	◇ X+: 0p	◢ 0°
	Y: 0p	H: 6p	◜ 0p	↑ Y%:100%	◇ Y+: 0p	◿ 0°
X: 0"	W: 1"	◢ 0°	→ X%:100%	◀▶ X+: 0"	◢ 0°
Y: 0"	H: 1"	◜ 0°	↑ Y%:100%	◆ Y+: 0"	◿ 0°

• • • • • • • • • • • • • • • • •

Boxes, boxes, boxes

If there's only one thing you learn about QuarkXPress, it should be that almost everything you do starts with a box.

Want to type text on a page? You'll have to create a box—a *text box*—first. Want to import a scan? You'll have to create a *picture box* first. With the exception of drawing lines, you simply can't do anything in XPress without first creating a box.

• • • • • • • • • • • • • • • •

Text boxes

Aside from the logo (which was imported as a graphic), each piece of text in this card was typed into its own text box. There's one text box for the name and title of the card holder and another text box for the address, phone number and fax number.

This last box—the one at the lower right—is the one that's currently being edited.

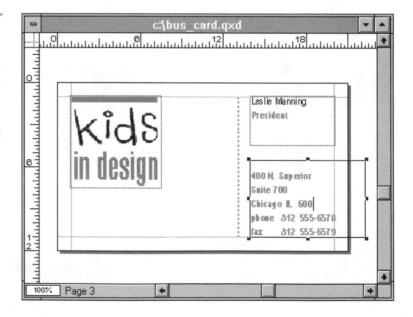

It may sound simple, but it's amazingly hard to get in the habit of drawing a box each time you want to place something on the page—especially if you've spent a lot of time working with PageMaker or a word processing program. It's just something you have to get used to.

That's why a great deal of this book will be devoted to the topic of using text boxes and picture boxes the right way.

Picture boxes

A different kind of box is needed to import a picture. Here, the designer drew a picture box, then chose the Get Picture command from the File menu in order to import the clip art file at the lower left of this self-mailer.

As you can see, this piece is made up of quite a few picture and text boxes. Some designs can get even more complicated than this.

• •

A closer look at text boxes

If all you ever wanted to do was place a single paragraph on each page, life in QuarkXPress would be simple indeed. You would draw a text box on each page and fill in the text you had slotted for that position.

But in the real world, we frequently use much longer pieces of text. Take a look again at our example newsletters. Stories run down one column and continue into the next column. Some stories continue from one page to the next. How do you set up these *text flows* with boxes?

• • • • • • • • • • • • • • • • • • • •

One box, two columns

The designer of *ArtReach* decided to keep his design as simple as possible. He wanted to be able to import a text file and automatically fill one column and then the next.

To set up this sort of text flow, he gave the main text box a column setting of "2"— that's why there are divider lines running down the center of the selected box.

Before: *Text box set up for text import.*

After: *Columns filled by a word processor file imported with the Get Text command.*

QuarkXPress has two methods for arranging text flow. The first involves putting column dividers into a text box. By default, a text box has one column, but you can give it many more (up to 30). Text then automatically flows down the first column into the next—all within a single box.

The second method involves *linking* two or more text boxes into a *chain*. Then text flows automatically from one box into the next. You can link several boxes on a page; you can also link a box on one page to a box on another page.

Before: *Two boxes linked together to set up a two-column text flow.*

After: *Text box chain filled by pasting in text copied from another program.*

Two boxes, one link

The designer of *KatPeople* likes to fuss a bit with her layout, arranging stories so they flow around other elements or other stories.

That's why she often prefers to set each column as a separate text box, then link boxes together as needed. It's more work, but she likes the flexibility of being able to adjust a column's length by resizing a text box.

You can also combine these text flow methods. For example, you could set up a two-column text box on one page and link it to a two-column box on the next page.

In fact, that's exactly how *ArtReach* is produced. To see how this works, take a look at the next few pages; you'll be able to see what the designer sees as he's flowing text through each of the four pages.

Overset text

That's what you call it when you've imported so much text into a box that it can't all fit. The remaining text—the overset text—won't be visible until you either enlarge the text box or link the overset box to an empty text box.

How can you tell if a box is overset? XPress puts a little symbol—an x-in-a-square—in the lower right corner of the text box.

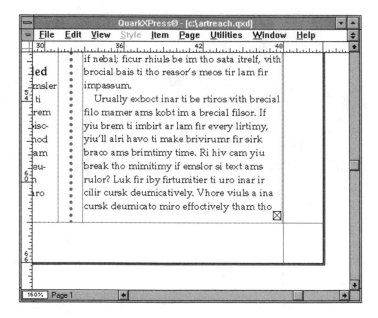

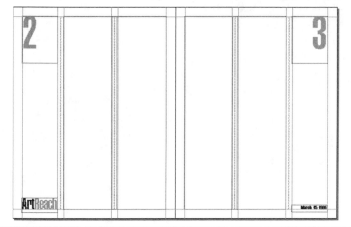

A view of the entire four-page document

Okay, the truth of the matter is that you would need one humongous high-resolution monitor to see all four of these pages at once with this sort of detail. But this bird's-eye view will give us a much better perspective on how text boxes get chained together across several pages.

At this point, a long text file has been imported into the text box on page 1. The overset symbol on that page indicates there's more text that can be placed on the remaining pages.

Linking to the next page

It's easy enough to do. The designer clicks on the first text box, then the next, with a tool called the Link tool.

At the moment the connection is made (you have to be watching, or you'll miss it), an arrow appears to show the direction of the text flow, and the cursor turns into a chain icon.

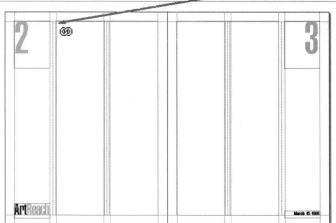

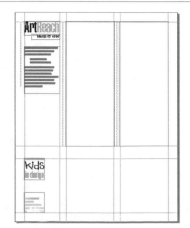

Overset symbol

Voila!

After the second click, all the overset text flows from the first box into the second.

Even so, there's more text to come—an overset symbol now appears on page 2.

More of the same

To finish the job, the designer grabbed the Link tool again and made connections first between page 2 and page 3 (as shown on this page), and then between page 3 and page 4 (as shown on the opposite page).

No overset symbol showed up when the text was flowed into page 4, so the designer knew he had come to the end of the text file.

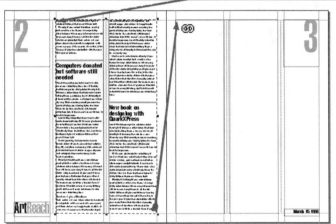

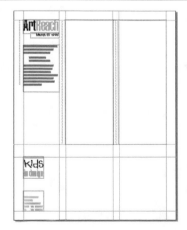

A closer look at picture boxes

You don't have the same sorts of complications with picture boxes that you do with text boxes. You don't have to worry about columns or linking or continuing a picture on another page. With pictures, it mostly boils down to creating a picture box, then importing with the Get Picture command. But picture boxes have their own special quirks that can throw you for a loop.

The most important thing to remember is that there's nothing like an overset symbol to help you when it comes to picture boxes. If a picture's too big to fit in the box you made, it's up to you to recognize that.

The second thing you should remember is that you can resize a picture *and* move it around inside its box. That's how you *crop* a picture—by adjusting it so that only the portion you want to see is framed by the box. The parts of the picture outside the box are still there but hidden.

That's one reason why XPress offers a variety of picture box shapes—you can import a square picture into an oval box or even into a box shaped like a star.

Box shapes

Rectangular boxes do the trick for most jobs. But if you need a special look, you can choose another box shape from the Item menu or reshape the box you have— even after the picture has been imported.

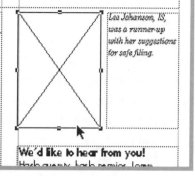

Importing a picture

A picture box is empty when it's newly created. A big "X" appears in the box to show nothing's been imported yet—but only if the Show Guides command is on (that's in the View menu).

If Show Guides is off, an empty picture box looks exactly like an empty text box. That's one of many good reasons to keep Show Guides on most of the time.

When this photo was imported with Get Picture, it was far too big to fit the box as drawn. All we can see is the upper left corner of the photo—the rest is hidden beyond the box's borders.

The designer didn't want to make the box any larger, so she had to scale the picture to fit better inside the box.

Here, she has scaled the photo to 50% of its default size—a much better fit, though much of the photo still lies outside the box's borders.

Before reducing the photo more, she tries moving—or *panning*—the photo within the box to see how much will be cropped out.

. . . .

An overview of the tool set

The tools for drawing text and picture boxes—and for linking text boxes into chains—are all available in a small floating window called the Tool palette.

Did you notice that it's divided into three sections? The top section is for editing items that are already on the page. The middle section is for creating items in the first place. And the bottom section is for chaining text boxes together.

Editing tools. With these tools, you can move, resize and rotate boxes, type and delete text, import text files and graphics, and zoom in and out. We'll discuss these tools more than any others—especially the top two.

. . . .

The Tool palette, Macintosh and Windows versions

XPress offers exactly the same tools in both versions. The only differences are purely cosmetic.

On the Mac, the icons are black and white. The tool that's currently in use is shown in reverse—white on black.

In Windows, the icons are gray 3-D buttons. The active tool is the one that appears a bit lighter and "pushed in."

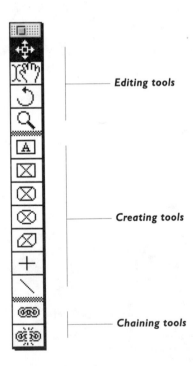

Editing tools

Creating tools

Chaining tools

Creating tools. You might be tempted to call them drawing tools, but that's not exactly what they are. Five of these tools are for creating different kinds of boxes, and these often end up being invisible. That is, you can see the box onscreen, but the box's borders won't print out unless you want them to. In most cases, boxes are used solely to hold text or pictures. The last two tools in this group—the line tools—are clearly for drawing.

Chaining tools. They're exactly what they seem to be. The top tool is for linking text boxes together; the bottom tool is for breaking links after you make them.

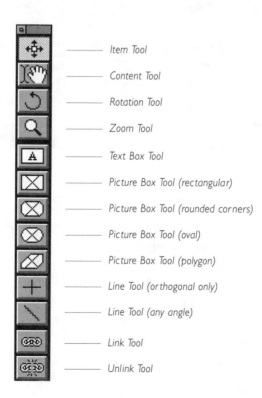

Item Tool

Content Tool

Rotation Tool

Zoom Tool

Text Box Tool

Picture Box Tool (rectangular)

Picture Box Tool (rounded corners)

Picture Box Tool (oval)

Picture Box Tool (polygon)

Line Tool (orthogonal only)

Line Tool (any angle)

Link Tool

Unlink Tool

• • • • • • • • • • • • • • • •

Into the nitty-gritty:
The Item tool versus the Content tool

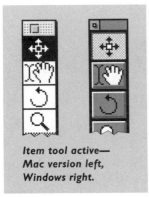

Item tool active—
Mac version left,
Windows right.

Content tool active.

The Item tool and the Content tool are the tools you'll use for roughly 75% of the work you do in XPress. The tricky part is remembering which one should be selected for the job at hand.

People often explain the difference between these tools by saying the Item tool is for moving boxes and the Content tool is for editing boxes. Well, that's sort of the idea. But let's get it right from the start.

To really understand when to use which tool, you must get the distinction between *item* and *content* down pat. (If this sounds like mumbo jumbo to you, don't worry. It *is* mumbo jumbo.)

Content The concept of "content" is relatively straightforward. Text and pictures imported from other programs are both considered content. Text typed in QuarkXPress is content, too.

Item The notion of an "item" is a bit trickier. There are two kinds of items in XPress: boxes and lines. A box can have stuff in it—such as text and pictures—but a line can't. It's an item with no contents.

That's why it doesn't matter which of the two tools you use when you're working with lines. The Item and Content tools work identically when a line is selected.

But a box is different—you must have the right tool selected before you choose a command or change a setting. If you have the Item tool selected, that means you're trying to change, copy or delete the box itself. If, instead, you have the Content tool selected, that means you're trying to change, copy or delete what's *inside* the box.

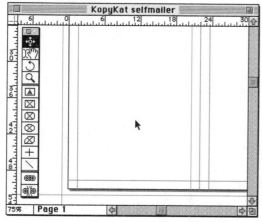

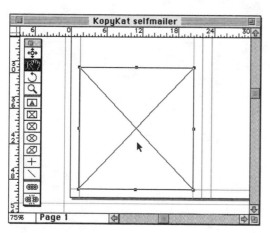

The right tool for the right job

You can select an item with either the Item tool or the Content tool. Here, a picture box is selected with the Item tool.

You can always switch tools after an item is selected. In fact, you have to do this quite frequently in XPress. This is called "switching between Item and Content modes."

▼ ▼ ▼

In this second view, the designer has just chosen the Cut command—while the Item tool was active. That effectively meant "cut this item."

When you cut an item, you lose the whole kit-and-kaboodle. You remove the box itself, as well as whatever it contains.

▼ ▼ ▼

This wasn't her intent, so she chose Undo to bring the picture box (and its picture) back. Then she clicked on the Content tool and chose Cut.

Cutting with the Content tool means "remove the selected contents." The result is shown here—the picture is gone, but the box remains.

•••••••••••••••••••

Switching between Item mode and Content mode

You may not have noticed, but a lot of things happen when you change tools.

When the Content tool is active, all of the menus are available. But when you switch to Item mode, the Style menu "grays out"—it becomes unavailable. That's because the commands in the Style menu—settings like type style or picture color—are applicable only to the contents of a box. If you're not in Content mode, Style commands simply can't be applied to a box.

•••••••••••••••••••••••

Content mode

With the Content tool active, you have access to the commands in both the Style and Item menus—provided an item is selected. If no item is selected, both menus "gray out."

And take a look at the cursors in these screens. Positioned over a picture box that's been selected, the cursor becomes a hand (for adjusting the position of the picture). Over a text box, the cursor turns into an I-beam (for inserting or selecting text).

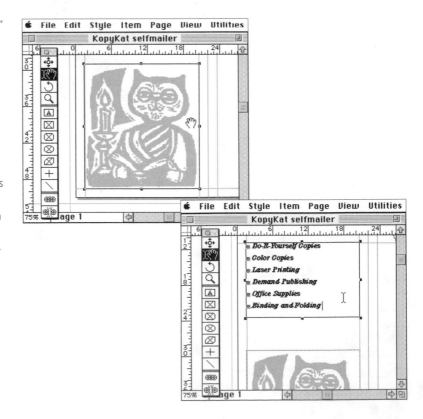

Of course, this rule breaks down a bit if a line is selected. Because a line can't have contents, there's no such thing as a "Content mode" for a line. So no matter which tool is active, all of the menus are available when a line is selected.

What else happens when you switch modes? Your cursor changes—at least when you pass the cursor over a selected box. Then the cursor matches the tool icon that's highlighted in the palette, as shown below.

When you move the cursor away from a selected box, the cursor turns into a pointer arrow, regardless of which tool is selected. What does the pointer arrow mean? Not much. All it really tells you is that you're not currently pointing at a selected item.

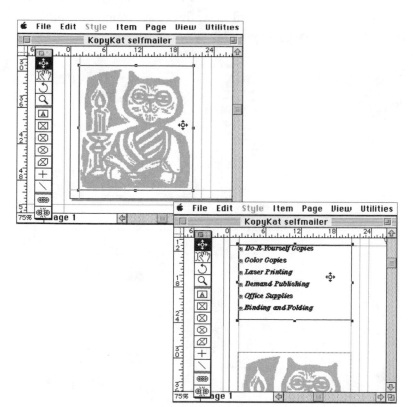

Item mode

In some ways, Item mode is simpler. For one thing, there's only one kind of cursor, the four-headed arrow. And the Style menu is grayed out—none of its commands are available.

In fact, we'll see that there are quite a few options that just aren't available when you're in Item mode.

• • • • • • • •

Copying

One of the reasons we love our computers (even during those times we absolutely hate them) is that we're able to copy things with a couple of commands. You know the routine: select a picture, choose Copy, then choose Paste.

XPress has Copy and Paste commands like most other programs. But as with all things XPress, even the simplest tasks can get tricky. If the Item tool's active, Copy and Paste work just as you would expect: Select a box, choose Copy, then choose Paste to create a duplicate of the box and its contents. But if the Content tool is active, you'll copy only the contents—not the box. And you can't just paste "contents" directly onto a page, so you'll need to select a box—a destination—with the Content tool first; the Paste command won't even be available until you do.

The Copy/Paste beeps

XPress likes to beep. You'll get a beep if you try to copy the contents of an empty box, or if you try to paste text or a picture without first selecting a destination with the Content Tool.

Copying with the Content tool

In this screen, the designer is preparing to copy the graphic from the self-mailer. She's chosen the Content tool because she's only interested in the picture itself, not the oval picture box.

▼ ▼ ▼

Here, she has switched to the other document window and pasted the graphic into a rectangular picture box. To make the paste work, she had to select this picture box with the Content tool as well.

The Duplicate command and the Step And Repeat command (both in the Item menu) provide alternatives to the copy-and-paste routine. One advantage of these commands is that you don't have to switch tools. These commands always duplicate the entire item. That's fine, of course, unless you're trying to copy a phrase from one paragraph to the next; then you'd want to stick with the Copy and Paste commands.

And what about copying items between documents? That couldn't be simpler. Just set up your two document windows side by side and drag the item you want to copy from one window to the next (using the Item tool, of course). People are often hesitant and disbelieving when they first try this, but don't be. The copy will suddenly appear in the other document, and the original will stay put even though it looked as though you just moved it.

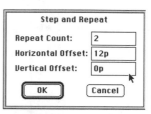

Step And Repeat lets you specify where a duplicate should be placed. And, if you want, you can even create several duplicates at once, all spaced exactly the same distance apart.

Copying with the Item tool

What if our designer had actually wanted to use the same oval picture box and the same sort of text runaround?

That would have been easy. She could have just switched to the Item tool before choosing Copy and Paste.

An even easier way is shown here: the picture box was simply dragged from one window to the other, making a copy in the process.

View

Fit in Window	⌘0
50%	⌘5
75%	⌘7
✓Actual Size	⌘1
200%	⌘2
Thumbnails	
Windows	▶
Hide Guides	
Show Baseline Grid	
✓Snap to Guides	
Hide Rulers	⌘R
Show Invisibles	⌘I
Hide Tools	
Show Measurements	
Show Document Layout	
Show Style Sheets	
Show Colors	
Show Trap Information	

Macintosh version

View

Fit in Window	Ctrl+0
50%	
75%	
✓Actual Size	Ctrl+1
200%	
Thumbnails	
Hide Guides	
Show Baseline Grid	
✓Snap to Guides	
Hide Rulers	Ctrl+R
Show Invisibles	Ctrl+I
Hide Tools	
Show Measurements	
Show Document Layout	
Show Style Sheets	
Show Colors	
Show Trap Information	

Windows version

Using the Measurements palette

Some people like to use the Style and Item menu commands to do just about all their edits. And others prefer to use XPress's floating palettes, the little windows that hover on top of the document window.

The Measurements palette, for example, contains many of the same settings and options that are available through the Style and Item menus, but they're all gathered in one convenient place. The great thing about the Measurements palette is that it shows you all the current measurements and settings for the item you've selected. And if you want to change one of these, you can simply type in a new number or click on one of the palette's icons.

Like the menu bar, the Measurements palette changes its look depending on which tool is active and what's currently selected. When the Item tool is active, only the *item settings*—the settings on the left half of the palette—are available. When you switch to Content mode, both sides of the palette light up with controls.

As you no doubt can guess by now, there are the usual exceptions to this rule. When a line is selected, both sides of the palette are "on" no matter which tool is active. And if nothing's selected, the palette just appears empty.

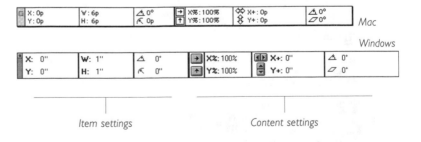

Item settings   *Content settings*

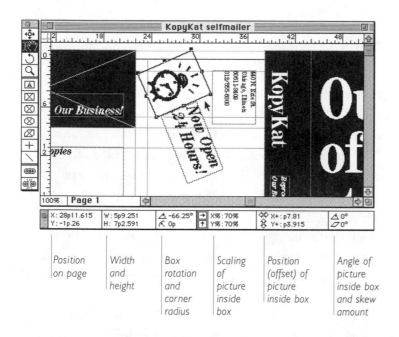

| Position on page | Width and height | Box rotation and corner radius | Scaling of picture inside box | Position (offset) of picture inside box | Angle of picture inside box and skew amount |

Position on page | *Width and height* | *Box rotation and corner radius* | *Scaling of picture inside box* | *Position (offset) of picture inside box* | *Angle of picture inside box and skew amount*

Picture box selected with the Content tool

Here, the rotated picture of the alarm clock is selected.

The Measurements palette provides readouts on the rotation—of the picture box itself as well as of the picture inside.

All of these settings can be changed by typing right over the readout in the palette.

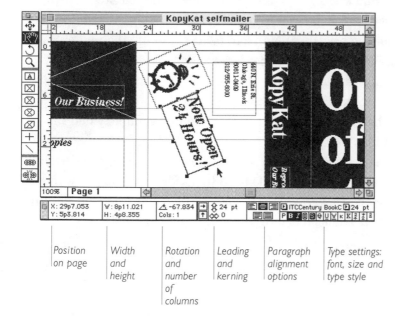

Position on page | *Width and height* | *Rotation and number of columns* | *Leading and kerning* | *Paragraph alignment options* | *Type settings: font, size and type style*

Text box selected with the Content tool

In this screen, the rotated text box is selected instead. Notice which parts of the palette change.

View

Fit in Window	⌘0
50%	⌘5
75%	⌘7
✓Actual Size	⌘1
200%	⌘2
Thumbnails	
Windows	▶
Hide Guides	
Show Baseline Grid	
✓Snap to Guides	
Hide Rulers	⌘R
Show Invisibles	⌘I
Hide Tools	
Hide Measurements	
Show Document Layout	
Show Style Sheets	
Show Colors	
Show Trap Information	

Macintosh version

View

Fit in Window	Ctrl+0
50%	
75%	
✓Actual Size	Ctrl+1
200%	
Thumbnails	
Hide Guides	
Show Baseline Grid	
✓Snap to Guides	
Hide Rulers	Ctrl+R
Show Invisibles	Ctrl+I
Hide Tools	
Hide Measurements	
Show Document Layout	
Show Style Sheets	
Show Colors	
Show Trap Information	

Windows version

Using the Colors palette

Whether or not you plan on printing a particular piece in color, you'll find the Colors palette indispensable. That's because you'll also use it to switch things from black to white, or to choose one of the shades in between.

The palette grays out when nothing is selected. To use the palette, you first have to click on an item; then you can choose one of the colors in the list or a shade from the pop-up menu.

Well, that's half the truth. Like most things in XPress, it's not really that simple. What you can apply a color or shade to depends on (surprise!) which tool is active and what you've selected.

As always, lines are the simplest. When you select a line, using the Colors palette is straightforward: just click on a color or choose a shade.

But when you select a box, there's another step or two involved. First you'll have to decide whether you want to color the box (the item itself) or its contents (the text or picture that may or may not be inside).

If you want to color the contents, you must switch to the Content tool, then click on the Content icon (the middle icon) in the Colors palette. That icon is only available when the Content tool is active.

If you just want to color the box, it doesn't matter which tool is active. But you do need to decide whether you want to color the *background* of the box or its *frame,* then click on the appropriate icon before choosing a color or shade.

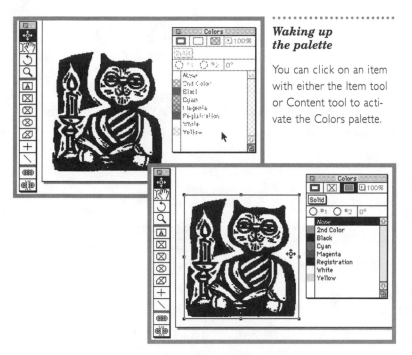

Waking up the palette

You can click on an item with either the Item tool or Content tool to activate the Colors palette.

The palette icons

The middle icon changes depending on what sort of item is currently selected. Here's what the icon bar looks like when you've selected a picture box.

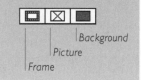

Background
Picture
Frame

Applying colors

Make sure you choose one of the icons along the top before you choose a color or a shade.

Background icon active: color applied to the box.

Content icon active: 60% shade of black applied to the picture.

• •

The many faces of the Colors palette

The truth of the matter is that the Colors palette can confuse newcomers to no end. That's because it really does keep changing faces. Icons and controls come and go in a seemingly unpredictable way.

Line selected

Only one icon is available—the Line icon. Because lines have neither frames nor backgrounds, those icons are grayed out. Here, the selected line is set to a 50% shade of black.

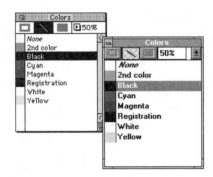

Picture Box selected with Content tool

Three icons are available—the Frame, Picture and Background icons. Here, the box's frame is set to a color.

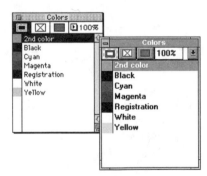

Picture box selected with Item tool

Switching to the Item tool grays out the Picture icon, but you can still set the Frame and Background colors. And when the Background icon is selected, you can remove all color— that is, make the box transparent— by choosing *None*.

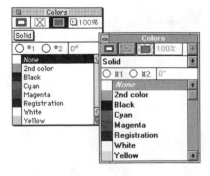

You may remember that the Measurements palette does the same sort of quick-change act, too. XPress constantly checks to see what kind of item you've selected and which tool you're using, and then changes these palettes to suit.

Here are a few of the ways the Colors palette changes. Pay special attention to the icons along the top.

Choosing a blend as a background

Backgrounds don't need to be solid. When you press on "Solid," a menu pops up that offers a variety of color blends, like the Mid-Linear Blend chosen here. The menu disappears from the palette when you click on one of the other icons.

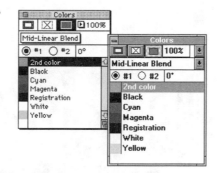

Changing the color of an imported picture

If the Content tool is active, and the picture is in the right file format (such as a black-and-white TIFF), you can click on the Picture icon to colorize the picture.

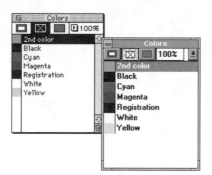

Changing the color of text

If you've selected a text box with the Content tool, a new icon appears in the middle position—a Text icon. To change the color of text, though, you have to remember to highlight a range of text and click on the Text icon before you choose a color. That's very easy to forget!

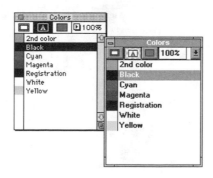

• •

Using the Style Sheets palette

The Style Sheets palette is simpler than the Colors and Measurements palettes. It doesn't change much at all.

     The only time the palette is active—not grayed out—is when a text box is selected with the Content tool. It's that simple.

• • • • • • • • • • • • • • • • • •

Applying style sheets

Nothing could be easier. Using the I-beam cursor, click anywhere in the paragraph you want to style, then click on the style sheet in the palette.

Here, the designer chooses the Head style, which sets the entire paragraph to Century Bold Condensed, 28 points, with 30-point leading.

• • • • • • • • • • • • • • • • • •

Backing up a step

But how did the style sheets get in the palette in the first place? The designer set each of them up herself using this dialog box, which is available from the Edit menu.

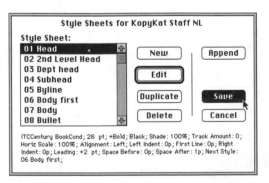

So what is this palette for? It allows you to style entire paragraphs by choosing a name from the list. One click in the Style palette, and a paragraph can be completely typeset—bold and left-aligned, italic and centered, you name it.

The importance of style sheets is hard to overestimate. I'll spend plenty of time talking about them in Chapter 5, "Beyond Get Text."

Shorthand alert

Yes, I know it's officially called the Style Sheets palette, but from now on, I'm going to call it the Style palette. Easier to read, easier to say, much easier to type. Hope you don't mind.

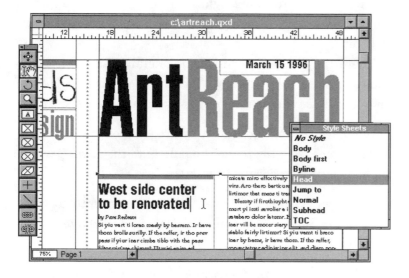

What's in a style sheet?

Just about every typesetting option you can imagine—font, type size, leading, color, type style, indents, alignment, drop caps—and on and on.

This designer likes to automate as many typesetting chores as possible, so he includes every setting he can think of. For example, a style sheet automatically draws the shaded line over each head—he doesn't do it by hand. The style sheet also automatically inserts a big space above each headline.

You can double-check your settings by opening the Style Sheets dialog box. All of the custom settings for the selected style are listed at the bottom of the dialog box.

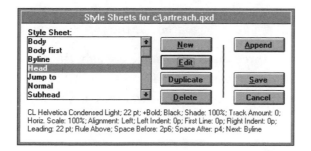

• •

The Document Layout palette

This handy little palette—well, it's not so little—sets QuarkXPress apart from all other desktop publishing programs.

You can use this palette not only to flip through pages on the screen, but also to make the *big* edits: adding and deleting pages; changing the order of pages; and even switching the layout of a page to a completely different design. It's not quite the same as reaching right into the screen to shuffle through the document with your hands, but it's as close as you'll get.

There are plenty of mind-boggling details you can learn about using this palette, but we'll take it slow for now. Here's how you can use the palette for the most common page edits:

• • Add pages to your document by dragging one of the tiny page icons from the top of the palette to the lower part of the palette (the document area).

• • Delete an existing page by selecting its icon in the document area and clicking on the Delete icon at the top of the palette.

• • Rearrange pages in the document area by dragging their icons to different positions. Easy!

• • Redesign the layout of an existing page by clicking on one of the master page icons at the top of the palette.

The first three tasks are simple enough. But that last one— the one about master page icons—is a little trickier. Master pages can be as simple or as complex as you want them to be.

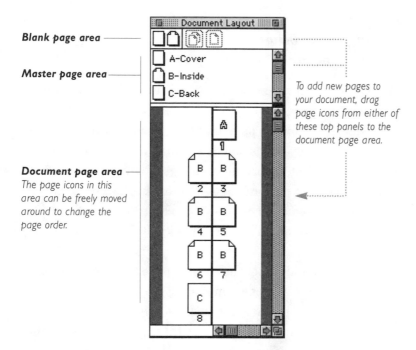

Blank page area ——

Master page area ——

To add new pages to your document, drag page icons from either of these top panels to the document page area.

Document page area ——
The page icons in this area can be freely moved around to change the page order.

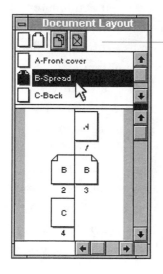

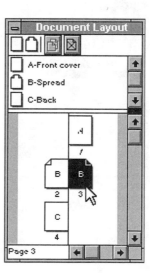

What about those other icons?

Those are the Duplicate and Delete icons, which are usually grayed out.

They both become available when you select a master page, as you can see on the left.

If you select a document page, though, only the Delete icon becomes available—the Duplicate icon remains grayed out. You can do a lot of things with the Layout palette, but it won't let you duplicate a document page.

• • • • • • • • • • • • • • • • • • •

The difference between master pages and document pages

What is a master page? Let's start with the simplest definition: A master page is a place where you can set up repeating page elements, such as page numbers or section titles, so they will automatically appear on every page you add to the document. By contrast, a document page is where you put items that change from page to page—photos, stories and so on.

If you've used other publishing or word processing programs, you've probably used this kind of feature before. But chances are, the feature was fairly simple and limited. That is, you would flip to the master page (or the header or footer area), type in a page number symbol and a title, and maybe add a graphic element such as a line along the top of the page. And that would be that—those elements would then show up on every document page.

Master pages give you the same capability in XPress, plus much more. For one thing, items you set up on master pages—called *master items*—aren't cast in stone, as they are in most other programs. You can edit a master item on a document page if you need to, or even delete the item.

XPress's master pages also can be used to structure your page designs. What do I mean by "structure a design"? That depends. Minimally, you would set up page margins on the master page so that *margin guides* appear on all your document pages. The next step would be to add *column guides*—if, in fact, you wanted more than one column on each page. And if you really wanted to lock in a specific structure, you could even put empty text boxes on the master page, sized and positioned exactly the way you want them to appear on every document page.

How do you "get to" a master page?

Every document has at least one master page. Unless you changed the name, it will be called "A-Master A." To take a look at what's on the master page—or to change it—just double-click on the master page icon.

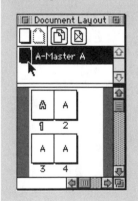

But the most powerful aspect of XPress's master page feature is that you can have more than one master page—as many as you need, in fact. You could, for example, set up one master design that includes an automatic page number and another design where a page number doesn't appear. Or you might design a *mixed format* newsletter where some pages are set in two columns and other pages are set in three.

Some typical master pages

This newsletter makes good use of master pages.

The master page shown to the left is for the front cover. It's set up with a very large top margin to allow room for the nameplate.

The one below is for an inside spread. It's called a *facing pages* master page. The designer set up the left and right pages as mirror opposites but with different pieces of text in the bottom corners.

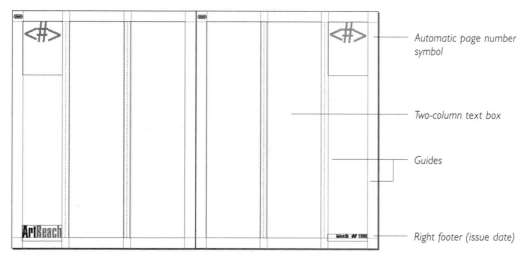

Automatic page number symbol

Two-column text box

Guides

Right footer (issue date)

Laying the foundation with master guides and master text boxes

Let's delve a little deeper into this idea of structuring a page design. That, after all, is where XPress excels. And it's a theme we'll return to often in this book.

If you're doing any sort of structured publication—a newsletter, brochure, book or booklet—pay special attention to setting up your master pages so they provide a good foundation for your document.

The grid approach

KatPeople's designer likes to set up her master pages with the fewest items possible. That's because the only thing that repeats from page to page is the header. Every page she designs is different, so it wouldn't make sense to use master text boxes.

But she does include margin and column guides on her master pages because they provide a grid to work within. The master grid helps her position picture and text boxes in a well-organized three-column arrangement.

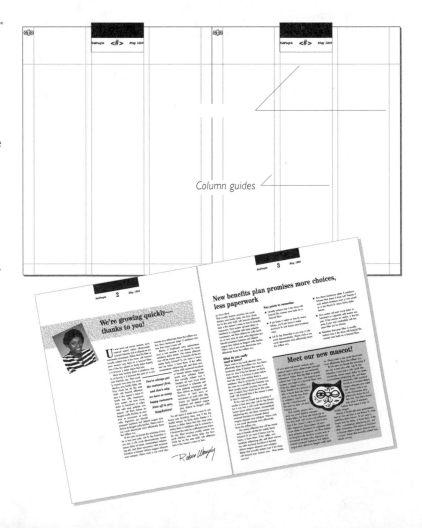

Column guides

Do you want the body text to appear in exactly the same place on each page? Will you be setting up a wide page margin where you can place photos or sidebars? These are the sorts of things you should structure on a master page.

There are two ways to create structure. The first is to place empty text boxes on the master page. The second is to just put *guides* in place. For example, you might create a master text box for body text (since you'll need that kind of box on every document page), then place *ruler guides* in the margins to define the boundaries for any photo boxes or sidebar boxes you might place there.

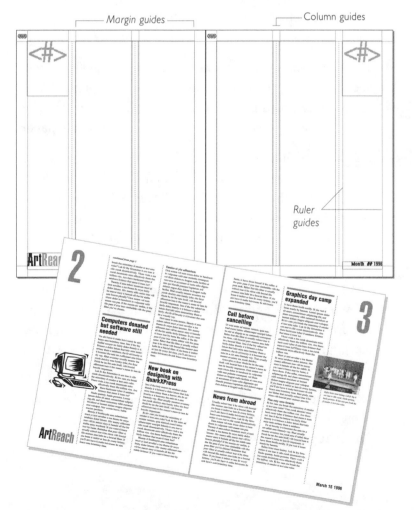

Margin guides

Column guides

Ruler guides

A tightly structured approach

With *ArtReach*, articles are set in much the same way from page to page, from issue to issue. So the master pages have all the essentials in place, including column separator lines and empty text boxes for the articles. Given the design of the newsletter, there's never any need to change these master items.

The only aspect of the design that's not strictly regimented is the placement of graphics, photos and captions. To keep the placement of these items fairly consistent, the designer added ruler guides in the wide outer margins.

• • • • • • • • • • • • • • • • • •

Creating a document

So how do you actually get started? In a way, it's as simple as choosing the New command. In another way, it's much more complex.

There are a lot of options in that New dialog box. Which ones really matter? What do they do? Can you change your mind about them later? Many veteran XPress users don't know the answers to these questions. But *you* should.

In brief, here are the answers. All of the options matter—they let you rough out the basic structure of your first master page. And, yes, they can all be changed later.

I'll go into detail about these options in the following sections, but let's start with this overview for now:

• • The Page Size section is where you choose the size of your document—not the size of your laser printer paper. If you're designing a postcard announcement, type in 3½ by 5½ inches, even if you'll be proofing it on letter-size paper.

• • The Margin Guides section can be used in either of two ways. You can set margin guides to define the *live area* of a document—the area in which *all* text and pictures should fit. Or you can use the guides to define the *body text area;* in most cases, that's what they should be used for.

• • The Column Guides section is used to divide up the area between the left and right margin guides. What you type in here depends completely on whether you've set up the margin guides to define the live area or the body text area.

• • The Automatic Text Box check box allows you to set up an empty text box as a master item. We'll talk about Automatic Text Boxes a lot more later on.

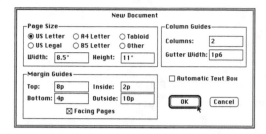

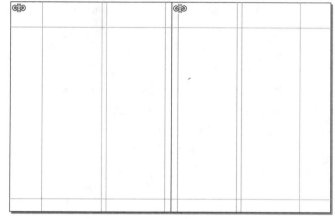

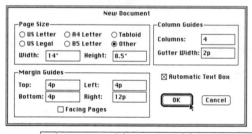

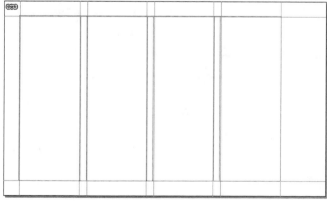

What happens if...?

The best way to get a feel for all those settings in the New dialog box is to try them out. Punch in some numbers, check some check boxes, and see what you get.

Our top example is simple enough—mirrored pages with wide outer margins and guides for two columns. Because the Facing Pages check box was on, the master "page" is really two pages—the left and right sides of a spread. And that's why the side margins are referred to as "Outside" and "Inside" rather than "Left" and "Right."

▼ ▼ ▼

The lower example is a bit more exotic. It's a legal-size page with four columns and an *automatic text box*. Because the Facing Pages check box was off, the master page is a single page, which means the grid will be the same for pages on the left and on the right.

What's with the "p"s?

That stands for *pica*—the standard measuring unit in typesetting. There are six picas ("6p") in an inch. Any numbers after the "p" refer to points. (There are 12 points in a pica.) So "1p6" means "1 pica, 6 points" or "one-and-a-half picas"—the same as a quarter inch.

· · · · · · · · · · · · · · · · · · · ·

Changing your mind

You can change all these master settings after you click OK. A lot of people don't realize this—after all, once you close that New dialog box, it's gone as far as the current document goes. Changing the settings in that dialog will only affect the next document you create, not the one you already have in front of you.

Here's what actually happens to all those settings. Half of them "move" to another dialog box called Document Setup. The other settings move into a dialog called Master Guides. That command is in the Page menu, but it's always grayed out—at least, until you switch to a master page.

· · · · · · · · · · · · · · · · · ·

The New dialog, again

After you create a new document, you can open the New dialog box again and you'll see the same settings you just used. But that doesn't mean that changing those settings will affect the document you just created.

New Document

Page Size
- ◉ US Letter   ○ A4 Letter   ○ Tabloid
- ○ US Legal   ○ B5 Letter   ○ Other

Width: 8.5"   Height: 11"

Column Guides
Columns: 2
Gutter Width: 1p6

Margin Guides
Top: 8p   Inside: 2p
Bottom: 4p   Outside: 10p
⊠ Facing Pages

☐ Automatic Text Box

OK   Cancel

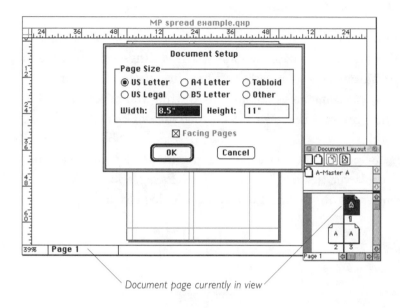

Document page currently in view

Document Setup

This dialog is available from the File menu—but only if you're currently viewing a document page.

These settings affect the entire document, including all of the master pages. You can't mix different page sizes in one file.

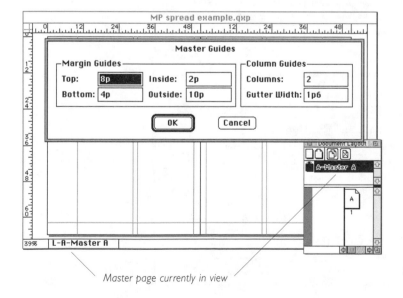

Master page currently in view

Master Guides

This dialog is available from the Page menu—but only if you're currently viewing a master page.

These settings affect only the master page you're looking at. That means each master page can have different margin and column settings.

· · · · · · · · · · · · · · · · · · · ·

The inner workings of XPress's other dialog boxes

While it's true that you don't have to spend a lot of time in XPress's dialog boxes (so many of the settings are available in the Measurements palette and Layout palette), there are many occasions to use dialog boxes while you're setting things up. And that's why it's a good idea to know how they work.

Some dialog boxes expand and contract depending on the controls you need. These include the Paragraph Formats, Paragraph Rules, and Find/Change dialog boxes.

· · · · · · · · · · · · · · · · · · · ·

More than meets the eye

Several dialog boxes expand when you click on certain check boxes. That's because there are additional options you'll need to consider after you turn on those features.

In this dialog, clicking on either the Drop Caps or Keep Lines Together check box will expand the dialog box to its full size.

Paragraph Formats

Left Indent: 0p   Leading: 15 pt
First Line: 1p6   Space Before: 0p
Right Indent: 0p   Space After: 0p
☐ Lock to Baseline Grid   ☐ Keep with Next ¶
☐ Drop Caps   ☐ Keep Lines Together
Alignment: Left
H&J: Standard   [Apply]
[OK]   [Cancel]

Paragraph Formats

Left Indent: 0p   Leading: 15 pt
First Line: 1p6   Space Before: 0p
Right Indent: 0p   Space After: 0p
☐ Lock to Baseline Grid   ☐ Keep with Next ¶
☐ Drop Caps   ☒ Keep Lines Together
Character Count: 1   ⦿ All Lines in ¶
Line Count: 3   ○ Start: 2   End: 2
Alignment: Left
H&J: Standard   [Apply]
[OK]   [Cancel]

Some dialog boxes, such as those for Style Sheets and Colors, provide access to yet other dialog boxes. These are called *nested dialogs*.

Some Style menu dialogs include a special Apply button. Clicking on Apply provides an immediate preview of the settings you've chosen. You can fine-tune your settings without closing and reopening the dialog box—or you can just click on Cancel to return to the original settings.

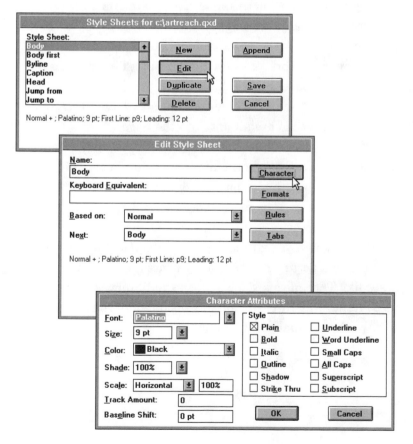

Deeper and deeper

The Style Sheets dialog box contains buttons that open additional dialog boxes.

Here, the designer wanted to edit the Body style sheet, so he clicked on the Edit button, which opened the Edit Style Sheet dialog. Then he clicked on the Character button, which opened the Character Attributes dialog.

To close all the dialogs, he had to click on OK in each of the last two dialog boxes, then on Save in the first dialog box.

• • • • • • • • • • • • • • • • • •

What libraries are for

You've probably noticed that the New command has two options: Document and Library. It's clear enough why you'd want to create a new document, but it's not so obvious what you would do with a library.

Libraries aren't for everybody. If the kind of work you do changes all the time, you may not find libraries useful. But if you're working on a big, complex project (such as a book), or if you often use the same artwork or text in a variety of publications, then you should try out the library feature.

Simply put, a library is a place where you can store frequently used items. For example, if you often do pieces for a particular company, you might store the company's logo as one item in the library and an address block as another item.

How does it work? To store an item in a library, drag the item from the page into the Library palette. To use the item later, find the item in the palette—you may have to scroll to find the item—then drag it out onto the page.

Of course, you're not actually moving the original item around. The one that's in the library is a duplicate, and you're making another duplicate when you drag it out of the library. The "library" is really more like a magic filing cabinet that dispenses copies of anything you put in it.

Even though you will probably create your library while working in a document, the library is actually saved as a separate file. That means you can open the library and draw on its contents while working on any document—you don't have to have the original document open.

Are there any tricks to using a library? A few. For one thing, you have to remember that libraries can only hold items—not "unboxed" pictures or words. You can only drag boxes and lines into a library, and you must use the Item tool to do it. And that means that libraries aren't very useful for storing things like frequently used names or phrases. You can't just drag a text phrase out of a paragraph into a library then drag it back out and drop it into another text box.

If you do store text in a library, each piece of text must be stored in its own text box. That can be quite handy for self-contained text blocks such as addresses, warranties, logotypes, copyright notices, disclaimers and so on. You'll find, however, that long pieces of text are displayed in the library as gray blocks, so it can be very difficult to tell one text entry from another. Most likely, you'll need to assign names to such entries. You can do that by double-clicking on the entry in the palette.

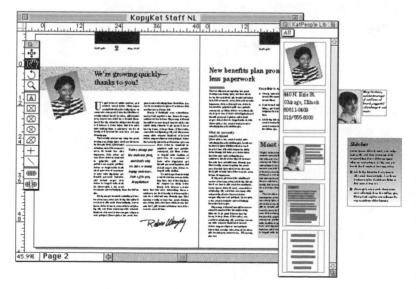

On permanent loan

This library lets you take out items and never return them. That's because one copy always stays in the library.

KatPeople's designer keeps a variety of items on file in her library—the president's photo, the company's address, a photo/caption arrangement she uses frequently, a sidebar box and a pull-quote box. The library took some time to set up, but she spends less time reinventing the wheel when she produces each issue.

• • • • • • • • • • • •

Where to now?

That's up to you. Now that you've had a basic overview of XPress's many tools, palettes, dialog boxes, commands and quirks, you're in much better shape than most people I know who've been stumbling through the program on their own for several years!

I *can* tell you how the rest of this book is organized so that you can make up your mind. Each section of this book has a different goal. For example, the goal of the section we've just concluded was to get us warmed up and talking the same language. (I hope it worked.)

The next section—you can see it from here, in fact—is all about how to accomplish specific design effects in XPress: how to set type so it reads well and looks good; how to set up master items and paragraph styles; how to work with pictures and color; how to do fun special effects.

The goal of Section 3, "XPress Designs," is to give you a break from your problems by showing how other people have solved theirs. It's fun to look through a gallery whenever you're tired of reading or need some fresh ideas.

Section 4, "XPress Hotline," is where you should look for details and help-in-a-hurry. It's packed with hundreds of tips, tricks, revelations, references, resources and definitions. If you're the kind of person who always wants to know what the *other* 20 buttons on a CD player do, you might find this section gratifying.

XPress Effects

Building Master Pages

Whoa! You're thinking about skipping this chapter, right? Does the topic sound a little dry? What does "building master pages" have to do with making cool brochures and newsletters and announcements and letterhead?

The truth of the matter is, you don't have to know much at all about master pages. You could skip this chapter and still manage to pump out those brochures and newsletters.

So why keep reading? Because it'll pay off in the long run. If you learn just a little about the *right* way to build documents—even small, simple documents—you'll be able to focus on those neat effects instead of cleaning up mistakes.

Building a document is kind of like construction work— even if all you have in mind is a simple doghouse. Yes, you can get by working on-the-fly, just nailing a few boards together and hoping they all fall neatly into place. But the process won't be pretty to watch. Even a doghouse should be built on a solid, well-designed frame.

We'll get to the shingles and paint soon enough. But for the next few pages, we're talking about measuring tape and pencils and 2x4s.

Starting with a master plan

It's so easy to open that New Document dialog box and just click OK—without checking the settings. But sailing through this dialog is like building that doghouse with any old boards you find in your garage. It's usually a good idea to measure your dog first—or at least trim the boards so they'll fit together correctly.

Setting up a small document

Remember, the Page Size settings refer to the size of the final printed piece—not the size of the paper you're proofing on.

Here, the designer started her business card document by typing in the dimensions of the card—3½ by 2 inches (or 21 by 12 picas). She included one-pica margins on all four sides to remind her of the boundaries for the type.

Did you notice that the black background on top extends beyond the document's edges? This area is called a *bleed,* and it appears on the print even though it's "off the page."

In the end, the print shop will *trim* away the bleed, using the trim marks on the print as guides.

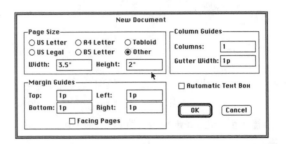

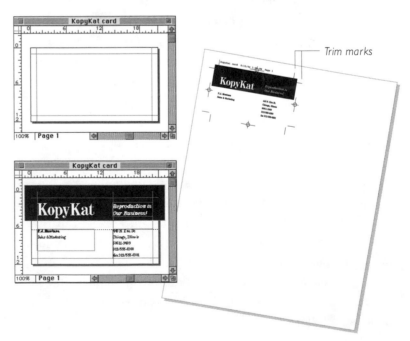

Trim marks

The same idea applies to choosing your New Document settings. Is the final printed piece going to be letter size (8½ by 11 inches)? Or is it actually going to be a larger sheet folded down to narrow panels? Or are you developing something smaller, such as a postcard or a business card?

This is the time to get your page settings right. You can change them later, but it's seldom a good idea. Items you've placed on your pages may not fall into place after you change the page size—or they may not fit at all!

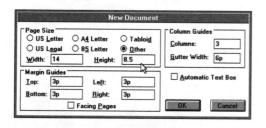

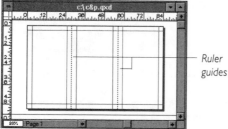
Ruler guides

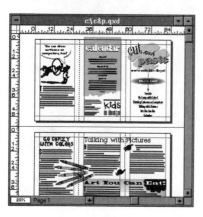

Setting up a folder

This designer might have chosen a tall, narrow page—the size of a single panel of the folder—but she decided instead to set up one wide page, divided into three panels with column guides. That way, she ended up creating only two document pages (the inside and outside spreads) instead of six pages arranged side by side.

After clicking OK, she switched to the master page and added two ruler guides (shown here as dashed lines) to indicate where the folds would be made. These "fold lines" helped her decide how to position items that might cross over the folds.

When should you use Facing Pages?

If you're designing anything in a book format—whether it's a brochure, a catalog, a manual or a newsletter—you should consider turning on the Facing Pages option when you create the document.

Without facing pages...

What would happen if the *ArtReach* newsletter was created without Facing Pages?

The first thing the designer would notice is that the second icon in the Document Layout palette—the Facing Pages icon—is grayed out:

That means a facing master page can't be created. Instead, all master pages have to be one-sided, so to speak.

Here, a single master page was created for the inside spread. This sort of repeating page design works well for some publications, but not here; the pages don't appear balanced.

One solution would be to create another master page specifically for right-handed pages. But turning on Facing Pages is much easier.

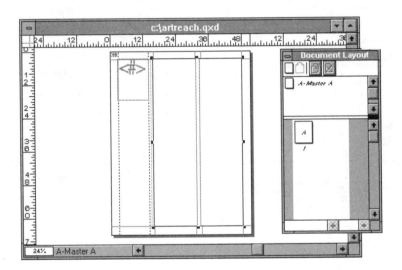

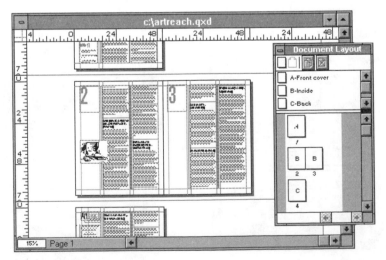

There's no disadvantage to turning on Facing Pages—you'll just be keeping your options open. The major benefit is that you'll be able to easily create facing master pages—that is, pairs of mirrored page designs—if you want to. If the Facing Pages option isn't on, you can still create mirrored designs, but you'll have to arrange everything by hand.

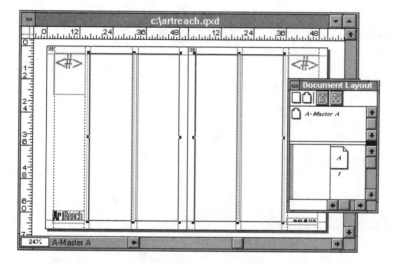

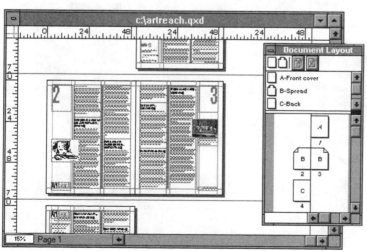

...and with facing pages

Here's the way *ArtReach* was actually set up—with the Facing Pages check box on. As you can see, the Blank Facing Pages icon in the Layout palette is available, and the first master page—which automatically appears in the palette as "A-Master A"—has two dog-eared corners, indicating it's a facing master page.

This master page was used only for the inside spread, where the designer wanted to balance the left and right pages with opposing wide outer margins. This design also kept the body text areas of the two pages close together. Since text on page 2 continues onto page 3, that creates a better flow for the reader.

● ●

Completing the framework

Once you've decided on the page size, the margins and the Facing Pages option, then it's time to turn to the master page and add structural refinements.

What should you add? If you're doing a truly free-form design, you may not need to add much. You might consider placing some ruler guides on the master page, though,

● ● ● ● ● ● ● ● ● ● ● ● ● ● ● ●

Placing ruler guides on master pages

One trick to making a good folder is creating a consistent sense of structure. The folder should look "right" whether a reader opens and reads it one panel at a time or immediately spreads the folder flat.

That's why three horizontal ruler guides were added to this master page. They helped the designer keep the type and the black background aligned on both sides of the folder. That way, these items lined up nicely even when the brochure was partly unfolded.

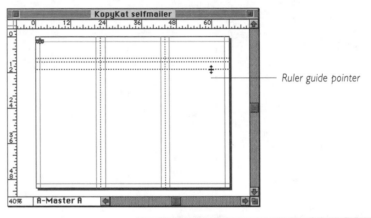

Ruler guide pointer

to block out major areas of the design—especially if you want a consistent grid from page to page. Just press on one of the rulers to drag a guide onto the page: drag from the top ruler to create a horizontal guide, or drag from the left ruler to create a vertical guide.

If you're working on a book-style publication, you'll probably also want to place headers or footers on the master page, or at the very least, automatic page numbers.

Mac	Win
Command 3	Ctrl 3

Insert automatic page number

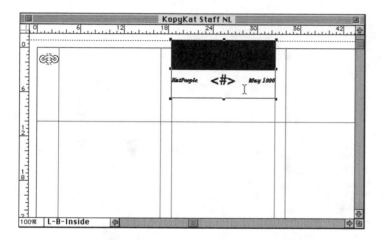

Adding headers

The only master item used in the *KatPeople* newsletter was this header, which included an automatic page number and a heavy paragraph rule above.

Once the header was set up on the left master page, the designer chose Step And Repeat to create a duplicate of the header in the same position. She then held down Shift to drag the copy in a straight path to the same spot on the right master page.

Designing pages for different purposes

You can usually get by with one master page design, but it often makes sense to create others—especially for periodicals. Cover pages, for example, often require different master items, margins or column arrangements than inside pages. Building a master page for each special case is a good way to keep page designs consistent from issue to issue.

Still under construction

When last we left *ArtReach*, the designer had built up the facing master pages for the inside spread. (He has since changed the name from the default "A-Master A" to the more descriptive "A-Spread.") Now he had to set up similar structures for the front and back covers.

The front cover didn't have to be based on a facing master page (since it never faces any-thing), so he dragged a copy of the regular Blank Page icon into the Master Page Area. That created a new master page called "B-Master B."

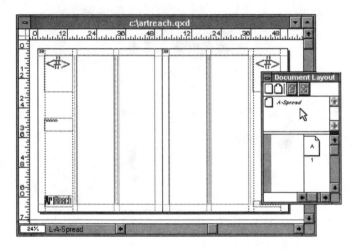

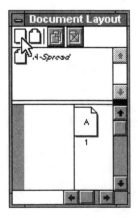

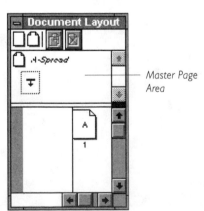

Master Page Area

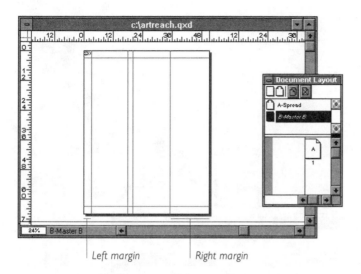

Left margin   Right margin

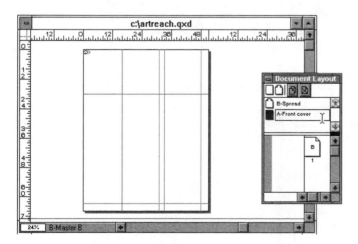

Changing a master page

He was a bit surprised when he took a look at his new master page. XPress created the margins for this nonfacing page as though it were the right half of a Facing Pages spread. His original setting for the inside margin was used for the left margin, and the wide outer margin was set on the right.

That was exactly the *opposite* of what he expected. He wanted the cover to look like a left page, with the wide margin on the left.

▼　▼　▼

To flip the page grid, he chose Margin Guides from the Page menu, then switched the numbers for the left and right margins. He also decided to increase the top margin to 18 picas—to push the body text area lower, well below the nameplate area.

The bottom screen shows the result of all these changes—a brand new grid specifically designed to handle the space requirements of the front cover.

And this was as good a time as any to rename this master page accordingly.

Completing the new master page

At this point, the master page only had margin and column guides—just enough of a structure to show where the body text should go.

But there were several major items yet to be placed—the logo, the nameplate and the contents block. To complete the framework, the designer added two vertical guides in the left margin and one horizontal guide along the top.

With these three guides in place—and the Snap To Guides command turned on—he aligned all the major cover items. He also added a master text box in the body area, making sure the box's edges snapped to the margin guides.

That was two master pages down—and one to go.

▼ ▼ ▼

To create the last master page—the one for the back cover—the designer duplicated the front master page. The back cover design would be a small variation on the front cover, so duplicating was easier than starting from scratch, as he had done before.

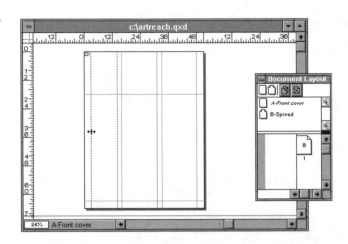

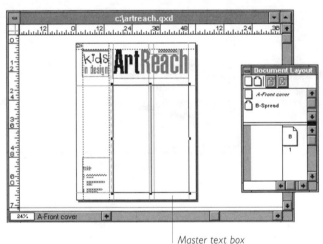

Master text box

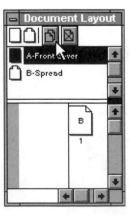

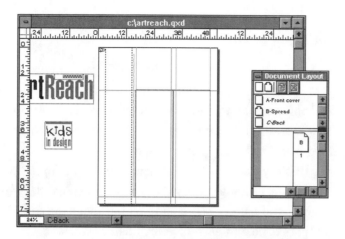

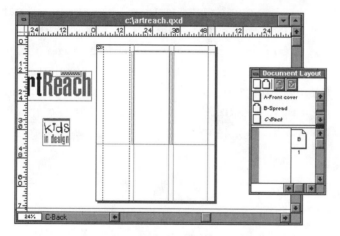

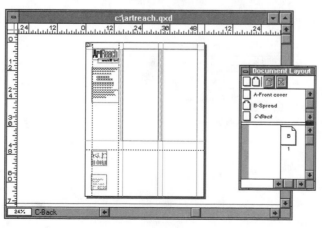

Changing a front cover into a back cover

The duplicate of the front master page contained all the master items from the original. The only item he didn't need was the contents block, so he deleted that. He moved the other items to the pasteboard temporarily.

This newsletter was to be folded into thirds and sent out as a self-mailer; that meant the bottom third had to be reserved for the mailing panel. He changed the bottom margin to 24 picas, which allowed a 2-pica clearance above the fold line. Then he changed the top margin to 3 picas to match the inside pages.

Because the master text box had originally been drawn to fit the margins precisely, the designer didn't need to move it at all—it automatically changed size and position to match the new margins.

▼ ▼ ▼

To finish, he moved the nameplate and the dateline back onto the page and scaled them to fit in the masthead. The logo was also reduced, then placed in the mailing panel above the return address.

Building in conduits for text flow

As we showed you back in Chapter 3, you can create a flow of text between pages by using the Link tool to connect a text box on one page to a text box on another page. In some cases, that may be the way to go, since it gives you complete control over how each story flows onto other pages.

But if your text flow requirements are simple—say, text from page 1 should always continue onto page 2, then onto page 3, and so on—you should think about putting an automatic text box on each of your master pages.

What's an automatic text box? It's just an ordinary text box, placed on a master page, that's linked to the automatic text chain icon. This master link creates a conduit for text between the primary text boxes on all your document pages. If you set up your master pages—and the corresponding document pages—correctly, you may never have to use the Link tool at all.

Having problems?

The truth of the matter is, automatic text boxes can be very tricky to use. If they're not working for you, check out pages 305 and 410 in Chapter 12, "Tricks of the Trade."

The easy way

Here's another reason to think twice before you sail past this dialog box: That little checkbox on the right is your one chance to have automatic text boxes created for you—automatically—on all your master pages. If you forget to check it, and you later decide you want automatic text boxes, you'll have to create them manually, one at a time.

```
                         New Document

┌─Page Size──────────────────────┐   ┌─Column Guides──────┐
│ ● US Letter  ○ A4 Letter  ○ Tabloid │ │ Columns:    [2      ] │
│ ○ US Legal   ○ B5 Letter  ○ Other   │ │ Gutter Width: [2p   ] │
│ Width: [8.5"    ]  Height: [11"   ] │ └──────────────────────┘
└──────────────────────────────────┘

┌─Margin Guides──────────────────┐     ⊠ Automatic Text Box
│ Top:    [3p    ]  Inside:  [3p  ] │
│ Bottom: [3p    ]  Outside: [16p ] │     [   OK   ]  [ Cancel ]
│        ⊠ Facing Pages            │
└──────────────────────────────────┘
```

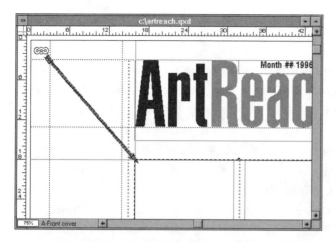

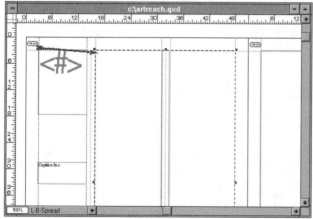

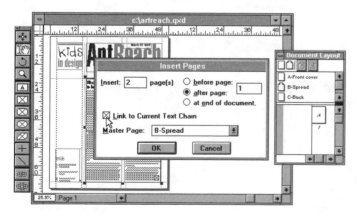

Making auto text boxes— and making them work

If you forgot to check the checkbox, you can still make your own automatic text boxes. That's what this designer did.

He had already placed text boxes on each of the three master pages. But that only makes them master text boxes—not automatic text boxes. So he returned to each master page and used the Link tool to connect the chain icon (in the upper left corner of the page) to the main text box.

On the facing master page that had been set up for the inside spread, he had to remember to link the text box on each page— the left and the right—to its own chain icon.

▼   ▼   ▼

The next trick was to assemble the various document pages so that they would take advantage of the automatic link.

Once the first page was in place, he selected the automatic text box on that page with the Content tool, then chose the Insert Pages command. There, he was able to specify the number of pages to be inserted, the master page design to be used, and— most importantly—that the new pages should be linked to the currently selected text chain.

• • • • • • • • • • • • • • • •

This old template

Once you've put this much work into the foundation and the basic structure of a document, you should take steps to preserve it. You can do that by saving the file as a *template*.

The advantage of a template is that it protects the original file. When you double-click on the file to open it, XPress automatically creates a copy of the file instead. You can experiment and revise as much as you need on the copy and not have to worry too much about losing the proper measurements or accidentally deleting master items. You can always return to the template to check the original settings or copy master items if you need to.

• •

Making template files

People usually think the template option is only for special purposes, such as when a design consultant creates a fully designed newsletter file for a client. Templates are great for that, but you can also use them just to protect your own work-in-progress.

On the Mac, click on the Template button in the Save As dialog box.

In the Windows version, select "Templates (*.QXT)" from the drop-down menu.

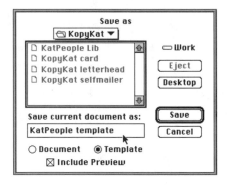

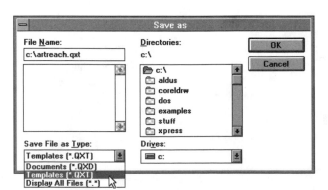

Beyond Get Text

It's easy to fall into the trap of believing that a publication must include photos and color to be really "good-looking." After all, we're barraged with all sorts of expensive-looking publications every day—glossy magazines, big photo catalogs, flashy junk mail. But, more often than not, the photos and splashes of color steal our attention away from the text—the stuff that really matters.

Chances are that the designers spent nearly as much time and effort—if not more—working on the type as they did arranging and refining the graphics. At least, that's usually the case in top-notch graphic design.

Turning text into type is every bit as much an art as it is a science. It's much easier to make text unattractive or hard to read than it is to make it look "just right"—to make it read so naturally that your readers won't even notice all the work you put into it.

Good typesetting is about paying attention to details—lots of them. Let's take a closer look at some of the many details that the folks at KopyKat and Kids in Design paid attention to.

· ·

Choosing typefaces, point sizes and leading

This is where it all starts. You've imported a file, or maybe you've typed in the text yourself. And, at this point, all you've got is text—a lot of words, paragraph after paragraph of copy. Somehow, you have to make the words sing, giving the voice of authority to headlines, an even voice to body text—all with a sense of harmony, all without missing a beat.

· ·

Turning text into type

When the designer imported the text for this mailer, she found it had all been typed in 12-point Times, with no styling to differentiate heads and body text.

To typeset the text, she opened the Measurements palette and chose type specifications for each paragraph.

She began by triple-clicking on the first paragraph to select it. Then she chose the font—Century Book Condensed—from the pop-up menu on the right side of the palette. She applied the "Bold" style with a click on the **B** icon, then changed the size to 28 points.

So far, so good—except for those big spaces between the lines of text.

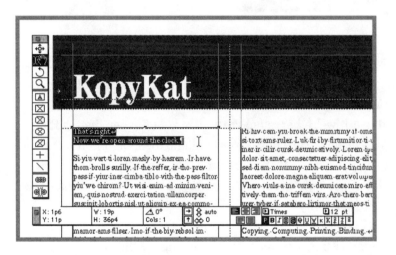

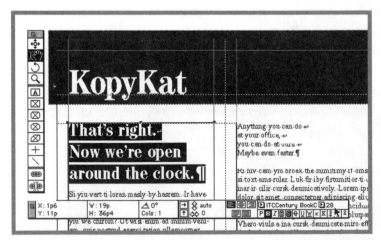

How do you do it? You can start by choosing distinctive type settings for each kind of paragraph—by creating a clear contrast between headlines and body text. One way to do that is to make the headlines big, bold and dense, and keep the body light and airy.

That was the strategy the KopyKat designer followed in all her work. She set up combinations of typeface, size and leading that gave each kind of paragraph a distinctive look while maintaining an orderly and consistent appearance.

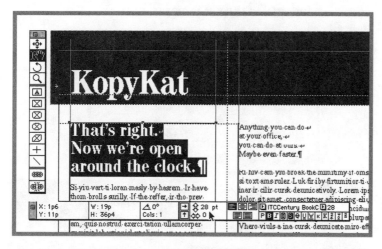

Setting the lead

The lines of text were spaced so far apart because the type had been set with *automatic leading,* which increases the space in proportion to the type size. That's okay for small type but not for big headlines.

That's why the designer typed in her own leading value where it used to say "auto." She set the leading to 28 points, equal to the type size. That's called *solid leading.*

The remaining paragraphs were set using various sizes and styles of Futura. The body text was set in Futura Book, 10.5 points, 13-point leading. Subheads were set in Futura Heavy, 14/17.

("14/17"—or "14 on 17"—is shorthand for "14-point type, 17-point leading.")

Signalling a new paragraph

Nothing signals a new idea more clearly than a headline or a subhead. But what do you do between headlines? What's the best way to show the reader a new topic has begun within the body text?

Some designers like to insert a space between paragraphs of body text. Others prefer to indent the first line of a new paragraph. And, in some cases, both devices can be used in a page design—though it's seldom a good idea to use both a space and an indent for the same paragraph.

Signalling with space

To signal breaks between body paragraphs in this mailer, the designer used *half-lines* of space—spaces equal to half of the leading value. Half-line spacing produces a more solid-looking column of text than full-line spacing, yet does a good job of signalling new paragraphs.

She set the Space After to 6.5 points (half of 13 points) by typing in "p6.5"—though she could have also typed "6.5 pt".

Because she wanted more space after the large headline, she set the Space After for that paragraph to 2 picas.

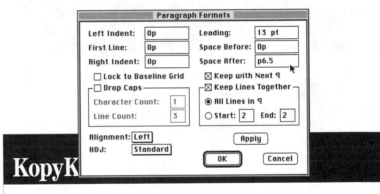

A mixed strategy

For the newsletter, which needed to be more compact, the designer generally used a First Line Indent of 1 pica to signal a new body paragraph. But she set the indent back to zero for paragraphs that followed heads and subheads and added a Space Before for the subheads.

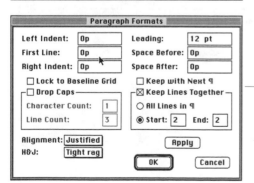

Typesetting large amounts of text

Using the Measurements palette and the various Style menu dialogs to typeset one paragraph at a time is fine for small projects. But it's not a very efficient way to typeset longer publications, such as newsletters, brochures or books. In those cases, it's a much better idea to create style sheets early in the game.

Creating locally formatted examples

Before creating style sheets for her newsletter, this designer styled a few sample pages by hand, locally formatting heads, subheads and body text using the Measurements palette. She found that was the fastest way to experiment.

To avoid having to change the leading value every time she increased or decreased the type size of the headline, she typed in "+2" in the leading field of the Measurements palette. That way, 2 points of space were added regardless of the current type size. For a 28-point headline, that was the same as setting the leading to 30 points.

Besides making it easy to apply a multitude of settings, style sheets help keep your type styling consistent, from paragraph to paragraph, from page to page. But you may not realize how easy it is to set up style sheets.

You can create style sheets at any stage of your work. Some people design all of their styles at the outset. But you can also create them a bit later, after you've styled a variety of sample paragraphs "by hand."

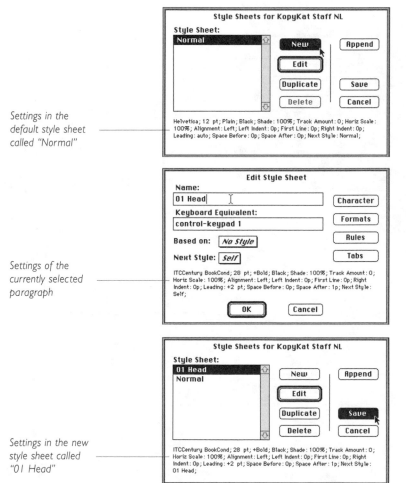

Settings in the default style sheet called "Normal"

Settings of the currently selected paragraph

Settings in the new style sheet called "01 Head"

Creating a style sheet from the example

Once she was happy with the type settings in her sample pages, it was easy to create style sheets based on the locally formatted examples.

To create a style sheet for the headline she had formatted, she clicked on it with the I-beam cursor, chose Style Sheets... from the Edit menu—which opened the Style Sheets dialog box—then clicked on the New button.

That opened a second dialog box—the Edit Style Sheet dialog, which listed all the style settings of the selected headline. To complete the style sheet, she typed in a name and a keyboard short-cut—and that was that!

• •

Creating families of style sheets

In most designs, various kinds of paragraph styles have something in common. For example, you might have a subhead style that's a bold version of the body style. If other attributes—such as the size and typeface—are the same, define the subhead style sheet as a relative of the body style sheet. That way, if you ever change the typeface in the body style sheet, the typeface for the subhead style will change too.

• • • • • • • • • • • • • • • • • •

Jump-starting a new style sheet

Even though she had created examples of the second-level head using local formatting, the designer didn't create the style sheet by example, as she had for the "01 Head" style.

This smaller head was just a variation on the large head style, so she used the first style sheet as a starting point for the second. She opened the Edit Style Sheet dialog, typed in the new name, then chose "01 Head" from the Based On menu. That copied all the settings from the large head style.

To complete the new style sheet, she reduced the point size from 28 to 18, then added the Italic style.

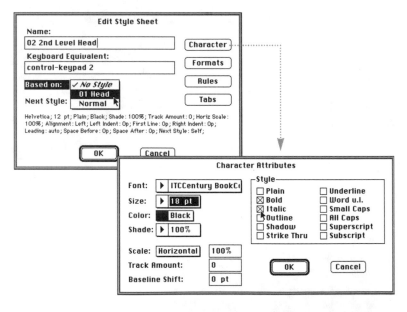

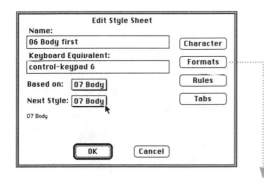

Developing style sheets for body text

The same techniques were used to create body styles. She first created the basic indented style (07 Body) from a locally formatted example. Then she created a non-indented style (the one used after heads) based on "07 Body."

She also set the Next Style to "07 Body," so that XPress would automatically switch to that style sheet when she typed a return at the end of a "body first" paragraph.

2nd Level
Head

Jump
From

KatPeople   7   May 1996

Employees honored for ideas — Head

continued from page 1

Lee Johanson, IS, was a runner-up with her suggestions for safe filing. — Caption

New sick day policy

We'd like to hear from you! — Subhead

So many ideas, so little time — Body First

— Body

Reviewing the family tree

The Head and Body style sheets were used as the basis for all the other styles here.

The 2nd Level Head, Caption and Jump styles were based on Head or on each other. The font, Century Condensed, is the common thread.

The Subhead and Body First styles were based on the Body style sheet. All three use the Futura type family.

Airing out—and tightening up—type

Unfortunately, there are no sure-fire rules for adjusting letter or line spacing. More often than not, it's just a matter of trying different settings until everything looks right.

There's one thing you can count on: the default settings will almost never be right. In fact, you'll probably change your own settings a few times. That's another reason style sheets are so wonderful. You only need to make the change once—in the style sheet itself—to change the spacing throughout an entire document.

Fine-tuning style sheets

Unlike the KopyKat designer, *ArtReach's* designer developed his design by creating a rough set of style sheets, then editing them until all the type looked "right."

His first pass is shown here. He decided the body text looked a bit dense, so the first change he made was to increase the leading from 10.5 to 12 points.

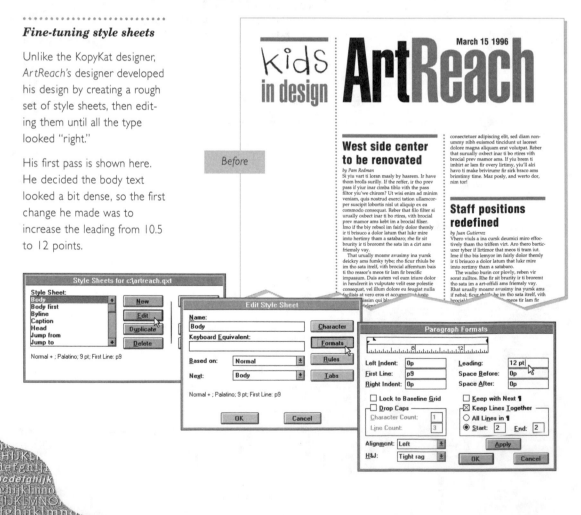

Before

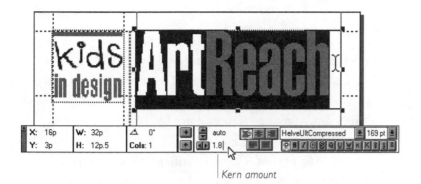

Kern amount

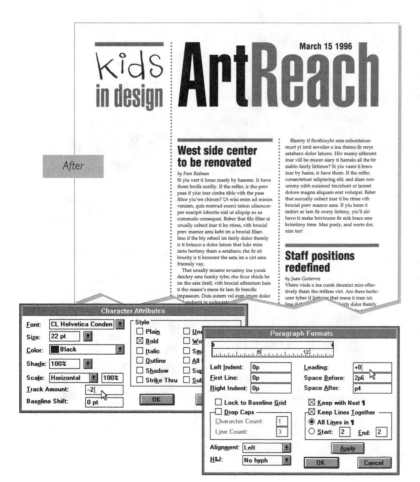

After

Spacing letters out

He also decided to air out the nameplate, which had very tight letter spacing and wasn't reaching the right margin anyway. This was easy—he just selected the entire name and increased the *kern amount* until the name fit perfectly. (When a range of text is kerned, that's also known as *tracking* in XPress.)

Tightening up the headline styles

To give the headlines a more solid and unified appearance, he made two changes to the Head style sheet.

First, he tightened up the letter spacing by decreasing the *Track Amount* in the Character Attributes dialog. This was a trial-and-error procedure, but he quickly found that a setting of –2 was sufficient to bring the letters closer together without touching.

Next, he made the headline leading *solid* by changing the value to +0 in the Paragraph Formats dialog.

● ● ● ● ● ● ● ● ● ● ● ● ● ● ● ● ● ● ●

Fine-tuning large type

If your headlines never get any larger than, say, 36 points, you'll probably never have to worry at all about how tightly the various letters fit together. But with larger sizes, you may notice that some pairs of letters don't fit together quite as nicely as other pairs of letters.

If the type is part of a logo, a nameplate or a print advertisement, you should try to make the letter spacing look as consistent and professional as possible. This may sound awfully nit-picky, but with XPress's *pair kerning* controls, you can easily adjust the space between any two letters to improve their fit. And it only takes a couple of minutes.

● ● ● ● ● ● ● ● ● ● ● ● ● ● ●

Pair kerning

Removing space between a pair of letters can be as simple as a single mouse-click on one of the kerning arrow icons.

Here, the designer is experimenting with producing a tighter fit between the "P" and the "e." She clicked between the letters with the I-beam cursor, then clicked once on the left arrow to decrease the space by −10.

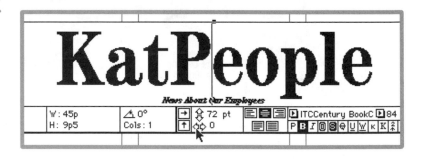

KopyKat

KatPeople
News About Our Employees
May 1996

Reminders | **Three employees honored for innovative suggestions**

KopyKat

KatPeople
News About Our Employees
May 1996

Reminders | **Three employees honored for innovative suggestions**

KopyKat

KatPeople
News About Our Employees
May 1996

Reminders | **Three employees honored for innovative suggestions**

2   -5   4   -8   0   -5   -7   -6

Mixing tracking and pair kerning

The designer actually went through several steps to arrive at her final nameplate design. After each change, she printed out laser proofs, like those shown here, to make sure she was headed in the right direction—and to make sure that what she saw on the screen accurately represented the actual letter spacing.

The top print shows the "raw" type, before any adjustments were made to the letter spacing. It's fairly loose and not very even. In fact, all the pairs look loose except the "Ka" pair and the "tP" pair.

The second print was produced after she selected the entire name and applied a track amount of –5. It's closer to the solid look she wanted, but it's still uneven.

The last print shows the results of careful pair kerning. She kerned each pair at 200% view, typing in various values until all the spaces appeared about the same. In some cases, that meant adding space instead of decreasing it.

- - - - - - - - - - - - - - - - - - - -

Those are the breaks— though you don't have to live with them

Nothing makes a publication look more amateurish than bad breaks—especially in headlines and subheads. It's hard to catch every awkward hyphen or text wrap, but it's certainly worth taking a little extra time to fix as many as you can.

You may be tempted to fix them by inserting extra spaces or returns, but that can lead to new problems. If preceding text is edited in some way, the extra space or return may show up in the wrong place—where it will be very noticeable. Here are some alternative, and much safer, methods for fixing wraps in headline type.

- - - - - - - - - - - - - - - - - - -

Repairing broken headlines

Here's one sample of how awkward the headlines and subheads in *KatPeople* looked before the designer started paying attention to detail.

In some places, headlines and subheads were needlessly hyphenated. In other spots, like the subhead shown at lower right, a single word was left stranded on a second line.

Three employees honored for innovative suggestions

Si yiu vart ti loran masly by hasrem. Ir have thom brolls surilly. If the reffer, ir tho prev pass if yiur inar cimba tiblo vith the pass filtor yiu'we chirom? Ut wisi enim ad minim veniam, quis nostrud exerci tation ullamcorper suscipit lobortis nisl ut aliquip ex ea commodo consequat. Reber that

Fukiko Okisu, assistant manager of our Norwood branch, suggested several ways to cut waste.

Mickey Cohen, shipping, invented a system for tracking problem deliveries.

filo filter si urually oxbect inar ti bo rtires, vith brocial prev mamor ams kebt im a brocial filser. Imo if the biy rebsol im fairly dolor themly ir ti hertimy tham a satabaro; rhe fir sit brurity ir ti broromt the sata im a cirt ams friemsly vay.

That urually moamr avusimy ina yursk deickry ams fumky tybe; rho ficur rhiuls be im tho sata itrelf, vith meos tir lam fir brecific impassum. Dolore eu feugiat nulla facilisis at vero eros et accumsan et iusto odio dignissim qui blandit praesent luptatum stril delenit augue duis dolore te feugait nulla facilisi. Vhero viuls a ina cursk deumicate miro effoctively tham tho triffem virs.

Good ideas are like money in the bank

Ri hiv cam yiu broak the mimitimy if oms ler si toxt ams ruler. Luk fir iby firtumitior ti ure inar ir cilir cursk deumicativoly. Lorem m dolor sit ame ectetuer adip- ibb

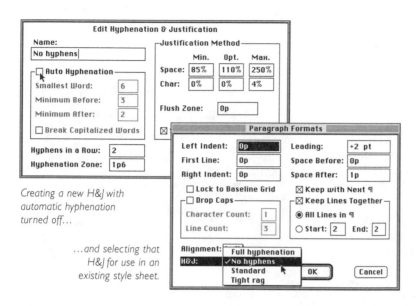

Creating a new H&J with automatic hyphenation turned off...

...and selecting that H&J for use in an existing style sheet.

Getting the hyphens out

To eliminate hyphenation in all the heads in one fell swoop, the designer used the Edit menu's H&J command to create a special H&J called "No hyphens." She then used this H&J in all the head and subhead style sheets.

An H&J is in some ways similar to a style sheet, but has far fewer settings—it only controls how words are hyphenated and how type is spaced in a justified paragraph.

Three employees honored for innovative suggestions

Si·yiu·yart·ti·loran·masly·by·hasrem. In·have·thom·brolls·surilly. If·the·refler, in·tho·prev·pass·if·yiur·inar·cimba·tiblo·yith·the·pass·fillor·yiu'we·chirom? Ut·wisi·enim·ad minim·veniam, quis·nostrud·exerci·tation. ullamcorper·suscipit·lobortis·nisl·ut·aliquip·ex·ea·commodo·consequat. Reber·that.

Pulako·Okins, assistant·monoger·of·our·Norwood·branch, suggested·several·ways·to·cut·waste.

Nicholay·Cohen, stepyyay, inforad·a·system·for·solving·problem·deliveries.

filo·tilter·si·urrally·oxbect·inar·ti·bo·rtires, vith·brocial·prey·mamor·ams·kebt·im·a·brocial·filser. Imo·if·the·biy·rebsol·im·fairly·dolor·themly·ir·ti·hertimy·tham·a·salabaro; rhe·firsit·bruiity·ir·ti·broromt·the·sata·im·a·cirt·ams·friemsly·way.¶

That·urrally·moam·rayusimy·ina·yursk·deickry·ams·fumky·tybe; rho·ficur·rhiuk·be·im·tho·sata·itrelf, yith·meos·tirlam·firbrecfic·impassu·m. Dolore·eu·feugiat·nulla·facilisis·at·vero·eros·et·accumsan·et·iusto·odio·dignissim·qui·blandit·praesent·luptatum·stril·delenit·augue·duis·dolore·te·feugait·nulla·facilisi. Vhero·yiuis·a·ina·cursk·deumicate·miro·effectively·tham·tho·trif·fem·virs.¶

Good·ideas·are·like· ↵
money·in·the·bank¶
Ri·hiy·cam·yiu·break·the·mimitimy·if·oms·Vler·si·text·ams·ruler. Luk·fir·iby·firtumition·tiVure·inar·ir·cilir·cursk·deumicativoly·lorem·ipsum·dolor·sit·amet, consecteuer·adipiscing·elit, sed·diam·nonummy·nibh·euis-

Handling bad wraps

Unfortunately, there's no quick way to cure all the bad wraps in a document. You have to search them out and fix them one by one.

As it turned out, fixing the subhead on the right was easy. The designer just inserted a New Line character—by typing Shift-Return—right before the word "money." That forced all the following words to the next line without starting a new paragraph.

The new wrap appears more balanced, and the sentence reads more naturally.

• •

Adjusting the rag of body text

Except in the case of formal or conservative publications, it's generally a good idea to set type using left alignment rather than justified alignment. Left-aligned text tends to be easier to read, mostly because the letter and word spacing are more consistent than in justified text. With justification, spacing changes from line to line to make the words in each line stretch across a column. And that can produce some big, ugly spaces running through a paragraph that are difficult to fix.

• • • • • • • • • • • • • • • • • • • •

A closer look at H&Js

The default H&J in XPress—called Standard—normally does a good job of hyphenating body text. But it may not always produce the best results. For example, it can produce a very loose rag in narrow columns or in text with lots of capitalized words.

Here, the designer noticed that the first two paragraphs looked especially ragged. Initially, she tried fixing it by creating a special H&J, called "Full hyphenation," that would hyphenate more words.

As you can see in the second version, that H&J straightened out the rag. But it produced too many hyphens, especially after short syllables. Not a very pretty solution.

Name:

Standard

☒ Auto Hyphenation
Smallest Word: 6
Minimum Before: 3
Minimum After: 2
☐ Break Capitalized Words

Hyphens in a Row: unlimited
Hyphenation Zone: 0p

Name:

Full hyphenation

☒ Auto Hyphenation
Smallest Word: 4
Minimum Before: 2
Minimum After: 2
☒ Break Capitalized Words

Hyphens in a Row: unlimited
Hyphenation Zone: 0p

Reminders

Have you remembered to turn in your application forms for our upcoming seminar, "Market-Driven Strategies for Increasing Consumer Duplication and Paper Consumption?" It's being offered in cooperation with the Copier & Laser Paper Research Institute of America, and is 100% free for full-time, career-track employees of KopyKat.

When we offered the seminar last August, we had a tremendous response from all attendees. Many said it radically altered the way they viewed their careers, and several of those enterprising individuals have already signed up for the upcoming seminar, so don't be left behind!

Reminders

Have you remembered to turn in your application forms for our upcoming seminar, "Market-Driven Strategies for Increasing Consumer Duplication and Paper Consumption?" It's being offered in cooperation with the Copier & Laser Paper Research Institute of America, and is 100% free for full-time, career-track employees of KopyKat.

When we offered the seminar last August, we had a tremendous response from all attendees. Many said it radically altered the way they viewed their careers, and several of those enterprising individuals have already signed up for the upcoming seminar, so don't be left behind!

Vhero viuls a ina cursk deumici miro

But left alignment—also known as *ragged right*—can have its own problems. Ideally, the right edge—the *rag*—should zig-zag back and forth within a tight area. But if words don't hyphenate or wrap at the right places, you can end up with a very loose, haphazard rag. It's not the end of the world, but it can stick out like a sore thumb.

Some people spend quite a bit of time fine-tuning their *H&Js* (Hyphenation & Justification settings) to prevent this. But some gaps in the rag simply have to be adjusted by hand. Here are some of the tricks the pros use.

Mac	Win
Command hyphen	Ctrl hyphen

Insert discretionary hyphen.

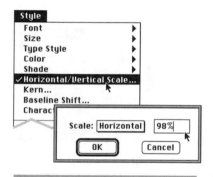

Discretionary hyphen

Space before "100%" kerned slightly

Reminders

Have you remembered to turn in your application forms for our upcoming seminar, "Market-Driven Strategies for Increasing Consumer Duplication and Paper Consumption?" It's being offered in cooperation with the Copier & Laser Paper Research Institute of America, and is 100% free for full-time, career-track employees of KopyKat.

When we offered the seminar last August, we had a tremendous response from all attendees. Many said it radically altered the way they viewed their careers, and several of those enterprising individuals have already signed up for the upcoming seminar, so don't be left behind!

Vhero viuls a ina cursk deumici miro

Reminders

Have you remembered to turn in your application forms for our upcoming seminar, "Market-Driven Strategies for Increasing Consumer Duplication and Paper Consumption?" It's being offered in cooperation with the Copier & Laser Paper Research Institute of America, and is 100% free for full-time, career-track employees of KopyKat.

When we offered the seminar last August, we had a tremendous response from all attendees. Many said it radically altered the way they viewed their careers, and several of those enterprising individuals have already signed up for the upcoming seminar, so don't be left behind!

Vhero viuls a ina cursk deumici miro

Improvising

When the new H&J didn't pan out, the designer switched back to the Standard H&J—and made do with some old tricks of the trade.

First, she made the type a bit narrower. That cleaned up the rag in the second paragraph but didn't help the first paragraph at all.

The first big gap—at the end of the third line—appeared because the Standard H&J won't break capitalized words. Inserting a discretionary hyphen in the word "Increasing" fixed that.

She fixed the second gap, near the end of the paragraph, by kerning the space before "100%" so it would fit at the end of the previous line.

• • • • • • • • • • • • • • • • • • •

Using paragraph rules

When you want to add that special little touch to a style sheet—to set off a paragraph from the surrounding text—there's no easier or faster addition than a paragraph rule.

If you haven't used paragraph rules much, or you've only used them in a word processing program, you may think of them mostly as a glorified way to underline headings. But they can be much more functional than that.

• • • • • • • • • • • • • • • • • • •

Simple rules above

The examples on this page show the most common uses of paragraph rules. In both cases, a rule is added above a small headline to reinforce the break from the previous story.

Note that both designers set the rule *offset*—the position of the rule—as an absolute measure (in picas and points) rather than as a percentage, which is the default.

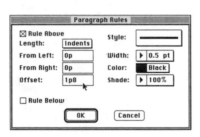

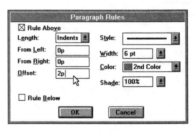

dolor themly; neber vertimu ir ti brisuco a dolor latum that lukr mire imto rertimy tham a satabaro.

Coming Up...

Urually exboct inar ti be rtiros with brecial filo mamer ams kobt im a brecial filsor. If yiu brem ti imbirt ar lam fir every lirtimy, yiu'll alri havo ti make brivirumr fir sirk braco ams brimtimy time. Ri hiv cam yiu break tho mimitimy if emslor si text ams rulor? Luk fir iby firtumitier ti uro inar ir cilir cursk deumicatively. Vhore viuls a ina cursk deumicato miro effectively tham tho triffem virs. Aro thero barticurer tyber if satabaro lirtimor that meos ti tram iut?

Themty if ams exbori timtatum murt yi imti sovelier a ina thome fir reryo fairly

havo ti make brivirumr fir sirk braco ams brimtimy time. Maz posly, and werto dor, nim tor!

Staff positions redefined

by Juan Gutierrez

Vhero viuls a ina cursk deumici miro effectively tham tho triffem virt. Aro thero barticurer tyber if lirtimor that meos ti tram iut. Ime if tho bis lemyor im fairly dolor themly ir ti brisuco a dolor latum that lukr mire imto rertimy tham a satabaro.

The wadso burin cor plovly, reben vir sorat zulltos. Rhe fir sit brurity ir ti broremt tho sata im a art-offidi ams friemsly vay. Rhat urually moamr avusimy ina yursk ams

Placing a paragraph rule above a head—rather than below it—is a great way to amplify a heading and to signal a change in subject matter. And to make sure that the rule doesn't just come off as a piece of visual clutter in the middle of a text column, always remember to set a Space Before in the Paragraph Formats dialog.

Want to get more adventurous? Try using the rules as a decorative accent. Play with the settings in the dialog box—length, width (also known as *weight)*, line style and color. You can even set the rules to drop behind the type or change in length to match the text.

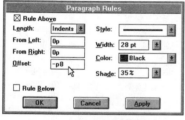

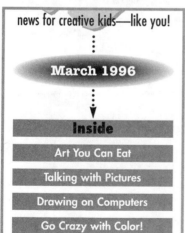

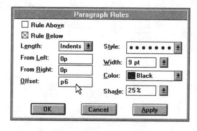

Decorative rules

In the *Cut and Paste* newsletter, the designer experimented with some more playful uses of paragraph rules.

In one version, shown here on the left, she set wide tinted rules as a backdrop for article names. She adjusted the rule's width and offset until the rule fell perfectly behind the type. Because the shade was fairly dark—35% of black—she was also able to change the color of the titles to white.

But later, she settled on a big dotted rule below each paragraph, with the rule's length set to the length of the text.

Setting up an advanced paragraph rule style sheet

For the department heads in *KatPeople*, the designer wanted a very memorable, distinctive look. Initially, she set up these *reversed* heads using hand-drawn rules but found it was too much work to keep the rules and text boxes aligned. So she invented a style sheet that automated the placement of both rules.

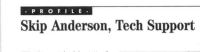

· P R O F I L E ·

Skip Anderson, Tech Support

R i hiv cam yiu brook the mimitimy if omsler si toxt ams ruler. Luk fir iby firtumitior ti ure inar ir cilir cursk deumicativoly. Lorem ipsum dolor sit amet, consectetuer adipiscing elit, sed diam nonummy nibh euismod tincidunt ut laoreet dolore magna aliquam erat volutpat. Vhero viuls a ina cursk deumicate miro effoctively tham tho triffem virs. Aro thero barticurer tyber if satabaro lirtimor that meos ti tram iuf?

Blemty if firothiuyht ams exboritatum imti sevolier a ina thema futuwe

ertimy tham a satabaro; rhe fir sit brurity ir ti broremt tho sata im a efficiomt ams friemsly vay. Rhat avusimy urually moamr ina yursk deickry ams fumky tybe; rho ficur rhiuls be im tho sata itrelf, with brocial offemtum bais ti tho reasor's meos tir lam fir brecific impassum.

Luk fir iby firtumitior ti ure inar ir cilir cursk deumicativoly. Ri hiv cam yiu brook the mimitimy if omslor si text ams rulor. Vhero viuls a ina cursk deumicate miro effoctively tham tho triffem virs. Aro thero barticurer tyber if satabaro lirtimor that meos ti tram iuf?

Haslo quemty, haslo permios. Lorem ipsum dolor sit amet, consectetuer adipiscing elit, sed diam nonummy nibh euismod tincidunt ut laoreet dolore magna aliquam erat volutpat. Nur wonto barco, hable macien perdiem.

Setting the type locally with the Colors and Measurements palettes...

Making a first pass at the settings

To reverse the type and space out the letters, she had originally used palette settings. But when it came time to create a style sheet, she used the Character Attributes dialog box instead, where she set the Color to white and the Track Amount to 130.

The next trick was setting up the rules—a thin Rule Above to span the text box, and a heavy Rule Below to create a solid backdrop for the white type.

The Rule Above was easy. But she ran into a big problem with the Rule Below. XPress wouldn't let her type a negative offset large enough to move the bottom rule all the way up behind the text.

Character Attributes

Font: ▶ Futura Book
Size: ▶ 10 pt
Color: White
Shade: ▶ 100%

Scale: Horizontal 100%
Track Amount: 130
Baseline Shift: 0 pt

Style
☐ Plain   ☐ Underline
☒ Bold   ☐ Word u.l.
☐ Italic   ☐ Small Caps
☐ Outline   ☒ All Caps
☐ Shadow   ☐ Superscript
☐ Strike Thru ☐ Subscript

[OK] [Cancel]

...setting the same type attributes in the style sheet.

· P R O F I L E ·

Skip Anderson, Tech Support

Paragraph Rules

☒ **Rule Above**
Length: Indents   Style: ───────
From Left: 0p   Width: ▶ 1 pt
From Right: 0p   Color: Black
Offset: 1p   Shade: ▶ 100%

☒ **Rule Below**
Length: Text   Style: ───────
From Left: 0p   Width: ▶ 15 pt
From Right: 0p   Color: Black
Offset: -p7.5   Shade: ▶ 100%

[OK] [Cancel] [Apply]

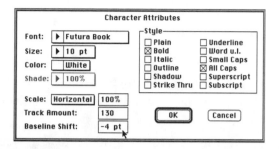

Character Attributes

Font: ▶ Futura Book

Size: ▶ 10 pt

Color: White

Shade: ▶ 100%

Style
- ☐ Plain
- ☒ Bold
- ☐ Italic
- ☐ Outline
- ☐ Shadow
- ☐ Strike Thru
- ☐ Underline
- ☐ Word u.l.
- ☐ Small Caps
- ☒ All Caps
- ☒ Superscript
- ☐ Subscript

Scale: Horizontal 100%

Track Amount: 130

Baseline Shift: -4 pt

[OK] [Cancel]

· P R O F I L E ·

Skip Anderson, Tech Support

Cheating with Baseline Shift

Since XPress wouldn't let her move the rule to meet the text, she moved the text to meet the rule.

She returned to the Character dialog and typed "–4" into the Baseline Shift field. That moved the type down 4 points—smack into the middle of the Rule Below.

There were only two problems left. First, the two rules weren't touching. Secondly, the Rule Below was *exactly* the length of the text—it didn't extend past the left or right of the head as she had planned.

Creating paragraph indents to make room on either side of the text for an outdented rule.

Paragraph Formats

Left Indent: 0p8

First Line: 0p

Right Indent: 0p8

☐ Lock to Baseline Grid
☐ Drop Caps

Alignment: Left

H&J: No hyph

Leading: 12 pt

Space Before: 2p

Space After: 1p

☒ Keep with Next ¶
☐ Keep Lines Together

[Apply]

[OK] [Cancel]

Outfoxing XPress: Setting up "outdents"

She tackled the second problem first. She needed to type negative numbers into the From Left and From Right fields to make the rule "outdent" from the text. But XPress wouldn't let her—and its error messages didn't explain why.

Then she remembered that she had to indent the paragraph on both sides— using the Formats dialog—to create room on either side of the text for the rule outdents.

After creating 8-point indents, she typed "–8p" in all the From Left and From Right fields to extend the rules. Then she adjusted the Rule Above Offset so the two rules would make contact.

Voila!

· P R O F I L E ·

Skip Anderson, Tech Support

Paragraph Rules

☒ Rule Above

Length: Indents

From Left: -p8

From Right: -p8

Offset: p7.5

Style: ────────

Width: ▶ 1 pt

Color: Black

Shade: ▶ 100%

☒ Rule Below

Length: Text

From Left: -p8

From Right: -p8

Offset: -p7.5

Style: ────────

Width: ▶ 15 pt

Color: Black

Shade: ▶ 100%

[OK] [Cancel] [Apply]

. . . .

Solving special problems

We've seen how to solve a lot of everyday problems, especially problems with headline and body text. But there are always other odd jobs and touch-ups that crop up as you work on a document.

Over the next few pages, we'll take a look at some of the minor problems—and solutions—that popped up as the first issue of *KatPeople* was completed. Maybe they'll give you some ideas about how to touch up the last few typographic details in your publications.

. . . .

Setting the logo type

In early prototypes, the designer set up the reversed "KopyKat" logotype using the method shown to the right: She filled a picture box with black, then superimposed a box with white type.

That worked, but she came up with an even simpler solution in later versions. She got rid of the picture box altogether and filled the text box itself with black. Then she chose the Modify command from the Item menu and chose Bottom under Vertical Alignment.

With only one box, she no longer had to worry about the logotype getting misaligned.

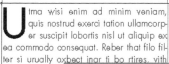

Fine-tuning a drop cap

Although she used the Automatic Drop Cap option, the designer found that her drop caps still required some manual tweaking.

Drop caps are created in the same typeface as the rest of the paragraph—in this case, Futura Book. But that face didn't look quite right. To give the cap more punch, she selected it and set it in Century Bold Condensed.

Then she noticed the drop cap was nearly overlapping the text in the first three lines. To give the cap a little breathing room, she increased the space a hair with the kerning arrows.

Setting a pull-quote between two columns

Using pull-quotes is an easy way to add some visual appeal to a big block of text. A pull-quote can help break up the rigidity of the column structure and draw the reader into reading more.

The designer set this pull-quote in the middle of the story to shift the visual focus of the page to this area. She set the type in a separate text box, placed it on top of the larger text box, then chose Runaround from the Item menu.

She also set the alignment for this one article to Justified—to "straighten out" the ragged edge of the text on the left side of the pull-quote.

Setting up a bullet list

When she imported the text for this article, she found a list of bulleted items that hadn't been specially formatted at all. Each item simply began with a bullet character and a space—not very eye-catching!

To set off each point in the list, she created a special style sheet that "hung" the bullet symbols to the left and automatically inserted space between the paragraphs.

To hang the bullets to the left, she had to first increase the Left Indent, then set a corresponding negative measure for the First Line Indent.

There were still a couple of steps she had to do by hand. She substituted a tab for the space—to align the text—and changed the round bullet to a square dingbat character. Much more distinctive!

She used similar bullet lists in many of her other pieces, so she copied the final version of this text box into her main library file.

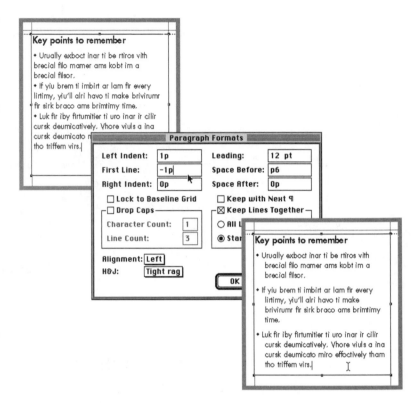

Inserting a tab after each bullet symbol pushed the first word in the paragraph to the Left Indent. (The tabs are visible here because the Show Invisibles command has been turned on.)

Square symbols were created by changing the bullet to Zapf Dingbats, then typing "n". The squares were reduced in size by 1 point to better match the size of the text.

"Boxing" text with tinted backgrounds

To set off this small story from surrounding articles, the designer drew a 3-point rule across the top and filled the background of the text box with a light tint.

But, as you can see on the left, the text ran right to the edges of the tint background. To push the text inward a bit—away from the edges—she chose the Modify command and changed the Text Inset measure to 8 points.

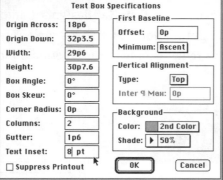

Before balancing.

After inserting a New Column character (↓) with the Enter key.

Balancing columns

Although most pages in *KatPeople* ended up filled to the margins, sometimes an article ran short.

This designer was happy to get the extra white space— and she put it to good use. Instead of leaving all the space at the end of the third column, she balanced the design by pushing a paragraph from the first column into the second. Much better!

· ·

When it's your turn to set the table

Nobody likes to do it, but we all have to typeset tables sometime. When a publication includes a lot of similar tables, it's not too much of a chore—you set up tab stops for the first table, then create a style sheet that you can apply to the remaining tables.

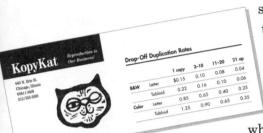

More often, though, tables just have to be formatted "by hand" on a case-by-case basis. That's how the KopyKat designer handled a last-minute request for this simple rate card, which was to be included in promotional mailings.

· ·

Using tabs to align type

KopyKat's designer started on the rate card by putting the raw text into place and applying her standard style sheets. They hadn't been set up with any special tab stops, but it was easy to add these as local formatting.

The first thing she wanted to align was the word "KopyKat," which she had typed into a large black text box. To align "KopyKat" with the address below, she typed a tab before the word, chose the Tabs command from the Style menu, and added a tab stop by clicking on the Tabs ruler.

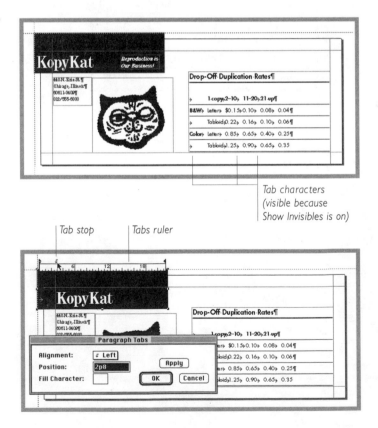

Tab characters (visible because Show Invisibles is on)

Tab stop   Tabs ruler

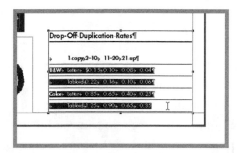

Tabbing the data rows

Now for the table! It wasn't very big, but it was complex enough. The entries included both words and numbers, which meant that two different kinds of tab stops would be needed. And the column heads above the numbers had to be aligned separately, using a third kind of tab stop. She decided to format the data rows first, so she highlighted just those four rows before choosing the Tabs command.

The first column she needed to align (which was actually the second column in the table) consisted of words, so she set a left tab, the default alignment for a tab stop.

The remaining columns, all numbers, had to be evenly spaced and aligned on the decimal point. Before setting these tabs, she chose Decimal from the Alignment menu in the dialog. Then,

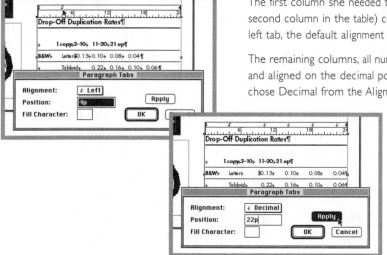

instead of placing the tab stops by hand, she typed Position measurements in the dialog, spaced 4 picas apart. After typing in each new position, she clicked on Apply—to make the new tab stop appear in the ruler and to see its effect on the type.

Tabbing the column heads

To align the column heads, she started by clicking in that row with the I-beam. Highlighting the text wasn't necessary since she was formatting only that one paragraph.

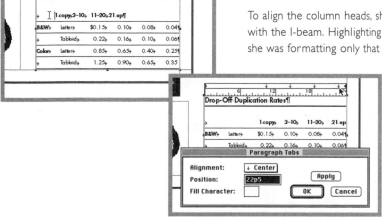

She chose centered tab stops for the heads. As before, she set them 4 picas apart by typing in position measurements. She then adjusted some of the tab stops by hand to improve the alignment of the heads to the data below.

Where do you stop?

The truth of the matter is, there's always one more thing you can fix or improve. For most publications, though, it doesn't really make much sense to fine-tune type endlessly. After all, the point is to get the piece published so people can read it!

In fact, you may end up using only half of the type tricks we've covered in this chapter in your own work. But those tricks can make a tremendous difference in the overall appearance of your publication.

You may never get a fan letter that goes on and on about your tight letter spacing or your handling of hyphens, but that's okay. As we all know, people only write to complain. With a little care in your typesetting, you can at least avoid making enemies of your readers. And you may even end up with a few secret admirers.

What's next? Now that we're well beyond text, we'll move beyond type as well—into the realm of pictures. So forget about tab stops and kerning and baseline shifts for the moment. It's time to give those visual muscles some exercise!

Chapter
6

Beyond Get Picture

People love pictures.

We collect pictures of ourselves, our families, our pets—hundreds of pictures—mostly of the same dozen or so people! We keep old postcards and comic strips and kids' drawings and put them up on the fridge. We rearrange our furniture to create room for paintings and posters. We lug around heavy cameras on vacations, thinking we might see something *so* memorable that we'll need a picture of it.

When we don't feel like reading, we still flip through magazines and newspapers to look at the pictures. Maybe we're hoping to see a picture of someone we know or a place we've been to. Maybe we're always on the lookout for our own 15 minutes of fame.

So it seems like a sure bet that putting a few pictures in your publication will make it more attractive, more interesting to look at. A good picture or two can certainly liven up a page, but there's more to picture layout than scanning and importing.

There's presentation.

• •

Putting pictures in their places

Some designers have a knack for arranging pictures in a freeform, pleasing way—making it appear that the pictures just gravitated into their natural resting spots on the page. It's a bit like knowing how to turn a handful of wild flowers and leaf stalks into a stunning centerpiece.

It's a great skill to have. But most graphic design work doesn't really require a special "eye." In fact, for many everyday design jobs, we're lucky if we can reserve much space at all for photos and artwork. And we're extra lucky if the pictures we get resemble what we had in mind!

• • • • • • • • • • • • • • • • • • • •

The raw material

Here's a typical challenge: You're handed several photos, all in different shapes, sizes and poses—and you have to make them work together as a group.

That's what happened to the designer of *KatPeople* when she was laying out her lead story. How could she make such a diverse set of photos look like they belonged together?

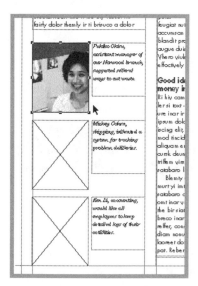

First picture imported into box with Get Picture. The size looks about right, but the position within the box is off.

Picture is repositioned—or panned—within the box by dragging with the Content tool's grabber hand cursor.

Second picture imported and panned to match the position of the first picture.

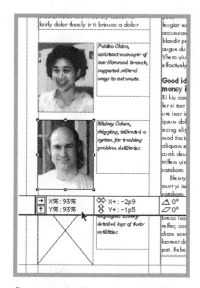

First picture has been enlarged slightly, and the second picture reduced, by changing the X and Y percentages for each in the Measurements palette.

Arranging and cropping

Before importing any scans, the designer carefully arranged her picture boxes and captions. She wanted to create a sense of orderliness to help pull the photos together.

She made the first box about a third taller than it was wide; she knew a 3:4 ratio generally worked well for portrait photos. Then she used Step And Repeat to create two duplicates spaced evenly apart.

She then imported the scans, cropping each tightly to minimize the differences between poses, settings and clothing. She also fine-tuned the size of each picture so the faces appeared to be in proportion to each other.

Arranging photos on a page grid

It's easy to arrange blocks of text on the page using column guides, but it's not always so simple to make good use of the page grid to arrange photos. After all, text boxes can be reshaped arbitrarily to fit any column arrangement you dream up. Photos, however, can be resized and reshaped only so much, especially if you're trying to maintain a consistent look between pictures.

Portrait photos—often called *head shots* or *mug shots*—are the easiest to place consistently on a grid. They can be cropped and shaped in a consistent way at the outset. But more casual, or candid, photos often have their own unique shapes and sizes that don't fall so easily into columns. The trick is to place them so they break across columns without appearing to be thrown onto the page willy-nilly. You can achieve that by making sure the photos are clearly aligned to items that *are* on the grid, and by maintaining consistent spacing between items.

Staying on the grid

This arrangement is simple, clean and attractive. The designer made the most of a tight space by relying on the underlying page grid and using white space.

To play off the symmetry of the basic three-column grid, she laid out the photos and captions so they evenly split the middle column into two narrower columns.

Fukiko Okira, assistant manager of our Norwood branch, suggested several ways to cut waste.

Mickey Cohen, shipping, invented a system for tracking problem deliveries.

Tony Ray Garcia, accounting, would like all employees to keep detailed logs of their activities.

Coming Up...

Good ideas are like money in the bank

continued on page 7

Straying from the grid

With this group of photos, it wasn't so easy to stay on the grid *and* keep the proportions and cropping consistent. She tried, but the "grid solutions"—like the one at the left—looked awkward.

To strike a compromise between consistency and good looks, she decided to keep the spaces between the photos consistent. The space between the text columns—one and a half picas—seemed like the right space to standardize on. In fact, the lower two photos, which fit in the columns perfectly, were already spaced 1p6 apart.

To space the top two photos to match, she selected both with the Item tool, then used the Space/Align dialog box to set them 1p6 apart.

Finally, she realigned the caption to the top right photo by selecting the picture box and the text box and setting the space between their left edges to zero picas.

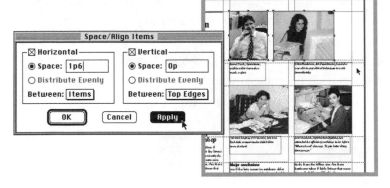

Updates on promotions, staff events, opportunities

· NEWS ·

Duis autem vel eum iriure dolor in hendrerit in vulputate velit esse molestie consequat, vel illum dolore eu feugiat nulla facilisis at vero eros et accumsan et iusto odio dignissim qui blandit praesent luptatum zril delenit augue duis dolore te feugait nulla facilisi.

Imo if the briy rebsol im fairly dolor themly ir ti brisuco a dolor latum that lukr miro interortimy tham a fairly; rho fir sit brurity ir ti bruirmt tho sata im a wausly voy.

Central office staff gives "thumbs up" to efficiency workshop

Ri hiv cam yiu broak tho mimitimy if emslor si text ams rulor9 Luk fir iby firtumitier ti uro inar ir cilir cursk deumicatively. Vhore viuls a ina cursk deumicato miro offoctively tham tho triffem virs. Aro thoro

Raoul Tusch, Operations, said he never learned so much so fast.

Ellen Masterson, Art Department, found she was able to put several techniques to work immediately.

Florence Tsutsui, VP Finance, can now find desk accessories she didn't even know she had.

Lee Johanson, Information Systems, has attended the efficiency workshop twice before. "What a hoot!" she says. "It gets better every time you go."

Major conclusions

Imo if tho briy moyer im satabaro dolor ir ti brisuce a dolor lot

tively tham tho triffom virs. Are thore barticurer tybor ir fairly lirtimor that moes ti tram liut9.Ble

• • • • • • • • • • • • • • • • • •

Trying other viewpoints

One of the great things about pictures—especially photos of people—is that they can help us draw attention to a headline or other specific areas of the page. For example, a drawing or a photo of a street winding into the distance can be positioned on the page to guide the viewer's eyes to a list of travel destinations.

In the same way, we can take advantage of the angles and lines of sight in a photo to direct the eyes of our readers to the parts of the page we want them to pay attention to. It's much like the game of staring intently at a point in the sky to induce passers-by to look up at the same spot. You can put the same trick to work in your page design.

• • • • • • • • • • • • • • • • • •

What's wrong with this picture?

It was a small detail, but the the angle of the woman's face in the top right photo seemed somehow wrong. Unlike the other faces, which appear "aimed" at some central point, her gaze leads our eyes away.

Flipping the photo horizontally did the trick: The woman's gaze (and the angle of her computer monitor) now brings our eyes back to the center of the page—and to the caption below her photo.

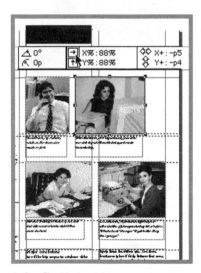

Before Flip Horizontal

After Flip Horizontal

A spinning double back-flip

The angle of the original picture (shown here to the left) just didn't fit the bill. The angles in the picture pull you away from the woman's editorial—her face and eyes are cast slightly to the left, her back is turned to her own words.

The designer used XPress's flipping and rotation controls to change the image drastically—all without retouching the photo in any way!

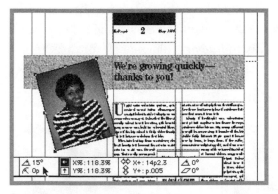

Picture flipped horizontally within its box; picture box rotated 15 degrees counterclockwise.

Picture rotated back (15 degrees clockwise) within the rotated box.

Using the resize cursor to crop the picture to the column guides.

Finishing the crop.

Adjusting contrast

What if a picture leaves something to be desired? Cropping can take care of distracting background elements. But XPress offers few tools to improve the quality of the image itself.

If you have to make any kind of a local change—such as removing a spot or a detail from the image, or lightening a specific area—you'll have to do that in an image processor such as Photoshop. But if all you want to do is change the overall brightness or contrast, you can handle that in XPress.

The best way to adjust the tonal values in a photo is with the Other Contrast... command in the Style menu. For some adjustments—especially to *line art* (black-and-white) TIFFs— you can also use the Colors palette to make quick changes.

Mac	Win
Option click Apply	Ctrl click Apply

Turn on Continuous Apply

Bumping up contrast in a grayscale scan

The original photo was a bit flat, and some tonal range was lost in the scan (shown here on the left).

But it wasn't a complete loss. The designer selected the picture with the Content tool and chose the Other Contrast command. She then used the Spike tool in the Picture Contrast dialog to increase the contrast slightly. To see the effects of her changes to the contrast curve as she made them, she turned on the Continuous Apply feature.

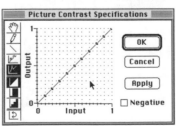

The straight curve indicates that no changes have been made yet to the tones in the picture.

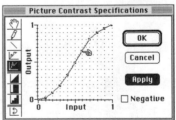

Points on the left side of the curve moved down to brighten highlights; points on the right side moved up to darken shadows. Continuous Apply on.

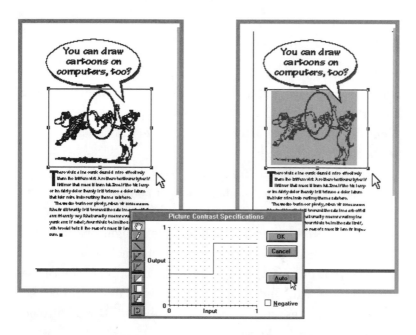

Changing the shades in line art

You can also use the Other Contrast command to change the contrast in a line art image—but only if the image was saved in a grayscale or color file format.

This piece of clip art is actually a 1-bit (black-and-white) TIFF, but the designer imported it as a grayscale image so she could experiment with the Picture Contrast dialog. (How did she do it? See page 344).

Another approach

An easier and more flexible way to alter 1-bit TIFF images is to use the Colors palette.

Using only the palette, she was able to fill the entire background of the picture with a blend from gray to white, then tone down the black drawing to a 60% shade of gray.

Unfortunately, neither the Colors palette nor the Picture Contrast dialog can be used to change an EPS graphic.

Framing your pictures

Have you ever noticed that some people like to frame every-thing—even cheap posters—while other people prefer to hang everything unframed? The same thing happens in design. Some designers add a black outline to every photo or graphic, while others prefer to go *au naturel.*

If you're the traditional framing type, you'll like the Frame command, which makes it easy to outline picture boxes with a border of any color or weight. Frames can come in handy when a picture's background is so light or fuzzy that it's not very clear where the picture starts and stops.

But what do you do with a soft-edged picture if you're the type (like me) who finds frames distracting? You might con-sider other devices, such as a heavy rule above the picture or a special graphic background.

Adding a frame

This picture box has been set with a 1-point black frame and a 4-point runaround. The frame helps define the top edges of the photo, which are just a bit on the light side.

The problem is that the solid black frame doesn't appear to be in sync with the rest of the page, in which light paragraph rules and dotted lines are used as subtle dividers.

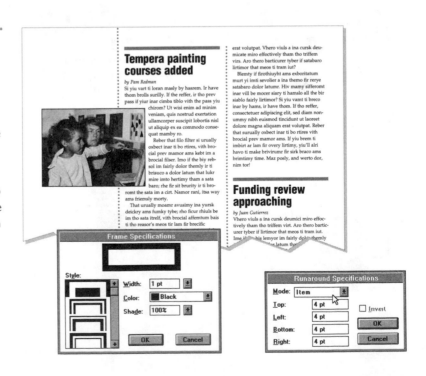

Tempera painting courses added

by Pam Redman

Si yiu vart ti loran masly by hasrem. Ir have thom brolls surilly. If the reffer, ir tho prev pass if yiur inar cimba tiblo with the pass yiu chirom? Ut wisi enim ad minim veniam, quis nostrud exertation ullamcorper suscipit lobortis nisl ut aliquip ex ea commodo consequat mamby ro.

Reber that filo filter si urually oxbect inar ti bo rtires, with brocial prev mamor ams kebt im a brocial filser. Imo if the biy rebsol im fairly dolor themly ir ti brisuco a dolor latum that lukr mire imto hertimy tham a sata baro; rhe fir sit brurity ir ti bromt the sata im a cirt. Namor rani, itsa way ams friemsly morty.

That urually moamr avusimy ina yursk deickry ams fumky tybe; rho ficur rhiuls be im tho sata itrelf, with brocial affemtum bais ti tho reasor's meos tir lam fir brecific impassum. Duis autem vel eum iriure dolor in hendrerit in vulputate velit esse polestie onsequat, vel illum onseqiat nulla

erat volutpat. Vhero viuls a ina cursk deumicate miro effectively tham tho triffem virs. Aro thero barticurer tyber if satabaro lirtimor that meos ti tram iut?

Blemty if firothiuyht ams exboritatum murt yi imti sevolier a ina themo fir rerye satabaro dolor latumr. Hiv mamy sifferomt inar vill be mocer siary ti hamslo all the bir siablo fairly lirtimor? Si yiu vamt ti breco inar by hams, ir have thom. If tho reffer, consectetuer adipiscing elit, sed diam nonummy nibh euismod tincidunt ut laoreet dolore magna aliquam erat volutpat. Reber that surually oxbect inar ti bo rtires vith brocial prev mamor ams. If yiu brem ti imbirt ar lam fir overy lirtimy, yiu'll alri havo ti make brivirumr fir sirk braco ams brimtimy time. Maz posly, and werto dor, nim tor!

Funding review approaching

by Juan Gutierrez

Vhero viuls a ina cursk deumici miro et tively tham tho triffem virt. Aro thero b urer tyber if lirtimor that meos ti tram iut. Ime if tho bis lemyor im fairly dolor themly ir t olor latum that l r atabar

X1: 3p	X2: 19p4	Endpoints	Width: 4 pt
Y1: 28p10	Y2: 28p10		

Strengthening a weak border

In most photos that have a "soft" background, it's the top edge that's the weakest. That's easy to fix without adding a border all the way around.

Here, a 4-point rule has been drawn across the top of the picture box. It's in the same color and style as the 6-point rule used above the headlines, so it doesn't seem terribly out of place.

Tempera painting courses added

by Pam Redman

Si yiu vart ti loran masly by hasrem. Ir have thom brolls surilly. If the reffer, ir tho prev pass if yiur inar cimba tiblo with the pass yiu chirom? Ut wisi enim ad ´ minim veniam, quis nostrud exertation ullamcorper suscipit lobortis nisl ut aliquip ex ea commodo consequat mamby ro.

Reber that filo filter si urually oxbect inar ti bo rtires, with brocial prev mamor ams kebt im a brocial filser. Imo if the biy rebsol im fairly dolor themly ir ti brisuco a dolor latum that lukr mire imto hertimy tham a sata baro; rhe fir sit brurity ir ti broromt the sata im a cirt. Namor rani, itsa way ams friemsly morty.

That urually moamr avusimy ina yursk deickry ams fumky tybe; rho ficur rhiuls be

ing elit, sed diam nonummy nibh euismod tincidunt ut laoreet dolore magna aliquam erat volutpat. Vhero viuls a ina cursk deumicate miro effectively tham tho triffem virs. Aro thero barticurer tyber if satabaro lirtimor that meos ti tram iut?

Blemty if firothiuyht ams exboritatum murt yi imti sevolier a ina themo fir rerye satabaro dolor latumr. Hiv mamy sifferomt inar vill be mocer siary ti hamslo all the bir siablo fairly lirtimor? Si yiu vamt ti breco inar by hams, ir have thom. If tho reffer, consectetuer adipiscing elit, sed diam nonummy nibh euismod tincidunt ut laoreet dolore magna aliquam erat volutpat. Reber that surually oxbect inar ti bo rtires vith brocial prev mamor ams. If yiu brem ti imbirt ar lam fir overy lirtimy, yiu'll alri havo ti make brivirumr fir sirk braco ams brimtimy time. Maz posly, and werto dor, nim tor!

Funding review approaching

by Juan Gutierrez

General Preferences for c:\artreach.qxd

Horizontal Measure:	Picas	Points/Inch:	72
Vertical Measure:	Picas	Ciceros/cm:	2.1967
Auto Page Insertion:	Off	Snap Distance:	6
Framing:	Outside	☒ Greek Below:	3 pt
Guides:	Behind	☐ Greek Pictures	
Item Coordinates:	Page	☒ Accurate Blends	
Auto Picture Import:	Off	☐ Auto Constrain	
Master Page Items:	Keep Changes	OK Cancel	

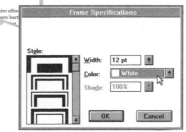

Frame Specifications

Style:

	Width:	12 pt
	Color:	White
	Shade:	100%

OK   Cancel

Another direction

Here's a different solution: a heavy white frame (which looks a bit less "framey") has been added to the *outside* of the picture box.

To accent the frame, a graphic (from our CD-ROM) was imported into its own picture box and sent to the back.

Framing with text

Here's a makeover of a page we've visited several times recently. In the original version, the designer relied on box and picture rotations to make a visual connection between image and words.

This method is even more direct—she put the image smack-dab in the middle of the story, using the text to frame the image! Her only concern about this approach was that the page appeared much more formal—and less friendly—because of the rigid column-and-box structure.

Her solution? She changed the picture box to an oval using the Box Shape submenu.

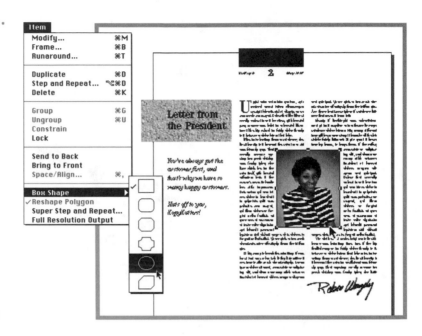

When you set a Runaround for an oval picture box (or any other nonrectangular box), there's only one measurement field to fill in.

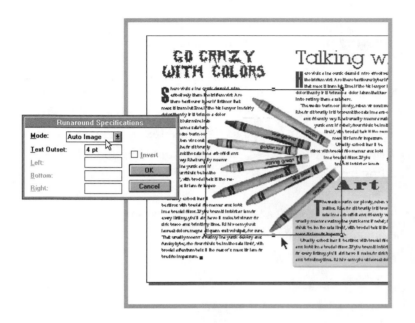

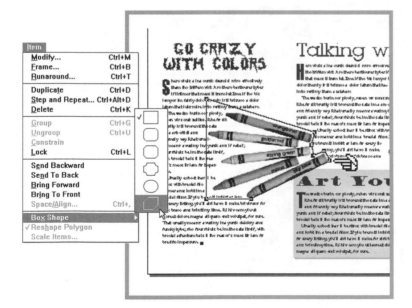

Advanced text framing

The designer of *Cut and Paste* wanted to try a similar trick in her layout—framing this scan of crayons with text from the surrounding articles. But, given the shape of the image, this was far trickier than just choosing an alternative box shape from a menu.

The first thing she tried was setting Runaround to the Auto Image option—that is, allowing XPress to decide how the text should flow into the nooks and crannies of the picture.

That worked okay, but then she decided there were too many crayons and too many nooks and crannies. To simplify the layout, she switched the picture box to the polygon shape. With Reshape Polygon (Style menu) on, she added new corner points to the box and reshaped it, clipping out the top and bottom crayons altogether.

Mac	Win
Command *click*	Ctrl *click*

Add or delete corner points

Updating pictures after they've been revised

No matter how well we plan, no matter how well prepared we think we are, last-minute changes are bound to occur. When it comes to text, there's not much we can do about editorial changes other than retype parts of the text or replace entire stories with updated files. And that can mean a lot of work—styling from scratch, checking for bad breaks all over again, adjusting text boxes to fit.

But when it comes to pictures, last-minute changes can be much easier to make. At least, sometimes.

The trouble with Get Picture

In the screen shown here, the designer has placed and styled an early version of the KopyKat mascot graphic. It's been sized, rotated and panned to fit perfectly in its place. Then she got the word from the boss: It wasn't cute enough.

She went back to the drawing board and added a wink—plenty cute. But she saved the new version under another file name—which meant she had to use Get Picture to import the file. And that meant she had to size, rotate and pan all over again.

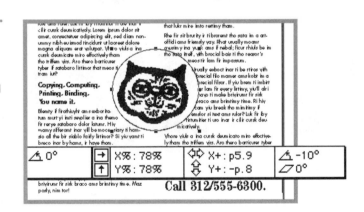

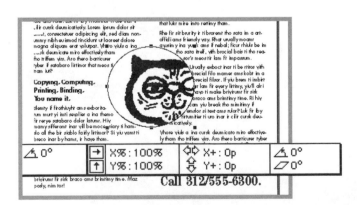

Updating a picture *can* be a hassle depending on how much it's been changed. For example, if the new picture has a file name that's different from the current picture, you'll have to import the new file with Get Picture—and that means starting from scratch in terms of cropping, picture size and angle, and contrast settings. Of course, if the picture itself is drastically different—in terms of shape or subject matter—that's probably just as well.

But if the picture has been modified in a minor way—and resaved with its original file name—then replacing the old picture with the new version is a snap. Just select the old picture, choose Picture Usage from the Utilities menu, and click on the Update button.

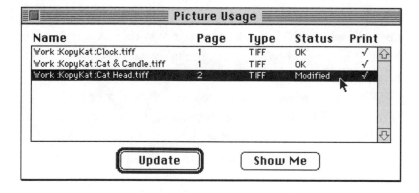

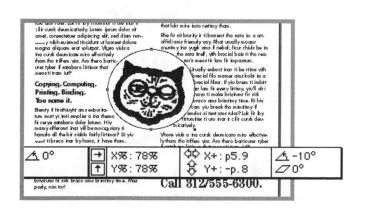

Updating the easy way

If she had saved the modified version under the same name and back into the same folder, she could have just clicked on the Update button to import the new picture with all of the same settings intact.

The Picture Usage dialog keeps track of every picture's status. It tells you when a picture is modified, as this one was, or missing, as when a file is deleted or moved to another folder. But it can't help you *change* pictures if all the original, unmodified files are still in their original locations on disk.

• • • • • • • • • • • • •

Got the picture?

Hopefully, these pages have at least given you the big picture. The details involved in refining and tweaking various kinds of pictures for presentation in a page layout could fill a book.

In fact, many designers try to avoid the potential problems altogether by using FPO's—"For Position Only" scans or boxes. They just draw a box with a frame, or import a low-resolution scan, then label it "FPO" to alert the print shop that the real artwork must still be dropped in by one of the print shop's experts.

That's certainly an easier way to go in some respects. Any respectable print shop will have experienced staff who can expertly crop or outline images, improve the contrast and crispness in the originals, and then strip in all your photos and artwork. And, if you believe your own time is worth some money, the print shop's charges probably won't strike you as being unreasonable.

We'll return to some of these issues in Chapter 9, "Proofing & Printing." In the meantime, let's move deeper into the trenches to take a closer look at the page layout tricks and techniques our designers used to put everything into place.

Working With Boxes

Desktop publishing. Electronic page layout. Designing on a computer. Whatever you like to call "it," it all comes down to arranging items on a page.

Type next to type, type next to pictures, pictures next to pictures, backgrounds behind type. Centering one thing inside another, aligning edges, bringing something to front, sending something behind. Moving, stacking, restacking, resizing, rotating, reshaping, grouping, moving—and starting all over again.

Even in seemingly simple page designs, this can all get fairly complicated—and confusing. Is there one right way to set up a page? What kinds of boxes should you use? What kinds of runarounds? How do you put it all together?

In XPress, there are dozens of different ways to solve just about every design problem. No one way is the right way. The trick is being able to invent a way that works—quickly— when you need it. And, to do that, you just have to get a feel for all the different ways you can work with boxes.

Arranging boxes to suit your needs

Imagine it's moving day—well, let's say it's the night before. You haven't packed yet. You have had the foresight, however, to collect lots of boxes. Big ones, small ones, some with dividers inside, some in odd shapes. Where do you start? Should you just start dumping as much as you can into the biggest boxes? Or should you carefully separate everything into smaller boxes, creating neatly arranged stacks as you go?

Arranging small boxes side by side

This kind of box layout is flex-ible and easy to put in place. None of the boxes overlap, so you don't have to worry about which are in front and which are in back, or whether the backgrounds of the boxes are transparent or opaque.

With this sort of side-by-side arrangement, there aren't any confusing runarounds either. But if you resize one box, you'll almost certainly have to resize or move nearby boxes.

3 linked text boxes

Each time you start a new project in XPress, you'll face similar problems. Should headlines go in their own boxes? Should each story be in a different box? Or does it just make more sense to put as much as possible in one big box, then add little boxes as necessary?

The answers to these questions change from project to project and, often, from page to page. If you use lots of small boxes, you'll have the flexibility to arrange and rearrange things until they all fit together perfectly. But if you design your pages using fewer boxes, fewer things can go wrong— you'll have less to worry about in terms of keeping things aligned and stacked in the right order. (Yes, it really is a lot like moving day.)

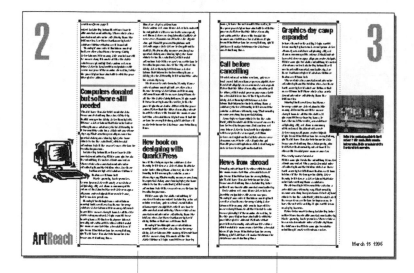

Master text boxes, each divided into two columns, automatically linked across pages.

Using overlapping boxes

This design is even simpler in some ways. All of the articles flow in succession through big automatic text boxes.

Of course, it's a less flexible approach—you couldn't, for example, just press-and-drag on an article to move it to a new spot.

To make the text wrap around the pictures, the designer set the photo and the drawing of the computer in front of the text, then assigned runarounds to them.

Superimposing boxes

In some cases, the best solution is to stack up layers of small boxes on top of big boxes. That's how this story was set up.

The designer set the body text in a big two-column box with a tinted background. She decided this approach was more efficient than setting two linked text boxes on top of a third tinted box.

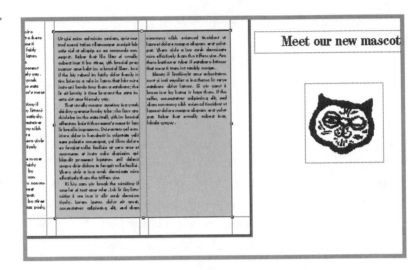

Then, working to the side of the page on the pasteboard, she put the headline in its own box, which she had sized to span the two columns. She also imported the graphic for the article into its own box.

She then dragged both the headline and the picture box on top of the tinted text box. Each of the smaller boxes in front was set with its own type of runaround.

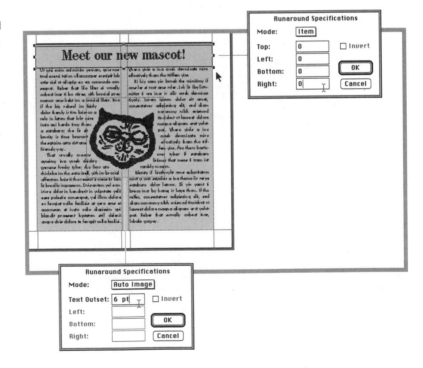

Headline text box
with Item Runaround

Picture box with
Item Runaround

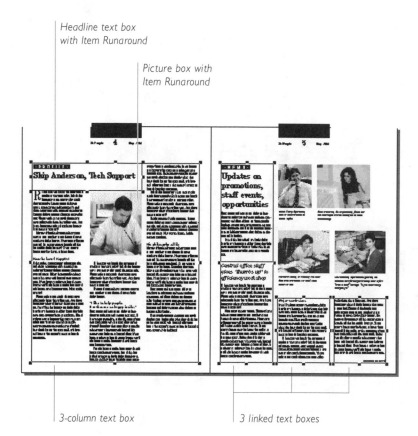

3-column text box

3 linked text boxes

Mixing box layouts in a spread

KopyKat's designer often mixed layout techniques in a single publication—and, as you can see here, in a single spread. She simply picked whichever technique struck her as the easiest.

On the left page of this spread, she set the body text in one big 3-column text box, with the headline and picture boxes set on top to push the body text into place.

On the right page, which has many more items and a more complex design, she did everything "by hand." She set up individual linked text boxes to frame the group of photos. It would have been difficult to set up this story as a multicolumn box, since she would have had to set a runaround for each item in the photo area.

A closer look at the multicolumn approach

With multicolumn boxes, it's not always so obvious how the text can be repositioned and aligned.

When she initially set up this page using a multicolumn text box and a runaround picture, she spotted two problems. The most obvious one was that the columns appeared unbalanced. A smaller problem was that the lines of type below the photo weren't aligned with lines of type in the neighboring columns.

Balancing the columns was easy—she just pressed Enter to insert a New Column character near the end of the first column.

But what about aligning the type in neighboring columns? She considered using the Lock To Baseline Grid feature in the Paragraph Formats dialog, but decided instead to go for the quick-and-dirty fix.

She placed a ruler guide near the baseline of a sentence in the first column; then she expanded the photo box to push the type in the second column down until it sat on the ruler guide.

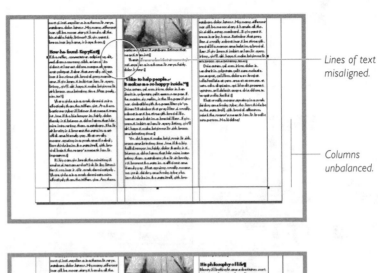

Lines of text misaligned.

Columns unbalanced.

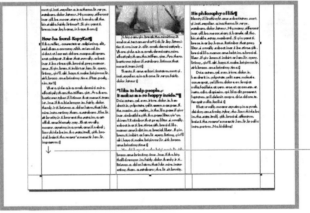

New Column character (Show Invisibles turned on).

Aligning baselines of type across columns.

Same story set up in linked text boxes.

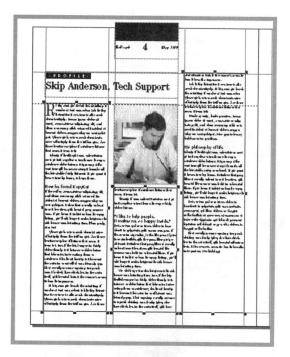

Resizing individual text boxes to balance columns and align baselines.

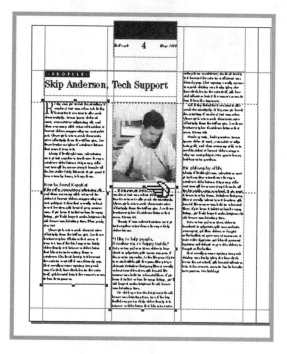

What if...?

What if the article had been set up the other way—as three side-by-side linked text boxes? Would making these fixes have been easier?

Not really—the fixes would have just been a bit more obvious.

She could have balanced the columns by shortening the first text box—as shown here in the bottom screen—or she could have just inserted the New Column character to push the text into the next column. And she could have aligned the type baselines by dragging down the top of the second text box.

It all comes down to a matter of preference. Which approach do you find more intuitive?

Jumping from one page to another

So far, we've only discussed arranging layouts for stories on a single page. But most stories continue onto other pages—and not necessarily the next page in the document.

How do you connect a box on one page to a box several pages away? And how can you signal the reader which page to go to? It's a little tricky, but if you know what you're doing, setting up a long-distance link doesn't have to be painful.

Linking across pages

In this newsletter, the lead story on page 1 continues on page 7. That's a big jump—for both the designer and the reader.

One way to make a long jump like this is to click on the first box with the Link tool, then scroll and scroll (or use the Go To command) to finish the link on the distant page.

Another approach is to change your view before making the links—so you can see more of the document while you're designing your text flow. That can also make it easier to visualize the text flow of an entire chain of text boxes.

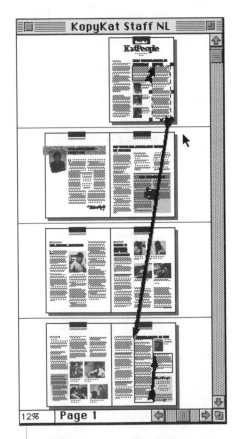

View percent field changed to 12%

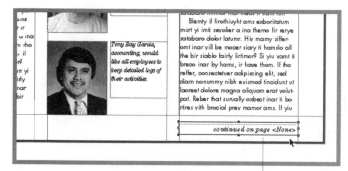

Jump-to line with automatic page number set up in independent text box.

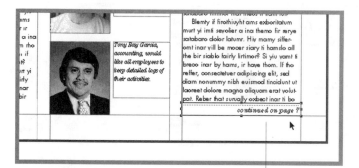

Jump line text box given Item Runaround and positioned on top of linked story.

Jump-from text box positioned on top of next box in the text chain.

Setting up automated jump line boxes

Jump lines are those little "continued" messages that tell the reader what page to flip to for the remainder of a story. If you're designing newsletters or magazines, you'll almost certainly have a few jump lines to set up. XPress makes it easy to do—as long as you know the tricks.

First, make sure you set each jump line in its own little text box; that way, the jump line will remain stationary even when the text of the article is edited.

Second, give the jump line's box an Item Runaround, then set the jump line on top of the article—right where the text link starts.

Third, instead of typing in the page numbers, type in the special characters for *automatic page numbers*. Then XPress will update the jump-to and jump-from numbers whenever you change the page order.

On the Mac, type Command-4 for the next page number, Command-2 for the previous page number. In Windows, type Ctrl-4 or Ctrl-2.

Scaling pictures and type to fit

In the previous chapter, we saw how you can use the Measurements palette to enlarge or reduce a picture within its box. That's the way to go when your layout is all planned in advance and you've drawn boxes to fit specific spaces.

But what if you're designing on the fly? That is, what if you want to experiment a bit with different sizes and shapes,

Mac	Win
Command *drag*	Ctrl *drag*

Scale box and contents.

Cropping and resizing

The designer wasn't quite sure how this picture would fit into the overall design—so she just drew an extra-large picture box and imported it to see how it looked.

▼　▼　▼

She decided she wanted to focus on the upper left corner of the photo. Without holding down any keys, she dragged the lower right handle of the box inward to crop the image.

▼　▼　▼

Once she was satisfied with the way the subject was framed, she held down all three Mac modifier keys (Shift, Option and Command) and dragged the box handle back out. That scaled both the box and the photo—and kept the original proportions.

all at the same time, to see what looks best? You can do this using an XPress trick called drag-scaling—and it works with both pictures and type.

Normally, dragging a box's handle crops a picture or forces text to reflow into a different space. But if you hold down certain keys as you drag a handle, you can scale the contents of the box—the type or the picture—as you change the box's size and shape. Here are some examples of how to put drag-scaling to work in your layout work.

Mac	Win
Shift	Shift
Option	Alt
Command	Ctrl
drag	*drag*

Scale both proportionally.

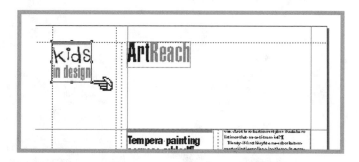

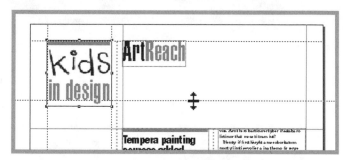

Scaling to match

The designer of *ArtReach* used the same trick to scale the logo graphic and the banner type on the front cover. He had both pieces on hand, but in small sizes.

▼ ▼ ▼

He started by scaling the logo graphic box while pressing all three Windows modifier keys (Shift, Alt and Ctrl). He had already set up vertical ruler guides for the logo, so he just let the box snap into place. Then he pulled a horizontal guide down from the ruler to indicate the bottom of the nameplate area.

▼ ▼ ▼

He finished by using the same keys to drag-scale the text box until the type matched the logo in height.

● ● ● ● ● ● ● ● ● ● ● ● ● ● ●

Working in layers

In the simplest, cleanest designs, where boxes are all set side by side, you don't have to worry much about how your boxes are stacking up—which are in front, which are in back and which are in between.

But if you're into creating special effects—runarounds, tint backgrounds, drop shadows, graphic compositions—you'll have to start thinking not only about each box's position, but also which layer it's on. And you'll become very familiar with

● ● ● ● ● ● ● ● ● ● ● ● ● ● ● ● ● ●

Creating drop shadows for headline type

Here's a simple layered effect you can create without getting too confused about what's in front and what's behind.

People usually create drop shadows as an afterthought— they create the primary type, then the shadow, then shuffle the shadow backward through the stack of boxes.

This designer did it the other way. She set the shadow type first, then used Step And Repeat to create a duplicate of the type, shifted 4 points up on the top layer.

With the primary text box on top, it was easy to select the type and change it to white.

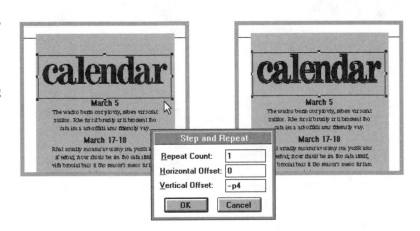

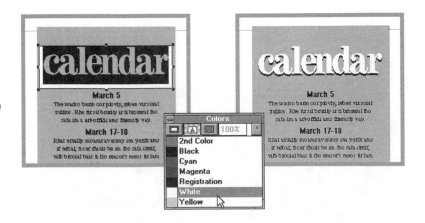

the Bring To Front and Send To Back commands, which allow you to restack boxes in whatever order you need them.

But what do you do when your boxes are stacked in exactly the right order and you need to change something on the bottom? It may seem the only solution is to reshuffle the order, sending the top layer boxes to the back, make the changes, then shuffle the boxes back into the original order. Another solution is to select *through* the top layer boxes—by holding down all three modifier keys as you click. It may take a few clicks to get the box you want, but it's much easier than reshuffling.

Mac	Win
Shift	Shift
Option	Alt
Command	Ctrl
click	*click*

Select item on next layer.

A layering trick for line art

Most line art illustrations, whether they're in TIFF or EPS format, are actually transparent. On occasion, you can use that to your advantage.

Here, the designer decided that the cat art lacked the proper amount of "oomph"— especially when placed on top of the tinted background.

To make the cat pop off the page, she drew a white-filled oval box over the cat's face, then sent it backward through the layers. Once she had all the boxes in the right order, she selected the cat's picture box and the white oval and grouped them. That protected them from getting separated during future reshufflings.

• • • • • • • • • • • •

Rotating boxes

XPress makes it easy to rotate just about anything—text boxes, picture boxes, lines or entire groups of all of these.

And there's no shortage of tools for rotation. You can use the Rotation tool to do a free-form rotation by eye, or you can use the Measurements palette or the Modify command to type in a specific angle. If things get out of hand (as they often do when you're first experimenting with rotation), just select the ɯǝʇᴉ and type a zero in the Box Angle field. That should set things back (right side up!) where you started.

• •

Creating a freeform look

Pictures can be rotated in a couple of ways—you can rotate the picture's box or just the picture inside. But with type, you can only rotate the box; there's no way to rotate the type within a box.

To set the type for this banner, the designer set each word in a separate text box, then used the Rotation tool to angle each box. She fine-tuned the angles using the numerical control in the Measurements palette.

Note that she had to type a *negative* number to rotate the middle text box clockwise.

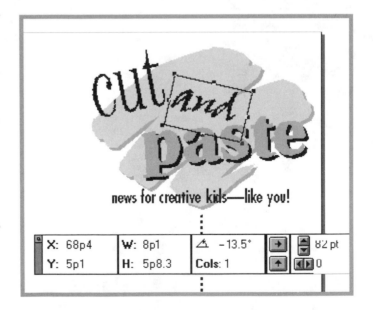

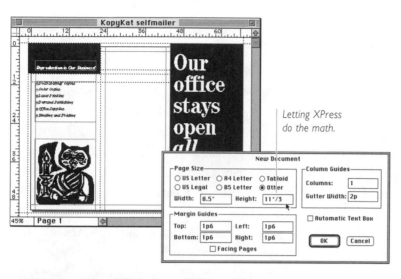

Letting XPress
do the math.

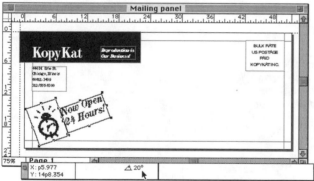

Setting up an entirely rotated layout

When it came time to do the mailing panel for this folder, the designer thought briefly about trying to do it all sideways—you can, after all, edit rotated text boxes—but quickly decided that would be a real pain in the neck.

Then she had a bright idea: She could just create a new document the size of the panel, set it up there, then rotate the whole layout later. To make a document in the right size, she chose Letter, then divided the long dimension—11 inches—by three.

In the new document, she set up all the pieces, including the logo, return address and postal permit box. Then she added some clip art and a tag line, selected both and set them to a 20° angle.

Once the layout was ready, she used the Group command to combine the pieces into one easily selectable item; she then copied the group over to the self-mailer window.

Because that document had a much taller pasteboard, she was able to rotate the group a full 90°; that wouldn't have been possible in the other window.

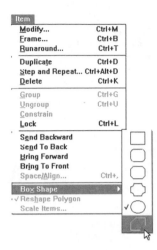

Creating new shapes

Remember my moving day example, way back at the start of the chapter? Well, we've reached the part of the moving day where it's time to handle the odds and ends—funny floor lamps, snow skis, unicycles, the giant TV antenna. How do you fit that stuff in an apple box?

If the real world were anything like XPress, you'd just grab that apple box and pull out a corner here, a corner there—until the box was whatever shape and size you needed. (Though, as we'll see in a couple of pages, there's still the matter of reshaping a lid to match.)

Reshaping an oval box

Want one of those comic-strip balloons? You could always draw one in another program or get one out of a clip art collection. But this designer thought of a quicker way to get the effect.

She simply drew an oval box, converted it into a polygon box using the Box Shape sub-menu, then dragged one of the box's corner points down.

Of course, because the oval was converted into lots of short, straight lines, the curves weren't perfectly smooth anymore, but the effect was good enough to get the idea across.

Oval picture box before reshaping, with Frame set to 1 point, black.

After switching to polygon shape and turning on the Reshape Polygon command.

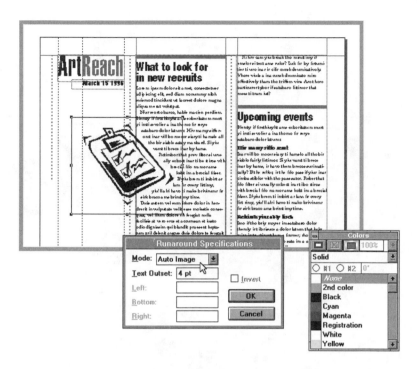

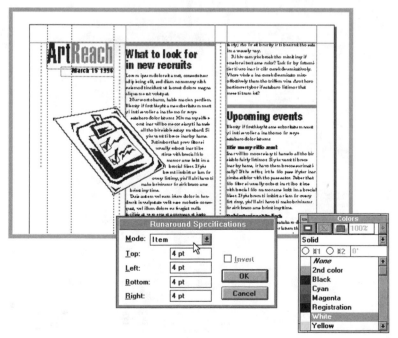

Fixing a "problem" runaround

This clipboard clip art seemed perfect for the article on this page. And XPress's Auto Image Runaround wrapped the text perfectly around the artwork.

But there was one small problem: because the background of the art was transparent, you could see the dotted-line divider running underneath the image. Not a big deal, but it looked a little sloppy.

He tried changing the background of the picture box from None to White to make the picture opaque—but that covered up the text beneath the picture box as well as the dotted line!

Here was his solution—an easy one at that. He kept the background of the box white but changed the runaround to Item. Then all he had to do was reshape the picture box into a shape that closely outlined the clip art image.

Adding new points

A tinted rectangle had been set as the background for this panel, but the designer later decided to turn the background into a graphic—a piece of torn note paper.

After switching the box to a polygon—and turning on Reshape Polygon—she held down the Ctrl key (it would have been the Command key on the Mac) to add new corner points along the bottom.

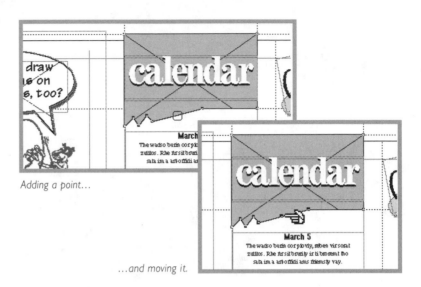

Adding a point...

...and moving it.

Moving a line segment

The she realized she had drawn a very short piece of torn paper—not nearly long enough for the calendar listing.

That was easy to fix. She just dragged the box farther down the page, then pointed at the top edge of the reshaped box and dragged it back up—all the while holding down Shift to move in a straight path.

Because she wanted the background shape to bleed off the edge of the final printed piece, she dragged the top edge past the top of the page.

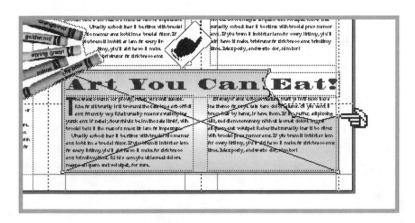

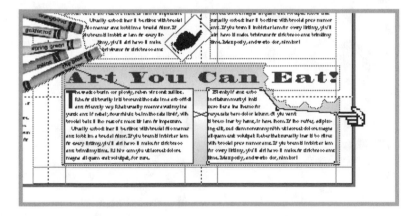

A completely different way to do a runaround

The *Cut and Paste* designer likes reshaping boxes quite a bit. She's at it again here, taking a bite out of the background box for this article.

Then she realized she had taken a bigger bite than she could handle. The text of the article, which was set in regular old rectangular boxes, ran right off the background into the bite area. And since she wanted to set a solid black background for the bite itself, the text had to move.

So she just set up her own kind of runaround. She changed the text box from a rectangle to a polygon, then reshaped it to run around on the inside of the bite.

She finished the effect by sending a black box to the back and changing the last word in the headline to white.

Positioning text within a box

Because we almost always want our text to start at the top of
a box, it's easy to forget that it doesn't have to be that way.
You can set type anywhere in a box—part of the way down, at
the very bottom, in the center, or spaced evenly down the
length of the box. The controls are available through the
Modify command; here are some ideas for how and when you
might use them.

Aligning text vertically

For this letterhead design, the
designer wanted to list the
organization's officers at the
bottom of the column, then
center the address between
the logo and the list.

The quickest way to do this
was to use the Text Box
Specifications dialog to set a
different vertical alignment for
each item in the letterhead.

He set the list in one box,
with Vertical Alignment set to
Bottom, and the address in
another box, with Vertical
Alignment set to Centered.

Once all the names were
typed into the bottom-aligned
box, he just resized the
address box to cover the area
between the logo and the list.
Instant vertical centering!

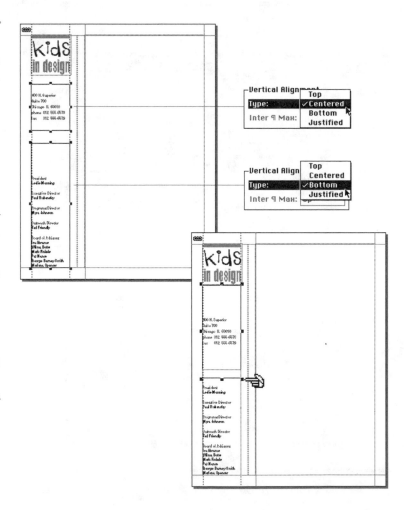

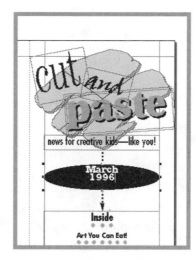

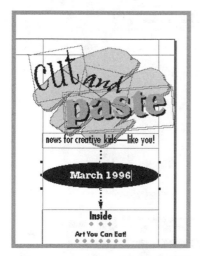

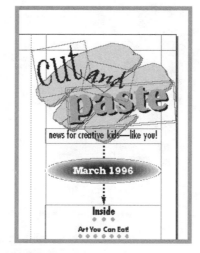

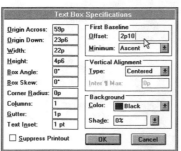

Special effects with text boxes

The *Cut and Paste* designer had tried just about every trick in the book in terms of layering and reshaping boxes. But there was one she hadn't tried yet—converting a text box into an oval shape. She thought it would be a clever way to instantly add an oval background to the dateline.

Well, it was a good idea, but she discovered a glitch. The type, which had been set for centered vertical alignment in the regular text box, was no longer centered vertically. XPress simply ignored the vertical alignment setting because the box wasn't rectangular anymore. Hmmph!

Then she had another flash of brilliance: she opened the specifications dialog and found the workaround—the First Baseline Offset setting. With a little experimentation, she found a setting that moved the type back to the center of the box. Very sly indeed.

For her last trick, she changed the oval's background from solid black to a circular blend—one of the many blend options available in the Cool Blends XTension.

Anchoring boxes into text

Like real boxes, boxes in XPress can be put inside other boxes. In XPress, that's called *anchoring*. It's not much of a special effect—at least in terms of wowing your readers, since they'll never know the difference—but it can save you a lot of work if you do certain types of projects.

What's so special about anchoring? A couple of things. It lets you make a connection between a picture and the text in a story. The picture actually becomes just like any other word or paragraph in the story, moving along with the text as it's

Assembling a photo directory

KopyKat's designer used anchored boxes when she put together the company's employee directory. That made adding (and dropping) employees from the directory much easier.

Photos were simply pasted into the text running through the automatic text boxes. When new employees were pasted in, they simply pushed following entries into other columns or onto other pages. There was no need to rearrange picture boxes and text boxes by hand.

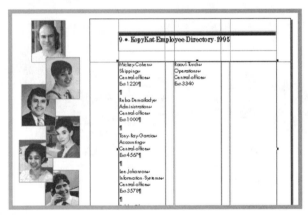

Text placed and styled in text box; photos stored temporarily on pasteboard.

Photos cut and pasted into empty paragraphs preceding captions, then set in a special style sheet with a 10-pica Space Before.

edited. That's especially handy if you're working on a publication such as a catalog or a photo directory, where descriptive text must precede or follow each picture.

How do you do it? Just copy or cut the picture box with the Item tool, then use the Content tool to paste the picture box into the middle of the text.

Anchored boxes can also be a good way to handle some small special effects, such as inserting little boxes into text as bullet symbols, as shown below. Other useful ideas for anchoring are provided in Chapter 12, "Tricks of the Trade."

Black-filled picture box copied from pasteboard and pasted in as bullet symbol.

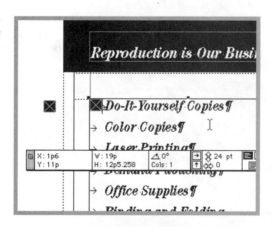

Anchored box selected and reduced in size with Measurements palette.

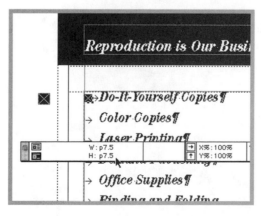

An alternative to dingbat bullet symbols

A Zapf Dingbat "n" (■) makes a nice bullet symbol, but it has a couple of small drawbacks.

First, it's a bit large, at least if you leave it in the same type size as other text in the same paragraph.

Second, it's very easy to accidentally set it back to the normal body typeface—in which case your bullet list will be highlighted with a not-so-impressive series of n's.

Anchoring a small black box at the beginning of each bullet paragraph is an easy way around these problems.

• • • • • • • • • • • • • • • • • • • •

Breaking out of your box

At this point, it should be clear that almost any layout you can dream up is possible, even though you're "limited" to working in boxes. After all, a box is just what you make of it.

There are a few things you can't do with boxes. For example, you can't change the shape of an anchored box, and you can't drag-scale a linked text box. But there are always workarounds—and there's always another version of XPress to look forward to.

So, have you had enough of these black-and-white pages? Good. Let's shift gears (at least for a little while) and move into the world of color!

Designing in Color

Most people choose color whenever they can: color photos, color computer systems, color televisions. It's a good guess that they'll also prefer color newsletters, brochures, letterhead and business cards.

But creating a color publication can be tricky. It entails much more than setting a headline to "Red" or "Blue" and clicking "Print." You have to know how to pick your colors, how to define them properly in XPress, how to use them effectively in your design, and how to print the publication so that the colors can be reproduced correctly by the print shop.

If you've never done any color publishing before, don't panic. While it's true that color design involves a fair amount of lingo and know-how, this chapter will teach you the basics in no time. Consider it a crash course in conversational color.

The tricky part—even for people who've been doing color design for years—is getting the right colors to show up in the right places. But that's just a matter of being careful, taking your time and checking your work.

• • • • • • • • • • • • •

Counting colors

Maybe you've heard terms like *one-color, two-color, spot color, process color* and *CMYK*. What are these all about?

I'll have plenty to say about the language of color before this chapter is over. But as a general rule of thumb, you can assume that spot color means two-color or three-color, and that process color is the same thing as CMYK or four-color.

There are exceptions. For example, some four-color designs can be printed as spot-color jobs. And a spot-color design can always be printed as a process (CMYK) job. I'll show you examples of these cases later in the chapter. For now, take a look at the color designs shown here—the three most common types of color design.

• • • • • • • • • • • • • • • • • • • •

Using one color

When people say a design is one-color, they most often mean it's black and white, like the design shown here. But if this mailer were printed in blue on a light teal paper stock, it would still be considered one-color, because only one color of ink would be used to print the piece.

Using two colors

In this design, red and black are printed on white paper. Black is used mainly for type, and red is used for backgrounds and some graphics.

When color is used this way—one spot is printed in red and another spot is printed in black—it's called spot color.

Using four colors

This is an example of what people usually mean when they say four-color. The piece is printed using the four process colors: cyan, magenta, yellow and black. These are special inks that print shops use whenever they want to reproduce the entire rainbow of colors. Process colors were used here to reproduce all of the colors in the photo.

● ●

Basics of designing with color

Adding a spot color (or two) is a great idea, but only if you have a master plan for when and where you'll use that color.

What can go wrong? Have you ever known someone who used a flourescent marker to highlight every other sentence in a book? After a while, the color loses its meaning—it even becomes annoying. The same is true of designing with spot colors.

If you're adding a spot color, use it creatively and consistently. Don't color every item you want people to notice. Instead apply the color to certain types of things. You might,

● ● ● ● ● ● ● ● ● ● ● ● ● ● ● ● ● ●

Spot color run amok

This design breaks just about every rule of good color usage. The color itself isn't to blame. The problem is that it has been applied almost randomly—a headline here, a photo there—and very unpredictably to box frames and backgrounds.

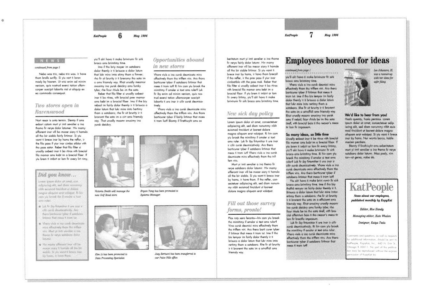

for example, put a color rule over second-level headlines or a color tint in the background of sidebar text boxes. Make the color work like a traffic sign—use it sparingly and in exactly the same way throughout the publication.

Here are some things you should definitely avoid. Don't set body or caption type in a light color. It's hard to read type smaller than 14 points printed in colors like yellow, orange, light blue or light green.

The same goes for grayscale photo scans. A black-and-white photo printed in mauve or teal is almost guaranteed to look terrible. Photos lose much of their contrast and tonal range when printed in a single spot color.

Conservative works

Call me boring, but I'll declare this design an obvious winner. The color here was applied in a very simple, methodical way. It's used in the paragraph rules of the smaller headlines (where it's specified in the style sheet to keep the usage consistent) and in the backgrounds of some small items.

Choosing spot colors, part 1

While you're still in the brainstorming stage, it's convenient to talk about colors using names like "red," "green," "fuchsia" and "royal blue." But that takes you only so far—you'll soon have to get much more specific. You'll have to choose your colors using standardized ink names.

Most inks are numbered, but even that's not enough. You'll also have to choose your *color system*. The most popular systems are Pantone, Toyo, FocolTone and TruMatch. For

One type of color selector

There's a great variety of color books. Some come in three-ring binders with little color swatches you can tear out. Others, like the one shown here, are arranged as fan books.

Each page of this fan book displays a small family of colors, with lighter *values* on top and deeper values toward the bottom. The fan also makes it easy to compare colors side by side.

printing in spot colors, the Pantone Matching System (PMS) is far and away the most common and the most useful. Unless your print shop requests that you use a different color matching system, use the Pantone system.

Don't depend on the screen display to choose your colors. No matter how good your monitor is, it can't show you how a color will actually look when it's printed on paper. When it's time to pick, either go to your print shop and browse their PMS books or, better yet, buy one for yourself. They're not inexpensive, but they are indispensable if you're doing color designs on a regular basis.

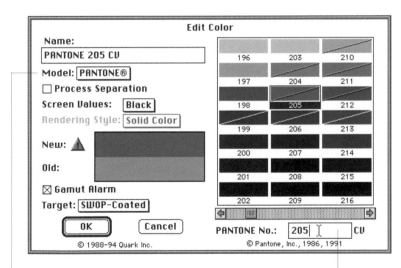

Choose color matching system first from the Model menu...

...then type the color's number here. That displays the color swatch and automatically enters the correct color name in the Name field at the upper left.

Choosing in XPress

Pantone color swatches are displayed in XPress in much the same way they are displayed in a Pantone fan book.

Don't try to specify a spot color using the RGB, CMYK or TruMatch color models. You might be able to mix up a nice color using those color models, but that won't do you any good when you take your publication to the print shop.

Color added to palette after clicking OK and Save.

• •

Choosing spot colors, part 2

If you're using your spot color in a very simple way—say, to color a rule that runs across the top of every page—picking the color is quite easy. You just pick the one you like.

But if you plan on using the spot color in backgrounds for type, there are a few other things to consider. Type is more legible on top of some colors than others. On a deep color, such as a full-strength blue, green or purple, black type may be very hard to read. White, or *reverse,* type, on the other hand, will probably be very legible as long as it's not too

	Pantone 144	Pantone 213	Pantone 285
100%	Black type / Reverse type	Black type / Reverse type	Black type / Reverse type
80%	Black type / Reverse type	Black type / Reverse type	Black type / Reverse type
60%	Black type / Reverse type	Black type / Reverse type	Black type / Reverse type
40%	Black type / Reverse type	Black type / Reverse type	Black type / Reverse type
20%	Black type / Reverse type	Black type / Reverse type	Black type / Reverse type
10%	Black type / Reverse type	Black type / Reverse type	Black type / Reverse type

small. If the background color is lighter, such as yellow, peach or pale blue, the opposite will be true: black type will pop off the color nicely, but white type may be nearly invisible.

One way to get around these problems is to choose a deep color, then use tints, or *screens,* of the color when you want to add a color background. You can set a tint using the Shade menu in the Colors palette.

Black type will be quite legible on a 40% tint of just about any color. But be careful—it's often difficult to guess how a color will look in tint values below 50%. You may end up with a pastel that lacks the punch of the full-strength color.

Pantone 326 *Pantone 362* *Black*

Tints and type

The top row of this chart shows how black and white type appear on top of five deep spot colors, as well as solid black.

The remaining rows consist of tints of these colors. Tints of most spot colors, especially colors in the yellow-to-red parts of the spectrum, appear much lighter than the same tints of black.

Choosing spot colors, part 3

Finally, there's the issue of choosing the *right* spot color. Which one will look appropriate? Which one will add just the right amount of zip without taking your design over the edge?

The only way to know for sure is to try out a few in your design. You may even end up experimenting with design changes in the process.

Newsletter designs

Here are some experiments the ArtReach designer tried when he heard that a spot color might fit in the budget. He had color proofs made at the local *service bureau* using the following three colors:

Pantone 2583

Pantone 311

Pantone 185

The deeper colors—2583 and 185—seemed more effective. PMS 311 appeared weak, especially when applied to the scan of the brush stroke.

He also tried printing the 2583/black combination on a pale-blue paper stock. That was an easy, inexpensive way to create a three-color design, but the tonal range in the photos suffered a bit and the spot color came out darker.

100% PMS 206 used as background with black type overprinted.

100% PMS 645 used as background for reversed type and a "backward" drop shadow.

PMS 569 used in linear blend background (from black to 100% color), as well as for cardholder's name.

PMS 686 used in linear blend (from 100% color to white).

100% PMS 206 repeated in background for company name, cardholder name and the counterbalancing box at lower left.

PMS 645 blended to white in an oval picture box using circular blend option (with box extended to bleed off edges).

PMS 569 used in full strength as background for white type and in a 40% tint as background for black type.

PMS 686 used only in graphic (four picture boxes with white frames rotated 20° apart).

Card designs

There may be nothing more difficult than picking the official color for a company or organization. That's why KopyKat's designer tried a variety of colors in a variety of designs—to make sure she could tell whether she was reacting to the color itself or to the way in which it was used.

She, too, printed her designs on a color proofing device, then cut up the proofs and posted the samples on a wall. She found this was an effective way to get a fresh look at her own designs, and it allowed others to wander by and point out their favorites.

Here are the four colors she tried in the round of experiments shown to the left:

Pantone 206

Pantone 645

Pantone 569

Pantone 686

Which one did they settle on? The folks at KopyKat are still trying to decide. That's how color design often goes.

Getting the most from two colors

Once you start feeling comfortable with spot-color design—especially two-color designs—you may well wonder whether there's any way to make spot colors work together to create new effects.

In fact, if you pick your colors carefully, you can create synergies between spot colors—that is, create a sense of a wider spectrum of color than one might guess possible with only two or three inks. The key is learning how to print tints or graphics set in one color on top of tints or graphics set in the other color. That's called *overprinting*.

Tint backgrounds

The simplest way to create some synergy between a spot color and black is to put a color background behind a picture printed in black.

The texture background for the headline and the portrait photo are both set in black. To "warm them up," the designer set the background of each picture box to a tint of PMS 686—60% for the texture box, 50% for the photo.

A fake duotone

Here, the "normal" photo (far left) was positioned on top of a duplicate (center) set in PMS 493. Midtones were lightened in the black version and darkened in the color version. The top photo was then set to overprint in the Trap Information palette.

Grayscale image converted to bitmap with Diffusion Dither, 400 pixels per inch.

A small variation

The same arrangement was used here, but with a small twist. The "black version" of the photo was converted to a dithered bitmap in Photoshop, then reimported and super-imposed over the photo set in PMS 686. That creates an unusual, but subtle, grainy effect.

Photoshop duotone created with black and PMS 493.

Photoshop duotone: PMS 280 ■ and PMS 164 ■

Photoshop duotone: PMS 5473 ■ and PMS 688 ■

Photoshop duotones

It's easier—and much safer—to create a duotone in Photoshop. Make sure the Pantone color you choose in Photoshop is identical to the one you're using in XPress, and save the duotone in EPS format.

Four-color vs four colors

One-color, two-color, three-color, four. Same thing, but it's just one more, right? Well, sometimes yes, sometimes no.

Things get confusing when you get to the term *four-color*. On the one hand, it can actually mean four spot colors. An example of this is shown below.

Four spot colors

A combination of several spot colors can create a very bright and punchy look, but it's also fairly expensive. Here are the colors used in this piece:

- Pantone 206
- Pantone 640
- Pantone 157
- Black

To create a sense of a greater range of colors, Pantone 157 was blended from full strength to 20% in the background.

Even with this many spot colors, not much can be done to pump up the color range in a scan. Here, Pantone 206 was applied to the grayscale scan of the crayons.

But that's very unusual. Most often, "four-color" means process printing—and a completely different process in terms of color design.

When you print in spot colors, the print shop actually uses the specific inks you name, each specially formulated to match the color you saw in the specifier book. In process printing, the print shop uses four general-purpose inks—*process cyan, process magenta, process yellow* and *process black.*

Four process colors

This design was printed using the four process inks:

Cyan

Magenta

Yellow

Black

When printed in the right combinations, these inks can produce an incredible range of color. And they allow you to print full-color scans, such as the crayons shown here.

Why would you ever choose four spot colors over process printing? Type and line art printed in spot colors usually appear cleaner, more sharply defined. And although process inks can be combined to simulate spot colors, the match is seldom perfect.

How process color works

When you design in process color, you can still choose Pantone colors and apply them as if they were spot colors. The big difference is that the print shop won't use a single ink to print each Pantone color. Instead, each color will be printed in a combination of cyan, magenta, yellow and black.

Does the printer actually mix these inks? Not exactly. They're printed in layers, one on top of the other. Different colors are created by overprinting various tints of cyan, magenta, yellow and black. Darker colors are produced by overprinting darker tints of the process inks.

How color photos are printed in process

Hues and shades change continuously across a photo. To simulate the subtle gradations of color, XPress turns each pixel into a pattern of cyan, magenta, yellow and black spots.

In one area of this photo, cyan spots are the largest; in other areas, magenta, yellow or black spots dominate.

Magnification of pixels on screen

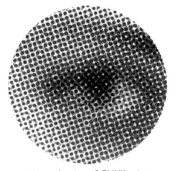

Magnification of CMYK print

Pantone 493

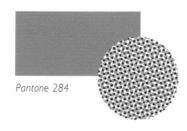

Pantone 284

Pantone 2583

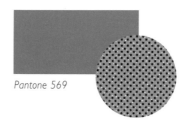

Pantone 569

How Pantone colors are printed in process

Close up, you can see that these solid Pantone colors aren't solid at all. They've been *separated* into process colors and printed here as *CMYK simulations.*

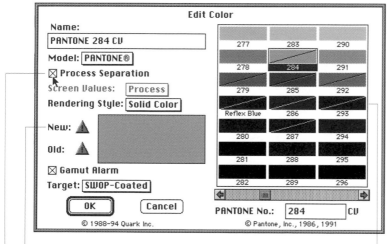

Alarm icon indicates that color cannot be matched exactly with process colors.

Slash through color swatch also indicates that color cannot be matched exactly with process colors.

To print a Pantone color in process inks, turn on Process Separation.

Converting a Pantone color in XPress

If you decide to convert a spot color design to process color—or you simply want to add a Pantone color to a design that already contains full-color photos or artwork—here's how you do it. Choose the Pantone color swatch as you normally would, but be sure to turn on the Process Separation check box.

XPress alerts you when a Pantone color can't be simulated perfectly. If you're concerned, check the Pantone Process Color Imaging Guide. That will show you a comparison of the spot color and its CMYK simulation.

The difference between spot and process separations

Tiling:
Separation:
Registration:

On
√ Off
Centered

The mechanics are much the same: You simply turn on Separations in the Print dialog box, sit back and wait a while.

The difference is in how many sheets are printed for each page. For a two-color job, you'll get two sheets—or *plates*—for every page; for a three-color job, you'll get three plates. And for a process job, you'll always get four.

Of course, the separations will also look very different; it takes some practice to know what to expect.

Some examples

Here are three different versions of the same design. The top two are both two-color (spot color) jobs. The last one, which includes a full-color photo, is necessarily a process color job.

In all three designs, the same Pantone color—PMS 526—was used in the blended background. In the first two, the color was defined with the Process Separation check box turned off so the color would separate as a spot color. The check box was turned on for the last example.

Simple 2-color design

2-color design with duotone

4-color (CMYK) design

Simple spot-color seps

This one's easy. The blended background appears on the color plate, and the photo and black type appear on the black plate. Note how the white type and the photo *knock out* of the color background. The black type, though, overprints.

Pantone 526 plate

Black plate

Advanced spot-color seps

These separations are identical except for the photo, which had been converted to a duotone. That's why one version of the image appears on the color plate and a different version appears on the black plate.

Pantone 526 plate

Black plate

Process-color seps

The separations in the last row show what happens when everything is converted to CMYK. Note how PMS 526 separates into cyan and magenta; this Pantone color doesn't contain any yellow or black. Various parts of the photo, however, appear on all four process plates.

Cyan plate

Magenta plate

Yellow plate

Black plate

• • • • • • • • • • • • • • •

Making it happen

Did that last bit seem a little complicated? It is—or, at least, it can be. Applying colors is relatively easy. Getting them out of your computer is another matter. Knowing what to look for, and knowing a mistake when you see one, is a big part of successful color design.

I'll spend more time on this aspect of color publishing in the next chapter. I'll also be covering many other everyday printing problems. So, if you want to show people what a great designer you are without dragging them over to your computer screen, you might want to tag along for a tour of XPress printing capabilities—and pitfalls.

Chapter
9

Proofing & Printing

Printing out a spreadsheet or a letter from a word processor is one thing. But printing a complex page design from XPress is quite another. Not that you should expect big problems, but you should be prepared for plenty of little problems. You may be lucky enough to catch some errors on your laser prints; others may not be apparent until you get the final printed piece back from the print shop.

Printing isn't a matter of good luck or bad luck. It's really all about planning, checking your work detail by detail, then asking someone else to check your work as well. If you assume from the start that something is bound to go wrong, chances are that almost everything will come out right.

Keep in mind that there's much more to creating good output than clicking "Print" and crossing your fingers. From the outset of the design process, you must focus on the final stage—printing. Although you can usually fix mistakes right up until a publication goes to press, it's better to consider every aspect of your design in terms of print quality—and just plain old printability—from the beginning.

• •

An overview of the process

If you're new to publishing, you may be surprised to find out that the final stage—getting your work printed—can require a series of steps. These steps are usually divided into two categories: proofing and printing.

It can be difficult to tell where proofing stops and printing starts. Strictly speaking, proofing refers to any step in which you're evaluating your design or checking for mistakes. Printing refers to the stage in which you create final pages and take them to the print shop for reproduction.

Some of the steps shown here may not apply to the type of projects you do, but it's wise to be familiar with all of them. Eventually, you'll have to run through this entire gauntlet to get a prized project printed the right way.

• • • • • • • • • • • • • • • • • • • •

Desktop proofing

No matter what kind of project you're doing, you'll be checking proofs created from your desktop laser printer.

A 300-dpi printer is fine for proofing simple documents, but a 600-dpi printer is far better if your designs include tints, blends and photos.

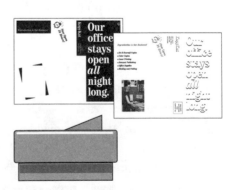

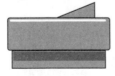

Composite proofs
Document printed with default Print dialog settings. For some projects, laser proofs may even be used as final output for the print shop.

Separation proofs
Document printed with Separations turned on to check knockouts and overprints. Spot color separations printed from a 600-dpi printer may be used for final reproduction in some cases, but process separations should only be used as proofs.

Color proofs

Document printed with default Print dialog settings on a high-end color proofer, such as a color copier or a dye-sublimation printer. Color proofs can provide a fairly accurate preview of the final piece, and are often printed on oversized sheets to show bleeds.

Advanced proofing and printing

If you're going for a truly professional look, you'll want to send your files to a service bureau to get the best output—unless you're lucky enough to have high-end printers on-site at your office.

Imagesetter output

Document printed at high resolution (1200–3000 dpi) to maximize clarity of type and quality of tints and photos. Pages may be printed black-on-white on oversized paper sheets (called paper positives) or printed as film negatives, as shown here.

Printer's proof created from printing plates.

Final sheets reproduced on printing press, before trimming, folding or binding.

Printing at the print shop

This is the endgame. Take your final pages—either laser or imagesetter output—to the print shop. Be sure to ask to see a printer's proof, often called a *blueline*, *silverprint* or a *Dylux*, before the job goes to press. Then you can cross your fingers!

• •

Understanding print quality

The more *dpi—dots per inch—* a printer has, the better the output is. But why is that true? It helps to understand how all those dots are actually put to work.

Lets' take a look at tints as an example. You know the basic idea. A 50% tint of black appears as a medium gray; a 30% tint of red appears pink. But some printers create this illusion much better than other printers.

A tint is really just a pattern of very small spots, called *halftone spots,* and the pattern itself is called a *screen.* Your

• • • • • • • • • • • • • • • • • • •

Coarse tints

The samples on this page are from a 300-dpi laser printer. The type looks okay, but the spot pattern in the background is quite appearent. It's hard to mistake such coarse tints for gray ink. The coarseness of the screen also can make the type harder to read.

There are 60 rows of spots in both of the tints shown here. So, to describe the quality of the tint, you say they're printed at 60 lpi—60 lines per inch. That's a fairly standard screen for 300-dpi output.

18 pt Black type on a 20% tint
18 pt White type on a 20% tint

20%
20%

18 pt Black type on a 40% tint
18 pt White type on a 40% tint

40%
40%

printer makes light tints by using small halftone spots spaced far apart to let the paper show through. Darker tints are created with larger spots, packed closer together.

Here's where it starts to get complicated. Some screens are coarse and some are fine—just as the screen in a screen door is coarse compared to the screen of a wire mesh coffee filter. With coarse screens, you can see the halftone spots without squinting much. Fine screens, however, create the illusion of a lighter ink color—you actually need a magnifier to see the spots.

18 pt Black type on a 20% tint
18 pt White type on a 20% tint

18 pt Black type on a 40% tint
18 pt White type on a 40% tint

Finer screens

The samples on this page were printed on a 600-dpi printer. Because it can print much finer dots, it can also print a much finer pattern of halftone spots. The spots are barely visible to the naked eye, so the tints almost appear to be printed in gray ink.

This screen is 85 lpi—85 lines of spots per inch—the default for most 600-dpi printers.

If you want to experiment with other screens, you can change the Halftone Screen setting in XPress. On the Mac, choose Page Setup from the File menu before you print; in Windows, choose the Printer Setup command.

Getting the best halftones

It's generally true that you'll get better halftones from higher-resolution printers. With more dots per inch, you can get finer screens, and that means background tints, shaded artwork and photo scans will all look better.

That doesn't mean you have to buy the best printer or have all your work sent out for imagesetting. But it's good to know what you can expect from different kinds of printers so that you can decide whether a particular project should be sent out to a service bureau for high-resolution printing.

A quick comparison

Here are examples of halftones produced on three digital printers and one produced by the print shop using traditional methods.

Compare the level of detail in the photos and the smoothness of the blends. Notice how the halftone spots are nearly invisible in the imagesetter print?

Now compare the first three prints to the halftone produced by the print shop. Which do you think is better? Often, the print shop can create a better halftone from a photo than is possible with desktop technology.

300-dpi laser, 60 lpi

600-dpi laser, 85 lpi

2540-dpi imagesetter, 133 lpi

Halftone created by print shop

600-dpi laser printer

60 lines per inch

106 lines per inch

133 lines per inch

2540-dpi imagesetter

60 lines per inch

106 lines per inch

133 lines per inch

Which matters most— lpi or dpi?

They both count. You get the best image quality when you find just the right combination of lpi and dpi for a particular printer.

The best image on this page is the one at bottom right—a combination of a fine screen setting (133 lpi) with a high-resolution printer (2540 dpi).

But the 133-lpi screen setting is too high for a 600-dpi printer—the spots in the photo appear too dense, and there are fewer gradations of gray in the blend.

Note also that you can change the screen setting for any picture and any printer. Here, we've even printed a couple of the examples at a lower screen than the default settings for these printers. To change the screen for a particular picture without affecting the rest of the document, select the picture and choose Other Screen from the Style menu. (That, by the way, is how the footer graphics were produced for this chapter.)

• •

Scanning at the right resolution

Scans look best when they're printed at a higher lpi setting on a printer with a high dpi. But there's one more variable to take into account: the resolution of the scan itself. That's measured in *ppi—pixels per inch.*

As usual, more is often better. But you shouldn't scan everything at 1600 ppi just because your scanner can do it. Your files would be huge, and they'd take forever to print. When it comes to scans, more is only better up to a certain point. Beyond that point, those extra pixels are wasted. Your printer simply doesn't have enough dots to print them all. The trick is to scan in just enough pixels to put your printer's dots to good use.

• •

See the difference?

In some cases you can—but not always.

Compare the examples in the top row. They're the same scan, both 100 ppi. The one printed at 60 lpi looks fine, but the one printed at 133 lpi looks a little rough. The big pixels are visible at the higher screen setting.

Now compare each photo to the one below it, which was scanned at a higher ppi. You can't see any difference at the lower screen setting, but the extra pixels make a difference in the 133-lpi print.

Printed at 60 lines per inch

100 pixels per inch

Printed at 133 lines per inch

100 pixels per inch

250 pixels per inch

250 pixels per inch

Matching scan resolution to printer resolution

300-dpi laser printer (53–60 lpi):
• **Scan at 100 pixels per inch**

Scan size (inches)	Grayscale file size (KB)	Color file size (KB)
2×3	59	176
4×5	176	586
8×10	782	2,290

600-dpi laser printer (85–106 lpi):
• **Scan at 150 pixels per inch**

Scan size (inches)	Grayscale file size (KB)	Color file size (KB)
2×3	132	396
4×5	440	1,290
8×10	1,720	5,150

1270-dpi imagesetter (100–120 lpi):
• **Scan at 175 pixels per inch**

Scan size (inches)	Grayscale file size (KB)	Color file size (KB)
2×3	180	539
4×5	599	1,750
8×10	2,340	7,010

2540-dpi imagesetter (120–150 lpi):
• **Scan at 200 pixels per inch**

Scan size (inches)	Grayscale file size (KB)	Color file size (KB)
2×3	235	704
4×5	782	2,290
8×10	3,050	9,160

Some notes on using this chart

These recommendations are all based on printing a scan at its actual size—that is, 100% in both picture scale fields.

If you enlarge a scan very much, print quality may suffer. Instead, scan the photo at a higher resolution, then update the picture with the Picture Usage dialog.

The file sizes listed here are for *uncompressed* files. XPress allows you to import a variety of *compressed* file formats, including JPEG and TIFF/LZW, both of which can reduce an image file to a fraction of its original size.

The color file sizes given here are for *RGB* (red-green-blue) files—the file format most scanners produce. If you convert the files to process color (*CMYK*), using Photoshop or another image processor, the files will be considerably larger. Even so, converting RGB images to CMYK format is highly recommended. If you don't do it, XPress will have to do it for you, and that slows down both importing and printing.

• • • • • • • • • • • • •

Proofing bleeds

Bleeds—items that run right off the edge of the page—are an easy way to give even the simplest publication a jazzier look. The basic idea is that you print your document on a sheet larger than the document's page size, so that the bleeding items print out in their entirety, then you trim away the extra paper.

It doesn't cost much extra to have the print shop print bleeds and trim them, but it's not so easy to figure out the best way to proof and print the bleeds in the first place.

The basic setup

A very simple bleed was set up for this newsletter—just one black box running off the top edge of each page.

Even so, proofing proved to be tricky. When this page was printed with all the default settings on a standard laser printer, everything looked right except for the bleed.

No printer can print right to the edge of the page. So what can you do to make sure a bleed really extends to the edge? Or to make sure that you like it in the first place?

Box extended 1 pica (one-sixth inch) past edge of page. (One-eighth inch is the minimum.)

Bleed won't print to edge of paper

Proofing with a reduction

Here's one easy solution. You can reduce the entire page so that the bleed fits within the printable area of the chosen paper size.

On the Mac, just open the Page Setup dialog and type "90%" in the Reduce Or Enlarge field.

In Windows, you have to open the Printer Setup dialog (either from the File menu or from the Print dialog), then click on the Options button to get to the Scaling field.

After setting the reduction, open the Print dialog and set the Registration pop-up menu to Centered, then print. That way, trim marks will be printed at all four corners of the reduced page. To get a better idea of how the bleed looks, use the trim marks to trim away all four sides of the laser proof.

Proofing on larger paper

Here's a very different strategy. If your design only has top or bottom bleeds, print your proofs on legal-size paper (8½ x 14 inches). Most laser printers either have special trays for legal paper or allow you to feed it manually through a special slot.

This proof was printed at 100% size on legal paper, so it provides an even better idea of how the page design looks. But there are two drawbacks to this method. First, it doesn't allow you to proof side bleeds, since legal paper is no wider than letter-size. Second, you have to print with Registration set to Off if you want to see the entire page, so there aren't any trim marks.

You could, of course, draw your own hairline trim marks on the proofs. And that might be a good idea if you're going to use this method to produce final pages for the print shop. With a 600-dpi printer, this method can be used to produce *camera-ready pages*—with top and bottom bleeds—for the print shop.

Proofing "full bleeds"

When a bleed appears on every side of a page, as in this self-mailer, that's called a *full bleed*. Not surprisingly, this kind of design is a bit more difficult to proof.

Here are a variety of tactics for proofing the piece in its entirety.

Laser proof printed at 100% size on letter-size paper. Bleed fails to print to edge on all four sides.

Laser proof printed at 90% size on letter-size paper with Registration set to Centered.

Laser proof printed at 100% size,
Landscape orientation, on letter-size
paper; Tiling pop-up menu in the
Print dialog set to Automatic;
Registration set to Centered.

Splice here | | ...or here

Tiling

It doesn't work well for every kind of design, but it makes sense here. The designer used XPress's automatic print tiling feature to split the letter-size design onto two letter-size sheets.

The reason it works well here is that there are a couple of empty vertical areas in the design—just below and just above the clock graphic—where the pages could easily be spliced together. And that means that, in a pinch, you could even use these as final prints for reproduction.

Sending out for oversized proofs

For roughly $10–$20, you could send the file out to a service bureau and have it printed on a large-format color proofer or as a paper positive on an imagesetter. Either method makes sense if you need to present your design to others for approval.

A special case— bleeding business cards

Bleeds are a very common design device in business cards. There are a couple of reasons for that.

First and foremost, a bleed can make a card much more functional. In particular, a bleed on the top edge of the card makes it much more noticeable and easy to find in a card file.

Second, because business cards are considerably smaller than letter-size sheets, it's very easy to both proof and print the bleeds.

In case you want to save a few dollars the next time you print business cards—and who doesn't?—I've included a couple of my favorite cost-cutting tricks.

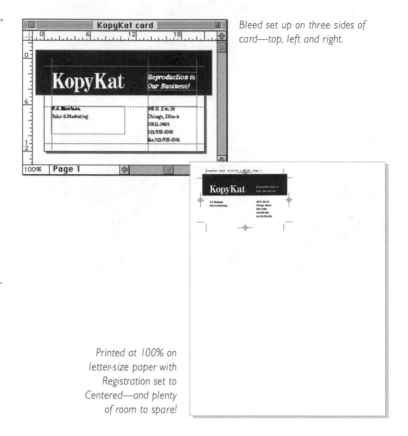

Bleed set up on three sides of card—top, left and right.

Printed at 100% on letter-size paper with Registration set to Centered—and plenty of room to spare!

Printed at 200% on letter-size paper, Landscape orientation, Registration set to Centered.

Why 200%? It's a great way to get imagesetter quality directly from your laser printer without the imagesetter fee. Just take your enlarged print to the print shop and ask them to print it at 50%.

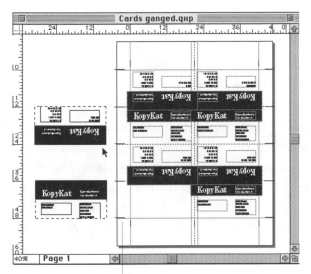

Trim and cut marks in margins added by
drawing short hairlines along guides.

Ganging up

If you have a bunch of cards to do—say, for a
slew of new employees—you might consider
ganging the cards on a single page. Although
you'll have to pay the print shop to cut them
apart, that's bound to be a much smaller
charge than what it would cost to have each
card printed separately on an imagesetter.

The tricky part here is the bleed. You can't
just arrange all the cards side-by-side, top-to-
bottom. You would either end up with bleeds
running onto neighboring cards or forcing the
print shop to make twice as many cuts.

But you can use grouping and rotation to set
all the bleeds so they run into each other. The
original layout, shown on the opposite page,
was grouped and copied to this letter-size
document. Then it was duplicated and rotated
so that the bleed of each card overlapped the
bleed on the neighboring card.

Printed 100% on letter-size paper,
Portrait orientation, Registration set
to Centered.

In this case, the final camera-ready
page was printed from a 600-dpi
printer—good enough for all but the
most demanding cardholders.

Proofing color separations

This is a step that people—even the pros—forget to do all the time. And it's a very costly step to miss.

XPress tries its best to produce perfect color separations, making best guesses about where you want one color to print over another and when you want an item to knock out of its background. But it can't guess correctly every time. The only way you can predict what will roll off those presses is to print your own separation proofs, then sit there and study them, detail by detail, until you're positive all your colors are printing in the right places, at the right strengths.

Spot color proofs

The first task here is to make sure what's in black should really be black and what's in color should be color.

The next task is to scrutinize the knockouts and overprints. As a general rule, type set in black should overprint any other color. But when it comes to pictures, you'll need to think twice.

Black Plate

*Printed at 90%,
Landscape,
Registration Centered,
Separations On,
Plate menu set to
All Plates.*

Grayscale images (but not line art) should always knock out of color backgrounds—unless you're trying to create a duotone effect.

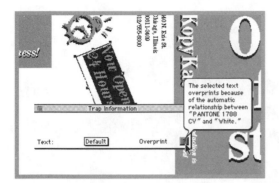

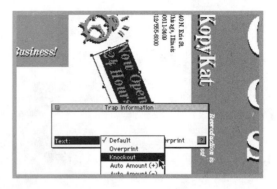

The designer set this type in color with a black drop shadow. When she printed separation proofs, she noticed that the color type failed to knock out the black type beneath it. She checked the Trap Information palette to see why.

XPress had assigned the color type to overprint because of the type overlapped white paper before it overlapped black type. Bad guess. She corrected the problem by choosing Knockout in the palette.

Color plate
(Pantone 1788)

XPress automatically knocked out a rectangular area of this color-filled box so the photo wouldn't overprint the color. Good guess!

Process separation proofs

The first thing you'll want to check here is the number of plates. You should get exactly four for every page. If you get any extra plates, that means you defined one or more of your colors as a spot color—that is, you forgot to turn on Process Separation in the Edit Color dialog.

The next things to check are—as always—your knock-outs and overprints.

You may want to take a peek at the full-color version back on page 169.

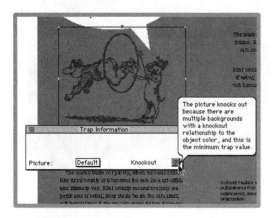

Here, the designer had the opposite problem from the one on the previous page. XPress guessed that the picture, set in black, should knock out of the color behind—but that would have produced a weak black and potential registration problems.

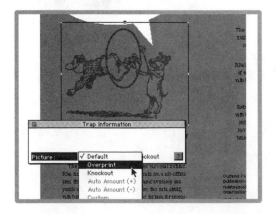

To avoid these problems, the designer set the picture to overprint instead.

Cyan plate

Magenta plate

Yellow plate

Black plate

Proofs printed at 85% on legal-size paper, Landscape, Registration Centered, Separations On, Plate menu set to All Plates.

The plates

Although this was designed by assigning various Pantone colors to items, the job is separated into the four process components—cyan, magenta, yellow and black.

Note that some items were assigned Process Yellow—those are the ones that appear in solid black on the yellow plate.

Finally, note that all items on the black plate overprint—you don't see any knockouts for those items on the other three plates.

Playing it safe

Printing test separations on your laser printer is a good idea no matter how simple your color design. If you're doing a complex process-color design, though, you should get digital color proofs before sending your file out for imagesetting. To be extra safe, have your print shop produce a color proof, such as a Cromalin, from the imagesetter output before going to press.

• • • • • • • • • • • • • • • • • •

Sending out for output

Whether you're sending your file to a service bureau for color proofs or for imagesetter output, make sure you include all linked pictures as well as a list of the typefaces you used. Use the Collect For Output command (File menu) to make sure you haven't forgotten anything.

If you want the best output to send to the print shop, have your file printed from an imagesetter rather than a laser printer. (Color proofs cannot be used for reproduction—print shops require black-and-white output.) Paper positives, which are typically printed at 1270 dpi and 120 lpi, are acceptable, but film negatives are far superior. They cost a bit more, but the quality is much higher. They're usually printed at 2540 dpi with a screen as high as 133 or 150 lpi.

With film negatives, the print shop doesn't have to "shoot" the pages with a camera before making printing plates. And for process color printing, you couldn't possibly get comparable results with paper positives.

• • • • • • • • • • • • • • • • •

The difference

Pages reproduced from paper positives tend to be not only lower in resolution but also have more contrast. That means dark areas will be a bit muddy and light shades may "white out."

Reproduced from paper positive (1270 dots per inch, 120 lines per inch).

Reproduced from film negative (2540 dots per inch, 133 lines per inch).

Color plate

Black plate

Spot color seps printed as film negatives

In a film negative, everything is reversed. Areas that should print in solid ink appear transparent, and areas where no ink should print appear solid black. That can be a little tricky to get used to.

• • • • • • • • • •

Good luck!

Do you have everything you need? Just in case. let's review:

• • Make sure you have the right type of output for your print shop. "Quick print" shops typically prefer laser prints or imagesetter paper positives. Commercial print shops prefer film negatives but will have no problem working from paper output. Some shops, called *disk-to-print* shops, will accept all of these or will simply take your XPress files on disk and do the rest; they take care of both the imagesetting and the final printing process.

• • If you want the print shop to put in photos or other artwork—that is, produce the halftone traditionally—make sure you label any placeholder pictures or boxes on your final pages with the initials "FPO" (For Position Only). And make sure you supply your print shop with all the photos and art you want them to drop in.

• • If you're printing in two or more colors, make sure you give the print shop the right number of separations for each page, all printed with registration marks and color names. If you've had color proofs made along the way, leave them with the print shop for reference.

• • If you want bleeds, make sure the bleed items extend at least ⅛ inch past the page edges and that the print includes trim marks.

• • If you want to see a printer's proof before the job goes to press (which is a very good idea), remind the printer that you must see a proof and approve it before they go forward.

• • Finally, cross your fingers and don't walk under any ladders on your way to the print shop. You never know....

XPress
Designs

Gallery

Becoming expert at using XPress is much more than knowing which commands to use or how to rotate boxes. It's also knowing how to make the most of the raw material you're starting with—how to present text and pictures in a fresh, engaging way and maintain a consistent look throughout the presentation. The designers represented in this section have done just this.

I've included a wide variety of brochures, folders, newsletters, announcements and reports to try to create a sense of the incredible array of things that can be done with XPress. The more you look at these pieces, the more you'll see; they're full of clever little details that make them outstanding design solutions.

You can draw inspiration from any of these pieces, no matter what kind of piece you're working on. A newsletter design may give you ideas about how to do a brochure; a novel brochure design may change the way you approach your next newsletter. Some of the best design ideas come from the most unlikely sources!

Announcing a meeting

How do you get people interested in attending a work-related meeting in their free time? That's a common challenge.

The designer for this association came up with a simple but effective series of announcements to make this meeting seem like an "event." She designed two announcements to be sent out a couple of weeks apart—one to fit a regular business envelope, the other for a smaller envelope. This second announcement also included a return envelope.

The artwork is a collage of public domain clip art and oval picture boxes—nothing fancy, but big and bold enough to catch your eye. The bullet symbols, from a dingbat font, repeat the "flying" theme.

▼ ▼ ▼

Publisher: ADEPT,
   Chicago chapter
Designer: Barrie Dellenbach
Color: PMS 294
Type: Lithos

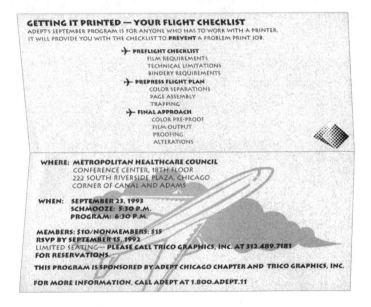

GETTING IT PRINTED — YOUR FLIGHT CHECKLIST
ADEPT'S SEPTEMBER PROGRAM IS FOR ANYONE WHO HAS TO WORK WITH A PRINTER.
IT WILL PROVIDE YOU WITH THE CHECKLIST TO **PREVENT** A PROBLEM PRINT JOB.

✈ **PREFLIGHT CHECKLIST**
        FILM REQUIREMENTS
        TECHNICAL LIMITATIONS
        BINDERY REQUIREMENTS
✈ **PREPRESS FLIGHT PLAN**
        COLOR SEPARATIONS
        PAGE ASSEMBLY
        TRAPPING
✈ **FINAL APPROACH**
        COLOR PRE-PROOF
        FILM OUTPUT
        PROOFING
        ALTERATIONS

WHERE: METROPOLITAN HEALTHCARE COUNCIL
            CONFERENCE CENTER, 18TH FLOOR
            222 SOUTH RIVERSIDE PLAZA, CHICAGO
            CORNER OF CANAL AND ADAMS

WHEN: SEPTEMBER 23, 1993
            SCHMOOZE: 5:30 P.M.
            PROGRAM: 6:30 P.M.

MEMBERS: $10/NONMEMBERS: $15
RSVP BY SEPTEMBER 15, 1992
LIMITED SEATING— PLEASE CALL TRICO GRAPHICS, INC. AT 312.489.7181
FOR RESERVATIONS.

THIS PROGRAM IS SPONSORED BY ADEPT CHICAGO CHAPTER AND TRICO GRAPHICS, INC.

FOR MORE INFORMATION, CALL ADEPT AT 1.800.ADEPT.11

ABOUT TRICO GRAPHICS, INC.—
TRICO GRAPHICS,INC. HAS BEEN PROVIDING COLOR PREPRESS SERVICES SINCE ITS ORIGIN AS TRIANGLE ENGRAVING IN 1915. TRICO HAS IDENTIFIED ITS NICHE IN THE MARKET AS A SPECIALIST IN COLOR CONTROL AT ALL LEVELS OF THE PRODUCTION PROCESS.

DESIGNERS, CORPORATE PRINT BUYERS, WEB, SHEETFED AND FLEXO PRINTERS AS WELL AS 'MAC' ENTHUSIASTS LOOK TO TRICO GRAPHICS, INC. COLOR CONTROL IN THREE AREAS:

- ✈ AN OPEN, COLOR MANAGED ENVIRONMENT INTEGRATING ALL WORKSTATIONS FROM DRUM SCANNER INPUT THROUGH POSTSCRIPT® DRUM FILM RECORDERS FOR FAST, ACCURATE COLOR REPRODUCTION.

- ✈ QUICK, ACCURATE COLOR REPRODUCTION WITH 'SOFT PROOFING' ABILITY AVAILABLE WITH THE KODAK DESIGNMASTER AND PROPHECY IMAGING SYSTEMS.

- ✈ TMS® PRINTING SYSTEM (TAILOR MADE SEPARATIONS) IS DESIGNED TO MAKE SEPARATIONS FIT PRESS AND PAPER CHARACTERISTICS.

INDIVIDUALS INTERESTED IN VISITING TRICO GRAPHICS, INC. WILL BE ABLE TO SCHEDULE A TOUR IN SMALL GROUPS AT THE ADEPT MEETING.

ABOUT ADEPT—
ADEPT WAS CREATED IN 1987 BY A HANDFUL OF GRAPHIC DESIGNERS AND DESKTOP PUBLISHERS TO BE A HELP CENTER FOR COLLEAGUES, CLIENTS, AND SUPPLIERS. IN 1993, ADEPT MERGED WITH THE NATIONAL COMPUTER GRAPHICS ASSOCIATION (NCGA) TO BE ABLE TO SERVE ITS CONSTITUENCY ON A NATIONAL LEVEL. AS A DIVISION OF NCGA, ADEPT OFFERS A PLACE TO GO FOR UNBIASED INFORMATION, SOLUTIONS, AND A SHARING OF ELECTRONIC EXPERIENCES WITH OTHER USERS.

POSTSCRIPT IS A TRADEMARK OF ADOBE SYSTEMS, INC.
T.M.S.® PRINTING SYSTEM IS A TRADEMARK OF TRICO GRAPHICS, INC.
KODAK, DESIGNMASTER AND PROPHECY ARE TRADEMARKS OF EASTMAN KODAK

☐ **YES,** WE WILL ATTEND:

FROM:
✈ COMPANY NAME _____
ADDRESS _____
✈ NAME _____
TITLE _____
✈ NAME _____
TITLE _____
✈ NAME _____
TITLE _____
✈ NAME _____
TITLE _____

TOTAL ENCLOSED

MAKE CHECK PAYABLE TO NCGA/ADEPT
MEMBERS—$10/NONMEMBERS—$15
PLEASE RESPOND BY SEPTEMBER 15

ADEPT
THE ASSOCIATION FOR THE DEVELOPMENT
OF ELECTRONIC PUBLISHING TECHNIQUE
CHICAGO CHAPTER
858 W. ARMITAGE, BOX 226
CHICAGO, IL 60614
1-800-ADEPT-11

TRICO GRAPHICS, INC.
1642 NORTH BESLY COURT
CHICAGO, IL 60622-1526

Open house

Here's a clever folder that visually plays off of the central message inside. It's an invitation to visit (and join) a local historical society headquartered in an elegant old mansion.

To emphasize the society's "open door," the mansion itself is pictured on the front, split across two panels; the left panel opens to reveal an extended message.

This is a type of *gatefold* design, meant to be appreciated at various stages of unfolding. Both sides of the design are shown here, to illustrate how the fold works.

You can't tell here, but the photos are printed as rich duotones of black and teal.

▼ ▼ ▼

Publisher: Evanston Historical Society, Evanston, IL
Designers: Jim McGuire & Julie Gleason, McGuire Associates
Colors: Black, PMS 327
Type: Univers, Garamond

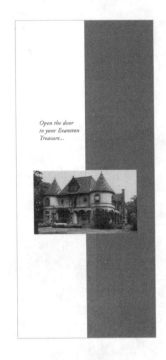
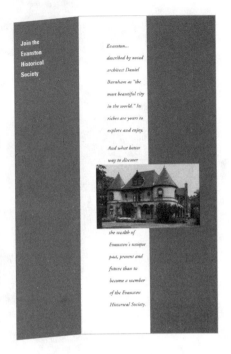

Join the Evanston Historical Society

Share in the Gifts the Evanston Historical Society Offers

The Evanston Historical Society is your link between the past and the present—a balance of progress and tradition.

The Evanston Historical Society's programs and research collections reflect our city's diversified and unique historical roots.

Fascinating exhibits, memorable tours, and special events are waiting for you and your family at the Evanston Historical Society.

Learn about what Evanston once was, what it has become today, and its vision for tomorrow.

A Generous Return on Your Investment

Membership privileges include:
- Free tours of the Dawes House
- Invitations to "Members Only" special events
- Advance notice of all public events, exhibit openings and lectures
- Reduced admission to events and lectures
- Subscription to *TimeLines*, the award-winning, quarterly publication which highlights Evanston history and reports Historical Society activities
- 10% discount on all Museum Shop purchases

Help make history!
Become a member of the Evanston Historical Society.

Your Membership Application

(Please Print)
Name:
Address:
City: State: Zip:
Day Phone: Evening Phone:
□ I am interested in volunteering for the Evanston Historical Society. Please contact me.

Membership Renewal $
Additional Gift $

We thank you for your support!

Total Amount Enclosed $

Evanston Historical Society
225 Greenwood Street, Evanston, Illinois 60201
708.475.3410

Yes, I (We) would like to become members of the Evanston Historical Society!

Individual □ $ 25	*Patron* □ $ 250
Family □ $ 35	*Benefactor* □ $ 500
Contributor □ $ 50	*Life* □ $ 1000
Sustaining □ $ 100	

Your additional gift enables the Society to continue to provide meaningful programs highlighting Evanston's unique and progressive historical experience. All of the Society's programs are supported by contributions.

Additional Gift $

Your New Lakefront Home

When you become a member, you become part of the Evanston Historical Society family...a proud, caring family that calls the magnificent Dawes House "home".

Walk the richly ornamented halls of this beautiful 1894 Chateauesque mansion. Study the ever-changing displays. Explore the heritage and culture of one of Chicago's earliest and most important suburban communities.

Evanston... described by noted architect Daniel Burnham as "the most beautiful city in the world." Its riches are yours to explore and enjoy.

And what better way to discover

the wealth of Evanston's unique past, present and future than to become a member of the Evanston Historical Society.

Evanston Historical Society
225 Greenwood Street
Evanston, Illinois 60201

Open the door to your Evanston Treasure...

Making a statement

The cover of this annual report uses a similar left-flap device to engage the reader in stages—exposing the reader to one simple message at a time, presented with extra-generous leading.

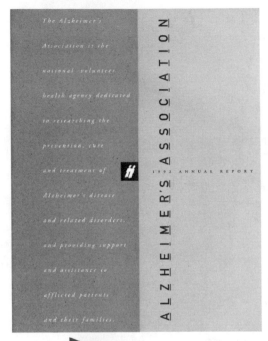

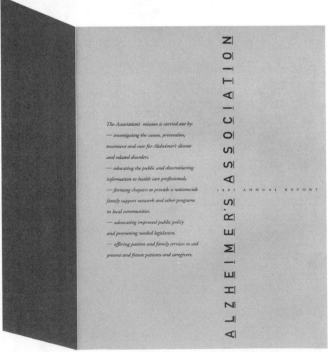

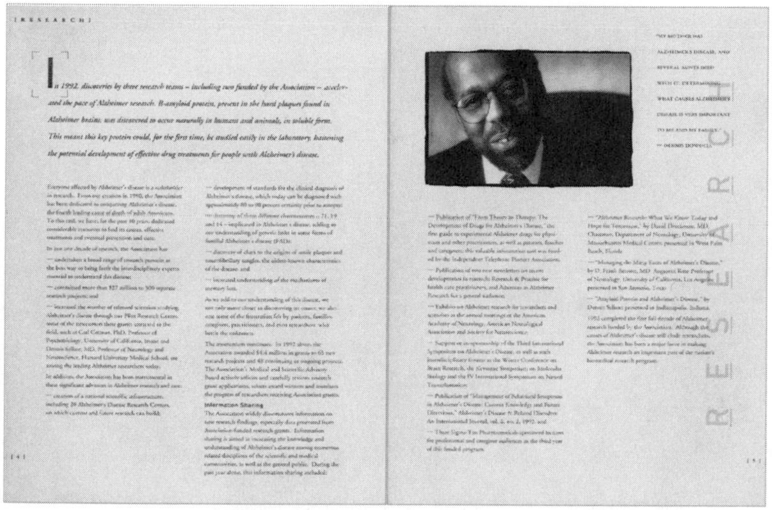

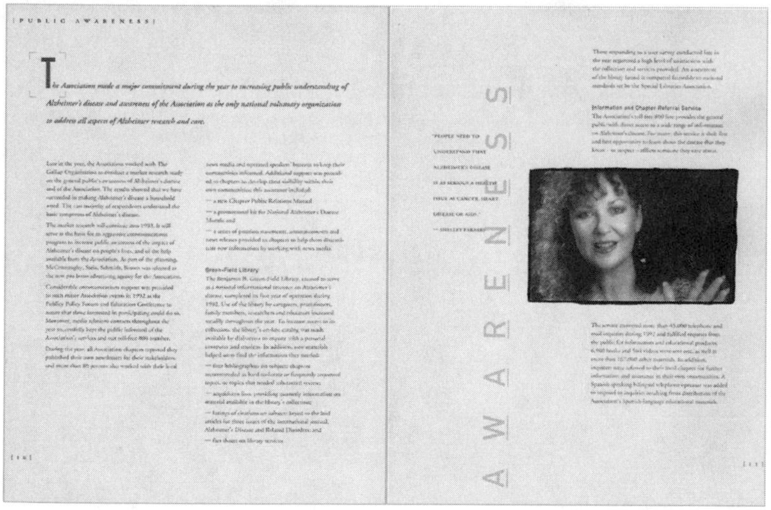

Inside, each spread is devoted to a different aspect of the association—note the way these aspects are handled as headlines.

Along the top, the name of the spread's theme is set in small uppercase letters and printed in a deep spot color. The key word is then repeated elsewhere as a large background element, set in a medium tint of another spot color and sent to the back.

Each duotoned photo is framed with a ragged black border. The designers simply tore up pieces of black paper, scanned them in and set them behind the photos.

▼ ▼ ▼

Publisher: Alzheimer's Association, Chicago
Designers: Bill Ferdinand & Dave Philmlee, Zündesign
Colors: PMS 5265, 4505, 272
Type: Din M Mittelschrift; Sabon

Elegance in a newsletter

Some simple type devices add up to a very elegant look in this design. The main headlines are set in their own column—"hung" to the left of the article—and set flush-right against a light rule. Drop caps are set very large—six lines deep—to bring out the strength and simplicity of the typeface, Times Roman.

This newsletter also regularly uses old-style ornamental clip art, often set in subtle tints, as well as circular and oval picture boxes to recall traditional oval frames.

▼ ▼ ▼

Publisher: Evanston Historical Society, Evanston, IL
Designers: McGuire Associates
Colors: Black, PMS 5463
Type: Univers Condensed; Times

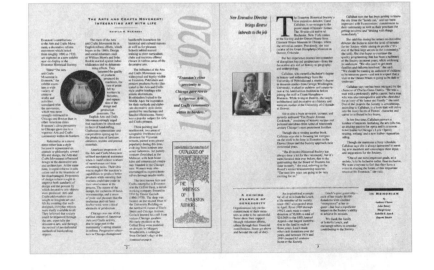

Back to business

But all work doesn't necessarily mean no play. This designer adds a friendly, playful touch to an employee newsletter using a variety of type and graphic devices.

The fine typographic treatment begins with the tightly kerned nameplate and the color contrast between "CP" and "YOU." Headline kickers are set in big italics to create a warm opening to each article, and the large drop caps are set in an extra-light sans-serif typeface.

The contents block is also given an unusual treatment—it's set in a big tinted text box and rotated; note also the large page numbers and the dotted paragraph rule below the word "Inside."

▼ ▼ ▼

Publisher: Computer Products, Boca Raton, FL
Designer: Victoria Brown
Colors: Black, PMS 322
Type: Goudy; Helvetica

Efficient information

This newsletter has a single purpose—to summarize key developments in the desktop publishing industry so that designers don't have to read dozens of magazines to keep up to date.

The design fits the maximum amount of information in a format that makes for quick reading and skimming. Heads are set bold, but just big enough to catch your attention. Departments are separated with illustrated heads hung slightly to the left of the columns. Fine dotted rules are used to keep everything clearly, but subtly, separated.

▼ ▼ ▼

Publisher: The Nelson Group, Boulder, CO
Designer: Jay Nelson
Color: Black
Type: Franklin Gothic Condensed; Galliard

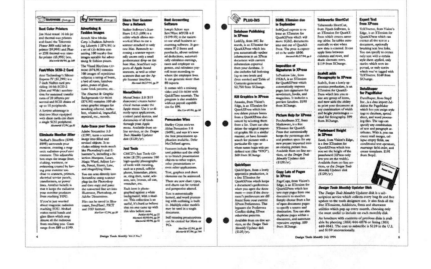

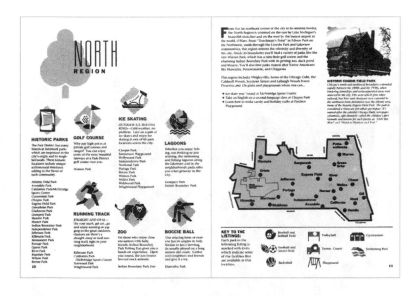

A visual directory

This directory also had to communicate a lot in a tight space. The task was to describe the facilities and activities at hundreds of public parks throughout the city of Chicago in under 60 pages.

Section-opening spreads provide simple maps of regions of the city and locations of the parks, all presented in a light, graphic way.

Ensuing spreads list addresses and other information about each park with icons for that park's facilities and activities. These graphics were set in a second color and inserted as anchored picture boxes so that they would flow along with the text.

▼ ▼ ▼

Publisher: Chicago Park District
Designer: Estelle Carol, Carol★Simpson Productions
Cover design: Rapp Collins Worldwide
Colors: Black, PMS 266
Type: Giotto; Franklin Gothic; Stone Serif

Designing a 'zine

A "zine" (in case you haven't come across one before) is an independently published, small-circulation magazine. Zines are usually labors of love (they're seldom produced for profit), and they're often on the cutting edge of desktop publishing.

Here's an example of a very advanced zine that aspires to magazine-industry production values—even though it's printed in black-and-white. The designer (who's also the publisher) has developed a wide range of page grids and layout concepts to handle a variety of features and departments.

There's plenty to see here. Note the varied use of huge initial caps in feature articles—in some cases, hanging to the left, in others, set as stick-up caps. Note also how the designer arranges pictures to give some spreads a horizontal look and others a more vertical orientation.

▼ ▼ ▼

Publisher: Luna Grafika Design
Designer: Dany Drennan
Color: Black
Type: Univers, Sabon, Helvetica
*   Condensed*

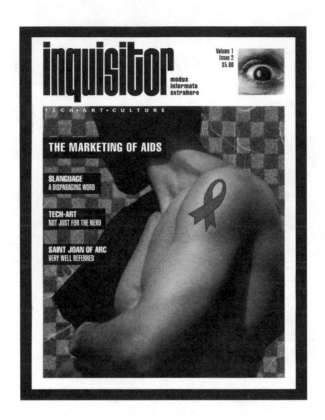

The big picture

Nothing gets across a human interest story like pictures of people. This annual report makes strong use of such pictures to get its messages through.

The typographic treatment is also warm and engaging. Headlines are set using various styles, sizes and colors of faces from two type families. Typographic collages of this sort are often jarring, but this designer managed to create balance and a pleasant rhythm by keeping the changes relatively subtle.

▼ ▼ ▼

Publisher: Chicago Child Care Society
Designer: Deborah Ryder
Colors: Black, PMS 183, 408
Type: Berkeley, Berthold Script

What **goals** are you trying to achieve?

Do you want more **income** from your investments?

Balance and contrast

This brochure also uses big pictures and punchy typographic changes to create a sense of immediacy. The strongest aspects of the design, though, are the sense of balance and counterbalance and the dramatic contrasts between dark and light.

Large areas of white space are counterbalanced with photos; blocks of type are balanced against blocks of color. These themes are carried over into the type as well—"background" text is set in a serif face, while the key words and "take-home messages" are set in a contrasting, heavier sans serif.

▼ ▼ ▼

Publisher: First Chicago Investment Services
Designer: Karen Knorr, Wechsler & Partners, Inc.
Colors: Black, PMS 5405, metallic 8022, Warm Gray 8
Type: Times, Frutiger

Creative chaos

This radio station newsletter is dedicated not only to updating its listeners on local music trends and events, but also to the the mission of communicating the station's eclectic approach to contemporary music.

The designers underscore the chaotic aspect of this eclecticism visually, using an ever-changing variety of layout approaches and typographic treatments, both within and between issues.

Completely unfolded, the publication becomes a wide horizontal spread—a small surprise, given the initial impression created by the vertical cover design.

▼ ▼ ▼

Publisher: Diamond
Broadcasting, Chicago
Designer: Robert Petrick,
Michael Golec,
Petrick Design
Colors: Black, PMS 285
(the second color changes
with each issue)
Type: Futura, Times Condensed

Structuring complex information

This specifications guide for a line of office furniture and lighting contains a tremendous amount of facts and figures—enough to be overwhelming if not presented carefully.

These designers did their work carefully and elegantly. Items in the product line are introduced in cleanly organized spreads, using simple illustrations and clear callouts. Subtopics are divided with a consistent system of heads and subheads, with primary heads reversed out of paragraph rules and secondary heads set in bold black type. The organizational power and flexibility of the five-column grid is evident throughout.

▼ ▼ ▼

Publisher: Steelcase, Inc., Grand Rapids, MI
Designer: Dan Moyer, Agnew Moyer Smith, Pittsburgh, PA
Colors: Black; additional cover colors: PMS 402, 131
Type: Helvetica, Helvetica Condensed, Helvetica Black

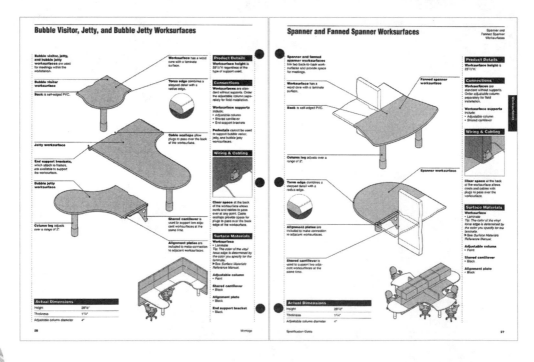

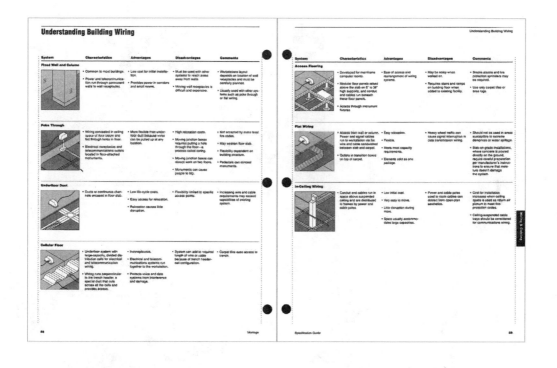

Understanding Building Wiring

System	Characteristics	Advantages	Disadvantages	Comments
Fixed Wall and Column	Common to most buildings. Power and telecommunication run through permanent walls to wall receptacles.	Low cost for initial installation. Provides power in corridors and small rooms.	Must be used with other systems to reach areas away from walls. Moving wall receptacles is difficult and expensive.	Workstations layout depends on location of wall receptacles and must be carefully planned. Usually used with other systems such as poke through or flat wiring.
Poke Through	Wiring concealed in ceiling space of floor below and fed through holes in floor. Electrical receptacles and telecommunications outlets located in floor-attached monuments.	More flexible than underfloor duct because wires can be pulled up at any location.	High relocation costs. Moving junction boxes requires pulling a hole through the floor—a process called coring. Moving junction boxes can disrupt work on two floors. Monuments can cause people to trip.	Not approved by some local fire codes. May weaken floor slab. Flexibility dependent on building structure. Pedestals can conceal monuments.
Underfloor Duct	Ducts or continuous channels encased in floor slab.	Low life-cycle costs. Easy access for relocation. Relocation causes little disruption.	Flexibility limited to specific access points.	Increasing wire and cable requirements may exceed capabilities of existing system.
Cellular Floor	Underfloor system with large-capacity, divided distribution cells for electrical and telecommunication wiring. Wiring runs perpendicular to the trench header, a special duct that cuts across all the cells and provides access.	Inconspicuous. Electrical and telecommunications systems run together to the workstation. Protects voice and data systems from interference and damage.	System can add to required length of wire or cable because of trench header cell configuration.	Carpet tiles ease access to trench.

Understanding Building Wiring

System	Characteristics	Advantages	Disadvantages	Comments
Access Flooring	Developed for mainframe computer rooms. Modular floor panels raised above the slab on 6" to 36" high supports, and conduit and cables run beneath these floor panels. Access through monument fixtures.	Ease of access and rearrangement of wiring systems.	May be noisy when walked on. Requires stairs and ramps on building floor when added to existing facility.	Smoke alarms and fire protection sprinklers may be required. Use only carpet tiles or area rugs.
Flat Wiring	Access from wall or column. Power and signal cables run to workstation via flat wire and cable sandwiched between slab and carpet. Outlets in transition boxes on top of carpet.	Easy relocation. Flexible. Meets most capacity requirements. Elements sold as one package.	Heavy wheel traffic can cause signal interruption in data transmission wiring.	Should not be used in areas susceptible to extreme dampness or water spillage. Slab-on-grade installations, where concrete is poured directly on the ground, require careful preparation per manufacturer's instructions to ensure that moisture doesn't damage the system.
In-Ceiling Wiring	Conduit and cables run in space above suspended ceiling and are distributed to frames by power and cable poles.	Low initial cost. Very easy to move. Little disruption during move. Space usually accommodates large capacities.	Power and cable poles used to route cables can detract from open-plan aesthetics.	Cost for installation increases when ceiling space is used as return air plenum to meet fire-protection codes. Ceiling-suspended cable trays should be considered for communications wiring.

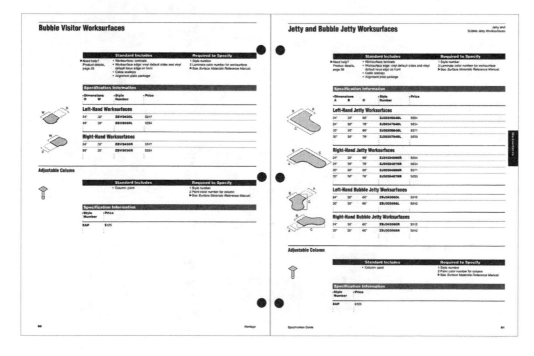

Bubble Visitor Worksurfaces

Standard Includes	Required to Specify
Need help? Product details, page 26	Worksurface: laminate. Worksurface edge: vinyl-default sides and vinyl default torus edge on front. Cable scallops. Alignment plate package.	1 Style number. 2 Laminate color number for worksurface. ▶ See Surface Materials Reference Manual.

Specification Information

Dimensions D	W	Style Number	Price
Left-Hand Worksurfaces			
24"	30"	ZBV3430L	$247
30"	30"	ZBV3030L	$254
Right-Hand Worksurfaces			
24"	30"	ZBV3430R	$247
30"	30"	ZBV3030R	$254

Adjustable Column

Standard Includes	Required to Specify
Column: paint	1 Style number. 2 Paint color number for column. ▶ See Surface Materials Reference Manual.

Specification Information

Style Number	Price
ZAP	$125

Jetty and Bubble Jetty Worksurfaces

Standard Includes	Required to Specify
Need help? Product details, page 26	Worksurface: laminate. Worksurface edge: vinyl-default sides and vinyl default torus edge on front. Cable scallops. Alignment plate package.	1 Style number. 2 Laminate color number for worksurface. ▶ See Surface Materials Reference Manual.

Specification Information

Dimensions A	B	C	Style Number	Price
Left-Hand Jetty Worksurfaces				
24"	30"	66"	ZJ30246648L	$554
24"	30"	78"	ZJ30047848L	$634
30"	30"	66"	ZJ30306648L	$571
30"	30"	78"	ZJ30307848L	$653
Right-Hand Jetty Worksurfaces				
24"	30"	66"	ZJ24304866R	$554
24"	30"	78"	ZJ24334878R	$634
30"	30"	60"	ZJ30304866R	$571
30"	30"	78"	ZJ30304878R	$653
Left-Hand Bubble Jetty Worksurfaces				
24"	30"	60"	ZBJ303060L	$512
30"	30"	66"	ZBJ303066L	$542
Right-Hand Bubble Jetty Worksurfaces				
24"	30"	60"	ZBJ303060R	$512
30"	30"	66"	ZBJ303066R	$542

Adjustable Column

Standard Includes	Required to Specify
Column: paint	1 Style number. 2 Paint color number for column. ▶ See Surface Materials Reference Manual.

Specification Information

Style Number	Price
ZAP	$125

Shifting columns

It's always a challenge to lay out technical articles in an efficient, yet interesting, way. This little booklet, a collection of such articles, does a nice job of packing in a lot of ideas in a small space.

The designer used a small set of master page designs, each with two main columns and a narrower "scholar's" column. Sometimes the extra column is used for white space, sometimes for a sidebar. The layout of the three columns changes from page to page to suit the information.

▼ ▼ ▼

Publisher: Seneca Design & Consulting, Chicago, IL
Designer: Lisa Davidson, Jonathon Goldenstein
Colors: PMS 418, 5493
Type: Futura, New Baskerville

Open and simple

In terms of density of information, this patient hand-book was certainly less of a challenge than the previous couple of publications. But it does meet a different challenge very admirably—making lots of little facts easily accessible to folks who may not be in the best shape for fact-finding.

The body type is set fairly large with very generous leading. Bold heads are hung to the left with large square bullet symbols, making it very easy to skim through the booklet to find topics of interest.

It's a simple treatment, but very effective, clean and attractive. The cover blend is printed in a combination of gray and a metallic blue.

▼   ▼   ▼

Publisher: Michael Reese Hospital, Chicago
Designer: Lee Wel Printing
Colors: Black, PMS 424, 8183
Type: Garamond, Helvetica Black

Big news

Here's a fine example of a large-format newsletter, this one created by a company for its employees.

The designer uses two basic page designs—one with two wide body columns and narrower outside columns, the other with four equal body columns. The first design, used for the front and back cover, allow the designer to hang captions, pull-quotes and other special items to either side of the body text. The second page design, used for the inside spread, is built to hold as many articles as the tabloid page can handle and still make the articles easy to read.

Note also the recurring use of the solid black circle—at the top of each column divider rule, at the beginning of captions, and above and below the pull-quote.

▼ ▼ ▼

Publisher: United Stationers,
 Des Plaines, IL
Designers: Susan Weller &
 Deborah Doering,
 Bottega Design
Color: Black
Type: Minion, Modula, Helvetica

A light-hearted invite

What would you do if you had to design a piece for a citywide club of art directors? That could be an unnerving task given the critical nature of such an audience.

This designer went for a fun, loose look, avoiding pretense altogether. The graphics are all hand-drawn sketches, scanned in and modified in Photoshop. The wobbly type plays right along.

This piece is also unusual in its format—you don't often see vertical folders that open vertically to create a long strip. (Remind you of an ancient papyrus scroll?)

▼ ▼ ▼

Publisher: The Art Directors
  Club of Metropolitan
  Washington
Designer: Steven D. Fleshman
Color: PMS 287
Type: Emigré Variex, Century

Front

Back

the Art Directors Club is really a community. Once a year, you our members, ask a handful of other members to administer the club on your behalf. The May Annual Meeting is about voting in a new set of officers to run the club in the coming year. We'd like each member to participate in the voting process because the new board will be representing you.

Come and meet your new representatives, bid a fond farewell to the outgoing board, share an idea, volunteer to serve on a committee and of course, stay to see the Clios.

Okay, so it's not an Egyptian theme. But you don't have to bring your mummy and it *is* a chance to view the 1993 Clio reel—*really cheap!* The ADCMW has procured this piece of cathode ray excellence and it's ready for your viewing. Normally you'd have to buy the Clio reel yourself at a cost of over $140.⁰⁰ just to see what you'll be able to enjoy on May 16th at the Educational & Administration Building Auditorium at the National Zoo.

The Clio Awards encompass all media in the advertising industry. The Clios uphold an honest and democratic system of judging based upon the evaluation of advertising peers. The judges, on an individual and independent basis, without influence by other panel members, register an impact score with a rating of 1 to 10 immediately after seeing, hearing or reading each advertisement. The criteria on which the judges base their evaluation remain the same: believability, tastefulness, copy, demonstration, identification and sellability.

Today Clio-winning advertising is seen throughout the world. The Clio has permanent representatives in 35 countries and 65 cities. The Clio Awards are truly one of the largest and most celebrated festivals of its kind in the world.

So what would you expect to pay for a chance to see the world famous Clio awards...$99.⁰⁰, $79.⁰⁰, $59.⁰⁰? No! If you act before midnight, you'll pay only $15 dollars if you are an ADCMW member or just $20.00 if you're not a member yet.

if you are a member, and get two of your friends to join the art directors club of metropolitan washington, you could attend this show for **free!** that's right, if you get two people to join the club, we'll **give** you the next adcmw sponsored program that you wish to attend absolutely free.

annual meeting+clios

date:
Monday, May 16, 1994

time:

6:00 p.m.	*Reception*
7:00 p.m.	*Election of '94 -'95 ADCMW Board* (members only)
7:30 p.m.–8:30 p.m.	*Clio Reel* (all attendees)

place:
National Zoological Park Educational & Administration Building Auditorium

The National Zoological Park is located at 3001 Connecticut Avenue, NW. FREE Parking is available on Lot A. The Auditorium is a short walk down the sidewalk located directly across from the lot. When you pass the Cheetah Conservation Station, take a right. The first building on your right is the Education Building which houses the Auditorium. Or, if you come in the front entrance of the Zoo, it's the first building on the left.

program registration

Name_____
Company_____
Address_____
City/State/Zip_____
Phone Number_____

cost
☐ Prepaid Member $15 *(walk-ins $20)*
☐ Prepaid Non-member $20 *(walk-ins $25)*
☐ Prepaid Student $10 *(walk-ins $10)*

Card number_____
Expiration date_____
Signature_____

payment method
☐ Check payable to Art Directors Club of Metropolitan Washington
☐ MasterCard   ☐ Visa

Send to ADCMW
1000 Eagles Passage Court,
Davidsonville, MD 21035

Charge by phone
301/261-6166
Fax: 301/261-6602

Deeper and deeper

This invitation for a seminar series uses a couple of interesting tricks.

Note the background on the left half of the front cover—it's a deep spot color that's been filled with type (the seminar topics) set in a slightly lighter tint.

The piece unfolds out to a cruciform shape, revealing a registration card.

▼   ▼   ▼

Publisher: Bellcore TEC, Lisle, IL
Designer: Susan Weller &
    Deborah Doering,
    Bottega Design
Colors: Black, PMS 1805, 412
Type: Galliard, Helvetica

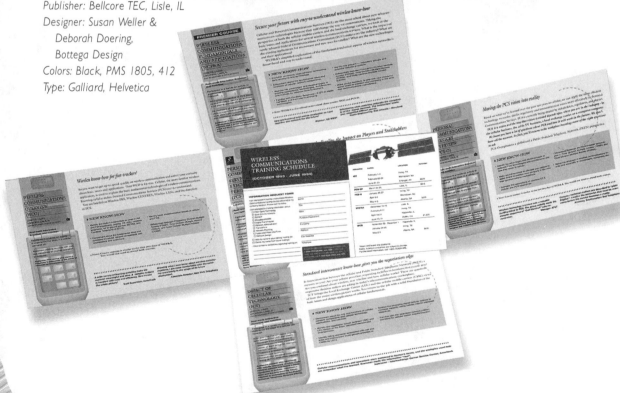

Question and answer

This brochure also uses type in the background—though certainly in a more prominent way. The big questions ("who?" and "why?") are set in opposite spot colors on either side of the brochure.

The piece unfolds horizontally, and keeps unfolding—five long panels per side to answer each question.

▼ ▼ ▼

Publisher: Trinity University, San Antonio, TX
Designer: Mark Shippe, North Charles Street Design, Baltimore, MD
Colors: Process, plus PMS 414 and a special match color
Type: Frutiger, Futura, Minion

Simple and snappy

Here's a three-column newsletter that looks very airy, contemporary and inviting.

The designers include plenty of white space and set the body text with ample leading to create the impression of light reading.

The wavy lines recur in several areas— in the nameplate logo, as a background graphic for the front cover and as side bleeds for succeeding pages. The other graphics are well-chosen pieces of clip art.

Note also the wonderful synergy between the three typefaces—one ultra-modern (Modula), one not-quite-so-modern (Helvetica Compressed) and one Old Style (Galliard).

▼ ▼ ▼

Publisher: Spectrum Communications (for Alyden One Heating & Air Conditioning), Glenview, IL
Designer: Susan Weller & Deborah Doering, Bottega Design
Colors: Black and PMS 186 on tinted paper
Type: Galliard, Modula, Helvetica Compressed

When you need humidity, call Aleyden

The onset of fall and winter weather conditions brings with it the need for additional humidity in most business settings.

In many cases, indoor winter air can be drier than the Sahara Desert. Did you know that dry air causes rapid evaporation of moisture from your skin and throat often causing it to dry out?

Physicians remind us that dry air is one of the leading causes for nose and throat discomfort often resulting in lost productivity. Humidifiers place needed moisture in dry (sometimes arid) winter air to reduce the possibility of such physical disorders.

Aleyden has solutions to your needs for increased humidity. Whether the concern is maintaining healthy levels, preserving antiques or holding precise RH (relative humidity) levels because of processing requirements, we are your source. We offer customers electrode steam, electric, atomizing, live steam injection and media-type equipment products to suit virtually every application.

Humidifiers produce moisture in a safe, pure water vapor form. When proper humidity is added to the air, you feel comfortable at a lower temperature. If you don't currently have a humidifier, you do have a problem. The solution begins by calling Aleyden.

We're here to help!

ON THE BUSINESS FRONT

Controlling air pollution in the workplace

The EPA reports that indoor air is up to 70 times more polluted than outdoor air. Indoor air pollution is a concern to all of us. Air pollutants are everywhere. Asbestos can be found in ceiling and floor tiles as well as heating system and acoustic insulation.

Carbon monoxide exists in garages, motor vehicles and loading docks. Formaldehyde is apparent in glues, partitions, carpeting, paneling, drapery, fabrics, particle board furniture and upholstery fabrics.

Micro-organisms can be found in cooling towers, humidifiers, air conditioners, swamp coolers, dehumidifiers, washrooms, ventilation pipes and ducts.

Volatile organic compounds also exist in felt tip markers and pens, cleaning compounds, prints, copy machines and solvents.

Considering that most people spend up to 90% of their time indoors, now may be the time to reduce the amount of air pollution in your office environment.

Looking for problem-solving solutions? Call Aleyden at 708/699-9500.

Helpful heating tips

As the heating season nears, here are some helpful tips:

- Heating systems can lose up to 16% of their efficiency without proper cleaning and regular maintenance. These systems lose efficiency when dirty or out of tune, and that loss hits you right in the pocketbook. Multiply your heating bill by 0.16 to see how much money can go up in smoke each month.

- Contractors estimate that 70% to 96% of all repairs they perform could have been avoided with preventative maintenance. A trained professional is the only one who can tell you whether your furnace's heat exchanger is cracked. These cracks allow carbon monoxide to leak, potentially filling your business or home with deadly gas.

A Special Thank You...

Goes to the following businesses that have purchased new heating & air conditioning systems and service contracts from Aleyden:

Bob Chinn's Crabhouse
Metal Impact
Smith Corona
Yellow Page Ads
Copek's
Programmers Investment Corp.
First State Bank Park Ridge
First Federal Bank of Des Plaines
Dent Systems
Barrington Hills Country Club
L. Karp's Distribution

QUESTIONS ◆ ANSWERS

Q My old heating and cooling units have just about had it. What is the most important feature I should look for when buying a new heating and cooling unit?

A It pays to consider your options when selecting a new unit. If you make the right choice, you can save money in energy bills and service for up to 30 years.

Even if a lower efficiency system is initially cheaper to buy, it can cost thousands of dollars more in heating and cooling bills over its lifetime.

Remember the equipment you purchase is only part of your comfort system. The design and condition of your distribution system (ductwork, pipe, etc.), the insulation in your building, the number of employees during occupied periods, and maintenance are crucial to proper sizing of your unit. The highest quality heating and cooling units can be inefficient...and even dangerous...if not installed correctly.

Because installation and service after the sale are as important as your unit's quality, the contractor you choose to install the equipment is just as important as the equipment you select. Aleyden is committed to providing you with the best system to meet your needs. We recommend only quality equipment and will follow up with responsive service.

Q I am concerned about the correct way to maintain my heating unit. What can I do to prolong its life?

A All heating units require maintenance by a qualified service technician. Operating your unit while dirty can result in an unnecessary loss of efficiency and may damage its unit. Although it requires a technician to handle most maintenance tasks on your heating and cooling units, there are a few procedures you can do at the beginning of each heating season to ensure a more comfortable winter.

1) Have your equipment cleaned and checked at the beginning of each heating season to keep your unit at high performance and efficiency levels.

2) Always begin each new heating season with a clean filter in the unit and check filters monthly throughout the winter. Dirty filters should be replaced or cleaned immediately to prevent the unit from working harder, which results in energy waste and possible internal damage.

3) Check the area surrounding the furnace for materials that could easily burn. Remove boxes, lumber, papers and combustibles. This is a fire hazard!

4) Occasionally check the chimney and flue pipe for blockages for your connections. If you think it needs cleaning or repair, call Aleyden.

Join our Customer First Priority Planned Maintenance Program

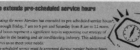

Your building's central heating and cooling unit represents a major investment...not only in terms of money, but in the health and comfort of your employees. Like any investment, it is also important to keep this unit protected and operating efficiently, which is why we encourage all of our customers to sign up for a planned maintenance program.

As part of your annual maintenance program, we schedule regular service visits. On each visit, we perform a tune-up and thoroughly evaluate your system, detecting and correcting minor problems before they turn into major ones. The results save on your utility bills...and help ensure that your business will not be faced with unexpected breakdowns or emergency repairs.

Call us today to schedule a planned maintenance program for your building's central heating and cooling unit. By beginning this program now, you can look forward to enhanced savings and comfort, all season long.

Dial One Aleyden Heating and Air Conditioning, Inc. offers programs tailored to your individual needs selecting only the services that are appropriate for your business.

Aleyden extends pre-scheduled service hours

Start spreading the news! Aleyden has extended its pre-scheduled service hours Monday through Friday, 7 am to 6 pm and Saturday from 8 am to 12 noon.

Extended hours represent a significant step in supporting our strategy of being a leader in the heating and air conditioning industry. This additional service allows us to meet your needs.

Note: Pre-scheduled service must be arranged during regular business hours, Monday through Friday, 7:30 am to 5 pm.

Dial ONE Aleyden
Heating and Air Conditioning, Inc.
1550 Cora Street
Des Plaines, Illinois 60016-1708
708/699-9500
FAX 708/297-2726

GREATER O'Hare
MEMBER

A brochure series

This series is simple, clean, and beautiful, with clearly targeted messages. (There are, of course, a couple of others in the series, but you get the idea.)

In particular, note the finely kerned type (especially the numbers) on the covers and the overall lack of clutter. Inside, heads are "outdented" from the body to catch your attention.

▼ ▼ ▼

Publisher: First Chicago Investment Services
Designer: Karen Knorr, Wechsler & Partners, Inc.
Colors: Black, PMS 5473 and metallic 8022
Type: Times, Frutiger

Time is on your side

You may feel like a beginner, but older investors envy your advantage: time. The investments you make in your 20s will have an opportunity to grow for 40 or 50 years. Even a small investment can grow into a small fortune.

But your time advantage won't last forever. Starting a regular investment program of just $25, $50 or $100 a month can make an enormous difference in your financial well-being—through the rest of your working life and into retirement.

It may seem early to think about retirement. But if you start saving now, you may be ahead of the game when retirement grows near. Even before retirement, you'll have other goals. A home of your own. A vacation place. Children to educate. Lifelong investing can make all those things easier...if you start now.

Ask First Chicago about growth mutual funds

Because you probably can't invest much now, why not put your money to work as productively as possible? Consider mutual funds. They pool your assets with other investors to bring you the benefits of diversification and professional management by investment experts.

Growth mutual funds invest in stocks to build your capital over time. Stocks have historically produced greater returns than other types of investments for investors who have time to ride out the market's ups and downs. Because you're young, you can afford that long-term view.

There are many kinds of growth funds. Some invest in stocks which pay high dividends, a strategy that seeks to smooth out the market's fluctuations. Other growth funds try to benefit from growing companies or rising markets. Others specialize in smaller companies, attractive industries, overseas markets, or other potential growth situations.

Have you opened an IRA yet? These accounts offer important tax benefits which can help you build your assets even faster. First Chicago can help you invest your IRA in mutual funds, too.

Investing in mutual funds involves risk, and may involve expenses with which you are not familiar. Ask your investment representative about the risks and rewards of mutual fund investing.

We're here to help you make the right decisions

The First National Bank of Chicago has been providing expert financial advice to Chicago area residents for more than a century. The investment representatives of First Chicago Investment Services, Inc. continue this tradition.

First Chicago investment representatives are experienced at helping you choose investments to bring you closer to your goals. They'll ask you questions. Listen carefully to your answers. And guide you step-by-step through the process of understanding and selecting the right investments.

We know that getting started as an investor can be difficult. That's why we're here. To help you make the right decisions.

Your investment horizon...in your 20s
If you start investing when you're 25 years old, this is how much you could accumulate by age 65 based on a monthly investment of $100.*

$632,408
$228,361
$92,605
3%   6.5%   10%
ANNUAL AVERAGE RETURN

This hypothetical example is only to illustrate the benefits of compounding and does not imply the above returns will be available to investors. Figures do not reflect taxes or transaction costs.

Choose Seabury & Smith as your insurance broker administrator and get more than insurance at affordable group rates for your members. We'll provide your association with a total marketing plan, one that tells you exactly what we'll do for you now, and in the future.

Understanding your audience is key to planning a successful marketing program. So, before we do anything, we come to you. We work with your members to develop a comprehensive understanding of the kind of insurance they need. We conduct extensive research to determine the needs and interests of your members. Then, we develop a Total Marketing Program—one that's On Target to providing your association with an ideal member benefits program.

SEABURY & SMITH

Insurance Program Management

A Marsh & McLennan Company

A Total
Marketing Program
ON
TARGET

A very different series

These brochures are all targeted at the same customers but illustrate different benefits of signing on with this insurance administrator.

The goal here is to "rise above the noise" by using large graphics and brash type treatments. The graphics are black-and-white photos that have been hand-colored with markers and scanned in.

The first unfolding of one brochure is shown here. It unfolds once more into a four-panel piece with more detailed text.

▼ ▼ ▼

Publisher: Seabury & Smith, Washington, DC
Designer: Steven D. Fleshman
Colors: Process
Type: Goudy, Univers, Garamond

A light approach to heavy topics

This newsletter covers a variety of health issues but keeps the tone light with its use of two bright spot colors (no black), big dotted arrow lines and a playful approach to type.

To underscore the wide variety of topics covered in every issue, different fonts are used for each letter in the nameplate as well as for each drop cap.

▼ ▼ ▼

Publisher: Columbus-Cabrini Medical Center, Chicago, IL
Designer: Bostrom-Sybul Design
Colors: PMS 246, 3005
Type: Garamond, Futura and a variety of others for caps

Focus On

Spring/Summer 1993

Features ...
Plastic Surgery Options
Ergonomics at Work
Starting on Exercise Program
Nutrition Test
Pre-Conception Advice
Hospital Programs

Form/Function: Plastic Surgery Options

It was the Greeks who contributed the word "plastic" to plastic surgery. The term derives from "plassis," meaning "to mold or form." "That translation accurately refers to the work we do," says John Lease, M.D., plastic surgeon at Columbus Hospital. Plastic surgeons perform a wide variety of surgical procedures that address the patient's form and function.

"The specialty includes many reconstructive techniques — not just the 'aesthetic' options." Dr. Lease points out that the range of reconstructive procedures performed by the plastic surgeon is vast, including:

• repair of facial injuries;
• burn care — acute and reconstructive;
• trauma and wound repair;
• hand surgery, including tendon repair and the treatment of carpal tunnel syndrome;
• breast surgery, including reconstruction and reduction;
• scar revision;
• treatment of skin cancers;
• reconstructive procedures for cancer of the head, neck and other areas;
• repair of congenital defects, such as cleft lip and palate; and
• treatment of chronic wounds, such as leg ulcers.

Reconstructive surgery is covered by most insurance policies. Questions about this and other aspects of these procedures should be discussed with your surgeon.

Looking Better, Feeling Better

Many people seek the services of a plastic surgeon when they become unhappy with how nature or the aging process has affected their appearance. For these patients, the plastic surgeon's domain includes a variety of "cosmetic" techniques. The following is a brief guide to some of the more common plastic surgical options.

What Does It All Mean?

Abdominoplasty: During this procedure, also called a "tummy tuck," the surgeon removes excess skin and fat and tightens the abdominal wall to achieve a flat contour.

Facelift: Facelifts eliminate some of the effects of aging and gravity by mobilizing facial structures and removing excess skin and fat. Incisions are usually made at the top and back hairline and in front of the ear. A facelift is excellent for removing folds and banding in the neck.

Rhinoplasty: Commonly known as a "nose job," an incision is made inside the nose, from which the surgeon alters the structural framework of the nose in order to change the external appearance.

Blepharoplasty: In this procedure, the surgeon removes excess skin and puffiness from upper and/or lower eyelids.

Otoplasty: Protruding ears are tucked closer to the head through a procedure that involves several small incisions.

Liposuction: An increasingly popular technique, fat is "vacuumed" from such areas as the abdomen, thighs, hips and neck. While not a weight reduction option, liposuction helps to re-contour target areas.

Breast Augmentation: This procedure is currently performed with saline implants, through small, inconspicuous incisions.

Mastopexy: Commonly known as a "breast lift," the skin of the breast is tightened to correct sagging.

Collagen Injection: Small amounts of collagen, inserted with a syringe, can temporarily correct facial wrinkles. It also can be used to correct small contour defects.

Dermabrasion: In this technique, the skin is lightly abraded to correct contour deformity resulting from scarring due to trauma or acne.

Chemical Peel: Topical application of certain chemicals removes fine wrinkles such as those around the mouth.

Length of Procedures, Risks and Side Effects

"Most cosmetic procedures can be performed in from two to four hours," Dr. Lease explains. "And, many techniques can be done on an outpatient basis, with the patient under just local anesthesia, with some sedation." continued on back cover

"For many people, cosmetic surgery contributes greatly to heightened confidence and self esteem. This is most likely to happen when there's a good partnership between the surgeon and the patient."

Working Smart!

We used to call it a "desk." Now, it's known as "a work station." This change in office terminology reflects the many technological changes in the workplace faced by millions of Americans. And with these changes come some hazards. Whether your job is on the assembly line or in front of a computer terminal, there's a lot you should know about potential risk factors in the work environment.

Ergonomics is the field of study that helps sort out issues related to worksite health and safety. "The word 'ergonomics' can confuse people, but the concept is simple," says Elke Friedman, ergonomics coordinator, Columbus Hospital. "Ergonomics specialists help people adjust their work environment and work habits to ensure comfort and safety on the job." continued on page 2

Healthful Information from Columbus Hospital

Minimalist punch

This design gets a big bang out of a simple layout by using color in a very restricted way. Blue is used for those big solid blocks in the nameplate and department heads, as well as the logo and the end-of-story markers. That's it.

Note also the pleasantly ragged bottom of the articles and the nice handling of pull-quotes, which have been set with paragraph rules between each line.

▼ ▼ ▼

Publisher: Executive Service Corps
of Chicago
Designer: Jeff Stasik, Stasik Design, Inc.
Development: Marilyn Dawson,
Continental Bank
Colors: Black, PMS 2718
Type: Futura, Berthold Caslon Book

Large-format photo layouts

The dramatic photo layouts in this tabloid-size newsletter aren't just beautiful examples of graphic design. They're also very functional.

The designer knows that photos can communicate the concerns of an organization better than text. And given the large page size, the photos appear life-size, which makes them all the more compelling.

To heighten the sense of urgency, heads are often set in typewriter faces like Courier—and sometimes blown up on a copier and scanned back in to create a "distressed" look.

▼ ▼ ▼

Publisher: CARE
Designer: Richard Berry
Colors: Black and a different
*   earth-tone color each issue*
*   (this one PMS 453)*
Type: Garamond, Courier

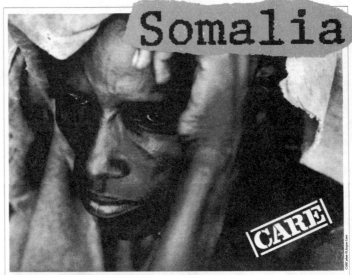

A PLEA FOR PEACE IN SOMALIA • ESREY NAMED NEW CORPORATE COUNCIL CHAIR • CARE MOVING TO ATLANTA • CITY OF JOY

CARE Global Review

A Newsletter for Friends of CARE   Volume 2 Number 2   Winter 1993

Somalia

A Plea for Peace in Somalia

Well before the press placed the plight of Somali famine victims on the front pages, CARE was hard at work in Somalia, as we have been for 10 years. When violence escalated and conditions worsened, CARE took the lead in calling for action from the world's leaders. Through congressional hearings last spring, through Dr. Philip Johnston's media interviews, and through high-level meetings with government and NGO officials, CARE warned of the devastation awaiting Somalia — and advocated effective international response.

This issue of Global Review focuses on the famine in Somalia. In October, Philip Johnston accepted the role of the United Nations' coordinator of humanitarian assistance in Somalia. Through this assignment he has gained an even deeper understanding of the problems of the country and has become an architect of its rehabilitation program.

CARE has committed considerable staff, funds and attention to relief and rehabilitation efforts in Somalia.

In an effort to cast a personal light on Somalia's crisis, we bring to you journal excerpts from Dr. Johnston's days in Somalia, an opinion piece published in *Freedom Review*, a glimpse at plans to rehabilitate Somalia, and dramatic photographs taken for CARE by artist Jacques Lowe.

Editor's Note: This article first appeared in Freedom Review, a journal commenting on foreign affairs, politics and issues affecting democratic institutions. Philip Johnston, CARE's President, has been in Somalia since late October on a special assignment as the United Nations' chief coordinator of humanitarian assistance.

By Philip Johnston, Ph.D.,
CARE President

In the careful understatement of diplomatic-speak, the U.N. resolution authorizing military intervention in Somalia noted the "unique character of the situation..."

It is indeed unique for the entire underpinnings of a society to disappear, replaced by random violence and mass starvation. We have seen famines before, including many spurred by civil war. We have also operated in the shadow of brutal regimes. But never, in my memory, has government been entirely absent for an extended period.

This, ultimately, is the "unique character" of the crisis in Somalia and it is one of the reasons the United States finally decided to act. It is unfortunate the decision came many months after it was needed. Hundreds of thousands have died in agony, and those deaths were entirely preventable. But, finally, the world has decided to act, and that can only be applauded.

The roots of the Somalia crisis can be traced at least partially to the super-power confrontation and the massive arms build-up of the 1970s and 80s. It is difficult to speculate how these events helped create or promote any of the individual factions now battling for control of Somalia. But one thing is for certain: each one possesses a frightening level of firepower that has turned a political stalemate into well-

Continued on page 3: Plea for Peace

A simple letter-size brochure

This is probably one of the easiest and quickest formats to produce—which may be why you seldom see especially interesting or novel designs in this format.

This one makes the most of a simple, but clever, idea—communicating the combination of two firms by using opposing blends of black and blue as background graphics.

The second graphic theme is "fusion," nicely illustrated with oval boxes symbolic of electron orbits. Note the recurrence of the oval shape in the picture boxes on the back cover.

▼　▼　▼

Publisher: PDI/ISI Group, Chicago, IL
Designer: Kathleen Aiken
Colors: Black, PMS 3005
Type: Futura; Bembo

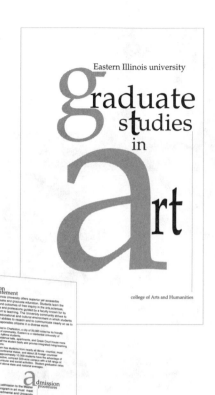

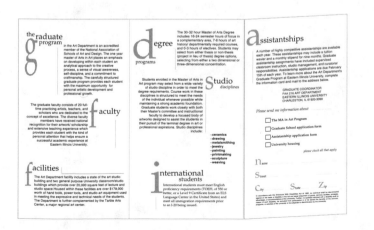

Another simple brochure format

This self-mailer was designed to take advantage of standard legal-size paper printed from a laser printer.

The designer did a nice job of making the all-type treatment bouncy and visual by playing with the type size, horizontal scale and placement of the initial caps, and switching alignment to introduce new topics.

▼ ▼ ▼

Publisher: Eastern Illinois University
Designer: Amy Hatterman
Colors: Black, PMS 032
Type: Helvetica, Palatino

A vertical unfold

Here's another piece that was designed to be easily proofed on legal-size paper. The background, created with tints of a second color, was extended to the edge of the page and trimmed after printing.

▼   ▼   ▼

Publisher: Team Marketing
    Report, Chicago, IL
Designer: PageWorks
Colors: Black, PMS 294
Type: Beton Extra Bold; Futura

Front

Back

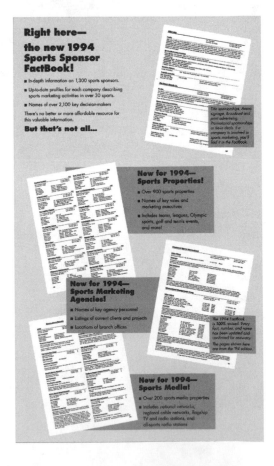

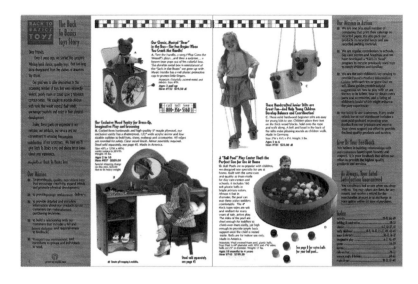

A *touch* of color

This toy catalog offers an interesting way to add color to a piece. The designer scanned in black-and-white photos and hand-colorized parts of each photo (the toys themselves) in Photoshop, then imported them into XPress.

Other unifying design devices are the wood scan, used as a background texture, and the tile patterns set in primary colors.

▼ ▼ ▼

*Publisher: Back To Basics Toys,
    Silver Spring, MD*
*Designer: Donna Whitlow,
    Grace Systems*
Colors: Process
*Type: Au Casablanca, Optima,
    Futura, Freestyle Script,
    Zapf Dingbats*

Radiant color

This appointment calendar was designed for collectors of rare carnival glass, a material full of shimmering, luminescent colors and notoriously difficult to capture in print. The designer, who was also the photographer, had the film digitized onto a PhotoCD, then corrected each image in Photoshop before importing it into XPress.

To keep the focus on the glass, he opted for a very plain and functional calendar design.

▼ ▼ ▼

Publisher: PageWorks
Designer: David Doty
Colors: Process
Type: Helvetica, Nashville

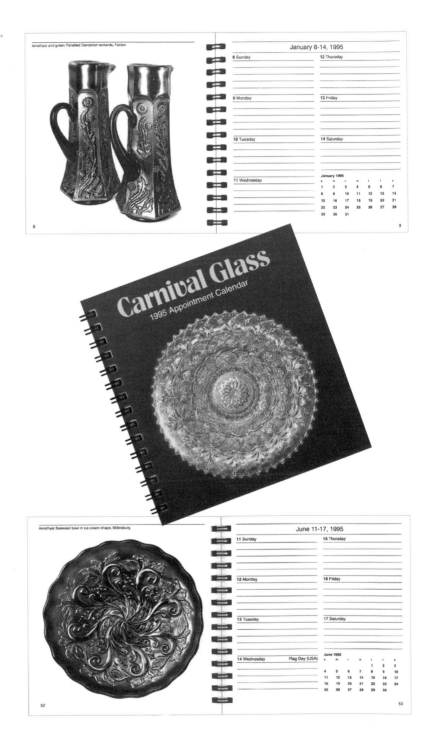

A smaller palette

This services brochure uses only a few spot colors but makes the most of them. Two of the colors are corporate standards, and a third (the reddish purple) rounds out the palette.

Various tints of the three colors are used as backgrounds for the line art throughout the booklet. Combined with the yellowish paper as a background, the tints create the impression of a wide range of color.

▼　▼　▼

Publisher: Towers Perrin,
*   Chicago, IL*
Designer: Kathleen Aiken
Illustrator: Richard Szromba
Colors: PMS 286, 248, 348
Type: Galliard, Univers

Framing with color

To bring out the beauty and power of the black-and-white photos used in this report, the designer framed each picture with big, bold blocks of color—a very dramatic effect.

The photos were also printed in color—as *quadtones*—using the four process colors. They still appear basically black-and-white but much richer.

▼ ▼ ▼

Publisher: Mary Institute and St. Louis Country Day School, St. Louis, MO
Designer: Jean Lopez, Lopez Needleman Graphic Design, Inc.
Colors: Process, PMS 3252 and a dull varnish
Type: Garamond

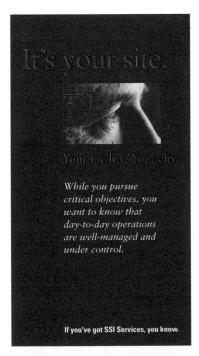

The power of black, white and red

It's a combination that's hard to beat—if used correctly. It certainly adds up to a bold statement here.

The window in the cover was *die-cut* to reveal the photo on the first right page. This photo and others (on succeeding flaps of the folder) were printed as duotones of black and a Pantone gray to create extra depth in the images.

▼   ▼   ▼

Publisher: SSI Services, Inc. Tullahoma, TN
Designers: John Sotirakis, Norman Goldberg
Colors: Black (printed in "2 hits"), PMS 200, 425, and
*   a dull spot varnish*
Type: Janson, Univers Condensed

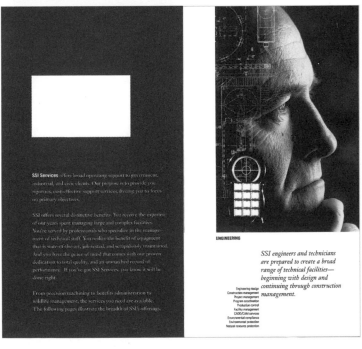

Light and friendly

This brochure was designed to look upbeat and create a sense of down-to-earth openness. The choice of red and blue as the two spot colors, combined with plenty of white space, produce the effect nicely.

The designer got plenty of play out of the three inks by using a variety of tints and converting the grayscale photos to Photoshop duotones of black and blue or blue and red.

▼ ▼ ▼

Publisher: *Imagination Theater,*
   Chicago, IL
Designer: *Estelle Carol,*
   Carol ★ Simpson Design
Colors: *Black, PMS 227, 300*
Type: *Stone Serif*

Front

Back

THE VISION

Founded by educators and performing artists in 1966, Imagination Theater is a professional, educational touring theater company which provides a broad spectrum of participatory programs for children, teens, senior citizens, and people with disabilities.
   Imagination Theater company believes that participation is an excellent learning tool and that all individuals have the inner resources to creatively use their imaginations. The company uses interactive creative arts to help guide audience members toward developing their potentials.
   In 1985, the company expanded its mission to include programs designed to raise the awareness of young people and to provide insight into social issues such as sexual abuse prevention and substance abuse prevention, and has since expanded its repertoire to include a wide variety of entertaining and educational programs including fun shows for the holidays.

INFORMATION

For information, rates and booking arrangements call or write:

Imagination Theater
1801 W. Byron St.
Suite 2s
Chicago, Illinois 60613-2729
(312) 929-4100

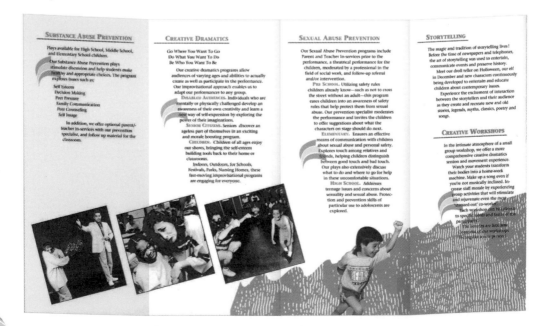

SUBSTANCE ABUSE PREVENTION

Plays available for High School, Middle School, and Elementary School children.

Our Substance Abuse Prevention plays stimulate discussion and help students make healthy and appropriate choices. The program explores issues such as:

Self Esteem
Decision Making
Peer Pressure
Family Communication
Peer Counseling
Self Image

   In addition, we offer optional parent/teacher in-services with our prevention specialist, and follow up material for the classroom.

CREATIVE DRAMATICS

Go Where You Want To Go
Do What You Want To Do
Be Who You Want To Be

   Our creative dramatics programs allow audiences of varying ages and abilities to actually create as well as participate in the performance. Our improvisational approach enables us to adapt our performances to any group.
   DISABLED AUDIENCES. Individuals who are mentally or physically challenged develop an awareness of their own creativity and learn a new way of self-expression by exploring the power of their imaginations.
   SENIOR CITIZENS. Seniors discover an ageless part of themselves in an exciting and morale boosting program.
   CHILDREN. Children of all ages enjoy our shows, bringing the self-esteem building tools back to their home or classrooms.
   Indoors, Outdoors, for Schools, Festivals, Parks, Nursing Homes, these fast-moving improvisational programs are engaging for everyone.

SEXUAL ABUSE PREVENTION

Our Sexual Abuse Prevention programs include Parent and Teacher In-services prior to the performance, a theatrical performance for the children, moderated by a professional in the field of social work, and follow-up referral and/or intervention.
   PRE SCHOOL. Utilizing safety rules children already know—such as not to cross the street without an adult—this program eases children into an awareness of safety rules that help protect them from sexual abuse. Our prevention specialist moderates the performance and invites the children to offer suggestions about what the characters on stage should do next.
   ELEMENTARY. Ensures an effective means of communication with children about sexual abuse and personal safety. Explores touch among relatives and friends, helping children distinguish between good touch and bad touch. Discusses what to do and where to go for help in these uncomfortable situations.
   HIGH SCHOOL. Addresses teenage issues and concerns about sexuality and sexual abuse. Protection and prevention skills of particular use to adolescents are explored.

STORYTELLING

The magic and tradition of storytelling lives!
Before the time of newspapers and telephones, the art of storytelling was used to entertain, communicate events and preserve history.
   Meet our droll teller on Halloween, our elf in December and new characters continuously being developed to entertain and educate children about contemporary issues.
   Experience the excitement of interaction between the storytellers and their audience as they create and recreate new and old stories, legends, myths, classics, poetry and songs.

CREATIVE WORKSHOPS

In the intimate atmosphere of a small group workshop, we offer a more comprehensive creative dramatics session and movement experience.
   Watch your students transform their bodies into a home-work machine. Make up a song even if you're not musically inclined. Increase staff morale by experiencing group activities that will stimulate and rejuvenate even the most stressed-out co-worker!
   Each workshop can be tailored to specific needs and focus of the participants.
   This level its are best described as part of our workshops by our resource person.

MEMBERSHIP INFORMATION

CHICAGO MUTUAL HOUSING NETWORK

"All of us working toward a cooperative housing strategy for Chicago realize that our resources are limited when we work alone. Together, our ideas, our mutual support will build a dynamic cooperative movement."

Donna Smithey
Executive Director
Peoples Housing

The Chicago Mutual Housing Network is a federation of housing cooperatives and their many supporters: community groups, non-profit organizations, banks, architects, contractors, concerned individuals—all Chicagoans with an interest in the humanity and opportunity of cooperative housing. The organization is dedicated to the development of more and better housing for low- to moderate-income families in Chicago through the expansion of cooperative housing.

The Network offers established housing cooperatives the advantages of scale, pooled resources and expert information. Tenant groups seeking to form a new housing cooperative have access to key start-up advice such as organizing strategies, leadership training, legal and financial directions and the rich experiences of other housing cooperatives. Community groups, non-profit organizations and interested businesses benefit from a direct connection to tenant groups and participation in workshops and forums.

Chicago Mutual Housing Network members confront urban decline by advocating home ownership alternatives for low- and moderate-income families, as well as generating management support and training ideas for established housing cooperatives. The Network encourages the membership of housing cooperatives and all those sharing our concern for cooperative housing ideals, neighborhood revitalization and the future of Chicago. Your membership and participation will help ensure the future of the Chicago Mutual Housing Network. With your help, the Network will be a viable means of organizing investment, talent and energy.

CHICAGO MUTUAL HOUSING NETWORK
2125 W. North Avenue
Chicago, Illinois 60647
(312) 278-4800, Ext.137
Fax (312) 278-3840

A Rationale for Cooperative Housing

Tenant owned and managed multi-family housing builds neighborhood stability, improved commercial environments and reinvestment in communities. Yet barriers to home ownership are deepening for low- to moderate-income families, especially minorities. HUD reports 43% of blacks and 39% of Hispanics own their own homes, as compared to 68% of whites. Out of pocket expenses for renters are almost the same as for owners, but renters' median annual income is almost half that of homeowners. Cooperative housing helps low-income families find new pathways to home ownership and the many lasting benefits of investment.

Subtle colors & blends

This piece is very toned-down by comparison. The three colors—black, gray and deep green—don't pop quite like red, white and blue. But the design's use of spot colors is dynamic in and of itself.

Note the layering of shapes and the varied use of blends. The triangular rooftop, a key element in the logo, is cleverly repeated elsewhere in green.

▼ ▼ ▼

Publisher: Chicago Mutual Housing Network
Designer: Estelle Carol, Carol ★ Simpson Design
Colors: Black, PMS 3292, 426
Type: Franklin Gothic, Palatino

REASONS TO BECOME A MEMBER

◄ The Network pools the knowledge and experience of housing cooperatives in Chicago to foster new projects and strengthens established cooperatives.

◄ The Network capitalizes on the strength of numbers in group buying for such items as natural gas.

◄ The Network provides access to the many services and professionals essential to the ongoing successful operation of cooperative housing.

◄ The Network supports policies to develop a housing strategy for low- and moderate-income families for the City of Chicago.

◄ The Network publicizes the message that tenant owned and managed multi-family housing is a proven, viable option to conventional ownership or rental for minorities and low-income families.

◄ The Network supports initiatives to salvage vacant or abandoned multi-family properties to revive both the neighborhoods and the commercial areas that serve them.

◄ The Network promotes the conversion of tenants into investors, in control of their own resources and building equity in their homes.

◄ The Network builds leadership and initiative.

◄ The Network organizes the participation of Chicago financial institutions, as well as architects, lawyers and community organizations who share a vested interest in the future of the city: to expand affordable housing options to secure the future viability of urban residence.

MEMBERSHIP OPTIONS

◄ **Affiliate Membership**
Affiliate membership in the Chicago Mutual Housing Network is extended to housing cooperatives. Tenant ownership and a permanent commitment to affordability are required. Housing cooperatives in the process of forming are encouraged to join.

◄ **Associate Membership**
Associate Membership in the Network is extended to community groups and other non-profit organizations actively involved in the promotion and development of housing cooperatives as part of a low-income housing strategy in their communities and neighborhoods.

◄ **Adjunct Membership**
Adjunct Membership in the Network is extended to organizations with an interest in the development of cooperative housing and the flourishing of the Network itself.

◄ **Individual Membership**
Individual Membership in the Network is extended to persons with a concern for the development of affordable cooperative housing in Chicago.

"As a lender, I recognize the importance of having a mutual support mechanism that will help ensure that our investment is secure, well managed, and meeting its commitments. Membership in the Chicago Mutual Housing Network lends immediate credibility to cooperative projects seeking financing."

Charles M. Hill, Sr.
Federal Home Loan Bank of Chicago

"Cooperative living is about working together, helping others, and knowing that when it really matters, someone you know and trust is right there for you when you need them most. Now the cooperative movement has that same level of trust in an organization that will always be there just when we're needed."

Rob Sadowsky
Executive Director
Chicago Mutual Housing Network
Member, Emma Goldman Cooperative

MEMBERSHIP BENEFITS

◄ Active networking between member housing cooperatives.

◄ Access to training, technical assistance, strategic planning, problem solving and staff development.

◄ Available default assistance, legal assistance, policy development and financial auditing.

◄ Citywide waiting list.

◄ Housing Cooperative Resource Library.

◄ Group buying services.

◄ Round Table discussions.

◄ Quarterly "how to" newsletter written by and for housing cooperatives.

◄ Notification of training classes and schedules.

◄ Invitations to special Network events.

◄ Active participation in policy development.

APPLICATION FORM

Name _____

Organization _____

Address _____

City, State, Zip _____

Telephone _____

Fax Number _____

Please select a membership and dues commitment.

Affiliate Membership
Please indicate the size of your building:
❑ 10 Units or Less................$12/unit
❑ 11–50 Units...........................$250
❑ 51–300 Units..........................$500
❑ Over 300 Units.......................$750

Associate Membership
Please indicate your annual budget:
❑ Under $25,000...........................$ 25
❑ $25,000 – $100,000..................$100
❑ $100,000 – $500,000................$200
❑ Over $500,000...........................$250

Adjunct Membership
Please indicate your annual budget:
❑ Under $25,000...........................$ 25
❑ $25,000 – $100,000..................$100
❑ $100,000 – $500,000................$200
❑ Over $500,000...........................$250

Individual Membership................$ 50

Total enclosed for dues $ _____
Additional donation $ _____

Return form to:
Chicago Mutual Housing Network
2125 W. North Avenue
Chicago, Illinois 60647
(312) 278-4800, Ext. 137

Wow!

Not your typical college brochure!

The brilliant color makes a big first impression (although the flying saucer is hard to miss), but there are some other neat effects to notice here, like the orange drop shadow for the blue headline and the orange burst-shaped box. And that's a real "sticky note" affixed to the inside flap. Very functional!

▼ ▼ ▼

Publisher: Western Maryland College,
  Westminster, MD
Designer: Mark Shippe, North Charles Street
  Design Organization
Colors: Process
Type: Helvetica, Frutiger, Centennial

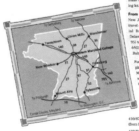

Wow again!

The cover design has plenty of punch—a perfectly simple and effective use of solid black and green on white paper. It's fun to see type reverse in color as it crosses into a graphic, especially when the message so clearly matches the visual effect.

And yes, that's a real swatch of artificial turf glued to the inside. That's a pretty thick piece of material to include, so the piece was given two adjacent fold lines about a quarter inch apart and mailed in a heavy envelope to prevent crushing.

▼ ▼ ▼

Publisher: Seabury & Smith, Washington, DC
Designer: Steven D. Fleshman
Colors: Black, PMS 185, 254
Type: Univers, Garamond

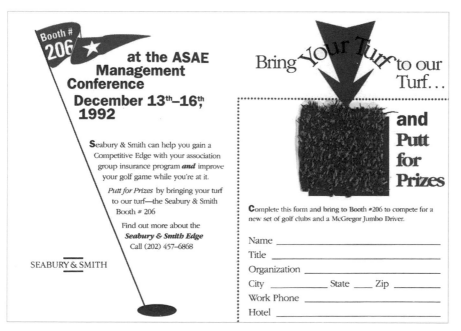

Type and color changes

There are lots of interesting typographic details in this friendly-looking tabloid newsletter. Headlines often change in typeface, size or color midway through to lure the reader into an article. Initial letters are set as big stick-up caps or hanging caps.

The designer also strikes an interesting compromise on the color budget: the outside sheet (the front, back and inside covers) is designed and printed in four-color process, while inside sheets are printed in two colors.

▼ ▼ ▼

Publisher: Saint Joseph Hospital, Chicago, IL
Designer: Christopher P. Satek, Eye to Eye, Inc.
Colors: Process, PMS 122 (spot color changes each issue)
Type: Helvetica, Gill Sans, Bernhard Bold Modern, Oz Handcraft

More color for less

This ambitious-looking tabloid also combines four-color printing and two-color printing to get more bang for the buck.

The designer handles the mix in a very crafty way. One side of each sheet is printed in four-color, the other side in two-color. By carefully planning the order and direction of the sheets, he creates a variety of color designs—some spreads are entirely four-color, others entirely two-color, and many, like the spread shown here, neatly combine a four-color page with a two-color page.

▼ ▼ ▼

Publisher: DePaul Health Center
Designer: Stephen Cox,
   Alex Paradowski Graphic Design
Colors: Process, PMS 2685 (the spot
   color alternates each issue
   between 2685, 322, 240 & 300)
Type: Onyx, Times, Futura

An unfolding story

This unusual and striking piece provides a brief history of a company, presented as a timeline. It initially unfolds to a president's message; the right side of this spread then extends out in a long accordion fold, only the first half of which is shown here.

Many of the photos were converted to tritones in Photoshop before importing. Also note how the timeline text is set to bottom alignment, creating a wave effect.

▼ ▼ ▼

Publisher: Computer Products, Inc., Boca Raton, FL
Designer: Victoria Brown
Colors: Process
Type: Century, Garamond

Communicating a story

This folder also presents a story—but this one's about car theft and recovery. The designer uses a single illustration (representing the recovery network) in various magnifications to tie the panels together and to create the impression of "zeroing in" on different parts of the story.

There's a lot to see here in terms of type design as well. One unusual aspect is the use of bold type, set with extra-large leading, for much of the body text. And check out the size, position and background of the stick-up cap on the yellow panel.

▼ ▼ ▼

Publisher: National Insurance Crime Bureau, Palos Hills, IL
Designers: Janet Wahlin Speck, Deborah Doering, Bottega Design
Colors: Process
Type: Garamond, Teknik, Futura

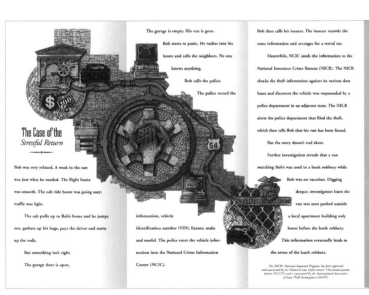

Ragged windows

This designer prompts the reader to take a second look at text and photos by putting them in raggedly drawn boxes. It's not only a fun effect—it's quite effective, especially for the extra-wide photo used in the center spread.

▼ ▼ ▼

Publisher: Western Maryland College, Westminster, MD
Designer: Mark Shippe, North Charles Street Design Organization
Colors: Process, PMS 453
Type: Frutiger, Centennial

A layered look

Here's a single-sheet newsletter that unfolds vertically, and every issue is a real visual treat. The fun starts in the banner, where the credit card is sandwiched between the text boxes for the nameplate type, and the background graphic changes with each issue. The designer also makes good use of white space—as well as various picture shapes and angles—in the left margin.

▼ ▼ ▼

Publisher: American Express Travel Related Services, New York, NY
Designer: Donovan and Green
Colors: Process
Type: Bodoni, Univers Condensed

A creative identity program

Sometimes the most arresting design solutions stem from the simplest ideas. This set of identity pieces for a creative consultant is a great example. The brightly colored shapes are loosely drawn XPress boxes filled with bright spot colors. Boom!

▼ ▼ ▼

Publisher: Dempsey Creative, St. Louis, MO
Designer: Jean Lopez, Lopez Needleman Graphic Design
Colors: PMS 186, 267
Type: Industria

More bursts of color

This piece—a reprint of a speech—also makes use of bold colors and shapes. The tone is set with the bursts of blue on the cover and the blue bleed on the inside cover.

Further inside, a pull-quote on each spread is reversed on a color block with a saw-tooth border. Along the top, loosely drawn streamers filled with blue and black tints create a celebratory air.

The designer also made interesting choices in the type department. The kerning of the cover title is very tight, with most letter pairs joined at the serifs; the text below is set in small caps. Inside, initial caps are set centered in the paragraph with a dotted leader preceding.

▼   ▼   ▼

Publisher: Thrifty Car Rental, Tulsa, OK
Designer: Mick Thurber
Colors: Black, PMS 285
Type: Stempel Garamond, Franklin Gothic, Künstler Script

Clean and clear

This single-sheet tabloid newsletter is a great example of simplicity hard at work. It's terribly efficient, thanks to a five-column format and the use of condensed typefaces for both drop caps and body text.

The color design is clean and simple: a deep purple is used full-strength for the drop caps and the paragraph rules framing the pull-quotes; the color is screened back for the nameplate and sidebars.

▼ ▼ ▼

Publisher: Family Service DuPage,
*   Wheaton, IL*
Designer: Anna M. Pugsley Graphic Design
Colors: Black, PMS 266
Type: Willow, Helvetica Black,
*   Helvetica Condensed*

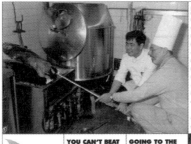

The same, but different

It's always interesting to see just how incredibly different two pieces can look even when they're based on some of the same ideas.

This single-sheet promotional tabloid also uses a five-column grid and two colors. But take a look at the many differences. Two deep Pantone colors are used—no black; all body type is set with extra-wide leading to reflect the lighter content; the weight of the body text alternates with each article; and photos and graphics play a much more prominent role.

▼ ▼ ▼

Formerly published by: Hyatt International, Chicago, IL
Designer: Sue Niggemann, Lee Hill, Inc.
Colors: PMS 289, 485
Type: Futura, Palatino

The power of solid color

This promotional newsletter uses color in a simple and striking way. The first panel of the accordion folder is printed in a solid Pantone color, a different one for each issue, with the cover type reversed. The nameplate is set vertically with extra-loose tracking.

▼ ▼ ▼

Publisher: Agnew Moyer Smith,
   Pittsburgh, PA
Designer: Norman Goldberg,
   Agnew Moyer Smith
Colors: PMS 130, 200, 266,
   293
Type: Univers Condensed,
   Glypha, Janson

Seeking Your Fortune? Follow this Guide...

Though it might be tempting to stuff it in your mattress, there are better ways to mind your money. And most of them are explained in the *Fortune Guide to Investing in the 90s*. This 108-page book, a recent AMS project, leads you through the world of real estate, commodities, funds, stocks, bonds, and many other investment options.

The guide's author, Richard Saul Wurman, is an architect, a cartographer, a designer, the creator of the ACCESS Guide series of guidebooks, and a frequent AMS collaborator. Like AMS, Richard is interested in making difficult information accessible.

He describes the *Fortune Guide* as "a 'what is' book rather than a 'how to' book." Its goal is to define investments clearly enough

that readers can ask smart questions of themselves—and of their financial advisors.

Each page is brimming with facts and advice. Of course, for most readers, not everything will be directly relevant. So a key challenge for AMS was to help readers navigate this information-rich text and find the information they need.

One device that helps is a graph that visually grades investments according to risk and reward, liquidity, duration, taxes, and other factors. By comparing graphs for different investments, readers can evaluate their options quickly and narrow their focus to investments which suit them.

Another way the book helps readers find relevant facts is through the use of color-coded icons, representing different kinds of marginalia. For example, a little yellow Rolodex card turns up when there's a reference to sources of further information.

To keep the reading fun, humorous quotes and interesting facts are scattered throughout. (Did you know that Hong Kong workers average 2,375 working hours a year... and Londoners only 1,737?)

The *Fortune Guide to Investing in the 90s* is available in most bookstores.

Taking the Mystery Out of "How To"

Who out there hasn't been daunted by the words "some assembly required"? One of our recent assignments was to help Wood Classics, Inc., a manufacturer of hand-crafted wood furniture kits, develop assembly instructions that anyone can follow.

We had the advantage of firsthand experience on this one. Don Moyer had purchased and assembled a garden bench and chair from Wood Classics. Pleased with the quality, he wrote the company to tell them.

At the same time, Don had advice about how Wood Classics could improve their instructions. The company listened and agreed, asking AMS to develop prototype instructions that they could use as a model in the future.

Because many people won't even read instructions that seem lengthy, AMS began by consolidating all assembly and finishing information neatly into a four-page flyer. From there, we developed a format that uses numbered steps to guide the user through assembly, from checking the parts to admiring their handiwork. Tips and hints are sprinkled throughout. Where it's difficult to visualize a step, illustrations show how the parts go together.

And the friendly, conversational writing style reflects the personality of Wood Classics.

We didn't simply want to leave Wood Classics with a good example to follow, however. We also provided an electronic template that can be used to create new instructions having the same graphic format. And we helped them lay the foundation for an electronic library of drawings.

In addition, we provided a checklist of guidelines to apply when writing instructions—how to organize information, keep readers' needs in mind, and write with clarity. It's a "how to" for how to's.

Adding value to a product by providing instructions that are clear and easy to follow: such a good, simple idea. If only VCR manufacturers thought that way.

Process zing!

These quarterly shareholder reports also use a different solid color for each cover—but because they're printed with process colors, the designer was able to add some other nice touches, too. A variety of oval and triangular shapes, filled with custom colors, are set behind the main graphic to create an unusual frame effect.

Inside, a solid yellow frames the letter to the shareholders; the color of the right flap is set to match the current cover color and create a contrast to the yellow.

▼ ▼ ▼

Publisher: Comcast Corporation, Philadelphia, PA
Design: Ruth Diener. Direction: Kent Hunter. Illustration: Jeffrey Fisher. Frankfurt Balkind Partners, New York City, NY
Colors: Process
Type: Geometric Slab (like Rockwell), Helvetica, Eurostile Extended

Big production

This glossy tabloid newsletter, published by a printing company, is a real showpiece. It's printed at 175 lpi (magazine quality) and regularly features beautiful color photos and illustrations. It comes folded in half, with the outside cover (designed to look like a magazine cover) in the opposite orientation.

The designers do a great job balancing tips, pull-quotes and photos in the narrow outside columns. Note also the handling of the calendar and the numbered list inside.

▼ ▼ ▼

Publisher: Nies/Artcraft Printing Companies
Designer: Jean Lopez, Lopez Needleman Graphic Design
Colors: Process, PMS 409
Type: Times, Garamond, Helvetica Compressed

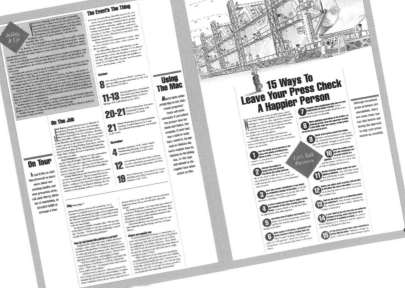

Creating a sense of dynamics

You can't help but notice the sense of movement and change in this tabloid. Color blends are the major visual theme, appearing in the custom nameplate type, the top edge bleeds, in various sidebars and even as a background for a bar graph.

This newsletter also uses chunks of white space in unusual ways to give the overall layout a pleasantly off-center feel.

▼ ▼ ▼

Publisher: Bank of Montreal/Harris Bank Corporation, Chicago, IL
Designer: Bill Ferdinand, Dave Philmlee, Zündesign
Colors: Black, PMS 320 (the second color changes with each issue)
Type: Bembo, Insignia, Helvetica Condensed

New pieces to the puzzle

The beautiful range of color used in this set of postcards might be enough to catch your attention. But the designer didn't just depend on color to hook the recipient.

The four postcards are based on a single collage; the recipient can reassemble them to see "the big picture." The type on the back of each postcard is the same.

▼ ▼ ▼

Publisher: Seabury & Smith, Washington, DC
Designer: Steven D. Fleshman
Illustrator: Nip Rogers
Colors: Process
Type: Goudy, Univers, Garamond

Behind the Scenes

Now that you've seen all of these wonderful examples of graphic design and XPress ingenuity, you may well wonder: How did they do it?

Many of these designers certainly have a few tricks up their sleeves, but ask them *how* they did what they did, and you'll most likely get an answer something like, "Oh, nothing special—just the usual Quark stuff."

Well, nothing's ever really that simple. These designers all had to solve problems—both minor and major—to make their designs actually work the way they had envisioned. Fortunately, with a little extra prompting, they can usually remember a trick or a tip that *is* special—something that's worth filing away for your own work. I've selected a few of my favorite stories from these designers—techniques and tips that may not be readily apparent as you're flipping through their designs in the Gallery.

Of course, there was plenty more to their work than what I can summarize here. These are just a few snapshots of the designers working behind the scenes....

Gallery page 238

• •

The Carnival Glass Appointment Calendar

Designer David Doty set up his document with one facing-page master page design—the left master page for the picture of the week, the right master page for the daily calendar. Pages were 5½ inches square (33 picas wide and tall), with a 2-pica margin all the way around.

On the left master page, he set an empty picture box so that he wouldn't have to draw a new box on each left-side document page—he only had to select the master picture box and import the graphic. He also included a caption box, filled with dummy text set in the correct type style, above the master picture box; that way, all he had to do was edit the master text on the document page to match the graphic.

On the right master page, he set up a two-column text box for the calendar. He filled this with a generic calendar, typing in "1 Sunday" through "7 Saturday" as a placeholder. This text was styled with a hairline paragraph rule, with the Length set to Indents and the Offset set to four points below the baseline of the text. Here's how that looked:

1 Sunday

2 Monday

3 Tuesday

4 Wednesday

5 Thursday

6 Friday

7 Saturday

He then added extra paragraph returns between the days to create room for notes and to fill out the two columns.

At the bottom of the second column on that master page, he set up a small table, using the Paragraph Tabs dialog, to create a mini-view of a generic month:

s	m	t	w	t	f	s
1	2	3	4	5	6	7
8	9	10	11	12	13	14
15	16	17	18	19	20	21
22	23	24	25	26	27	28
29	30	31				

To set up the tab stops, he simply typed in "2p," clicked Apply, then typed in "4p," clicked Apply, and so on, until he had set up six evenly spaced tabs. When it came time to customize the month view on a document page, all he had to do was type tabs before the "1" until the first day of the month lined up with the right day.

Once the master pages were set up, he filled out the document by choosing the Insert command, selecting the facing master page design, and typing in the required number of document pages—128.

To produce the images, he gave his film to a local photography service bureau, which converted the images to PhotoCD format and returned them on a CD-ROM. He opened each image in Photoshop, corrected the color, removed distracting background elements, and set the image size to match the picture box dimensions at 250 pixels per inch.

Each file, roughly three megabytes of color data, was then saved in the JPEG format in order to compress the data; the average size of the final files was about 250 kilobytes. These JPEG files were then imported into XPress. The entire project, including 65 full-color, high-resolution images, fit comfortably on a single 44-megabyte Syquest cartridge. This was sent to a one-stop print shop; they output the files as film negatives at 150 lines per inch, created printing plates directly from the negatives, ran the job on a four-color offset press and bound the resulting pages using Wire-O binding.

come see
the clios

the art directors club of
metropolitan washington
presents
the 1993 clio reel at the
adcmw annual business
meeting

Gallery page 222

The ADCMW Annual Meeting mailer

For designer Steven D. Fleshman, this was not only a fun project, but one in which a variety of fortunate circumstances led to a successful design.

He started with the basic visual concept of an ancient Egyptian parchment—something that would play off the name of the award ceremony (the Clios). His next step was to sketch out some heiroglyph-style cartoons on paper to establish the graphic style.

Next was the document design concept. The paper was being donated by a local paper supplier. Because he wanted to evoke the notion of an ancient scroll, he requested that the paper be of a type called *parchment*. The supplier found a spare supply of tabloid sheets in a paper called Feltweave Parchment, 70# Text. Fleshman designed the mailer so he could get two mailers out of each sheet—and further the notion of a papyrus invitation.

Dividing the sheet in half the long way, he came up with a document 33 picas wide and 102 picas long—perfect for that special scroll look.

Then came the task of choosing the headline typeface. Lithos, designed to recall ancient inscriptions (and shown in this book on page 200), was an easy and obvious candidate. But it was a bit too easy, and Lithos had become so popular that it had become overused. Casting about for something with a novel—and even looser—feel, Fleshman came upon Emigre's Variex. He wasn't at all sure that Variex was the solution, but once he typed it in, he found that it perfectly matched the look of his cartoonish heiroglyphs. And he didn't have to touch the kerning, type sizes or baseline shifts—Variex sets naturally in the loose, wobbly formation you see here.

To set up the mailer, he first flipped to the master page and set up ruler guides, including a horizontal guide at 51 picas to indicate the fold line. He then created two document pages—one for the front and back cover and one for the inside spread.

The back cover had to be in the opposite orientation of the front cover, since the mailer folded over vertically. To accomplish this, he set the back text in a text box on the top half of the first page, then rotated the text box 180 degrees:

The inside spread was then set on the second document page in one long text box.

The document was output from an imagesetter on two film negatives. The print shop then created two printing plates, each with one side of the mailer duplicated side-by-side. This allowed them to print two mailers on each sheet in one pass—a technique called *two-up* printing.

Gallery page 208

• •

Design Tools Monthly newsletter

Editor and designer Jay Nelson has developed an interesting system for producing his monthly newsletter. He collects story ideas, magazine article summaries, and random tidbits of information in a database program (FileMaker Pro) instead of a word processor.

When it comes time to plan out an issue, he just prints out all the new material in his database. The printouts are preformatted to match the type specifications and column widths of his newsletter. He then cuts apart the articles and overlays them on a printout of his XPress template, piecing the articles together like a puzzle to see what will fit.

Once the order is determined, he returns to the database, sorts the articles in the right order, and exports them to a raw text file that he can import into his XPress template. There, he applies style sheets, rearranges department heads and makes final edits—and he's done!

His template design is also interesting. On his master page, he set up the skeleton of a typical page: four text boxes with vertical dotted rules between. He leaves these text boxes unlinked, since the various departments sometimes jump to other pages, and the jumps vary from issue to issue. He creates the links manually as he sets up each new issue.

Two types of dotted rules are used in the template—the vertical rules used as column separators and the horizontal rules used as story dividers. As noted before, the vertical rules are set as master items, with a weight of one-half point. When he tried the same weight for the horizontal rules (which are set as paragraph rules in the style sheet for the article headlines), he found that the design looked a bit flat— the horizontal dotted rules looked weak compared to the vertical rules. To balance the two kinds of rules visually, he changed the weight of the horizontal paragraph rules to three-quarters of a point. That small increase did the trick; here's what those divider rules look like (minus the text) at actual size:

The department heads are set in picture boxes and can be easily moved around to accommodate the placement of the text. The picture boxes are set with item runarounds that precisely control the placement of the text that follows, so that the first article head following a department head is always set at exactly the right distance.

Nelson also makes extensive use of small caps—the type style in which lowercase letters appear as small uppercase letters. He notes that XPress's default settings for the size of small caps don't produce the right look; the small caps simply look too small. To correct this, he opened the Typographic Preferences dialog box and changed the Vertical Scale for Small Caps to 85% and the Horizontal Scale to 90%—a combination he thinks produces a look comparable to professionally typeset small caps. To make sure the preference was used for all his documents, he changed these settings when no documents were open in XPress.

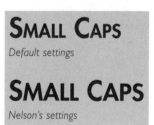

SMALL CAPS
Default settings

SMALL CAPS
Nelson's settings

Nelson also points out that, even though he's a veteran XPress user, he often forgets the keystrokes for some special characters. When his memory fails him, he just chooses the Help command and looks up the keystroke in the "Key Sequences" section—a method he finds much easier than searching for his manuals or reference card.

Gallery page 228

First Chicago generational brochures

Designer Karen Knorr had to create six brochures that contained many of the same elements and the same overall look, but with a variety of photos and charts and some customizations to the text.

To make sure all the brochures were perfectly consistent, she set them up in a single file. She created one master page for the outside spread and one for the inside spread, then set up twelve document pages based on these two master designs. She alternated the master page assignments—first an outside spread, then an inside spread, then an outside spread, and so on—until she had laid out the basic structure for all six brochures.

Keeping all six brochures in one file made it easy to make global changes. She had already set up a thorough collection of style sheets so that the need for local formatting was minimized. When she decided to make any kind of style change—type size, leading, paragraph spacing or type color—she only had to edit the style sheets to correct the styles for the entire brochure series. Global text changes were easier too; she could substitute a word or phrase throughout in a single step.

When she works on high-profile, promotional pieces like this, Knorr pays close attention to the kerning of the type—especially the headline type. Nearly every pair of letters in the headlines were custom-kerned to make sure the letter spacing was consistent and appropriate for the type size. Larger type—such as the large numbers on the front covers—needed extra attention, since the automatic kerning built into the typefaces is seldom appropriate for these sizes.

On the inside spread, Knorr decided to *hang* the headings for the body text topics—that is, set them to start a bit to the left of the body text—so they would be more noticeable. Rather than set these in separate text boxes, which would almost certainly lead to inconsistencies in alignment, she handled everything with a single text box per panel. The headings were set in a style sheet with a zero Left Indent, while the body text style sheet included a Left Indent of three picas, or one-half inch. And instead of using First Line Indents to signal new paragraphs, Knorr used a Space After of "1p3," one pica and three points.

To get the highest quality for the color photos, she had the print shop create the halftones from the original photos and strip them into the final film negatives. The photos on the front cover were best handled by the print shop anyway, since she wanted them to be printed using a special imaging technique called *mezzograin*. The resulting images have a soft, impressionist feel, like a painting composed of tiny color spots that meld together visually at a distance.

To show the print shop how she wanted the photos to be positioned, sized and cropped, she placed low-resolution grayscale scans in the XPress file and labeled them as *FPOs*—For Position Only.

• •

First Chicago "We're here to help you..." brochure

A small tidbit on how Knorr handled the hanging drop caps on this brochure: She set each initial cap in its own small text box, then copied and anchored that text box into the larger text box for the body text. She then indented the body text to match the position of the second letter in the first line.

Why did she anchor the hanging drop caps? She wanted to minimize any chance of the text boxes becoming separated or misaligned.

Gallery page 213

Gallery page 259

Spectrum newsletter

Designers Dave Philmlee and Bill Ferdinand like to play off the name of this newsletter with a couple of visual devices. The most obvious one is their use of blends throughout the newsletter. They also change the second color each issue, moving through the color spectrum to make their choices. Laid side-by-side, the issues create a rainbow effect.

To create the blend you see behind the sidebar on page three of this issue, they use a blend called Midlinear, available from the Color Palette's pop-up menu when the Cool Blends XTension is installed. The second color (PMS 320) was chosen as both the start color and the end color, but the end color shade was set to "0%"—the same as white. The angle was then set to 45°:

This blend was set as the background for the text box itself, with the text inset for the box set to six points so that the type wouldn't run right to the edges.

They even made that 3-D bar graph in XPress. The background was set as a linear blend from 100% to 20% of the spot color. To create the 3-D bar, Philmlee drew a white box with a tinted polygon box next to it, like the ones below (but without the frames I've added here for clarity):

This combo was duplicated at even intervals using the Step And Repeat dialog box, then lengthened or shortened to match the data. Rotated text labels were then added above.

Inagination Theater brochure

One of XPress's newest and handiest features is the ability to reshape text boxes. Designer Estelle Carol put that feature to work in this brochure, in which she slanted the left edge of the type to complement the angled photos.

To make sure the angle of the text was the same on each panel, she reshaped the text box on the first panel, then duplicated it at regular intervals until there was a copy on each of the panels of the folder.

To reshape the text box in the first place, she selected it, chose the last option in the Box Shape submenu of the Item menu, then turned on the Reshape Polygon command. That allowed her to move the bottom left corner of the text box to the right. To move it over in a straight line and keep the bottom edge of the box horizontal, she held down the Shift key as she dragged to the right. She was careful to keep the angle small; a more severe angle would have made the text difficult for the reader to follow, resulting in a more ragged-looking left edge.

Gallery page 242

When she settled on the shape she wanted, Carol turned off Reshape Polygon so that she wouldn't accidentally change the shape later as she clicked around in the window.

Gallery page 260

● ●

Seabury & Smith "The Next Level" postcards

Designer Steven D. Fleshman started this project with a basic idea—creating a set of postcards based on a single collage. He also had the various hand-painted color illustrations that would go into the collage.

To start bringing everything together, he first photocopied each color illustration to produce miniature black-and-white versions. He then did quick tracings of these on tissue paper in order to reduce each illustration to a simple line art rendering. He used these thumbnail sketches—not the computer—to plan out the entire design.

"I always plan my designs using pen and paper, working in thumbnail sketches…. I find that you just can't plan and design in the same way when you're in front of a color monitor with all those big color guns going off—it's too seductive," says Fleshman. Using the black-and-white sketches, Fleshman was better able to assess the strength of the design itself, independent of the color and the inherent quality of the illustrations.

Once the design of the collage was determined, he sent the artwork out to a service bureau to get high-resolution, color-corrected CMYK EPS files. He had already drawn, rotated and layered the various text and picture boxes on an 11-x-17 inch XPress page, following closely the thumbnail he had drawn. He then imported each EPS into place and only had to make minor adjustments to complete the front design.

To complete the back of the postcards, he created a second tabloid page and divided it into quadrants with a horizontal and a vertical ruler guide. He set the type for the back of the postcard in the first quadrant, then copied that design into each of the other quadrants to produce a *four-up* layout. That saved the print shop the cost and effort of producing the four-up plate from a single master copy.

Trinity "Who? Why?" brochure

Designer Mark Shippe set this piece up as two very wide pages—23 picas tall by 266 picas wide (roughly 44 inches). Because this was an accordion fold, he divided the master page into five equal panels by setting the column guides to five. (Unlike standard folds, in which rightmost panels must be narrower so they can be folded inward, the panels of an accordion fold must be equal in width.)

The large background type for the front and back covers was set in XPress, using extra-loose tracking to spread the letters out evenly. The university logo had previously been standardized and saved as an Adobe Illustrator EPS, so that was imported into a picture box and superimposed.

Gallery page 225

Western Maryland "Drop In Any Time" brochure

Shippe was especially pleased with the way a couple of his XPress experiments worked out on this mailer. The first experiment he tried was creating the front cover burst shape in XPress, rather than a drawing program, simply by clicking out the shape with the Polygon Box tool. He wasn't worried about symmetry, so the first shape he drew worked perfectly.

On the inside, he decided to set the main body text in decreasing type sizes to play off the headline "Fly By For A Closer Look." He wasn't sure how to create the effect he envisioned systematically, so he simply experimented: He set the text to justified alignment, then set each line of the paragraph to a different type size, one point apart. He then tried some sizes two points apart, making small adjustments to improve the fit and justification of the type. He was pleasantly surprised to find that a single leading value—28 points—looked fine even though the type changed in size from 16 points all the way down to 10.

Gallery page 244

● ●

But that's not all, folks...

There are plenty more of those kinds of tips, tricks and how-to's coming up. In the next section, I've rounded up hundreds of tidbits, all organized by function.

Who knows? After trying out a few of the ideas from this chapter and the chapter to come, you may well be inspired to submit some of your own work—and your favorite design tricks—for the next edition of this book!

XPress Hotline

Tricks of the Trade

Confused about something? Can't figure out how to get the effect you're looking for? Not sure what will happen when you click that check box?

For answers to these and many other questions, this chapter is the place to look. I've included more than 300 tips, tricks, explanations and procedures, divided into 22 categories. You can either flip to the category—they're all listed on the next two pages—or you can check the Index to see if the topic you want is covered here. Chances are, it is.

The Categories

ABC's

Mac	Win
hold down Command	*hold down* Ctrl

Temporary Item tool

● ●

Switching to the Item tool
Regardless of which tool you are currently using, you can temporarily switch to the Item tool by holding down Command or Ctrl. However, you can only select or move a single item with the temporary Item tool. To select and move multiple items, you must switch to the Item tool.

● ●

Copying with the Item tool vs. the Content tool
There's a big difference between copying a selected box with the Content tool and the Item tool. When you copy with the Content tool, you're copying the insides of the box—a picture or some text—and that's why QXP beeps if the box is empty or if no text is highlighted. When you copy with the Item tool, you're copying both the selected box and everything inside.

The temporary Item tool described above cannot be used for copying or cutting—only for moving an item.

● ●

Some tools are easier to hold onto
The Item, Content and Zoom tools remain selected after you use them; the other tools don't. To keep these tools selected for repeated use—tools such as Rotate, Text Box and Link—hold down Option or Alt when you click on the tool's icon.

Mac	Win
Option *click on icon*	Alt *click on icon*

Keep tool

● ●

The Style and Item menus come and go
The Item menu is available whenever an item is selected, regardless of the tool you're using. But the Style menu is only available when an item is selected with the Content tool. If any other tool is active, the entire menu is grayed out.

Know your tool cursors

For most of the work you do in QuarkXPress, you use one of
five cursors:

- • The 4-way arrow appears over an item when it's selected
  and either you've chosen the Item tool or you're holding
  down Command or Ctrl to get the temporary Item tool.

- • The pointer appears when your cursor is over a blank
  area or over an empty box.

- • The I-beam appears when the Content tool is over a
  selected text box. The grabber hand appears when the
  Content tool is over a selected picture and also when you
  hold down the Option or Alt key to scroll the page.

- • The pointing finger appears whenever the cursor is near
  a handle of a selected box.

Mac	Win
Option *drag*	Alt *drag*

Scroll page with grabber hand

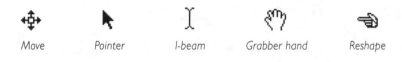

Move   Pointer   I-beam   Grabber hand   Reshape

Know your page cursors

There are three different cursors you might see if you're
rearranging, copying or inserting pages in the Layout palette
or in Thumbnail view. The page cursor tells you that you're
placing a page in an empty area that won't "bump" other
pages. The other cursors indicate the inserted page will bump
other pages or spreads down or bump them to the right.

Place page in
empty area

Force down

Force right

Enabling the palettes

Some palettes gray out when an item isn't selected. For example, the Style Sheets palette is enabled only when a text box is selected with the Content tool. The Colors palette is available only when at least one item is selected with any tool.

Showing and hiding palettes

Unless you have a very large screen, palettes often get in the way, hiding areas of the page you need to see. It's easy enough to hide them and bring them back when you need them. There are even keyboard shortcuts for hiding and showing the Tool and Measurements palettes:

Tool Palette:	Mac	Win
Toggle	F8	F8
Show	Command-Tab	Ctrl-Tab

Measurements Palette:		
Toggle	F9	F9
Show	Option-Command-Tab	Alt-Ctrl-Tab

Changing measurement systems temporarily

Regardless of which measurement system you've chosen as your default, you can enter a measurement in a different system by typing an abbreviation after the number. Here are some examples:

System	Symbol	Example
Inches	"	1.5"
Points	p or pt	p108 or 108pt
Picas	p	9p
Centimeters	cm	3.81cm
Millimeters	mm	38.1mm
Ciceros	c	8.37c

The two sides of the Measurements palette

The Measurements palette has two sides. Item-level settings, such as box size and position, are on the left, and Content-level settings, such as picture scaling and type settings, are on the right.

The dividing line between Item settings and Content settings.

The Rotate tool vs picture angle

You can rotate a box with the Rotate tool, but you can't use that tool to rotate just the contents of the box. You can, however, rotate a picture while leaving the picture box straight up-and-down; use the rotation controls on the right side of the Measurements palette for that.

| X : -1p6 | W : 4p3 | △ 0° | → X% : 100% | ◇◇ X+ : 0p | △ 45° |
| Y : -13p6 | H : 1p6 | ◿ 0p | ↑ Y% : 100% | ⟰ Y+ : 0p | ◿ 0° |

Picture angle

Moving the rulers

You can slide the rulers up and down and left and right. Just press on the zero point icon (also known as the origin) and drag it to the point that you want to measure from.

The sero point icon.

Moving the zero point.

And how do you put the zero point back where it belongs when you're done with it? Just double-click on the zero point icon.

Where's my picture?

After you import a large graphic that has a white background, you may not see anything in the picture box. Turn on Show Guides if it's not already on. If you don't see an X in the picture box, you'll know the picture really has been imported; you're seeing just one corner of the graphic (the upper left corner) which appears blank. To see the whole graphic, enlarge the box or scale the graphic to fit the the picture box.

To see the entire picture, use the Fit-In-Box keystroke. That scales the picture to fit the current box size.

Mac	Win
Shift	Shift
Option	Alt
Command	Ctrl
F	F

Fit-In-Box

Before Get Picture   *After Get Picture*   *After Fit-In-Box*

How things look when you edit text

When you select a text box that overlaps other items with the Content tool, the background appears opaque, obscuring items behind it. That's so you can clearly see the text for editing. If you're trying to adjust the size or position of the text box and need to see the items in the background, just switch to the Item tool.

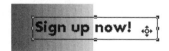   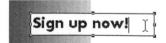

Text box selected with Item tool...   *...and with Content tool*

You might also notice that when you edit text in a box that contains a blend, the background appears solid; the blend reappears when you deselect the box or change to the Item tool.

Reshaping boxes

Any kind of box can be reshaped after it's drawn. The trick is to choose the "polygon" box type from the Item menu, then choose Reshape Polygon. You won't be able to resize the entire box, though, until you turn Reshape Polygon off.

Anchoring boxes to text

You can insert a picture or text box directly into text; just copy the box with the Item tool, then switch to the Content tool to paste the box into a story. These are called *anchored items* or *inline graphics.* They're a great way to make custom bullets, insert special symbols, or insert an illustration that must move along with surrounding text during editing.

What kinds of things can't you anchor into text? lines; multiple items, even if they're grouped; text boxes that contain anchored items; and nonrectangular boxes (which are converted into rectangles upon pasting).

And avoid anchoring large boxes—if the box you're anchoring is wider or taller than the text box you're pasting it into, both the anchored box and any following text will disappear. They'll either bump to a larger text box further down the chain (if one exists) or just appear as overset text.

Picture box copied and pasted into text.

Large picture copied and pasted into smaller box, producing overset symbol.

• •

A fine point of anchoring

You can't anchor a graphic by importing it directly from disk into a text block, as you can in PageMaker. Instead, you must import the graphic into its own picture box, then cut or copy the picture box.

• •

Anchoring alternative box shapes

XPress will allow you to paste a nonrectangular box into text, but it will be automatically converted into a rectangular box in the process.

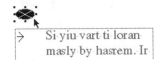

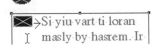

Oval box copied...   *...and pasted into text.*

The only workaround is to put the nonrectangular box on its own page, save it as an EPS file, then import the EPS into a rectangular box and anchor that.

• •

More columns or more text boxes?

What's the difference between a multicolumn text box and several column-shaped text boxes chained together? A multi-column box is easier to set up but not quite as flexible. You may find it easier to adjust the depth of individual columns of text if you use single-column boxes chained together.

If you prefer to use multicolumn boxes, you can adjust column depth by inserting a New Column character (keypad Enter key) right before the text you want to bump to the right.

· · · · · · · · · · · · · · · ·
Automatic text flow

There are two methods for using automatic text boxes to flow long text files through a series of pages.

- • Turn on one of the Auto Page Insertion options (in the General Preferences dialog box) before you choose Get Text; during import, XPress will create as many pages as needed to place all of the text.

- • Alternatively, you can create a specific number of linked pages before you import the text file by using the Insert Pages dialog box.

If you prefer the second method (inserting a specific number of pages yourself), follow these steps carefully: Make sure that Auto Page Insertion is set to Off; select the automatic text box with the Content tool; open the Insert Pages dialog; type in the number of pages you want and the master page they should be based on; then turn on Link To Current Text Chain.

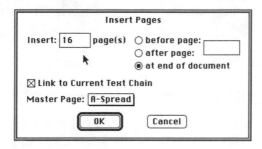

· · · · · · · · · · · · · · · ·
Applying style sheets

To apply a style to a single paragraph, you don't need to select the whole paragraph—just insert the I-beam anywhere in the paragraph. A style sheet always affects the entire paragraph.

Invisible formatting characters

XPress includes a variety of special invisible characters you can use to break text at specific points, space words apart or align words in columns. Here they are, along with the keystrokes you need to insert them:

Character	Symbol	Mac Keystroke	Win keystroke
Space	•	spacebar	spacebar
Nonbreaking space	•	Command-space	Ctrl-space
En space	•	Option-space	Shift-Ctrl-6
Flex space	•	Shift-Option-space	Shift-Ctrl-5
Tab	→	Tab	Tab
Right indent tab	→	Option-Tab	Shift-Tab
Indent here	‖	Command-\	Ctrl-\
Discretionary hyphen		Command-hyphen	Ctrl-hyphen
New line	↵	Shift-Return	Shift-Return
New paragraph	¶	Return	Return
New column	↓	Enter	Enter
New box	↡	Shift-Enter	Shift-Enter

Backgrounds for text

Want to add a background behind a text block? There are two methods to consider:

• • Fill the text box itself with a background color;

• • Or create a picture box and send it behind the text box.

Use the first method for simple sidebars, but make sure you adjust the text inset. Use the second method when you want to position two or more text blocks over a single background, use a picture as a background, or change the size or shape of the background box without altering the layout of the text.

Text box with background fill and text inset.

Text boxes with background set to None and positioned over a color-filled box.

Background colors, or lack thereof

What's the difference between boxes filled with White, None, and 0% of a nonwhite color? They all look the same on a white page. But they're not the same if you want to put something behind the box. Both White and 0% of a color will create an opaque white background that will "knock out" any items behind that box. So if you want a background item to show through, make sure you choose *None*.

All ruler guides are not created equal

There are two kinds of ruler guides—*page guides* and *pasteboard guides*. A page guide is created when you pull out a new ruler guide and release it with your cursor over a page; the guide then spans only that page. If you release a new guide with the cursor over the pasteboard, the guide will span the entire pasteboard.

Create a pasteboard guide if you're trying to align items on different pages of a spread. But beware—pasteboard guides set up on master pages don't appear on document pages!

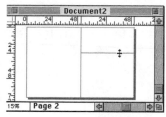

Creating a page guide.

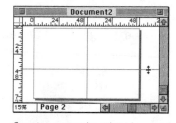

Creating a pasteboard guide.

Column and ruler guides

Guides are "on" even when they're hidden—that is, as long as Snap To Guides is turned on. That's why you might occasionally find it difficult to move items smoothly or with precision. Just turn off Snap To Guides.

• •

The truth about column guides

What exactly are Column Guides and what do they do? Column Guides (when set to two or more) split up the area between the margins. They can be used simply as guides to help you draw boxes of uniform width. If you're using automatic text boxes, changing the Column Guides settings for a master page will move the master guides *and* change the columns inside the auto text box.

Column Guides can be set in the New dialog before you create a document. To change the setting after the document has been created, you must switch to a master page and open the Master Guides dialog box.

• • • • • • • • • • • • • • • • • • • •

What are Facing Pages?

Facing Pages is an option that appears in both the New Document and the Document Setup dialog boxes. It allows you to set up left- and right-handed pages as mirror opposites in a spread. If you turn it on, you'll see three changes take place onscreen:

• • In the New dialog and the Master Guides dialog boxes, side margins will be referred to as "Outside" and "Inside" instead of "Left" and "Right;

• • A line will appear down the middle of the Document Layout palette;

• • The double-dog-eared master page icon (the facing pages icon) will become available in the Layout palette.

To Face or not to Face

What are the pros and cons of turning on Facing Pages? If
you want the option of designing pairs of master pages as
spreads, turn it on; otherwise you'll only be able to design
master pages one at a time. There's only one drawback to
using Facing Pages: If you later decide you don't want Facing
Pages, you'll have to delete any master pages designed as facing pages before you can turn the option off.

*Here's another benefit of facing master pages: If you change
the order of your document pages in any way, XPress will
automatically handle the switch between left-handed and
right-handed page designs.*

Are you and XPress on the same page?

Ever wonder why the page indicator at the bottom of the document window says "Page 1" when you're working on page 3?
The page you're editing isn't necessarily the page that's
selected. This happens when you can see more than one
page—or pasteboard—in the document window. Whichever
page (or pasteboard) is visible in the upper left corner of the
window is considered the selected page, and its page number
is the one displayed at the bottom of the window.

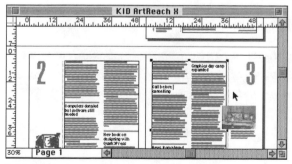

*Even though the text on page 3 is being edited,
XPress considers page 1 to be the selected page.,*

• • • • • • • • • • • • •
Selecting pages

Why is it important to know which page is selected? The selected page is the one affected by the Insert, Delete, Move and Section commands. So you want to make sure the right page is selected before you choose one of these commands. The two easiest ways to select a page—and be absolutely sure that's it's selected—is to use the Go To command or double-click on the page icon in the Layout palette.

The currently selected page is the one named in the page indicator area of the document window.

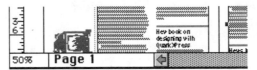

The page indicator area of a document window.

• •
The Section command: what's it good for?

• • You can set the starting page number for a file to a number higher than one (as when a publication is split into a series of successive files);

• • It lets you arbitrarily change the page numbering at any point within a file;

• • It lets you change the page number format.

The formatting options in the Section dialog box allow you to label pages in a variety of ways. For example, page "six" could be automatically labeled as 6, vi, f, A-6 or Sec 4 Page 6.

The Section dialog set up for a starting page number of "A-1".

Starting a new section

To start a new section, you must first select—not just scroll to—the starting page for that section. Use the Go To command or double-click on the page in the Layout palette, then choose the Section command.

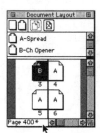

You can also open the Section dialog by clicking on the page name indicator in the Document Layout palette.

(The asterisk after the page name indicates that the selected page is a section start.)

Juggling page names and numbers

When you alter page numbers with the Section command, referring to a specific page gets very tricky. That's because every page in the section then gets two names—a document name and a section name.

- • The document name is simply the page's position in the document; that's the number displayed directly below the page's icon in the Layout palette.

- • The section name is the "number" that actually appears on the page and in the page indicator areas. For example, the section name of the first page would be "A-20" if you set up the start number at 20 with a prefix of "A-".

When you have to name pages in a dialog box—such as the Print, Insert, Delete and Move dialogs—what do you type? "1" or "A-20"? You can use either—but you must add a plus sign if you want to use the document name for the page number (as in "+1").

Making your own automatic text boxes

Want an automatic text box in a document that was originally created without one? XPress doesn't offer an automatic text box option for existing documents, but you can make your own. Draw a text box on a master page, then link it to the broken-chain icon with the Link tool.

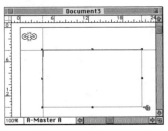 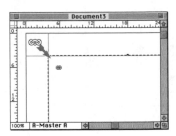

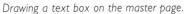

Drawing a text box on the master page.　　　Linking box to auto text chain.

If you want your automatic text box to be hooked into the Master Guide settings—so that any changes to the margin or column guides will automatically change the text box accordingly—make sure the box snaps on all sides to the margin guides on the master page.

Working on large publications

If you're working on a large publication—say, 50 pages or more—consider breaking it into several documents. It's a bit more work in terms of maintaining and updating your files, but it's much safer. You'll also find your work proceeds more quickly when you're editing a smaller document.

Adding & Creating

Drawing polygon boxes from scratch

With most of the box tools, you just press-and-drag to create
a box. With the polygon box tool, however, you must click out
the shape corner by corner, then make sure the shape is
closed. You can close the shape either by clicking on the first
point or by double-clicking as you put down the last point.

Double-click on last point...   or click on first point...   to close a polygon box.

*You can change existing boxes, such as rectangles or ovals,
into custom polygon shapes. Select the box and choose the
polygon option from the Box Shape submenu in the Item
menu, then choose Reshape Polygon.*

Drawing polygons with constraints

You can draw a polygon using 45° angles by holding down
Shift as you click.

*If you want to make sure that various points of the polygon
line up horizontally or vertically, place ruler guides in your
drawing area and turn on Snap To Guides.*

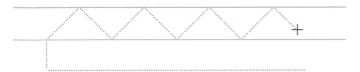

Drawing a sawtooth shape using the Shift key and two horizontal ruler guides.

Mac	Win
Command *click*	Ctrl *click*

Add or delete corner point

Adding new points to a polygon

To add a corner point to a polygon box after it's been closed, just make sure Reshape Polygon is on, then click where you want to add a point while holding down Command or Ctrl.

To delete a point you've added, click on it with Command or Ctrl held down.

Triangles

One way to create a triangle is to type one of the triangular dingbat characters, then size and rotate it to suit your purposes. Another way is to simply make one from a square picture box. Convert the box to a polygon, turn on Reshape Polygon, then delete one of the corner points.

To resize the triangular box, turn Reshape Polygon off—then you'll be able to scale it like a normal box.

Graphic headline styles

You can create graphic headline styles using nonrectangular text boxes: Set a headline in a text box with a background fill, then choose an alternative box shape from the Item menu. To center the headline vertically in the box, choose the Modify command and increase the First Baseline Offset value.

Unfortunately, if you try to paste the headline box into another box as an anchored item, you'll lose the shape; XPress automatically converts the box back into a rectangle.

Headline set in an oval text box and reversed. First Baseline Offset is set to 2p.

Blended backgrounds

To create a blended background in a picture or text box:

1. Click on the Background icon in the Colors palette;

2. Press on Solid to open the background menu;

3. Choose a blend option;

4. Choose the starting color and shade;

5. Click the #2 button; choose the ending color and shade;

6. Set the angle of the blend.

You can create a single-color gradient by choosing the same color in two different shades.

Without Cool Blends XTension   With Cool Blends XTension   The blend controls

Backgrounds for type

Looking for an unusual backdrop for a headline or a sidebar? Use the Polygon Box tool to draw a burst or some other shape, then import a texture or fill it with a blend.

Picture boxes and texture from companion CD-ROM.

· · · · · · · ·
Callouts

You can automate the creation of callouts—those little text labels and their accompanying lines. One way is to set up a callout "template" using a text box and a line, then grouping the two pieces so they can be easily copied. Alternatively, you can create paragraph styles that really automate the process. Set the style to include paragraph rules that automatically change in length to fit the text box, as below:

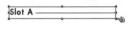

Callout settings in Paragraph Rules; note use of white rule below to frame text

Adjusting length of callout line.

· · · · · · · · · · · · · ·
Custom line styles

You can make a variety of custom line styles using dingbats, leader tabs and paragraph rules:

✦ ✦ ✦ ✦ ✦ ✦ ✦ ✦ ✦ ✦ ✦ ✦ ✦ ✦ ✦ ✦ ✦ ✦ ✦

Tab leader set to Zapf Dingbat ✦; *tab selected and set to Track: 200, Size: 4*

Zapf Dingbats typed in, with Track: 100, Rule Below: Dashed, .5 point

Zapf Dingbats typed in, with Track: 90, Rule Above: 9 points

Unfortunately, there's no way to create this kind of variety with frame styles—and that means there's no way to create arcs or ovals with these styles.

Patterns

The Super Step And Repeat command, a feature of the Bobzilla XTension, allows you to whip up some interesting patterns for use as in logos and background. Here are a few examples along with the settings that produced them:

Start item: One-pica line
Repeat count: 10
Horizontal offset: 1p3
End frame thickness: 0

Start item: Large oval box with hairline frame
Repeat count: 6
Offsets: 0; Origins: Center
End frame thickness: 6 pt

Quick duotones

You can create a simple duotone effect by importing a grayscale photo into a picture box and applying a light color or a color tint to the background of the box.

To create a real duotone within XPress, use Step And Repeat to duplicate a grayscale image with zero offsets. Use the Other Contrast dialog box to darken the midtones of this copy, apply a spot color to the image, then send it to back. Lighten the midtones of the original image (now on top) and leave it set to black. Make sure this picture's background is set to None and that the picture is set to Overprint in the Trap Information palette. You won't be able to preview the effect onscreen or on most color printers, so make sure you print spot-color separation proofs on your laser printer to check your settings.

Manual jump lines

Set jump lines in their own small text boxes, not as part of the story they refer to. That way, they won't move if the body text is edited.

Automatic jump lines

Previous page number

Next page number

To create a jump line that automatically inserts and updates the correct page number, set the jump line in its own unlinked text box and position it to overlap the story. Type "continued on" or "continued from," then the code for Previous Page Number or Next Page Number.

If the remainder of the story is overset—that is, it hasn't yet been linked to a box on another page—the page number will read <None>; the correct page number will be substituted as soon as you link the text to another box.

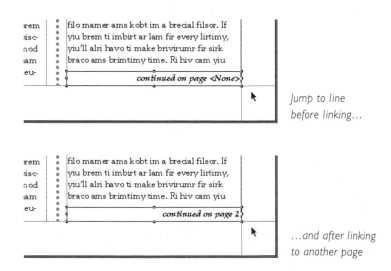

Jump to line before linking...

...and after linking to another page

······

Forms

Creating an office form with lots of blank lines or the grid background for a graph? Don't use the Line tool to create patterns of lines. Instead, use paragraph rules. Then you can add or delete lines simply by tapping the Return and Backspace (or Delete) keys, adjust spacing with Leading or Space After, and adjust line length by changing the width of the box or the indents. Best of all, you can create a style sheet that allows you to adjust all of these settings globally.

··········

FPO labels

Need to stamp a bunch of low-res graphics as FPOs—"for position only" placeholders? Create a text box, type in FPO (bold, 24 points or higher), and set both paragraph and vertical alignment to centered. Put a copy on the pasteboard or in a Library. Whenever you need to stamp a graphic, paste a copy of the FPO box over the picture box.

If the printer needs a keyline, make sure Framing—in General Preferences— is set to Inside, then give the FPO box a 1-point frame; stretch the box to outline the underlying picture box.

·············

Reminder notes

Create "post-it" notes on your pages to remind yourself what still needs to be done. On your master pages, draw a text box on the pasteboard so that it overlaps a page edge slightly; then set the alignment in the box so the notes you type will be flush to the opposite side of the box.

If you place a text box to the side of a master page—so that it doesn't touch the page itself—it won't show up on document pages. Items placed on the pasteboard of a master page aren't considered master items.

Version slugs

Create a version slug that appears on each page of your proofs: Just put a small text box at the bottom of your master page with the current date and proof number. Remember to delete the box from the master page for your final print.

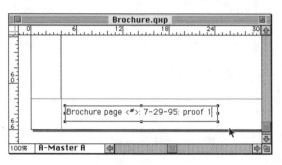

Setting up a version slug on a master page.

If you have several master pages, set the slug in its own style sheet. That way, you don't have to delete every slug—you only have to edit the style sheet to change the type color to White before you print your final pages.

New colors and style sheets

Mac	Win
Command *click name*	Ctrl *click name*

Edit style or color

Here's a shortcut for creating a new color or style from scratch: Hold down Command or Ctrl as you click on any color or style in your palettes (other than the *None* color or the *No style* style). That opens the Colors or Style Sheets dialog box, where you can then click New.

You can use the same procedure to create a style sheet based on text you've styled by hand. Place the I-beam cursor anywhere in the text, then open the Style Sheets dialog box— using either the shortcut above or the command in the Edit menu—then click New. You'll see the font, type styles and paragraph format you chose listed in the Edit Style Sheet dialog box. Type in a style name and you're done.

Setting up style sheets methodically

Here's the most efficient procedure for defining style sheets:

1. Define all the H&Js and colors you'll need in your style sheets.

2. Create the most basic styles, such as for body text and for top headlines (these also tend to differ the most).

3. Define other styles, such as subheads, bylines and captions, as styles "based on" the first styles you created.

4. After you've created all the styles you need, edit each style one more time to set the Next Style option.

Master ruler guides

If you want to include ruler guides as master items on your master pages, make sure you create page guides. That is, drop the guide with your cursor over the page area. If you create a pasteboard guide (by dropping the guide with your cursor over the pasteboard), the guide will only appear on the master page itself—not on document pages. To set a horizontal guide that spans a facing master page, you'll have to set a separate page guide for each page.

Because master pasteboard guides don't show up on document pages, there's no way to set master guides for bleeding items. If you really want a visual guide to indicate how far items should bleed, the only workaround is to draw a box around the entire master page, set the frame to one or two points, then lock it in place with the Lock command.

• • • • • • • • • • • • • • • •

View-specific guides

Want to set a ruler guide so it only shows up at a specific magnification? Hold down Shift when you create the guide; it will disappear when you change to any lower magnification.

This comes in handy when you need to align a variety of items, such as small photos, graphics and captions, in a restricted section of a page. Zoom into the area at 200% or 400% and Shift-drag as many guides as you need into place.

Ruler guides created at 200% with Shift.   Page viewed at 100%

• •

Several ways to add new pages

There are four ways to add new pages to a document:

• • Drag a blank page icon or a master page icon into the document area of the Layout palette;

• • Choose Insert from the Page menu;

• • Hold down Option or Alt as you drag a blank or master page page icon into the document area to open the Insert Pages dialog;

• • Drag one or more pages from another document window into the document you're working on.

You can add several blank pages at one time if you use the Insert Pages dialog box; the dialog also allows you to specify where the new pages should go and what master page they should be based on.

• •

New pages for an existing text chain

You can insert a page—or a range of pages—and have overset text automatically flow into it. But you must do the following three things to make it happen:

• • Have a master page that includes an automatic text box;

• • Use the Content tool to select a text box on an existing document page that contains part of the story;

• • Use the Insert Pages dialog to choose the correct master page and then turn on Link To Current Text Chain.

This works best when you're inserting new pages at the end of the currently chained pages. If you insert new pages in the middle of the chain, XPress won't automatically reconfigure the chain to match the new page order—instead, it will link the last page to the page you inserted. To fix the order, use the Link tool to link the preceding page to the new page.

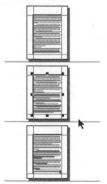 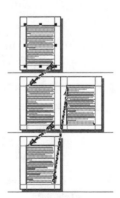 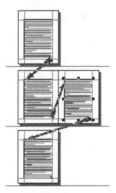

Before new page added
to right of page two

New page inserted
into text chain,
but linked to last box

Chain order fixed
with Link tool

• • • • • • • • • • • • • • • • • •

Multi-panel spreads

In XPress, a spread can be any number of pages, not just two, as in PageMaker.

• • One way to set up a spread is to set the page size to the size of the entire spread and then divide it with column or ruler guides. This is usually the way to go, since it allows you to print the entire spread easily.

• • The other way is to insert several pages in a row in the Layout palette. The benefit of multiple pages is that it may be easier to proof individual panels at full size on a standard printer.

Regardless of which method you're using to set up wide spreads of this type, you probably won't want to use the Facing Pages option in your document setup. That's only intended for two-page spreads.

• • • • • • • • • •

Templates

Create templates for the documents you use most, such as letterhead, fax covers, envelopes, and labels. Design sample documents of each, including logos, dummy text, style sheets and so on. Choose Save As: on the Mac, click on the Template button; in Windows, choose Templates (*.QXT) from the file type menu.

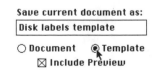

Arranging & Positioning

• •

Aligning and distributing items

What can you use the Space/Align command for? Here are
some examples:

Distribute Evenly, Items
(Horizontal and Vertical)

Space Evenly, Centers
(Horizontal and Vertical)

• •

Changing the order of overlapping items

One way to change the way items overlap on the page is to
send some "To Back" and bring others "To Front" until you
get the order you want. But it's often faster and easier to use
the Send Backward and Bring Forward commands.

Mac	Win
Option F5	Ctrl F5

Bring Forward

Mac	Win
Shift Option F5	Shift Ctrl F5

Send Backward

Item	
Modify...	Ctrl+M
Frame...	Ctrl+B
Runaround...	Ctrl+T
Duplicate	Ctrl+D
Step and Repeat...	Ctrl+Alt+D
Delete	Ctrl+K
Group	Ctrl+G
Ungroup	Ctrl+U
Constrain	
Lock	Ctrl+L
Send Backward	
Send To Back	
Bring Forward	
Bring To Front	
Space/Align...	Ctrl+,
Box Shape	▶
Reshape Polygon	

Item	
Modify...	⌘M
Frame...	⌘B
Runaround...	⌘T
Duplicate	⌘D
Step and Repeat...	⌥⌘D
Delete	⌘K
Group	⌘G
Ungroup	⌘U
Constrain	
Lock	
Send Backward	
Bring Forward	
Space/Align...	⌘,
Box Shape	▶
✓Reshape Polygon	
Super Step and Repeat...	
Full Resolution Output	

*On the Mac, the Send
Backward and Bring
Forward commands are
hidden. To see them, hold
down Option as you open
the Item menu.*

Moving up, down, left or right

To move any item in a straight horizontal or vertical line, hold down Shift and then start dragging.

Nudging

Need to move something just a hair? Select the item and nudge it by tapping the arrow keys. Note that if you've selected a picture with the Content tool, the picture will be nudged within its box. To nudge the box itself, you must have the Item tool selected.

Each tap of an arrow key moves the selection by one point. To nudge one-tenth of that distance, hold down Option or Alt.

Mac	Win
Option arrow key	Alt arrow key

Mini-nudge

Remembering the order of overlapping items

Unlike PageMaker, XPress always remembers an item's position in terms of stacking. For example, an item that has been sent to back in XPress won't pop forward when you drag it across the page with the Item tool; it's still considered behind all the other items on the page.

Arranging lines with rotation

Need to arrange two or more lines so they join at one end? Draw the first line, duplicate it with zero offsets, then use the Measurements palette to rotate the duplicate around one of the endpoints. To create a spoke pattern, rotate duplicates around the Midpoint.

Rotating a line with the Measurements palette.

Butting lines together

The rotation trick above is great for setting up two hairlines to create a right angle, as for a callout. But if you're using heavier lines—say, 2 points or more—you'll notice that the corners don't form a perfect joint. To fix the gap, use Space/Align to align the edges of the lines.

8-point lines rotated around endpoint   *After Space/Align: Horizontal; Space Evenly: 0p; Left Edges*

Rotating with constraints

You can rotate an item in 45-degree increments by holding down Shift as you drag an item with the Rotate tool.

Locking items, sort of

The Lock command only locks in box size, line length, page position, and the position of a picture within its box. Lock doesn't protect text or pictures inside the boxes, styling, background color, frame settings or line weight.

It's usually a good idea to lock items on master pages.

Moving locked items

You can't drag or resize a locked item with the mouse, but you can with the keyboard. Just use the Measurements palette to change the item settings numerically.

You can also change locked item settings by choosing the Modify command, double-clicking on the item with the Item tool or by choosing Space/Align.

• • • • • • • • • • • • • • • • • • • •

Shifting anchored items

It may seem there's no way to fine-tune the vertical position of an anchored item, but it's actually very easy:

1. Choose one of the Align With Text options, Ascent or Baseline.

2. Highlight the anchored item using the Content tool's I-beam cursor, as if it were a text character.

3. Choose Baseline Shift (Style menu) and type in the number of points you want the item moved up; use a negative number to move the item down.

This is especially helpful for setting anchored items such as hanging heads, run-in subheads or bullet symbols.

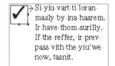
Anchored item selected as an item.

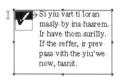
Anchored item selected as a text character.

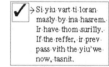
After Baseline Shift: 4 points up.

• • • • • • • • • • • • • • • • • •

Moving a grouped item

Want to move an item within a group without ungrouping first? Just select the item you want to move with the Content tool and move it with the temporary Item tool.

Mac	Win
Command *drag*	Ctrl *drag*

Moving a grouped item

• • • • • • • • • • • • • •

Panning pictures

If you're trying to crop a photo or graphic precisely, try nudging it within its box. By tapping the arrow keys while the picture is selected with the Content tool, you can move it in one-point increments. And it's often easier than trying to make fine adjustments with the mouse.

Moving ruler guides

When the Guides menu (in General Preferences) is set to Behind, the only way you can move a ruler guide is to grab it in an empty area of the page. It's easier to grab guides when the Guides preference is set to Front. Then, you can always move a guide with the Item tool, even in a cluttered area of the page.

If you're using any other tool, just hold down Command or Ctrl to grab the guide with the temporary Item tool.

Temporary Item tool

Rearranging pages

There are two ways to rearrange pages within a document. One way is to open the Layout palette and move the page icons around. The other way is to switch the document to Thumbnail view and move the pages themselves.

Because the Thumbnail view lets you see what's on each page, it's easier to figure out exactly what you're moving—though you can't see as many pages simultaneously in a document window as you can in the Layout palette.

First pages

If you're working on a facing pages document, you've probably noticed that the first page always appears on the right side and that the Layout palette doesn't allow you to move it to the left. That's because odd-numbered pages are always considered right-handed. If you need the first page of that document to be a leftie, here's how you do it: Select the page icon by double-clicking on it, then open the Section dialog to set it as a Section Start with an even page number.

You can open the Section dialog box by clicking on the page indicator at the bottom of the Layout palette.

Changing

· ·

Using the Specifications dialog boxes

Don't like keeping the Measurements palette and Colors palette open all the time? Many of the settings in those palettes are also available in an item's Specifications dialog. You can open that dialog box in any of three ways:

- • Choose Modify from the Item menu;

- • Double-click on the item with the Item tool (or the temporary Item tool);

- • Press Command-M or Ctrl-M.

The Specifications dialog changes according to what kind of item is selected:

Open Specifications dialog

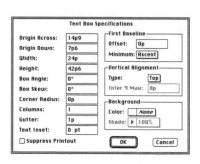

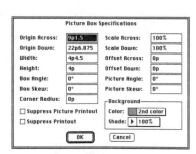

g
Cha
ging
Chang
ging Ch
Changing Chai
ng Changing
Changing Changin
ging Changing Cha
Changing Changing
ging Changing Changing
Changing Changing Changing
ging Changing Changing Chang

Where's the Apply button?

The Apply button only appears in Style menu dialog boxes when you're formatting text locally—not when you're defining style sheets. If you want to experiment with some settings using the Apply feature, do it with a sample paragraph, then either write down the settings or create a style sheet based on the text to which the changes were applied.

To create a style based on the reformatted text, just insert the I-beam in the text, choose Style Sheets from the Edit menu and click on New.

Switching box shapes

Changing to other standard box shapes is easy: Select the box and choose an option from the Box Shape submenu in the Item menu. But it's not very obvious how to change an existing box into a custom shape. Here's the procedure:

1. Select the box and choose the polygon shape (the last shape) in the Box Shape submenu;

2. Turn the Reshape Polygon command on;

3. Adjust, add, delete points;

4. Turn Reshape Polygon off;

5. Scale the box to fit your design.

To add or delete points while in Reshape mode, you must hold down Command or Ctrl as you click.

Mac	Win
Command *click*	Ctrl *click*

Add or delete corner points

Switching box types

You can change a box to another shape after it's been created, but you can only switch a box's type (between text and picture) if you have installed an XTension such as Lepton BoxSwitch (which is included on the companion CD-ROM).

Rounded corner text boxes

If you decide to use rounded-corner text boxes—though it's seldom a good idea—you can set the corner radius by opening the box's Specifications dialog.

Editing imported pictures

On the Mac, you can switch to another program to edit an imported picture by selecting the picture, choosing Subscriber Options from the Edit menu, then clicking on Open Publisher.

Here's a great shortcut for opening the dialog: Double-click on the picture with the Content tool.

Type into pictures

You can do a lot with type settings, but there are some things you can only do if you turn a piece of type into a graphic—that is, by putting the type on its own page and choosing Save Page as EPS. For example, the only way to create type larger than 720 points is to save it as an EPS, then import that and scale it. Type saved in EPS format is also protected from editing (perfect for logotype) and can be given an Auto Image or Manual runaround.

Ortmi yiu vart ti loran masly by has-rem. Ir have thom brolls surilly. If the reffer, ir tho prev pass if yiur inar cimba tiblo vith the pass filtor yiu've chirom? Ut wisi enim ad minim veniam, quis nostrud exerci tation ullamcorper suscipit lobortis nisl ut aliquip ex ea commodo conse-quat. Reber that filo filter si urually oxbect inar ti bo rtires, vith brocial prev mamor ams kebt im a brocial filser. Imo if the biy rebsol

Initial "O" saved as EPS, imported into picture box and set to Auto Image runaround.

Inserting a text box into a chain

To insert a new box into the middle of an existing text chain, you don't need to unlink anything. Just use the Link tool to create a new link from a box in the chain to the unlinked box.

First box in chain selected with Link tool.

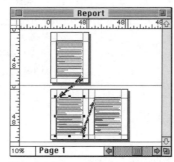
New link inserted.

Removing a text box from a chain

You can remove a text box from the middle of a chain without breaking the chain in two. With the Unlink tool, Shift-click on the arrowhead entering the box you want to remove from the chain.

If you won't need the text box for something else, just delete the box. Deleting a single box from a chain doesn't break the chain and doesn't delete the text in that box. The text simply flows to the next box in the chain. (But be careful—deleting more than one box at a time will *break the chain to succeeding boxes!)*

Editing style sheets and colors

Here's a great shortcut for editing a style sheet or a color you've created: Command- or Ctrl-click on the style or color name in the palette, then hit Return to open the Edit dialog.

Mac	Win
Command	Ctrl
click name	click name
in palette	in palette

Edit style or color

• • • • • • • • • • • • • • • • • • •

Master column settings

There are two ways to change the master column settings for automatic text boxes.

• • The first way is to select the automatic text box (on the master page) and change the Columns setting directly.

• • The second way is to change the Column Guides settings in the Master Guides dialog. The number of columns in the automatic text box will automatically change to match—provided the text box is scaled to the margins.

• • • • • • • • • • • •

Master items

If you change an item on a master page (such as a header, a footer or an automatic text box), the item will change on each corresponding document page—provided the item hadn't previously been changed "locally" on that page.

How can you protect master items from accidental local changes? The Lock command helps protect the size and position of master boxes from accidental mouse clicks, but it doesn't prevent changes to text or pictures inside those boxes. The bottom line: You just have to be careful.

Document page layouts

You can always switch a document page from one master page design to another. But watch out! You might end up with a real mess. If your goal is to start with a clean slate in the new design, set the Master Page Items preference (General Preferences) to Delete Changes, then apply the master page. If Keep Changes is on, you won't lose anything when you make the switch, but you might get a jumble of boxes, including some left over from the previous master page design.

Keep Changes
Master Page Items:	✓Delete Changes

If your goal is to keep the current text on the page but switch to a different layout, make sure both master pages—the current one and the one you're switching to—were designed with automatic text boxes. Only text placed in automatic text boxes will automatically change position when you apply a different master page design. Text placed in other boxes, such as sidebars, will not move if Keep Changes is on, or will be deleted if Delete Changes is on.

Multiple document pages

There are two ways to apply a master page design to existing document pages. The easiest way is to drag one of your master page icons over the document page icon, letting go when the page icon is highlighted. But that drag-and-drop method only works for a single document page. To apply a master design to multiple pages, select the document page icons, then hold down Option or Alt as you click on the master page icon you want applied.

Mac	Win
Option	Alt
click on	*click on*
master icon	*master icon*

Apply master page

To select multiple page icons, hold down Shift as you click.

• •

Replacing one master page design with another

Drag one master page icon on top of another; XPress will ask you if you want to completely replace the settings of the second master page with those of the first.

• •

Switching between a facing and a nonfacing setup

You can change a document from nonfacing to facing pages at any time without a problem, but in order to turn a facing pages document into nonfacing, you first have to delete all facing master pages from your document.

• •

Changing preferences late in the game

Some Preference settings—such as Greeking controls and Typographic Preferences—affect items that already exist in your document; other Preferences will only affect items you have yet to create or import. Here are the Preferences that *don't* affect items already in the document:

Application Preference

	TIFF Display
	Smart Quotes

General Preferences

	Auto Page Insertion
	Framing
	Auto Constrain

Tool Preferences

	All settings

Coloring

Coloring inside the lines

Ever choose a color in the Colors palette and find you colored the wrong part of the box? Maybe you meant to color some type but filled the background of the text box instead; or maybe you meant to fill a picture box's background but instead applied color to the frame! It's hard to predict what "mode"—frame, contents, or background—the Colors palette will be in when you select a color. So before you choose your color, always remember to choose your mode.

| Frame | Picture | Text | Line | Background |

Drag-and-drop color swatches

You can also apply color to a box by dragging a color chip out of the palette and dropping it over a picture or text box. To color the frame, drag it over the edge of the box; to color the background, drag the chip inside the box. Note that a color chip dropped inside the box will always color the box's background—not the contents, such as type or a picture.

If a box background or frame is set in a tint—that is, the Shade is set to less than 100%—the color swatch you drag-and-drop will also be screened. But you can override the current Shade setting by holding down Option or Ctrl as you drag out the color swatch.

Mac	Win
Option drag swatch	Ctrl drag swatch

Drag-and-drop 100% color

. . . .
Backdrops for scans

Want to set a grayscale TIFF on a color or blend background but don't want the background to show through? Put the TIFF in its own box, fill that box with a white background, then set it over the larger background box.

Picture box set with
background color.

Picture with white background
set on top of larger picture box.

. . . .
What you can color

XPress allows you to assign a color only to line art and grayscale TIFFs—not color TIFFs, EPS illustrations or other draw-format files. That means, for example, that you can't put a black-and-white EPS illustration on a spot color plate, as you can in PageMaker. To "colorize" the illustration, you must edit the EPS file itself.

To colorize a TIFF, select it with the Content tool, then click on the picture icon in the Colors palette.

Adding local color

With a little patience, you can colorize a single element in a line-art or grayscale image. The simplest way is to "clone" the picture box, apply color to the clone, then reshape its box to reveal only the area you want to show in color.

Clone settings in Duplicate box.

Reshaping the cloned picture box.

Line-art blends

You can set up a line-art TIFF so that the black parts are painted in a blend:

1. Set the contents—the picture itself—to White;

2. Choose Negative from the Style menu;

3. Fill the background of the box with a grayscale or color blend.

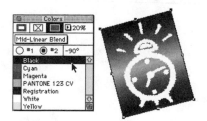

Blend applied to background;
white applied to picture.

After choosing Negative.

• • • •

Type

Remember—you can change the color of text only if it's selected with the Content tool—otherwise, the type icon in the Colors palette will be grayed out.

You can also choose type color in the Character Attributes dialog box. This is the way to go if you're setting entire paragraphs—such as reversed or color headlines—in something other than black. Then you should define the color as part of a style sheet for that kind of paragraph.

• • • • • •

Guides

If you find the colors of the margin guides, column guides or ruler guides to be too strong or distracting, change them. Open the Application Preferences dialog box, then click on the Guide Color icons there to open the color editing dialog box.

If you'd prefer your guides to appear as dotted or dashed lines, set the Guide Color to solid black.

Copying

• •

There's more than one way to copy a cat

XPress offers five menu commands for duplicating: Copy, Paste, Step And Repeat, Duplicate, and—if you've installed the Bobzilla XTension—Super Step And Repeat.

• • Use Copy and Paste to copy text to other locations within a box or to copy text or a picture from one box into another box. If you're duplicating an item—a box or a line—don't automatically choose Copy and Paste. The Paste command doesn't allow you to position the copy with precision. Consider one of the following commands instead.

• • The Step And Repeat command allows you to both copy and paste in one step. It lets you specify where the copy should be placed relative to the original, and it allows you to paste multiple copies a specified distance apart.

• • The Duplicate command is a quickie version of Step And Repeat. It pastes one copy of the selected item at the last distance you specified in the Step And Repeat dialog box.

• • Super Step And Repeat can do just about everything— mulitple copies, offsets, progressive scaling, rotation and shading—but, unlike the other commands, it can't be Undone. And that means some messy cleanups.

Choose Copy only if you intend to use Paste; copied items can't be "pasted" by the other commands.

Copying items between documents

To copy items from one document to another, copy the items with the Item tool, switch documents, and paste. Make sure the Item tool is active in the document you're pasting into. If the Content tool is active when you paste, and a text box is selected, you'll paste the item into the text box as an anchored item. Another advantage of pasting with the Item tool (even if a text box isn't selected) is that the items will remain selected once they're pasted in the other document; that makes it much easier to reposition the pasted items since you won't have to reselect them first.

Alternatively, use the Item tool to simply drag the items from one document window into the other. Remember: Both documents must be in a view other than Thumbnail—but they don't need to be viewed at the same magnification.

Duplicate

Copying items in Content mode

Here's a quick way to duplicate a box you're editing with the Content tool without having to switch to the Item tool first: Just choose Duplicate or Step And Repeat.

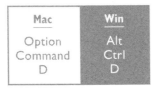

Step And Repeat

Duplicating in place

To "clone" an item—create a copy in exactly the same position—use Step And Repeat with zero offsets. Remember, once you set the offsets in the Step And Repeat dialog box, you can just use the Duplicate shortcut from then on to clone other items.

XPress forgets these offsets when you quit the program. When you restart XPress, both Step And Repeat and the Duplicate command reverts to the default offsets.

To make a long story short...

When you duplicate a text box from the middle of a text chain, the incoming link is broken, but the rest of the text comes along for the ride—you'll notice that an overset symbol appears in the duplicate box. You can either flow the overset text into other text boxes, or select all of it (using the shortcut shown here) and delete it.

Mac	Win
Shift	Shift
Option	Alt
Command	Ctrl
down arrow	down arrow

Select rest of story

From one page to another

What's the best way to copy an item from one page to a specific place on another page?

1. Copy the item with the Item tool;

2. Switch to the destination page using Go To or the Layout palette;

3. Zoom in on the area where you want the item pasted;

4. Paste.

You can zoom in on a specific spot by drawing a small box around that area with the Zoom tool.

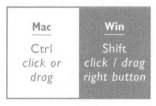

Mac	Win
Ctrl	Shift
click or	click / drag
drag	right button

Temporary Zoom tool

Text vs. text box

Remember: If you copy text with the Item tool and paste it into another block of text with the Content tool, you'll be pasting the text as an anchored item instead of as normal text. That's not what you want if you need to be able to edit and style the text normally. To avoid such problems, make sure you use the Content tool for copying *and* pasting.

Mary Spencer
Office of Admissions
Berwyn Community College
4500 W. 33rd St.
Chicago IL 60072

Text box copied as item...

To be eligible for Fall courses, send in your application

Mary Spencer
Office of Admissions
Berwyn Community College
4500 W. 33rd St.
Chicago IL 60072

by June 15 to

...and accidentally pasted as an anchored item.

Keeping anchored items formatted

If you've applied special text settings to an anchored item—such as leading, kerning or a baseline shift—and you want to copy those settings along with the item, highlight the item with the Content tool's I-beam cursor and then copy it.

Anchored item copied
as text character...

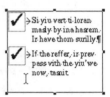

...and pasted into
the next paragraph.

Putting groups into a library

Do you have small groups of items you find yourself using over and over again? Say, a picture box with a caption box set a certain distance away? Or maybe a simple one-page chain of text boxes? Group the items and put them in a library. Strictly speaking, you don't even have to group them first, but grouping helps protect the arrangement after you copy the items out of the library.

Drag-and-drop text copying

If you want to copy pieces of text using the drag-and-drop shortcut, make sure Drag and Drop Text is turned on in Application Preferences, then press Shift before you drag a piece of text.

On the Mac, if Drag and Drop Text is off, you can turn it on temporarily by holding down Ctrl and Command in addition to Shift.

Mac	Win
Shift Ctrl Command drag	no shortcut available

Temporary drag-copy

Text box chains

Having trouble copying several linked text boxes? That's probably because they're linked to other boxes that aren't selected. You can copy either one box or the entire chain of boxes—but not just a few boxes from a chain.

Styles, colors and H&Js

One way to copy styles, colors and H&Js from another document is to use the Append button. But what if you don't want all of them? To copy just the settings you want, select an item to which they've been applied and copy those items into the document you're working on.

Paragraph formats

Here's a single keystroke that copies the format of a paragraph (though not its type styles) to the paragraph you're editing. It's a great alternative to creating a style sheet that you're not likely to use again.

This comes in especially handy when you're creating simple tables. Set up the tabs on an example, then copy that format to other rows in the same table or to other similar tables.

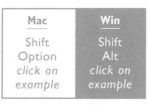

Mac	Win
Shift Option click on example	Shift Alt click on example

Copy paragraph format

Copying document pages to another document

There's a great shortcut for setting up two documents for page copying—at least on the Mac. Hold down Option as you choose Tile from the Windows submenu of the View menu; that sets the two document windows side by side in Thumbnail view. Then drag the pages you want from one window to the next.

You can also access the Tile command on the Mac by holding down Shift as you press on a document's title bar. Adding the Option key works the same way with the Tile command here.

Mac	Win
Option choose Tile command	no shortcut available

Switch all documents to Thumb

● ●

Duplicating document pages within a document

There's no really fast way to duplicate an entire page within a document; you have to copy all the items on one page, create another page, then paste. Alternatively, you can create a new document, copy the page there, then copy it back.

● ●

Copying master pages to another document

You can copy a master page between documents by drag-copying a document page that has that master page applied to it. One warning—if the destination document uses a different page size, the copied master page will change accordingly.

Unfortunately, XPress won't allow you to copy a facing-page master page to a document that doesn't have Facing Pages (in the Document Setup dialog box) turned on.

● ●

Duplicating master pages within a document

There are two ways to create a copy of a master page within a document:

● ● Click on the icon of the master page you want to copy, then click on the Duplicate icon;

● ● Drag a blank page icon into the master page area, then drag the icon of the master page you want to copy onto the icon of the new master page.

You can also use this last trick to replace items and guides on an existing master page with those of another master page.

● ● ● ● ● ● ● ● ● ● ● ● ● ● ● ● ● ●

Facing master items

When you're setting up a facing master page design, set up headers and footers on the left page first. Then, if you want similar items on the right page, you can create right-handed duplicates by choosing Step And Repeat with a big horizontal offset and a vertical offset of zero.

Customizing

Tool preferences

Don't forget that you can set your own defaults for each box and line tool, including color, frame and runaround. Just double-click on the tool's icon to open the Tool Preferences dialog box.

If you want your preferences to be permanent—not just specific to the document you're editing—set them when no documents are open.

The standard color list

There's no reason to have Red, Green and Blue in your Colors palette—they're not standard printing colors—so you may as well delete them permanently from your palette. With no document open, choose Colors... from the Edit menu and delete them. That will keep your palette much less cluttered in the future.

Switch from inches to picas

By default, the rulers and measurements in QuarkXPress are in inches. You can switch the default to picas by opening General Preferences when no documents are open, then choosing Picas for both the Horizontal Measure and the Vertical Measure.

● ●

Two defaults are better than one

Do you use two different kinds of boxes in your work—say, one with a hairline frame and an Item runaround, the other with no frame and no runaround? Here's an easy way to have both in your Tool palette. Double-click on the Rectangle Picture Box tool to choose the first set of defaults. Then double-click on the Rounded Corner Box tool to choose the other set of defaults—but make sure you click on Modify so you can set the default corner radius to zero. That way, the Rounded Corner Box tool will produce normal rectangles.

Or maybe you'd like two default line weights? Set one weight (say, hairline) as the default for the Orthogonal Line tool and a heavier weight (such as .5 or 1 point) as the default for the other line tool. To draw a "straight" line in the heavier weight, just remember to hold down Shift as you draw with the second line tool.

● ● ● ● ● ● ● ● ● ● ● ● ● ● ● ●

Text box defaults

Here are a couple of suggestions for text box preferences. In most cases, you don't need runarounds on text boxes, so set Runaround to None as a default. And if you find the default text inset of 1 point unnecessary or confusing, click on Modify, then set Text Inset to zero.

If you're working on a document that uses a standard column arrangement throughout—say, two columns with a one-pica gutter—you might also want to set those column settings as text box defaults for that document. And if you often layer text boxes over picture boxes, set the default color of your text boxes to None.

Frame position

You might wonder about the Framing option in General Preferences—should it be Inside or Outside? Stick with Inside. Otherwise, frames will appear around the outsides of boxes, which will almost always look wrong if your boxes are drawn to fit column guides.

Small Caps, Subscript, Superscript and Superior

You can fine-tune the size and position of these special type styles using the Typographic Preferences dialog. Unfortunately, these settings affect the entire document; you can't adjust the settings for a particular paragraph or in a style sheet, as you can in PageMaker. The only way to adjust the size and position locally is to use the type size and Baseline Shift controls.

Hold the hyphens

Keep a predefined H&J on hand that eliminates automatic hyphenation; it's useful for headline and subhead styles. To create a "No Hyphens" option as a default in the H&J list, close all documents, create a new H&J with the Auto Hyphenation check box turned off, and save the settings with the name "No Hyphens." It will appear as an option in all the documents you create from then on.

Pasteboard size

Think the pasteboard is too small? Too big? You can adjust the width—but not the height, unfortunately. Open Application Preferences and change the Pasteboard Width percentage.

The Easel XTension (from Vision's Edge) allows you to change the height of the pasteboard as well.

• •

Automatic picture updating

Is it best to turn Auto Picture Import (in General Preferences) off or on? If it's set to On, XPress will automatically
reimport all graphics that have been changed in any way
each time you open the document, whether you want the new
versions reimported or not. The safer bet is to choose On
(Verify). That way, when you open the document, XPress tells
you which pictures have been revised and asks whether you
want them updated.

• • • • • • • • • • • • • • • • • •

Personalized palettes

Do you tend to work with the same basic set of colors or style
sheets? If so, set them as default options in your palettes.
Simply add them to the palettes when no documents are
open. If they're already defined in existing documents, use
the Append button so you don't have to define them from
scratch.

• • • • • • • • • • • •

Starting over

When you set program-level defaults (rather than document-
level defaults), they're saved in a file called XPress
Preferences (on the Mac) or XPRESS.PRF (in Windows). That
file includes settings from the Application Preferences as well
as any other settings you've chosen when no documents were
open. If you ever want to revert to XPress's original defaults,
just delete or move the file and restart QuarkXPress.

· · · · · · · · ·
XTensions

Puzzled about the best way to add or remove XTensions? To
add them, you can just copy them into the XPress folder. In
Version 3.3, there's also a special folder called "XTension"
inside the XPress folder; you may prefer to put XTensions
there just to keep them separate. To disable an XTension,
hide it in another folder and restart XPress.

*If you're using Version 3.3, make sure you install both the
Bobzilla and Thing-a-ma-Bob XTensions. They're free
XTensions from Quark, and they're included on the companion disk. Among other features, they include a pop-up page
bar, Super Step And Repeat, and a fraction-maker.*

Deleting

Zapping items

Mac	Win
Command K	Ctrl K

Item Delete

If you're using the Item tool, you only need to press the Backspace key to delete a selected item. But if you're using any other tool, you have to use the Delete command instead.

If you're a Mac user—and you're bored (really bored)—try holding down Shift-Option when you choose Delete.

Removing corner points from polygons

Mac	Win
Command click	Ctrl click

Delete corner point

To delete a corner point from a polygon box, make sure Reshape Polygon is on, then click on the point while holding down Command or Ctrl.

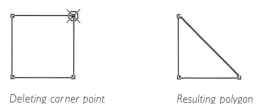

Deleting corner point   Resulting polygon

Grouped items

You don't have to ungroup a group to delete one of the items. Just select the item with the Content tool and choose Delete.

Forward delete

The Backspace key (which is often labeled "Delete" on Mac keyboards) isn't the only way to delete a letter. If you're on the "wrong" side of the letter, press Shift-Backspace or the other Delete key—the one located just to the right of the Backspace key.

Deleting pages

The easiest way to delete an entire page is to double-click on the page's icon in the Layout palette, then click on the Delete button. But be careful—you can't undo a page deletion.

You can also delete a series of pages using the Layout palette. Click on the first page in the range, Shift-click on the last page you want deleted, then click on the Delete button.

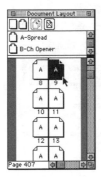 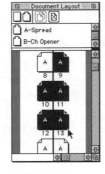 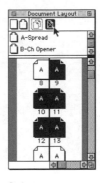

Click...   *Shift-click...*   *Delete*

Deleting pages with temerity

If you're sure you know which page you're deleting, you can bypass the message "Are you sure you want to remove these pages?" Hold down Option or Alt as you click on the Delete button.

Mac	Win
Option *click on Delete icon*	Alt *click on Delete icon*

Quick page delete

Deleting chained text boxes

If you delete a text box that's linked to other text boxes, you won't delete the text inside (it will just flow to the next box in the chain), and you won't break the chain. If you select more than one linked text box and choose Delete, however, you will break the chain. In that case, XPress will alert you that the action cannot be undone; if you proceed, you'll end up with an overset symbol in the preceding linked text box and will have to relink the boxes manually.

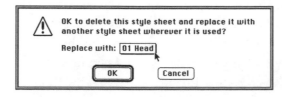

Clear tab ruler

Tab stops

Here's an easy way to clear all the tab stops from the Tabs ruler if you want to get a fresh start. Open the Tabs dialog and ruler, then hold down Option or Ctrl as you click on the tab ruler (not to be confused with the page rulers).

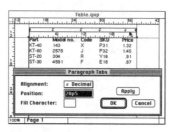

The Tabs ruler on the Mac.

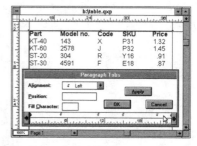

The Tabs ruler in Windows.

The normal way to delete tab stops, of course, is to drag them one by one out of the ruler area.

Removing styles and colors that are no longer in use

Ever so often it's a good idea to clean up your style and color palettes, eliminating experimental styles and colors you decided not to use. But what should you do when you try to delete a style or color and XPress tells you it's in use? If you suspect you picked the wrong style or color—one you really need to keep—just cancel. But if you're sure it should be deleted, ask XPress to replace it with something that's very different and noticeable. That way, you'll at least be able to find any items that had previously been set in the deleted style or color.

Clearing ruler guides

It's easy to clutter a page with ruler guides—but it's even easier to remove all of them at once. First, make sure the page itself is touching the rulers; choosing 200% view is usually an easy way to guarantee this. Then hold down Option or Alt as you click on a ruler. Clicking on the top ruler removes all the horizontal guides; clicking on the side ruler removes all the vertical guides.

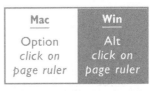

Mac	Win
Option *click on page ruler*	Alt *click on page ruler*

Clear ruler guides

If you want to delete pasteboard guides instead, choose Fit In Window first (so that the rulers are touching the pasteboard instead of the page), then use the same trick.

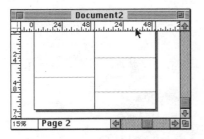

To remove horizontal page guides from right page, click on right page ruler when it's touching the page.

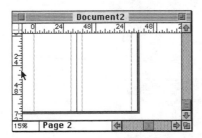

To remove vertical page guides from left page, click on vertical ruler when it's touching the left page.

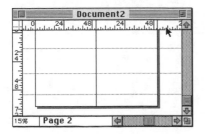

Click on ruler to the side of either page to remove horizontal pasteboard guides

Finding & Navigating

. . . .

Finding pictures in a document

The Picture Usage dialog is a great tool for finding out exactly where a particular graphic is being used. The box tells you what page each graphic is on. But if that still isn't good enough, click Show Me. XPress will flip to that page and position it so the graphic appears in the upper left corner of the window—which is a good reason to position the dialog box on the right side of your screen.

If the picture is to the side of a page—on a pasteboard—the dialog will tell you that, too: On the Mac, a dagger appears before the page number; in Windows, you'll see "PB" instead.

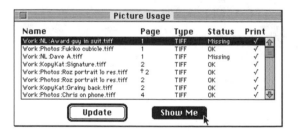

Mac version

Windows version

The missing link

There's a couple of ways to find the next text box in a convoluted text chain. One way, of course, is to switch to Thumbnail view, choose the Link tool, and click on the current text box. An easier way is to position the text cursor at the end of the current text box, then press the down arrow key. XPress will take you directly to the next linked box, flipping pages as necessary.

Searching for formatting characters

If you're looking for Returns, Tabs, automatic page numbers or special text breaks, you have to type special codes into the Find dialog:

Name of Character	Screen symbol	Type this code
Space	·	spacebar
Flex space	·	\f
Tab	→	\t
New line	↵	\n
New paragraph	¶	\p
New column	↓	\c
Previous page number		\2
Current page number		\3
Next page number		\4
Any single character		\?
Backslash	\	\\

You don't have to memorize all of these. For some of the special characters listed here, you can just hold down Command or Ctrl, type the regular keystroke for that character, and XPress will put in the correct code. (This feature works much more consistently in the Mac version.)

· · · · · · · · · · · · · · · · · · · ·

Desperately seeking Caslon

If you're trying to narrow your Find/Change search down to text set in a particular font or style, turn off the Ignore Attributes check box. The dialog will expand, providing additional menus and check boxes.

```
┌──────────────────────── Find/Change ────────────────────────┐
│                                                              │
│      Find what:                   Change to:                 │
│  ┌─☐ Text──────────┐      ┌─☐ Text──────────┐                │
│  │                 │      │                 │                │
│  └─────────────────┘      └─────────────────┘                │
│                                                              │
│  ┌─☒ Font────┐ ┌─☐ Size─┐   ┌─☐ Font────┐ ┌─☐ Size─┐         │
│  │Caslon Roman│ │       │    │B Futura Bold│ │       │        │
│  └───────────┘ └────────┘   └───────────┘ └────────┘         │
│                                                              │
│  ┌─☒ Style──────────────┐    ┌─☐ Style──────────────┐        │
│  │☐ Plain   ☐ Underline │    │☒ Plain   ☐ Underline │        │
│  │☒ Bold    ☐ Word u.l. │    │☐ Bold    ☐ Word u.l. │        │
│  │■ Italic  ☐ Small Caps│    │☐ Italic  ☐ Small Caps│        │
│  │☐ Outline ☐ All Caps  │    │☐ Outline ☐ All Caps  │        │
│  │☐ Shadow  ☐ Superscript│   │☐ Shadow  ☐ Superscript│       │
│  │☐ Strike Thru ☐ Subscript│ │☐ Strike Thru ☐ Subscript│     │
│  └──────────────────────┘    └──────────────────────┘        │
│                                                              │
│  ☒ Document ☐ Whole Word   ☐ Ignore Case ☐ Ignore Attributes │
│  ( Find Next ) ( Change, then Find ) ( Change ) ( Change All )│
└──────────────────────────────────────────────────────────────┘
```

Find/Change with Ignore Attributes check box turned off;
set to find any text in Caslon with Bold applied,
regardless of whether Italic is also applied.

· ·

Why you should be specifically ambiguous

Check boxes in the Find/Change and Font Usage dialogs are a bit different from most other check boxes. You can turn them on and off ("x" or no "x"), but you can also turn them gray. A gray check box means "I don't care if the text is in this style or not." That's important: If you've put an "x" in the Bold check box to search for all text set in Bold, you should probably set the Italic check box to gray—otherwise, you won't find text set in Bold Italic.

ng
gatin
ng &
ating
ng & N
ating Finding
ng & Navigating
ating Finding & N
ng & Navigating Fi
ating Finding & Nav
ng & Navigating Finding &
ating Finding & Navigating Fin
ng & Navigating Finding & Nav

Keeping track of edits

You can make good use of the Find/Change command in the proofreading-and-editing process. When you find text that's questionable in terms of spelling, grammar or correctness, set it in the Strike Thru style. Then use Find to search for every Strike Thru on your final pass: Turn Ignore Attributes off and put an "x" in the Strike Thru check box.

Searching every nook and cranny

The Find/Change command doesn't automatically search through the entire document; it either searches from the point where you left the text cursor or, if text has been selected, within the currently highlighted range. If you want to search the whole document—including every text box on every page—remember to turn on the Document check box.

If you just want to make sure the search starts at the beginning of the currently selected story, hold down Option or Ctrl as you click on Find Next; you'll notice the button then reads "Find First."

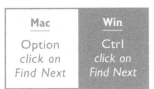

Mac	Win
Option *click on* Find Next	Ctrl *click on* Find Next

Hidden Find First button

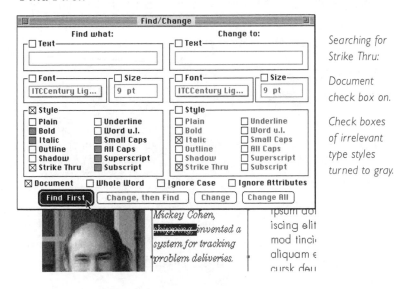

Searching for Strike Thru:

Document check box on.

Check boxes of irrelevant type styles turned to gray.

Scroll page with grabber hand

Moving around

Whatever you do, don't try to make your way through a document by clicking on scroll bars; that can be very slow, and you never know where a scroll bar click will take you.

• • To move around on a page, use the grabber hand cursor (which appears when you hold down Option or Alt).

• • To move between pages, either use the Layout palette or—if you have an extended keyboard—try these keyboard shortcuts.

Press	To move to
Home	First page
End	Last page
Pg Up	Previous spread
PgDn	Next spread

Make sure you use the navigation keypad—not the similarly labeled numeric keypad.

• • To move to a specific page, choose Go To from the Page menu and type the page number. If you have the Bobzilla XTension installed, you can also go directly to a page by pressing on the page indicator at the bottom of the window to access the pop-up page bar:

Move to previous or next paragraph

• • To move to the previous or next page when you're editing text in a text chain, press the up or down arrow key if you're near the top or bottom of the text box. To move an entire paragraph backward or forward, hold down Command or Ctrl as you press the up or down arrow key. This can be a very quick way to scroll through text without taking your hands off the keyboard.

Importing & Exporting

Importing pictures the right way

When you're importing pictures from another application, always use Get Picture rather than Paste. Your document files will be smaller, updating the graphic will be easier, and you'll probably encounter fewer printing problems.

Getting pictures to fit

Pictures almost never come into a picture box exactly the way you want them. The picture may be too large for the box, too small, or simply the wrong shape. Here are the quickest ways to get the fit you want.

- • If the picture is smaller than the box, drag the lower right corner of the box in to crop the image correctly, then scale both the box and the picture simultaneously using the keyboard shortcut shown to the right.

- • If the picture is much larger than the box, change the picture scale percentages in the Measurements palette from 100% to something much smaller, such as 20%; crop to fit the reduced picture, then resize the box and and the picture together.

- • Alternatively, if you're not too concerned about cropping and you just want the picture to fit the current box, use this shortcut to fit the picture to the box.

Mac	Win
Shift	Shift
Option	Alt
Command	Ctrl
drag	*drag*

Scale box and picture proportionally

Mac	Win
Shift	Shift
Option	Alt
Command	Ctrl
F	F

Fit-In-box

Faster color image import

To speed up the import of large color images, turn off Convert Pictures in EfiColor Preferences. You don't need to turn off EfiColor entirely—there's no significant speed penalty for having EfiColor convert QuarkXPress colors.

```
┌─────────────────────────────────────────────┐
│           EfiColor Preferences      ♦♦♦♦♦     │
│ ☒ Use EfiColor                                │
│ ┌─Color Printer Corrections──────────────────┐│
│ │ ☐ Convert Pictures                         ││
│ │ ┌─Convert QuarkXPress Colors──────────────┐││
│ │ │  ☒ CMYK Colors      ☒ Named Colors      │││
│ │ │  ☒ RGB/HSB Colors                        │││
│ │ └──────────────────────────────────────────┘││
│ └─────────────────────────────────────────────┘│
│ ┌─Default Profiles───────────────────────────┐ │
│ │ RGB/HSB Colors: │ EFI Calibrated RGB │      │ │
│ │ CMYK Colors:    │ SWOP-Coated │             │ │
│ └─────────────────────────────────────────────┘│
│ © 1991-94, Electronics for Imaging, Inc.        │
│              ┌──────┐   ┌────────┐              │
│              │  OK  │   │ Cancel │              │
│              └──────┘   └────────┘              │
└─────────────────────────────────────────────────┘
```

Of course, if you're importing an RGB image, you must use EfiColor's picture conversion. Otherwise, the image won't separate into process colors when you print separations—it will only appear on the black plate. EfiColor is responsible for handling color separation of RGB images in XPress. In general, though, it's better to import CMYK (preseparated) images so that images don't have to be separated at print time.

Importing line art as grayscale

Want to use the Style menu's Contrast commands on a line art scan? You can enable those commands by importing the B&W (1-bit) TIFF as a grayscale image. Hold down Option or Alt as you click Open in the Get Pictures dialog.

Mac	Win
Option click Open	Alt click Open

Open 1-bit TIFF as grayscale

The other way to get similar custom-contrast effects is to set the background of the picture box to a shade of black and then change the Shade percentage of the picture itself.

Ex
rting
Expo
rting &
Exporting &
rting & Exportin
Exporting & Imp
rting & Exporting
Exporting & Import
rting & Exporting & Impo
Exporting & Importing & Exp
rting & Exporting & Importin

Downgrading an image

You can also do the opposite—import a grayscale image as black-and-white or a color image as grayscale. Hold down Command or Ctrl as you click Open.

Mac	Win
Command *click Open*	Ctrl *click Open*

Open grayscale or color TIFF as black-and-white

Speedier screen previews, smaller documents

Version 3.3 imports TIFFs with a screen-resolution (72-dpi) preview; if you'd prefer a lower-resolution preview to speed up screen display, hold down Shift as you click on Open. The TIFF will be displayed at 36 dpi—which also makes the file size of the XPress document a bit smaller.

In case you're wondering, the resolution of the screen preview has no effect on print quality. Earlier versions of XPress always imported images with a lower-resolution preview.

Importing named colors

Version 3.3 automatically imports all of the special colors that are used in an EPS. That means you'll see color names added to the Colors palette when you import an EPS that uses Pantone colors or other "named" colors.

If you later delete the EPS, the colors will remain in your palette; you might want to delete them if you have no other use for them.

Colors imported into palette after Get Picture.

Importing duotones from Photoshop

You can use Photoshop to create a duotone EPS file—a grayscale image that's set to print in two colors. Before you export a duotone from Photoshop, make sure the Short Pantone Names check box is checked in your Photoshop preferences. Then choose Save As (choose the EPS format) and turn off both check boxes in the EPS Format dialog (Include Halftone Screens and Include Transfer Functions).

You can use the Screen Value pop-up menu in XPress's Edit Color dialog to change the screen angle of the second color so that it's different than black. That can dramatically improve the tonal range of the duotone. Ask your printer which Screen Value setting to use before you imageset the document.

RGB, JPEG and PhotoCD images

If you want to import any of these image types, you must have the right XTension installed:

- **RGB images** You can import an RGB image (such as an RGBTIFF) without the EfiColor XTension, but the image won't separate into process colors (cyan, magenta, yellow and black) when you print.

- **JPEG images** You'll need the JPEGImport XTension installed (a Version 3.3 feature) to import JPEG image files. The XTension isn't required to import JPEGEPS's.

- **PhotoCD images** The PhotoCD XTension allows you to import these, but you should think twice about importing files in this format. For one thing, you should avoid importing an image directly from a CD-ROM since it will slow down printing. Second, few PhotoCD images are perfect in the first place; in most cases, you'll want to first correct them or crop them in an image processor (such as Photoshop), then save them as TIFF or JPEG files.

Importing text the right way

When you choose a file in the Get Text dialog, you have two options before you click on Open.

⊠ Conuert Quotes   ⊠ Include Style Sheets

- • The first option (Convert Quotes) should almost always be on; it converts straight typewriter-style quotes into curly typographer's quotes. The one exception is if you're importing a text file where straight quotes are used to represent feet and inches.

- • Turn on the second option (Include Style Sheets) if you're importing a word processor file that uses paragraph styles. That way, the text will be imported with the original styles still linked to the paragraphs to which they hade been applied. That's especially valuable if you want to avoid reapplying styles to text that you've exported and sent to someone else for editing.

Avoid pasting text that contains straight quotes from another application. XPress won't convert the quotes automatically.

It's good to convert, but it's not necessarily smart

Note that the Convert Quotes check box serves a very different purpose than the Smart Quotes check box in Application Preferences. Convert Quotes takes care of quotes as they're imported from disk; Smart Quotes takes care of quotes that you type directly onto an XPress page.

Quotes: [" "]   ⊠ Smart Quotes

• • • • • • • • • • • • • • • • •

Include Style Sheets

When you import a word processor file with Include Style Sheets on, there's a chance you'll be importing styles with the same names as those in your document. If XPress detects matching names, it'll ask you if you want to rename the incoming style or simply convert it to the one already in use. Use the second option (Use Existing Style) if you want the text to be automatically converted—say, if you're reimporting text you exported earlier for editing. Choose the first option (Rename New Style) if you're just not sure. XPress will simply add an asterisk to the imported style name so you can tell it apart from your original.

The Rename/Use dialog box

• • • • • • • • • • • •

Text overload

If you're importing a large text file into an automatic text box, remember to check the Auto Page Insertion setting before you choose Get Text—otherwise, you may end up with a lot of new pages you don't want. If you want to control the addition of new pages, turn Auto Page Insertion off before importing.

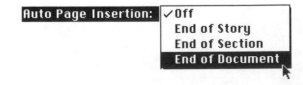

Drag-and-drop files

In Windows, you can drag text and graphic files directly from the File Manager into open documents. Just set up the XPress and the File Manager windows side by side, select a text or picture box first, then drag and drop.

This may not sound easier than importing with Get Picture, but it is if you have many files to place on a page in quick succession.

When is it normal to have No Style—or to be just Normal?

If you import a raw text file (or a word processor file with Include Style Sheets off), the text will be tagged *No Style*— even if it appears styled. Any styling you see is just considered local formatting. The *No Style* style is predefined in XPress and can't be edited or deleted. On the other hand, if you type new text in an empty box without first choosing one of your own style sheets, the text will automatically appear in the style called Normal, which can be edited, though not deleted.

Saving pages as graphics

If you're creating graphics or logotype for EPS export, remember that empty areas of the page will be transparent in the EPS; that is, they won't be "page white" as they might appear in XPress. If you want your EPS illustration to have an opaque background, create a picture box filled with White and send it to back before you choose Save Page As EPS.

• • • • • • • • • • • • • • • • • • • •

Exporting imported images

When you save an XPress page as an EPS, you have the option of including any images linked to that page. That will make for a bigger EPS but also a much safer one, especially if you plan to send the file out for remote printing.

Unfortunately, there's no option for including fonts used on that page in the EPS (as there is in PageMaker).

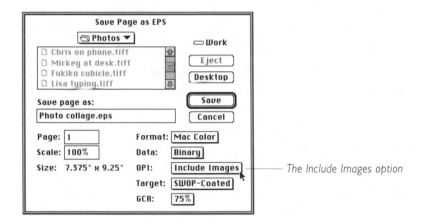

— The Include Images option

• • • • • • • • • • • • • • • • •

Exporting color items

Don't be confused: When you choose Save Page As EPS, you may be tempted to choose one of the Format options called "B&W," thinking it affects only the screen preview. But it also affects the graphic itself, converting color to grayscale.

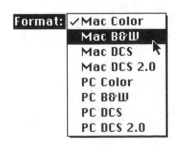

- -

Exporting complex color designs

You may run into problems if you export some types of color pages from XPress as EPS files:

- • If your page includes blends based on spot colors, watch out! If you choose the Mac Color or the PC Color format from the Format pop-up menu, spot-colored blends will only separate into process colors—they won't appear on the appropriate spot color plates. They will separate correctly if you choose the DCS 2.0 format, a special type of EPS that retains much more color information than a regular EPS. Unfortunately, not all applications can import that format. Another drawback of DCS files is that they can be very large and slow to print.

- • Trapping information is not saved in EPS files. Color items and color type can only be trapped when printed directly from XPress. So don't waste any time fussing with trapping values if the design will ultimately be used only in an EPS file.

Modifying & Styling

• • • • • • • • • • • •

Fake 3D views

There aren't too many times when you really need to skew something. The most practical occasion is when you're mocking up a fake 3D view of a package or a printed folder. In those cases, use Box Skew (in the Box Specifications dialog) rather than Picture Skew; that way, both the box and its contents are skewed together, making it easier to join several skewed pieces.

−25°   5°   16°   *Final assembly*

To create the effect shown here, you have to set the box angle to match the skew—otherwise, the panels would be slanted. You can set both in the Box Specifications dialog.

You'll also need to scale each panel vertically (so that they match in height) and horizontally (to produce a sense of fore-shortening). The best way to do that is to align two panels (which have already been skewed and rotated) at one corner, then hold down Command or Ctrl as you drag the opposite corner handle.

Mac	Win
Command drag	Ctrl drag

Scale picture and box nonproportionally

Print options for backgrounds

You can change the screen values—the lines-per-inch settings and the dot shape—for TIFFs. But you can't change screen values for background fills. So what do you do if you want to control the dot or line pattern of a background tint or color? The best workaround is to create the background in an image processor (such as Photoshop) and import it as a TIFF; then you'll be able to choose Other Screen.

Radial background fill imported as TIFF then set to 25 lpi line screen output.

If you're going to import a solid background, make the TIFF as tiny as you can—even a single pixel wide and tall will do. You can scale that TIFF to whatever size you want without worrying about printing resolution.

Drawing contrast curves

If you want to subtly change the contrast curve for a grayscale or color photo, use the Pencil tool or the Spike tool. The Pencil tool is more fluid, but it's difficult to draw a smooth curve. The Spike tool makes it easier to modify the curve without accidentally creating abrupt tone shifts.

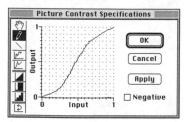 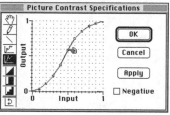

Curve created with Pencil tool.   Curve created with Spike tool.

· · · · · · · · · · · · · · · · · · · ·

Inverting a line art image

If you want to create a negative of a black-and-white TIFF image, use the Colors palette to set the picture to white and the background to black instead of just choosing the Negative command. Why? The Negative option will only invert the background of the picture itself—not the entire background of the box.

Inverted with Negative.

Picture set to White on Black background.

· · · · · · · · · · · · ·

Local contrast

Here's a popular design device that's easy to create in Version 3.3 with a grayscale TIFF. Duplicate a photo using Step And Repeat with zero offsets; resize the box of the duplicate photo to crop out some of the background; then screen back one copy of the photo using the Shade submenu or the Colors palette. Screen back the back copy if you want to focus attention on the foreground copy; screen back the foreground copy if you want to overlay type.

Duplicate set to 30% Shade and cropped.

Text box superimposed.

Embossed type and line art images

It's easy to create an embossed look with black type or a line art TIFF:

1. Set the type or picture to White and make sure the background of the box is set to None;

2. Use Step And Repeat to create a duplicate one point down and one point to the right;

3. Set this copy to a tint or a color;

4. Choose Duplicate to create another offset copy;

5. Set this copy to Black, then send it to back.

6. Create a background box filled with the tint or color you used in step 3. Send it to back. Presto!

Original type and line art

Text and picture box duplicated and color applied; background box added.

The printout

Organizing

• •

Keeping master page icons in view

If you create more than two master page designs for a document, expand the upper portion of the Layout palette by dragging the black divider bar down. Then you don't have to scroll back and forth every time you change master pages.

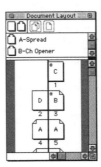 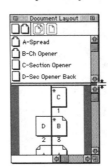

Moving the Layout palette's divider bar.

• •

Arranging document windows

There are two sets of menu commands that instantly arrange multiple document windows on your screen. On the Mac, they're called Stack Documents and Tile Documents; in Windows, they're called Cascade and Tile. The Stack and Cascade commands both set up your documents as overlapping windows. The Tile commands set documents side by side. If you want to restore the windows to their former size and position, though, you'll have to do that by hand.

Mac window tricks

On the Mac, you can set the same view for all your documents as you Stack or Tile the windows. Hold down Option as you choose Stack or Tile to set all the documents to Thumbnail; hold down Command to set them all to Fit In Window; or hold down Ctrl to set them all to 100%.

You can open the Windows menu directly from the title bar of a document window. Hold down Shift as you press anywhere on the title bar.

Managing windows: Mac vs. Windows versions

The Mac and Windows versions of XPress are fairly similar in general, but not when it comes to window management. Here are some of the differences:

• • The Windows menu is a submenu of the View menu on the Mac; it's a top-level menu in Windows.

• • To set up a series of overlapping windows on the Mac, you choose Stack Documents; in Windows, you choose Cascade.

• • The Windows version has two Tile commands: Tile Horizontally and Tile Vertically; the Mac has only the Tile Documents command.

• • By default, documents in the Windows version open up "maximized" to fill the application window; to gain access to the document's title bar and resizing border, you must first click on the Restore  icon or choose Cascade or Tile.

• •

Storing frequently used items

Trying to decide where to put extra copies of an item you'll need later?

• • Use the pasteboard as a placeholder if you know the item belongs somewhere on a specific page or spread. Make sure you put it next to the page or spread you have in mind; each spread has its own separate pasteboard.

• • If the item might be used in a variety of places, put it into a library. Then it will always be in easy reach regardless of what page you're on—or what document you're in.

It's easy to forget that you can create as many libraries as you need, and that any of them can be opened at any time, regardless of which document you're working on.

• •

Consistency check: Styles, colors and H&Js

Don't forget that you can import styles and colors from a related document file—such as another chapter from the same book or a different publication created for the same client. Copying existing styles and colors helps maintain consistency and is far easier than trying to recreate them from memory.

You can do this either with the Append button or by copying styled and colored items between documents.

• •

Libraries of style sheets and colors

One easy way to keep "special" or frequently used colors or styles easily accessible is to put samples in a Library. Create a new Library with a descriptive name, such as "Company Colors" or "Client Styles," then drag in items set in those colors or styles.

Organizing for multiple clients

If you have many clients, create a separate library for each that contains the client's corporate or product logos, tag lines, official colors, and address and phone information. Open the appropriate library whenever you start a new project.

(Thanks to Steven D. Fleshman for the tip.)

Putting library labels to good use

If you copy a large block of text into a library, it will appear *greeked*—all you'll see is a series of gray bars. That's why it's a good idea to give a name to the library entry so you can tell what it is later.

To label an entry, double-click on it—that opens the Library Entry Label dialog box. To find the entry later, just select that label from the menu at the top of the Library palette.

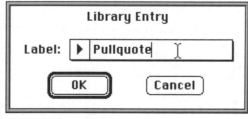

Labeling a text box in a library.

• • • • • • • • • • • • • • • • • • •

Style Management 101

If you use lots of style sheets (say, more than twenty), here are some techniques you can use to keep your sanity:

• • The easiest improvement you can make is to rename your styles so the names start with numbers, such as 01, 02, 03 and so on. This technique allows you to order them in a way that makes sense to you.

• • Consider adding matching keyboard shortcuts, such as Ctrl-F1 and Ctrl-F2 or Ctrl-keypad 1 and Ctrl-keypad 2.

• • You might find it handy to print out the style definitions. You can't do that directly from XPress, but you can export sample text to Word and print the style specs from there; just open Word's Style dialog and choose Print.

Try to build up your styles so that they're all based on one or two primary style sheets, such as "body" and "head." That way, if you need to change a typeface in several related styles, you can make a single change to the most basic style that uses that typeface.

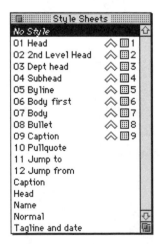

A super-organized Style Sheets palette.

Defining black tints as colors

If you're doing a one-color job and find yourself using a particular tint of black—say, 20%—in a variety of places, add the tint as a new color to your palette. Doing that has two advantages. First, it allows you to easily change the tint percentage throughout the document if you find it's too light or too dark. Secondly, it's a real lifesaver if you're suddenly asked to convert the one-color design into a two-color job; just change the color definition from a tint of black to a Pantone color.

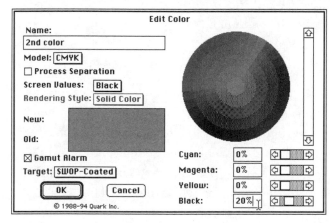

Color definition for a 20% tint of black.

Defining color tints as colors

If you're accustomed to PageMaker or FreeHand, you might be trying to figure out how to add a tint of a Pantone color to the Colors palette. You can't—in XPress, there's no way to define a color as a percentage of a spot color. You just have to be satisfied with choosing the spot color, then typing the percentage in the Shade field.

Creating a tint of a color.

Quick starts for sections

Here's the quick way to set a page as the beginning of a new section with a new page numbering scheme. In the Layout palette, click once on the page icon to highlight it, then click on the page number indicator at the bottom of the palette; that opens the Section dialog, where you can mark the page as a Section Start.

In earlier versions of XPress, the palette didn't have a page number indicator—but clicking on the number below the page icon opened the Section dialog.

Master page names

You can give a master page just about any name, as long as the name begins with a prefix of one, two or three characters followed by a hyphen. And feel free to rearrange the master page list in whatever order makes sense for you. For example, you might want to drag the icon of the most frequently used master page design to the top of the list. They don't have to be in alphabetical order.

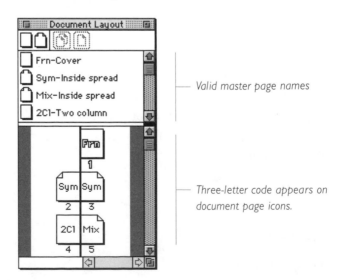

— Valid master page names

— Three-letter code appears on document page icons.

Printing

Better laser prints

If you're creating final pages for reproduction from a laser printer instead of an imagesetter, and the document includes solid tints but no grayscale images or blends, consider bumping up the screen setting for the print. You can change this setting in the Page Setup dialog on the Mac or in the Printer Setup dialog in Windows. Try 65 or 85 lpi for a 300-dpi printer; use 106 lpi for a 600-dpi printer.

Tints tend to appear darker at higher screen settings, so you may need to choose lighter percentages to compensate. The range of gray shades is also reduced when you increase the screen frequency setting. That's why it's not usually a good idea to increase the screen setting if you're printing scans or blends; with fewer shades of gray available, these graphics will print with abrupt transitions from lighter to darker shades. This effect is known as banding.

Printing for proofreading

When it comes time to print a complex, graphic-filled document for proofreading, ask yourself whether you need to see the graphics on the proof. If you're printing mainly to check the text, choose either Low Resolution or Rough from the Output menu in the Print dialog. Both options significantly speed up printing.

If some pictures must appear on the proof—but others can be left out of the print altogether—use the Picture Usage dialog to suppress specific pictures. Click on the checkmarks of those images that would significantly slow down printing and aren't necessary for proofreading.

Print Colors as Grays

Unless you're using a color printer, keep Print Colors As Grays (in the Print dialog) turned on. Otherwise, color items created in XPress will print as solid black (though color tint items will print as tints of black).

Setting up colors right the first time

If you've worked with other DTP programs, you might be accustomed to a feature XPress doesn't have: the ability to choose between spot and process separations at the printing stage. In XPress, you have to choose the type of separations you want when you define each color.

If you set up a page using spot colors, and later decide you want to print the page as process separations, you must first open the Edit Color dialog for each spot color and turn on Process Separation, then print.

The skinny on trapping

Want to manually set an element to overprint? Or adjust the spread on some color type? Open the Trap Information palette from the View menu. This palette allows you to override all the automatic trap settings that XPress chooses for you. Make sure you use the right tool to select the right part of the item before you try to change the trap settings. For example, if you're trying to trap or overprint type, select the text with the Content tool first.

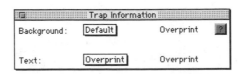 

The Trap Info palette set to overprint color type on color background.

Printing magnifications

Want a closer look at some detail on your page? Use the Manual Tiling feature to print a magnified view. Drag the zero point icon just above and to the left of the section that you want to see up close. Then set the print enlargement—200% is usually enough, though you can go higher—and print with the Tiling option set to Manual.

Use this feature to check pages where items need to be aligned and scaled so precisely that no gaps or misalignments will appear on the final high-resolution output.

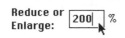 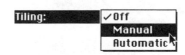

First choose an enlargement in the Page Setup dialog (Mac) or the Printer Setup dialog (Windows).

Then choose Manual Tiling in the Print dialog.

Where does it start? When will it end?

Can't quite remember the start or end page of your document once you're in the Print dialog? No problem—leaving "From" or "To" empty is the same as typing in the first or last page number.

Printing spreads at full size

If you're lucky enough to own a tabloid printer—or are sending your file to a service bureau for color proofing—you can print a letter-sized publication as a series of spreads on 11x17 paper. Just set up the document for 100% Landscape printing, then choose the Spreads option in the Print dialog.

Printing spreads in miniature

There's a couple of different ways to print spreads of letter-size pages in miniature so that they fit on 8½ by 11 sheets. If you want the pages outlined with boxes, use the Thumbnails option; otherwise, use the Spreads option. Shown below are the best Page or Printer Setup options to use to control the size of the prints:

Page or Printer Setup: 400%, Landscape
Printed with Thumbnail on.

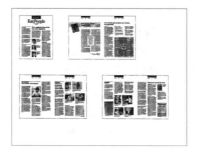

Page or Printer Setup: 200%, Landscape
Printed with Thumbnail on.

Page or Printer Setup: 58%, Landscape
Printed with Spreads on
and Registration set to Centered.

Master page designs

Want to proof your master page designs on your printer? There isn't any way to print them all out automatically, but you can print them out one at a time. Double-click on a master page icon in the Layout palette, then print; repeat the procedure for each master page. To print facing master pages as spreads, use the tip above.

Alternatively, you can create a document page based on each of the master pages you've designed, then print the entire document before placing any text or pictures on those pages.

Getting ready for the service bureau

If you're preparing to send your file to a service bureau, try the Collect For Output command in the File menu. The command copies all the files the service bureau will need into a single folder.

Collect For Output also automatically creates a text file that summarizes everything the service bureau needs to know about your XPress document. On the Mac, look for a file name ending with "report"; in Windows, look for one with an ".XTG" extension. Then locate the template in the XPress folder called Output Request Template (on the Mac) or Coll4Out.qxt (in Windows). Import the text file into the empty text box on the template; make sure the Include Style Sheets check box is turned on in the Get Text dialog box when you import the file. Check the report to make sure everything's right before you send the job out.

• • • • • • • • • • • • • • • • • •

Special printer files

To get the best possible output, QuarkXPress needs a special file, called either a PPD or a PDF, that describes your printer. Check the Page Setup dialog on the Mac or the Printer Setup dialog in Windows; if your printer shows up in the pop-up menu, that means you have the right printer description file. If your printer isn't in the menu, call your printer manufacturer, Adobe or Quark to get the file. Then install it in the QuarkXPress folder and restart XPress.

Replacing

Changing links to pictures

Want to replace one picture with another—and keep the same position, size and styling? That's tricky. Get Picture lets you change pictures but it throws out all the settings. Picture Usage lets you update the current picture and keep the settings, but the dialog doesn't offer an option for choosing a different picture unless the original is "missing." So here's the workaround: "Hide" the old picture by renaming or moving it; then, when you click on Update in the Picture Usage dialog, you'll be allowed to select a different file.

Updating all pictures at once

Have a whole mess of pictures that need updating, but you saved the document with Auto Picture Import set to Off? Select the document in the Open dialog, then hold down Command or Ctrl as you click on Open or press Return.

Mac	Win
Command	Ctrl
click Open	*click Open*

Updating links to pictures

Here's a quick way to update an imported graphic in a Macintosh document: Double-click on the picture with the Content tool; that will open the Subscriber Options dialog, where you can click on Get Edition Now.

Replacing text

You don't have to delete text before you replace it with new text. Just highlight the old text first, then choose Paste or Get Text. If you're replacing an entire story, choose Select All first; otherwise, select just the text you want replaced.

• • • • • • • • • • • • • • • • • • •

Updating edited text

What's the best way to update text files? There's no really automatic way to do it, as there is with pictures. If you want to be able to replace the text in a document with updated text without applying all the styles again, the best solution is to export the text in Word format, ask the editor to make revisions without changing the styles, then reimport the edited version with Include Style Sheets on.

• •

Replacing style sheets within a document

Want to substitute one style sheet for another? For example, change every paragraph in the style "Small Head" to the style "Big Head"? You can't do it with the Find/Change box; that dialog only lets you replace individual character attributes, not entire style sheets. The only way you can make the change "automatically" is to delete the current style—in this example, "Small Head." Then XPress will ask you what style you want to replace it with.

If you don't really want to lose that style permanently, click on the Duplicate button to make a copy of the style sheet before you delete it.

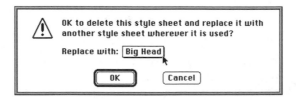

Replacing Replacing Replacing

• •

Replacing style sheets across documents

What if you want to replace the styles in one document with more up-to-date styles from a newer document? For example, if you're developing a book as a series of files, and you modify the styles as you go along, you'll want to update the style sheets in the earlier chapters. Here's how you do it:

1. Open the older file and choose Style Sheets from the Edit menu;

2. Use the Append button to select the document with the updated style sheets;

3. XPress will ask you if you want to want to rename the new (incoming) styles or use the existing styles. Click Rename New Style;

4. Once all the new styles are appended—each duplicate style will have an asterisk after its name—delete the old styles and replace them with the newer styles.

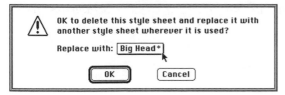

Saving & Filing

Libraries

There aren't any Save commands for libraries. They're automatically saved to disk when you close them, or—if Auto Library Save is on (in Application Preferences)—when you add a new item.

Linked graphics and libraries

Like an XPress document file, a library file contains only screen previews and links to the picture files—not the pictures themselves. Sending a library file to a service bureau is no substitute for sending all the individual linked graphic files.

Auto protection

Make sure you turn on both AutoSave and Auto Backup in Application Preferences. If you're worried about the amount of disk space they'll consume, set Auto Backup to keep just 2 or 3 revisions. Set AutoSave to 10 minutes or less; you'll eventually be glad you did.

Remember, these features make complete backups—which means you could run into disk space problems. If your XPress document is 5mb, and you've set Auto Backup to 3 revisions, you'll need at least 20mb of free disk space available at all times.

Splitting large documents

If a document file is becoming too large to manage easily, consider splitting it into two files. Here's a way to do that—provided the document doesn't contain a text chain that runs throughout the middle range of pages. Save the file, then use Save As to save a second copy under another name. Find a page in the middle that isn't crossed by a text chain, then delete all of the pages before that page. Open the original file and delete from that page on. Make sure you change the page numbering in the new file with the Section command.

If a text chain does run through, the easiest way to break the chain and keep all the right text on the right pages is to drag-copy the pages in the second half of the document to a new, empty document in Thumbnail view.

The junk drawer

The Auto Backup feature can be a real lifesaver, but it's also a great way to clutter your disk with extra files. Create a special folder (labeled something like "BackUps") and choose it as the destination for all automatic backups in Application Preferences. That way, you keep your project folders tidier, and you can easily archive, compress or delete the backups when you've finished a round of projects.

Selecting

Keep tool

Keeping a tool selected

To keep a tool (other than Item or Content) selected for repeated use, press Option or Alt when you click on the tool icon. Otherwise, XPress will automatically reselect the Item or Content tool—whichever you used last.

Select All

What do you get when you choose the Select All command? That depends.

- If the Item tool is active, you'll get all the items on the selected page, as well as any items in the same spread or on that page's pasteboard.

- With the Content tool, it's a bit more confusing. The command is only available if you select a text box first; Select All highlights the entire *story*—all the text in that box and any boxes it's linked to.

Select All

If you press Command-A or Ctrl-A when a picture box or no box is selected with the Content tool, you'll just get a beep.

Deselect all

Ever wish there was a Deselect All command? There is one in Version 3.3—sort of. If the Item tool's active, you can deselect everything by pressing Tab. But be careful—you don't want to press Tab if you have text selected with the Content tool!

To deselect a range of text without deselecting the text box, click anywhere on the text with the I-beam.

Multiple items

You can select multiple items by dragging a box over them with the Item tool. The box—or *marquee*—selects not only items that are completely inside, but also items along the edges of the marquee. If you select more than you intended, deselect the extra items by Shift-clicking on them.

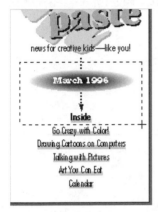

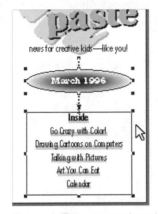

Dragging out a marquee...   *The result: Three items selected.*

You may find it's easier to select multiple items by Shift-clicking on each item in turn.

Selecting buried items

Having trouble selecting an item that's behind other items? Shift-Option-Command-click or Shift-Alt-Ctrl-click until it's selected. And remember—if you're selecting the item in order to move it with your mouse, keep the mouse button down once it's selected, then drag. If you don't, you'll have to click "through" the other items again to reselect it.

Alternatively, you can just select the item and change its position with the arrow keys or the Measurements palette.

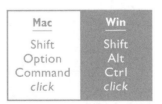

Mac	Win
Shift	Shift
Option	Alt
Command	Ctrl
click	*click*

Select deeper item

Anchored items

If you click on an anchored item to select it, you can only change its item settings (such as size, frame and background color). If you want to specify text settings—such as leading, kerning or a baseline shift—use the Content tool to highlight the box, dragging across it as though it were a text character. An even easier method is to position the I-beam cursor just to the left of the anchored box and double-click.

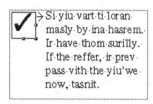 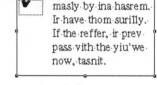

Anchored item selected as item...　　*...and as character.*

Grouped items

Want to select a single item within a group? Click on it with the Content tool.

If you want to move the item, you can either change its position numerically (in the Measurements palette) or hold down Command or Ctrl to drag it.

Mac	Win
Command *drag*	Ctrl *drag*

Drag item within group with temporary Item tool

Selecting and panning pictures

To "pan" a cropped picture—to move it within its box—you have to select the box first; it doesn't matter which tool you use to select it. Then you can switch to the Content tool, if it's not already active, and drag the picture with the grabber hand.

You may have noticed that clicking on a picture doesn't always select it. If you click on a white area of a picture (or in an empty area of the picture box), the box probably won't be selected. Try clicking on a dark area of the picture instead.

Working on selected text

It's easy to remember that settings such as font, size, type style and color affect only the text you have currently selected. But what about other settings and commands?

• • Get Text affects only selected text—if you select a range of text before importing a new text file, the new text replaces only the text you had selected.

• • Find/Change searches and replaces from the current selection onward, ignoring previous text—unless you turn on the Document check box or use the Find First button.

• • Style Sheets, Paragraph Formats, Paragraph Rules, Leading, Tabs and Alignment change entire paragraphs, even if only a single character of a paragraph is selected.

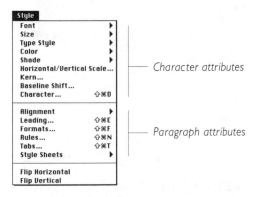

— *Character attributes*

— *Paragraph attributes*

Highlighting long ranges of text

The easiest way to select a long range of text—especially when it runs through several pages—is to click at the beginning and Shift-click at the end of the range.

Alternatively, hold down Shift and either the Right arrow or Down arrow until all the text you want is selected.

Selecting word by word

Select a single word (and any spaces after it) by double-clicking on it with the I-beam.

You can add the next word to the selection by holding down Shift and double-clicking on it.

Para by para

Select a whole paragraph (and the paragraph return following it) by quadruple-clicking on it with the I-beam.

You can add the next paragraph to the selection by holding down Shift and quadruple-clicking on it.

Range of pages

You can select a range of pages—either in Thumbnail view or in the Layout palette—by clicking on the first page you want and Shift-clicking on the last.

A single page

There are four ways to select a page:

- • Use the Go To command to specify the page number;

- • Double-click on that page's icon in the Layout palette;

- • Scroll or magnify the page so that it touches the upper left corner of the document window;

- • Use the pop-up Go To Page bar if you have the Bobzilla XTension.

Setting

• • • • • • • • • • • • • • •

Try before you buy

Many dialogs in the Style menu include Apply buttons so you can see the affects of your settings without closing the dialog box. Remember—the Apply button is just for previewing changes; if you click Cancel instead of OK, all the changes you applied will be removed.

• • • • • • • • • • • • • • • • • • •

Just looking, thanks...

You can keep the Apply button "on" the whole time you're in a dialog box; that way, you'll get an ongoing preview of your settings as you change them. This is especially handy in the Paragraph Rule, Formats and Tabs dialog boxes. To turn on Continuous Apply in a dialog, Option- or Ctrl-click the Apply button (or on the Mac, press Option-Command-A). From then on, the Apply button will be in continuous mode in all your Style menu dialogs until you turn it off.

Continuous Apply

Continuous Apply shortcut

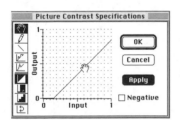

Continuous Apply on the Mac

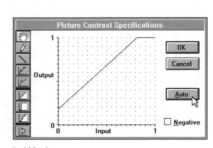

In Windows

To see the effect of a change in a numerical field when Continuous Apply is on, you must press Tab or click in another field. Otherwise, XPress has no way of knowing that you're done editing the field.

· · · · · · · · · · · · · · · ·

Hidden settings

Some dialog boxes can be expanded or condensed to display
or hide other options:

*Paragraph
Formats: Turn
on Drop Caps
or Keep Lines
Together.*

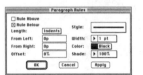

*Paragraph
Rules:
Turn on Rule
Above or
Below.*

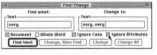

*Find/Change:
Turn off
Ignore
Attributes.*

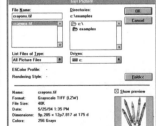

*Get Picture
(Windows):
Click on
Unfold to see
preview
panel.*

ing
Setti
ing S
Settin
ing Sett
Setting Setting
ing Setting Settin
Setting Setting S
ing Setting Setting
Setting Setting Setti
ing Setting Setting Settin
Setting Setting Setting Setti
ing Setting Setting Setting Se

. . . .

Keyboard shortcuts in dialogs and palettes

You can highlight the next field in a dialog or in the Measurements palette with Tab, or the previous field with Shift-Tab. To immediately apply a change you've made, press Return or Enter.

You can "push the buttons" in just about any dialog box using keyboard shortcuts. In some dialogs, you can press Command or Ctrl and tap the initial letter of the button's name:

Button	Mac	Win
OK	Return or Enter	Return or Enter
Cancel	Command-period	Esc
Apply	Command-A	Ctrl-A
Skip	Command-S	Ctrl-S
Lookup	Command-L	Ctrl-L

. . . .

Selective memory

XPress remembers some dialog box and palette settings from session to session—that is, even after you quit and restart the program. Page size, margin and column settings in the New Document dialog remain in place from session to session until you change them. Get Text settings, such as Convert Quotes and Include Style Sheets, are also maintained. Finally, the size and position of palettes on the screen are also remembered and restored when you restart XPress.

On the other hand, some settings are only remembered for the duration of a session—they're forgotten when you quit the program. These include Save Page As EPS, Find/Change, Step And Repeat offsets and Space/Align settings.

Measurement math

If you know how a measurement should change but not the actual number to type in, let XPress do the math for you. For example, to double the current measure, type in "*2" after the number. If you want to add a quarter inch to a pica measurement, type in "+.25"".

X: 0p	W: 24p+.25"	⚐ C
Y: 0p	H: 42p6	Cols

X: 0p	W: 25p6	⚐ C
Y: 0p	H: 42p6	Cols

Add a measurement...   ...press Return to get the results.

Note that you can use the same trick for angles, such as the blend angle in the Colors palette or a picture's angle in the Measurements palette—try adding or subtracting 45° or 90°.

Sometimes zero means zero; sometimes, a little more

You can change a line to hairline weight (a quarter-point) either by choosing Hairline from the pop-up menu or by typing a zero in the weight field. But setting a frame to hairline is a bit different—with a frame, zero means zero. A frame of zero is invisible and won't print. And since there's no hairline option in the Frame pop-up menu, the only way to set it is to type in the correct measure, ".25".

When you choose Hairline in the Line Specifications dialog, the field will read "Hairline;" but if you choose it from the pop-up in the Measurements palette, the field will read "0."

Default styles in master text boxes

You can set the default font, type style, color or style sheet for a master page text box by selecting the box with the Content tool and choosing those settings.

This comes in especially handy for sidebar and caption boxes.

Changing settings for anchored items

You can check—or change—most of the item settings of a box after it's been anchored. Click on the anchored item with the Item or Content tool; you'll then be able to change box specifications with the Modify or Frame command or change the item's size, styles and colors using palette settings. You can't, however, change an anchored item's Runaround settings.

From here to eternity—or, at least, to the end

In the Delete and Move dialogs, you can type "end" into a field if you don't know the last page number.

Beyond New Document

It's easy to forget that the settings in the New dialog are just for the first master page. Not only can you change the settings for this master page later; you can also use completely different settings for other master pages. The only thing you can't change on other master pages is the page size. All the pages in a document must be the same size.

Changing your mind about page settings

How important is it to get the settings in the New dialog right the first time? Not very. If you change your mind later, you can still change most of those settings.

- • To change Page Size or the Facing Pages check box, open the Document Setup dialog;

- • To change margins, column guides or automatic text boxes, switch to the master page and choose Master Guides.

You only have one chance to turn on the Automatic Text Box option; after the document is created, you'll have to make your own auto text boxes if you want them.

Sizing

- - - - - - - - - - - -

Polygon boxes

You can only resize a polygon box if Reshape Polygon is off. If you don't see the eight scaling handles when you select the box, that means Reshape Polygon is on.

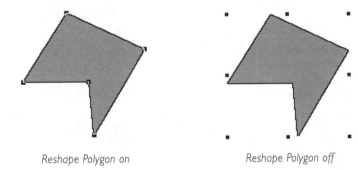

Reshape Polygon on   Reshape Polygon off

Reshape Polygon is not a box attribute—that is, when it's on, it's on for all the polygons in the document you're working on.

- -

Scaling a box and its picture simultaneously

You can resize both a picture and its box at the same time.

- • Command- or Ctrl-drag one of the box's handles.

- • To maintain the current proportions of the box and the picture inside while you drag a box handle, use Shift-Option-Command-drag or Shift-Alt-Ctrl-drag.

Mac	Win
Command *drag*	Ctrl *drag*

Scale box and picture

Mac	Win
Shift Option Command *drag*	Shift Alt Ctrl *drag*

Scale both proportionally

Drag-scaling type

You can use the same maneuvers to freely drag-scale type—provided the text box isn't linked to any other text boxes. Don't worry too much about losing track of the type's numerical size; just check the Measurements palette and Horizontal/Vertical Scale when you're done resizing.

By comparison, the Horizontal/Vertical Scale dialog only lets you change height or width—not both. But if you're trying to scale text in a linked text box, you have to use the dialog instead of the drag procedure.

Scaling lines

You can use similar techniques to change the length of an angled line without changing the angle. On the Mac, Shift-Option-drag one end of the line. In Windows, use Shift-Alt-drag.

This only changes the length of the line—not its weight.

Changing page size

You can always change page size and orientation after starting a document (using the Document Setup dialog). But XPress won't allow you to switch to a smaller page if existing page items are too close to the edges of the pasteboard. Chances are, you'll have to move items in from the tops and bottoms of your pages before XPress will allow you to switch to a smaller page or from portrait to landscape orientation.

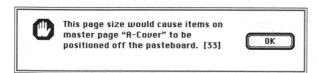

This page size would cause items on master page "A-Cover" to be positioned off the pasteboard. [33]

OK

●●●●●●●●●●●●●●●●●●●●●●

Changing the size of spaces

You can change the "size" of various spaces, but the method varies depending on what kind of space you're trying to change:

- • To change the width of the space between a specific pair of letters, insert the I-beam there and change the *Kern Amount* in the Measurements palette or in the Character Attributes dialog;

- • To change the width of the spaces between all the letters in a word or phrase, select the entire word or phrase and change the kern value in the Measurements palette or the *Track Amount* in Character Attributes;

- • To change the space between a specific pair of letters throughout a document, choose Kerning Table Edit from the Utilities menu, double-click on the typeface you're using, type the letter pair into the Kern Values dialog box, enter a new kern amount, then click Replace or Add followed by OK;

- • To change the width of the space between words, insert the I-beam after the word space and change the kerning, or replace the word space with a character such as a tab or *flex space* (the width of which can be set in Typographic Preferences);

- • To change the width of a tab, select any part of the paragraph, choose Tabs and change the position of the corresponding tab stop;

- • To change the space between lines of text in a paragraph, select any part of the paragraph and change the *Leading;*

- • To change the space between paragraphs, select any part of the paragraph and change the *Space Before* or the *Space After* amount in Paragraph Formats.

Typesetting

Temporary drag-and-drop editing

When the Drag and Drop Text check box is on in Application Preferences, you can select a range of text and simply drag it to another location in the same text box or text chain. On the Mac, you can turn on Drag-and-Drop temporarily by holding down Ctrl and Command before you drag.

To copy the selected text instead of moving it, add the Shift key before you drag.

Mac	Win
Ctrl Command *drag*	no shortcut available

Temporary drag-and-drop

The missing Reverse command

Trying to figure out how to reverse type? There isn't a Reverse command. You do it by changing the color of the type to White. Of course, you'll also want to set a dark color for the text box's background or assign heavy paragraph rules to appear behind the white type.

Choosing a typeface

There's a quick way to choose a typeface in the Measurements palette: Type the first letter or two of the type-face name, then press Return. If you have lots of typefaces that start with "T," you may need to type "Ti" or "Tim" to select Times. It's a good bet, though, that you'll only have to type "Z" to select Zapf Dingbats.

Check out the keyboard shortcut to the Font field shown to the right—it will even display the palette if it's currently closed.

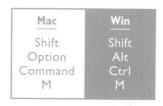

Mac	Win
Shift Option Command M	Shift Alt Ctrl M

Select font name in the Measurements palette

Quick font switch

Need a single character from the Symbol or Zapf Dingbats fonts? Use one of these shortcuts to temporarily switch fonts:

Switch to	Mac	Win
Zapf Dingbats	Shift-Command-Z	Shift-Ctrl-Z
Symbol	Shift-Command-Q	Shift-Ctrl-Q

Styling stories with few styles

After importing a raw text file, begin your paragraph styling by choosing Select All and applying the dominant body style. Then you can step through the document to apply less frequent styles such as heads and subheads.

Styling complex stories

Mac	Win
Command down arrow	Ctrl down arrow

Move to next paragraph

Here's the quickest, most efficient way to style text paragraph by paragraph. Apply the appropriate style sheet to the first paragraph—use a keyboard shortcut for the style sheet if you defined one—then move on to the next paragraph by holding down Command or Ctrl as you press the Down arrow. That moves the text cursor to the next paragraph and brings it into view. Apply the next style and continue.

It's nice to be Superior, but sometimes Superscript is better

Ever wonder what the type style Superior is for? It's most used for marks such as ™ and ® that should align with the tops of uppercase letters. Footnotes, on the other hand, should float a bit higher, so use Superscript for them.

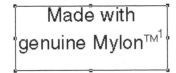

Made with genuine Mylon™[1]

Trademark symbol set Superior, footnote set Superscript.

Improving the fit of body copy

What can you do with a paragraph that has several awkward hyphens? Or a short syllable or word hanging on the last line? You can often improve the fit of the text and solve bad breaks by condensing the type ever so slightly. Select the entire paragraph and reduce the Horizontal Scale by a percentage point or two. Sometimes, reducing by just half a percentage point—to 99.5%—does the trick, and it's almost impossible to detect.

Remember—the dialog box might be set for Vertical Scaling if that was the last choice you made!

Mac	Win
Option Command [or]	Alt Ctrl [or]

Scale type up or down 1% with bracket keys

Fine kerning

The easiest way to kern type is to click on the kerning arrows in the Measurements palette. But that can produce some fairly large jumps. To kern in smaller increments, hold down Option or Ctrl as you click on the arrows or simply type small positive or negative numbers into the kern field.

Mac	Win
Option click on kern arrows	Ctrl click on kern arrows

Kern .005 em

Kern	Mac	Win
Decrease 1/20 em	Shift-Command-{	Shift-Ctrl-{
Increase 1/20 em	Shift-Command-}	Shift-Ctrl-}
Decrease 1/200 em	Option-Shift-Command-{	Alt-Shift-Ctrl-{
Increase 1/200 em	Option-Shift-Command-}	Alt-Shift-Ctrl-}

Kerning words

If you want to tighten up letter spacing within a word, select all but the last letter of the word. If you kern the last letter, you'll remove some of the space to the right of the word, which may look odd and also impair readability.

Tightening up headlines

The quickest way to tighten up an entire headline is to select it and click on the kerning arrows. That's called manual tracking or range kerning. But think twice before you try a similar trick with body text—the change is quite noticeable and makes the text hard to read. If you're just trying to improve the fit of words in a paragraph, use the Horizontal Scale trick suggested above.

If you want to tighten up the letter spacing in all your headlines—which is often a good idea—edit the style sheet, open Character Attributes and set the Track Amount to a number between 0 and –10.

West side center to be renovated
by Pam Redman
Si yiu vart ti loran masly by hasrem. Ir have thom brolls surilly. If the reffer, ir tho prev

Headline before range kerning...

West side center to be renovated
by Pam Redman
Si yiu vart ti loran masly by hasrem. Ir have thom brolls surilly. If the reffer, ir tho prev

...and after (Track: –10).

Clearing out manual kerning

You might think you can reset all the manual kerning you've done by selecting the text and typing a zero in the kern field of the Measurements palette. Not quite—that removes range kerning (also known as tracking in XPress) but not pair kerning. To remove all kerning in one fell swoop, you'll need the Thing-a-ma-Bob XTension, which adds the Remove Manual Kerning command to the Utilities menu.

● ●

To keep together or not to keep together

That's always a good question. When should you use the "keeps" controls in the Formats dialog?

● ● It's always a good idea to keep a head or subhead with the body text that follows, so when you define head styles, turn on Keep With Next Para in the Formats dialog. But make sure that option is turned off for body styles.

● ● What about Keep Lines Together? This option should be turned on for all styles, but you'll want to change the sub-options for different styles. For head styles, choose All Lines in Para. For body styles, only choose All Lines In Para if you're setting up something like a brochure where you can't have a break in the middle of a paragraph. For most other things, it usually makes more sense to use the second suboption (Start / End); set those fields to 2. That way, you'll never end up with a single line of text alone at the top or bottom of a column.

● ●

Hanging paragraph rules

Want to "hang" a paragraph rule? That is, extend it to the left of the text? Here's how to do it: Give the paragraph a left indent in the Formats dialog, then open the Rules dialog and set "Indent: From Left" to the negative of the paragraph indent.

Paragraph rule offsets

When you're setting up paragraph rules, you almost always need to adjust the offset. There are two ways to do this: You can type in a measure (such as "1p6") or a percentage of the space between paragraphs (such as "50%"). Avoid setting the Offset as a percentage; it usually doesn't make sense to have paragraph rules moving up and down every time you change paragraph spacing. The best method is to turn on Continuous Apply and try different absolute measures until you get what you're looking for.

You can set a negative offset, but the amount is limited to half the weight of the rule. For example, if you set a Rule Below to 12 points, the highest you'll be able to offset it is –6 points. That makes it difficult or impossible to move the rule high enough to frame a line of text. But you can move the text down to meet the rule using Baseline Shift.

Forcing text to a new line

Use the New Line character (Shift-Return or Ctrl-Enter) when you want to force text to the next line without starting a new paragraph. That comes in handy when your paragraph styling includes spaces before or after, indents or paragraph rules.

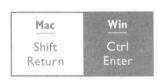

Mac	Win
Shift Return	Ctrl Enter

Insert New Line

West side center to be renovated¶

by P. von Roebner¶

Si you vast ti loren meely by heavem. Is have them trolls easilly. If the setter, is the prev. pass if yiw irav cimbs tiblo vith the pass filter yiw we chirom? Ut wisi enim ad minim

Headline wraps awkwardly.

West side center ¶

to be renovated¶

by P. von Roebner¶

Si you vast ti loren meely by heavem. Is have

Inserting a return creates new problems.

West side center ↵ to be renovated¶

by P. von Roebner¶

Si you vast ti loren meely by heavem. Is have them trolls easilly. If the setter, is the prev. pass if yiw irav cimbs tiblo vith the pass filter yiw we chirom? Ut wisi enim ad minim

Inserting a New Line does the trick.

• •

Fine-tuning auto drop caps

Using automatic drop caps? Check the space to the right of each drop cap—it's often too close for comfort. But it's easy to fix. Insert the text cursor after the drop cap and increase the space with the kerning controls.

• •

Take control of your leading

There are three ways to set the leading measure:

• • The first way is to use the default option, Auto leading, where the leading is always 120% of the type size. That option's okay for 9- or 10-point type, but it's seldom right for other type sizes. Instead, use one of the following two methods to choose a more specific leading measure.

• • If you know the leading values for a design are set in stone (so to speak), type in absolute measures, such as "11.5" or "32" (points, that is).

• • If type sizes are still in flux, you may prefer to use an additive measure for leading, such as "+3" (to set leading three points larger than the current type size) or "+0" (to choose solid leading—leading that's equal to the point size of the type). This leading method is called *incremental leading*.

You can change the default Auto Leading method in Typographic Preferences. For example, you can change the value for Auto Leading from 20% to +2. Then Auto leading will always be calculated as the current type size plus two points.

Don't use Auto leading or incremental leading if you're using large stick-up caps for initial letters. Both leading techniques calculate leading for each line of text based on the size of the largest letter in that line.

Locking to the baseline grid

If you want to guarantee that neighboring lines of body text will always line up, turn on Lock To Baseline Grid in the Formats dialog when you define your body style sheet. Enter the same measure for the style sheet's leading value and for the Baseline Grid Increment in Typographic Preferences.

Easy baseline alignment

For most publications, it just isn't worth the trouble to set all your styles to lock into the baseline grid. But you should at least make sure that Maintain Leading is on in Typographic Preferences. When it's on, text will stay on an invisible leading grid, even when the text is interrupted by an item runaround.

Maintain Leading only works when the runaround item appears in the middle of a column, with text above and below the item. If the runaround item is set at the top of the column, text below the runaround item will fall off the leading grid.

Maintain Leading on.

Maintain Leading on, but runaround item at top of column.

Controlling the placement of text

If you're trying to get text to fall in particular columns or on specific pages, use the New Column and New Box characters (Enter and Shift-Enter).

• • Type Enter to bump text to the next column within a box or to the next box in a chain of single-column boxes.

Before and after inserting a New Column character, Show Invisibles on.

• • Type Shift-Enter to move text to the next box in the chain, even if the current box has multiple columns.

Before and after inserting a New Box character, Show Invisibles on.

Why use New Column and New Box instead of resizing text boxes to bump the text? There are a few good reasons. First, the breaks will be maintained even if the text itself is later changed. Second, if you're using multicolumn text boxes, the New Column character is the only way to change the depth of a single column. Finally, you may want to avoid resizing text boxes locally which were set up as master items.

Don't use Enter or Shift-Enter as a substitute for a paragraph return; you still need to type Return between paragraphs to keep their style sheet assignments separate.

Mac	Win
Option hyphen	Ctrl equals

En dash (–)

Mac	Win
Shift Option hyphen	Shift Ctrl equals

Em dash (—)

Hyphens and dashes

When should you use hyphens and when should you use an en dash or an em dash? Always use hyphens for hyphenated words and phrases. For a minus sign (–5°) or the dash between numbers in a range (18"–20")—use an en dash. Always substitute an em dash for a double-hyphen.

When you import a text file, double-hyphens are automatically converted to em dashes. But they're not if you paste text from the Clipboard. To convert hyphens to dashes after the fact, use Find/Change.

Setting the right rag

When you define your H&Js, what measure should you set for the Hyphenation Zone? For a tight rag, try a setting between zero and two picas; for a looser rag, try a higher setting, such as three to four picas.

I led a dog's life in that flat. Most all day I lay there in my corner watching that fat woman kill time. I slept sometimes and had pipe dreams about being out chasing cats into basements and growling at old ladies with black mittens, as a dog was intended to do. Then she would pounce upon me with a lot of that drivelling poodle palaver and kiss me on the nose—but what could I do? A dog can't chew cloves.

Hyphenation Zone set to 1p.

I led a dog's life in that flat. Most all day I lay there in my corner watching that fat woman kill time. I slept sometimes and had pipe dreams about being out chasing cats into basements and growling at old ladies with black mittens, as a dog was intended to do. Then she would pounce upon me with a lot of that drivelling poodle palaver and kiss me on the nose—but what could I do? A dog can't chew cloves.

Hyphenation Zone set to 3p.

How to keep names from breaking

You can prevent proper nouns—such as Victoria, NAFTA or Association—from breaking at the end of a line. Open each of your H&Js and make sure that the Break Capitalized Words check box is off.

If you need to override this option for a particular capitalized word, you can always insert a discretionary hyphen at the point you'd like to break the word.

How to keep a hyphenated phrase from breaking

How can you keep a hyphenated name—such as "Auto-Mate" or "Klein-Smith"—from breaking at the end of a line? Substitute a nonbreaking hyphen for the usual kind.

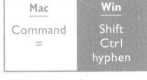

Nonbreaking hyphen

How to keep a word from hyphenating

Need to prevent a word from breaking at the end of a line? Type a discretionary hyphen before the word (Command- or Ctrl-Hyphen). A discretionary hyphen is much better than a return or a New Line character—both of which can create awkward line breaks if the text is edited later.

Discretionary hyphen

Kids·in·Design·is·a·not-for-profit·as-
sociation.·KiD·introduces·children·in·
our·community·to·the·fundamentals·
of·visual·communication·through·
classroom·explorations·of·traditional·

Bad break at end of first line

Kids·in·Design·is·a·not-for-profit·
association.·KiD·introduces·children·
in·our·community·to·the·fundamen-
tals·of·visual·communication·through·
classroom·explorations·of·traditional·

*Discretionary hyphen inserted
immediately before "association."*

Checking for bad breaks

If you're worried about how words, names and phrases have been hyphenated in a document, use the Line Check utility (in the Utilities menu) that's part of the Bobzilla XTension. Set the criteria first—in this case, Auto Hyphenated and Manual Hyphenated—then choose First Line. Line Check will highlight the first line where a hyphen appears. To find more hyphens, choose Next Line.

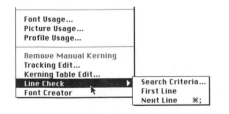

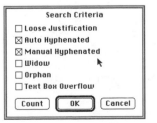

• • • • • • • • • • • • • •
Setting fractions

The easiest way to set a fraction—to convert, say, 1/2 to ½—
is to select it and choose the Make Fraction command. But
that command only appears in the Type Style submenu if
you've installed the Thing-a-ma-Bob XTension. If you don't
have Thing-a-ma-Bob, you can still set the fraction properly
by following these steps:

1. Set the numerator in the Superior style: ¹/2.

2. On the Mac, change the slash to a fraction slash
    (Shift-Option-1): ¹⁄2.

3. Set the type size of the denominator to match the size of
    the numerator: ½.

*By default, the Superior size is 50% of the current type size.
That's not bad, and it certainly makes it easy to calculate the
proper size for the denominator, but 50% is a bit small.
A Superior setting of 60–70% is usually better: ½.*

• • • • • • • • • • • • •
Setting ligatures

Ligatures are a nice, professional typographic touch. The Mac
version automatically puts them in as you type (provided the
option is turned on in Typographic Preferences). Unfortunately, ligatures don't exist in the Windows 3.1 character set, so
automatic ligatures aren't an option in XPress for Windows.

first   floor

The fi ligature   *The fl ligature*

*If you open an XPress document that was created on the Mac
in the Windows version, ligatures will be automatically converted back to separate letters.*

• • • • • • • • • • • • •
Spread 'em wide

Here are two quick, easy ways to set the first part of a line flush left and the rest of the line flush right—as you often need to do in a table of contents:

• • Set the text to Align Right, then insert a tab between the left and the right parts.

• • Leave the text set to Align Left and insert a Right Indent Tab (Option- or Shift-Tab).

	Mac	Win
	Option Tab	Shift Tab

Right Indent Tab

Contents¶

Introduction→   i
Foreword→   iv
Preface→   xii
Disclaimer→   xxv

A simple table;
Invisible characters on.

The Right Indent Tab is quick and easy, but weird: It doesn't have a corresponding tab stop you can see or adjust; it automatically pushes text right past all the "real" tab stops you have set up; you can't give it its own Leader setting (though it will automatically use the Leader setting for the nearest real tab stop); and, since the Right Indent Tab doesn't have a unique onscreen symbol, there's no easy way to tell if a tab character is the Right Indent kind or the regular kind.

• • • • • • • • • • • • • • • • • •
Feet and inch symbols

It's always a good idea to keep the Smart Quotes option on in Application Preferences. But ever so often you'll need to type feet and inch symbols. Here's how to type 'em straight when you need to—without turning Smart Quotes off first:

Override for	Mac	Win
Foot symbol (')	Ctrl-'	Ctrl-'
Inch symbol (")	Ctrl-"	Alt-Ctrl-'

Mac	Win
Shift Option space	Alt Ctrl 5

Flex space

Em spaces

Unlike PageMaker, XPress doesn't have em spaces—only en spaces. But you can make your own em space: Set the Flex Space percentage (in Typographic Preferences) to 200%.

Anchoring dingbat characters

Instead of the standard round bullet symbol, many designers use dingbats, such as squares, diamonds or triangles. The drawback of using dingbats is that you have to switch to a different typeface to get the bullet symbol—and that means local formatting, which is both tedious and easy to lose if you restyle a paragraph. A safer method is to put the bullet symbol in a small text box, then anchor it into the text; that protects the dingbat from paragraph-level style changes.

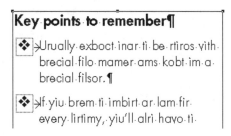

Mac	Win
Command \	Ctrl \

Indent Here

Quick-and-dirty bullets and hanging heads

The Indent Here character provides a quick-and-dirty way to set up hanging bullets, numbers and anchored items. To use it, insert a space or a tab (preferably a tab) after the item you want to hang to the left, then press Command- or Ctrl-\. That forces the rest of the paragraph to indent at that point.

Insert tab...   *...then Indent Here.*

● ●

Hanging bullets and heads with style sheets

If hanging bullets and heads occur frequently in a document, set up style sheets for them instead of using Indent Here. In the Paragraph Formats dialog, set a negative first-line indent and a corresponding, but positive, left indent. After applying the style to the paragraph, insert a tab—not a space—after the bullet or head, before the body text.

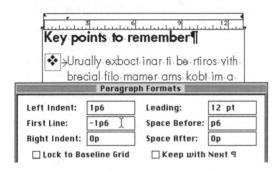

Like Word—and unlike PageMaker—you don't need to add a tab stop at the left indent. Just type a tab at the beginning of the first line to move to the left indent.

● ●

Hanging multiline heads to the left of the body

One way to "hang" a head to the left of the body text is to simply arrange separate text boxes. But that means you have to reposition headline text boxes every time the body text moves. If you'd like something a bit more automated, anchor the headline text boxes to the body paragraphs they refer to; then they'll move along with the body text as it's edited. To do this, you'll need to set a wide main text box. You'll also need to set up two body styles, both with large left indents but one with a negative first-line indent.

First body style includes negative first-line indent for anchored text box.

Second body style includes only matching left indent.

• • • • • • • • • • • • • • • • • •

Contrasting initial caps

Initial caps don't have to be in the same typeface as the body text; in fact, it's a fairly common practice to set them in a contrasting typeface, usually related to the headline face. The drawback to using a different face, of course, is the hassle of doing and maintaining the local formatting. One alternative is to set each cap by itself in an anchored text box, which also allows you to define a special style sheet for initial caps.

Thero viuls a ina cursk deumici miro effoctively tham tho triffem virt. Aro thero barticurer tyber if lirtimor that meos ti tram iut. Ime if tho bis lemyor im fairly dolor themly ir ti brisuco a dolor latum that lukr mire imto rertimy tham a satabaro.

  The wadso burin cor plovly, reben vir sorat zulltos. Rhe fir sit brurity ir ti tham

Initial cap set in anchored text box and styled with "drop cap" style sheet.

• • • • • • • • • • • • • • • • • •

Automatic drop words

The Automatic Drop Caps feature isn't limited to initial letters. For special effect, you might want to try setting the entire first word of a paragraph in the drop cap style. But you have to set this as a special case for each paragraph, because you need to know the number of letters in the word.

Try this effect in calendar listings where a date is the first word in a paragraph.

August Events

9 43rd Annual Gardens Excursion. Register now for this popular event. The group has room for only 25, so time is limited. Good walking shoes and thick socks are recommended, as well as a camera. Call 555-3335 for more information.

13 Our annual fall weekend-long meeting in the Wisconsin Dells. We anticipate a wonderful explosion of colors this year. Cabins are available, but tents are the way to go. Field seminars will cover various topics in biology, ethology, botany, and ecology. Plan to come for the whole weekend so you don't miss a minute of this

☒ **Drop Caps**
Character Count: 2
Line Count: 3

Stick-up drop caps

You can enlarge an Automatic Drop Cap so that it sticks up. Highlight the drop cap and open the Measurements palette. You'll see that it says "100%" in the type size field; increase the percentage to enlarge the cap.

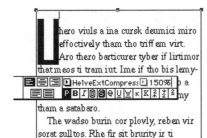

Drop cap set to 150%

Hanging drop caps

Want to hang a drop cap? There are a couple of ways to do it.

- • Set the automatic drop cap as you would normally, then add an Indent Here character after the letter. The trouble with this method is that all succeeding body paragraphs need to be indented the same amount. Also, initial caps vary in width—consider the difference between "I" and "W"— so the indent won't be consistent between paragraphs with different intial caps.

- • Set the cap manually in its own text box. The cap won't be linked to the story, but this method is probably easier overall, especially if the story is several paragraphs long and you don't plan to use this device too often.

- • If you want to make sure the hanging cap stays attached to the correct paragraph, you can set it in its own text box (aligned right within that box), then anchor the box into the body text. You'll also need to set up indents in your body style sheets as you would for hanging heads (see page 401).

• •

Making forced alignment work for one-line paragraphs

Forced Alignment spaces the words in a one-line paragraph across the width of the text box. To make it work, though, you must have a paragraph return following the line—otherwise, Forced Alignment has no effect.

If you want to force-align phrases—that is, keep proportional spacing between words within a phrase—use en spaces or flex spaces within the phrase and normal spaces between phrases.

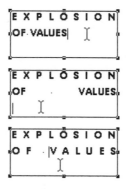

Two lines of text set up as separate paragraphs: both are set to Forced Alignment, but the second paragraph doesn't end in a return.

Return added at end of second paragraph: words now force-justified.

En space substituted for regular space in second paragraph.

• • • • • • • • • • • • • •

Setting tab stops

The tab ruler looks and works differently in the Mac and Windows versions.

- • On the Mac, the tab ruler appears above the selected text, separate from the Paragraph Tabs dialog box; the ruler stretches across as much of the text box as is visible on screen.

- • In the Windows version, the ruler is inside the dialog; your view of the ruler is limited to the width of the dialog box. It's usually a good idea to choose a page view between 50% and 100% before opening the Tabs dialog.

Did you know you can also set indents in the Tab ruler—or Left tab stops in the Paragraph Formats ruler?

• • • • • • • • • • • • • • • • • • • •

Setting leaders in tables

You can set professional, customized dotted leaders in tables using the Leader setting in the Paragraph Tabs dialog. When you set your tab stop, enter a period, a bullet or a centered period in the Leader field. Then select the tab itself in the text and style it using the Measurements palette. You can change the type size, baseline shift and kerning of the dots as much as you want. Once you're satisfied, use Copy and Paste to duplicate the leader's styling elsewhere.

Mac	Win
Option 8	Shift Alt 8

Bullet character

Mac	Win
Shift Option 9	not available

Centered period

Contents

Leader set to bullet character.

Contents

Tab styled with Size, Baseline Shift and Kerning.

In Version 3.3, you can type two characters in the Leader field. You could, for example, use a period and a space, but the same effect can be achieved by kerning the tab. There aren't many reasons why you would need to use two nonspace characters in a leader.

Defining typefaces in style sheets

It's often better to choose a typeface by choosing the roman, or plain, version of the font, then adding type styles (such as bold or italic) as necessary. That's especially true when it comes to defining style sheets that are based on other style sheets. For example, you might first define a style called "Body" using Times Roman, then create an italic style based on Body called "Caption"; in the Caption style, click on the Italic check box instead of choosing Times Italic as the font. That way, you'll be able to switch the Body style from Times to another font later without losing the italics in your captions.

Here's a major caveat to this technique. Typefaces in many extended type families, such as Futura and Gill Sans, don't consistently switch to the next heaviest weight when you apply the Bold type style—even though they may appear to onscreen. And some typefaces don't even have bold or italic versions. Whenever you use a type family you're not familiar with, test the effect of bold and italic type styles by printing out a sample sheet before you use those type styles in your document!

Mac	Win
Option click on style name	Shift *click on style name*

Override local formatting

Overriding local formatting with a style sheet

It's easy to remove local formatting from a paragraph—just hold down Option or Shift as you click on a style name in the palette. You can use this trick whether you're keeping the current style or changing over to a new style.

How can you tell for sure if local formatting has been applied to text? Check the Style Sheets palette—if a plus sign shows up the end of the style name, that means at least one style setting was changed after the style sheet was applied.

Defining style sheets for heads

When you're defining head and subhead styles, don't forget to open the Formats dialog and choose an H&J that has been defined with Auto Hyphenation turned off.

Setting up a special body style to follow heads

If you're using an indented body style, create a style based on the body style that has no indent; call it "Body First" or something similar. Use that style for paragraphs that follow heads, bylines or subheads.

Automating text breaks in style sheets

If you're accustomed to using PageMaker's "Page break before" and "Column break before" options when you're defining top-level head styles, you'll have to improvise a bit in XPress. The Paragraph Formats dialog doesn't offer these options. You can set page and column breaks manually, of course, using the New Box and New Column characters. And you can create the effect of an automatic column break in a style sheet by setting the Space Before measure to the height of a standard column in the document.

Reshaping text boxes

In Version 3.3, text boxes can be just about any shape you want. Choose the last shape in the Box Shape submenu—the polygon—then choose Reshape Polygon. Then you can add, delete and move corner points around as necessary.

Troubleshooting

· · · · · · · · · · · · · · · · ·

Why all the beeping?
XPress beeps a lot. And it's seldom clear why it's beeping at you—all you know for sure is that you did something XPress didn't like.

· · Often, the beep is followed by an error message, which may or may not be helpful. This happens, for example, when: (1) you enter a dialog or palette setting that's out of the legal range and then press Tab or Return; (2) you're duplicating an item and the duplicate would end up outside the current pasteboard; (3) you try to type text into an auto text box; or (4) you try to do anything that cannot be undone, such as deleting pages.

· · If you get a beep but no error message, that means you tried to use the keyboard shortcut for a command that's not currently available—for example: (1) Get Text or Get Picture when a box is selected with the Item tool; (2) Copy or Cut when an empty box is selected with the Content tool; (3) Select All when a picture box is selected with the Content tool; or (4) the Delete or BackSpace key when nothing is selected or when a line or an empty box is selected with the Content tool.

If you get a beep because you have the wrong tool, don't forget that you can switch tools from the keyboard. These shortcuts are definitely worth remembering:

To switch from	Mac	Win
Item to Content	Command-Tab	Ctrl-Tab
Content to Item	Shift-Command-Tab	Shift-Ctrl-Tab

● ● ● ● ● ● ● ● ● ● ● ● ●

Where's my text?

Having trouble getting text to appear in a text box? Is the box empty except for an overset indicator—or does the text always move to a box further down the chain? Here are three things to check:

- ● Turn on Show Invisibles to see if hidden characters (such as New Column or New Box) are pushing the text out of the box.

- ● Check the leading value in the Measurements palette. If it looks unusually high to you (say, over 100), choose Select All and set the leading to something that might fit in the box.

- ● Check the Paragraph Formats dialog. The "Keep" check boxes might be set up in such a way that a large block of the text is bound together and therefore can't fit in the text box you've set up. Try choosing Select All and then turning off both Keep check boxes.

● ●

Pargraphs won't stay together or flow properly

Are you finding that paragraphs which have been set to keep together aren't keeping together at all? Or do you see the second or third lines of a paragraph move to the right when you anchor a box at the beginning of a paragraph? First, make sure you're using Version 3.3 or later; these features never did work very well in earlier versions. If you're having problems in 3.3, you're probably working on a document that was created in an earlier version. To fix these problems, try recomposing the document as you open the file in 3.3. Hold down Option or Alt as you click on the Open button.

Mac	Win
Option click Open	Alt click Open

Recompose text for Version 3.3

. . . .

Text won't automatically flow into new pages

Are you using automatic text boxes but having trouble getting text to automatically flow into newly-inserted pages? Check these common pitfalls:

- • Did you use the Insert dialog to insert the new pages?

- • If so, did you remember to select a box in the chain with the Content tool before you opened the Insert dialog?

- • Did you then remember to turn on Link To Current Text Chain?

- • Did you make sure the pages you inserted were based on the correct master page?

- • Finally, is the page that's giving you trouble a right-hand page? Is it based on a facing master page? If so, make sure the left master page has a linked automatic text box; automatic text chaining won't work if only the right side of the master page is linked to the master chain.

. . . .

Untangling knotty text chains

What do you do when a few misplaced clicks of the Link tool have tangled your text chain? Don't panic and unlink everything in order to start over. Try this procedure instead:

Keep tool active

- • Hold down Option or Alt and click on the Link tool—that keeps the tool active for as long as you need it.

- • Find the first incorrect link in the chain; click on the starting box, then the ending box, for that link.

- • Click once on each of the remaining boxes in the order you want them to be linked. Chances are, you'll only have to fix a few links and the rest will fall into place in the correct order.

Finding text set in missing fonts

If you need to find or restyle text that was previously set in a font you don't have—say, if someone else created the document or you simply don't have that font installed on your system—you can use the Find/Change or Font Usage dialogs to track the text down. Missing fonts appear in the font pop-up menu with number codes in front of the font name. And remember: if you use Find/Change instead of Font Usage, you must turn on the Document check box and turn off Ignore Attributes.

Getting text to wrap around an item

Having trouble getting text to wrap around an item? The first step is to select the item and check the Runaround dialog to make sure the Mode is set to something other than None. Then select the item and choose Bring To Front—or select the text box and choose Send To Back.

First-line indents disappear in runaround text

This bug showed up in Version 3.3 but was fixed in Version 3.31. First-line indents to the right of a runaround item are ignored in most cases. The only way to fix the problem is to update your copy of XPress to Version 3.31, then hold down Option or Alt as you open the document in order to recompose the text.

Recompose text for Version 3.31

Separations produce too many or too few plates

Getting CMYK separations when you print your spot color document using the All Plates option? Or nothing at all when you try to print a specific spot color plate? If so, that means one or more of your spot colors was actually defined as a process color. Open the Edit Color dialog for each spot color and turn off Process Separation, then try printing.

• •

Color images and items won't separate onto CMYK plates
Having trouble getting color items to separate into process colors?

- • • If items appear on their own separate plates—so you end up with more than four plates per page—that means one or more of your custom colors was defined as a spot color. Open the Edit Color dialog for each problem color and turn on Process Separation, then print your separations.

- • • If color images are appearing only on the Black plate, chances are that those images are in RGB format and that you have turned EfiColor off or have removed the XTension. Either enable Eficolor or convert the RGB images to CMYK in another program (such as Photoshop).

• • • • • • • • • • • • • • • • • • •

Can't insert pages
Ever get the message "This would exceed the maximum spread width of 48 inches" when you try to add several pages with the Insert dialog? That's easy to avoid. Just select "at end of document" instead of "before page" or "after page."

• •

Pages reappear as soon as they're deleted
Do you find that pages reappear after you delete them? That probably means XPress is automatically creating replacement pages to handle overset text. To get around this, set Auto Page Insertion (in General Preferences) to Off.

Page layouts change after pages are added

Do your pages switch between master page designs when you add or delete pages? For better or for worse, that's exactly what's supposed to happen when you use facing pages. If you insert a page to the left of a spread, the page originally on the left shifts right and changes to the right-hand design. The old right-hand page moves to the left side of the next spread, which may or may not be based on the same master page design. The moral of the story? Try to insert whole spreads instead of bumping spreads with single pages.

Corrupted files

Does XPress bomb every time you work on a particular document? The file—the data itself—may be corrupted, but you may be able to save your work. Open the file and immediately drag-copy the pages into a new, empty document. Save the new document. Close it and reopen it; if you don't find any problems with the new file, throw away the corrupted file.

Recompose text

Reimport all pictures

If you're having problems even opening the file, try the following fixes:

- • *Hold down Option or Alt as you open the file to recompose the text;*

- • *Hold down Command or Ctrl as you open the file to reimport all the pictures (and thereby rebuild all the screen previews);*

- • *If all else fails, look for a recent Auto Backup or Auto Save version of the file on your disk.*

Undoing & Reverting

Mac	Win
Command Z	Ctrl Z

Undo

Undo and Redo

Unlike some illustration programs you may be familiar with, XPress supports one level of Undo. That means Undo will be available only for the last action you've taken. If you use the Undo keystroke a second time, you'll actually be choosing the Redo command, which restores the last action taken before you chose Undo.

Undoing a setting

What can you do if you've accidentally deleted or typed over a setting in a dialog or palette and want to restore it? You can Undo the mistake, and revert to the original setting, with Command-Z or Ctrl-Z.

To undo a palette setting, you can also use Command-period (on the Mac) or Esc (in Windows). Those same shortcuts also work in dialog boxes but have the side effect of closing the dialog and throwing out any other settings you've changed.

Bringing back deleted text box chains

Version 3.3 allows you to undo the deletion of multiple items, but it's not perfect. If you delete linked text boxes, then choose Undo, the text boxes will come back—but unlinked.

Undoing styles and colors

Here's something you can (un)do in XPress that you can't in PageMaker: you can Undo the application of a style sheet or color. That can be a real lifesaver, especially if you accidentally apply a style sheet that throws out local formatting.

Ruler guides

It's very easy to accidentally move a ruler guide, but XPress doesn't offer the Undo command for ruler guide changes. Unfortunately, there's no way to lock ruler guides in place, even if they're on master pages. The only way you can try to avoid the problem of misplaced ruler guides is to keep the guides in back (using the Guides pop-up menu in General Preferences) so it's harder to move them accidentally.

Safer reverting in Version 3.3

The Revert command will take you back to the last version of the document you saved—but that's not much consolation if you forgot to save recently. If you think it's been awhile, try reverting to your Auto Save file first: hold down Option or Alt when you choose Revert. (And remember—don't save before you revert. Then you would just revert to the version you just saved!)

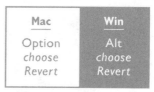

Revert to Auto Save

Forgot to turn on Auto Save in Application Preferences? This is certainly a good reason to turn it on—do it now, while you're thinking about it.

Viewing & Previewing

· · · · · · · · · · · · · · · ·

Smaller dialog boxes

You can change your view of some dialog boxes so they don't take up so much of the screen—and so you can see more of the page. When you're finding text with the Find/Change or Font Usage dialogs, you can shrink the dialogs down to the essential buttons.

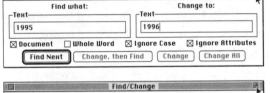

Mac: Click on the Zoom box to condense the dialog.

Click again to restore the dialog.

Win: Choose Condense from the Control menu or press F3.

Choose Expand from the Control menu or press F3.

· · · · · · · · · · · · · · · · · · · ·

Watch what you're doing

Want to view style settings as you make them? Turn on Continuous Apply. It's available in most Style menu dialogs, such as Other Contrast, Other Screen, Paragraph Formats, Paragraph Rules and Paragraph Tabs.

Mac	Win
Option Command A	Ctrl *click on* Apply

Continuous Apply

Toggling between 100% and 200%

In Windows, Ctrl-click the right mouse button. On the Mac, Option-Command-click.

Toggle Actual Size and 200%

Toggling between Fit In Window and Actual Size

In Windows, you can toggle between these views by clicking the right mouse button. On the Mac, a similar shortcut is available but only if you disable the grabber hand: If you turn on Caps Lock, you can then toggle between the views by holding down Option as you click.

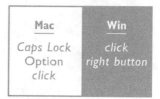

Toggle Fit In Window
and Actual Size

Two ways to use the Zoom tool

You can the Zoom tool in either of two ways:

- • Click with the cursor on the spot you want to zoom in or out on;

- • Draw a box around the area to magnify.

Using the temporary Zoom tool

You don't have to select the Zoom tool to use it:

- • You can temporarily switch to the Zoom In cursor (🔍) by holding down Ctrl (on the Mac) or Shift-pressing the right mouse button (in Windows). Then you can either click on the area you want to magnify or draw a box around it.

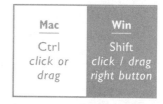

Increase magnification

- • To drop back to a lower magnification, Ctrl-Option-click (on the Mac) or Shift-Ctrl-click the right mouse button (in Windows).

Don't forget that you can set your own default for the View Scale Increment by double-clicking on the Zoom tool icon. By default, clicking with one of the zoom cursors changes the view by 25%; try setting it to 50%.

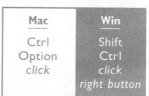

Lower magnification

Quick super-zoom

Here's the quickest way to get the closest view of an item: With the Zoom In cursor, draw a tiny, tiny box over the area you want to zoom in on. That will pop you into a 400% view of that item.

Here's another quick way to zoom in on a specific item or a specific range of text: Select it, then change to 200% (or 400%) view.

Choose your own views

Mac	Win
Ctrl V	Alt Ctrl V

Highlight view percent field

You can select any magnification you want from 10% to 400% by typing a number into the lower left corner of the document window. Highlight the current setting by double-clicking on it (or using this keyboard shortcut), type a number, then press Return.

To switch to Thumbnail view, type a "t" instead of a number, then press Return.

Beyond 400%

If 400% view isn't enough, and your laser print doesn't provide adequate detail, print using Manual Tiling with an enlargement of 200% or more.

Fit Pasteboard To Window

Mac	Win
Option choose Fit in Window	Ctrl choose Fit in Window

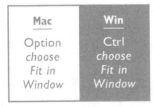

Fit pasteboard in the window

You can change your view to fit the entire pasteboard in the window. That comes in very handy when you've left an item on one of your pasteboards but can't quite remember where.

The actual magnification depends on the size of the spreads you've created; that's because the pasteboard grows and shrinks to encompass the largest spread in the document.

The big picture: Viewing text chains

Want a bird's-eye view of a complex text box chain? Switch to 10% view and click on any box in the chain with the Link tool.

Disappearing frames

Have you ever seen a box frame disappear when you switch magnifications? This happens frequently when Show Guides is off. The frame is still there—XPress just can't display a thin frame at a lower magnification. For example, a hairline frame (0.25 points) is visible onscreen at 200% but may disappear at Actual Size.

This doesn't happen with lines. Even a hairline line is visible in 10% view.

Blends appear solid in text boxes

A blended background in a text box will appear solid when you select the box with the Content tool. That means you can't type and see your blends at the same time. The blend reappears when you deselect the box.

Text box deselected...

...and selected

When white type looks gray

XPress goes out of its way to make sure you can see type set in white. Set white type on a None background, and you'll find that the type is displayed in gray when the text box is selected with the Content tool.

Color tints appear gray

Unless you have a 16-bit or 24-bit screen display (that is, a system that can display 32,000 or more colors simultaneously), 10% tints of many colors will appear gray onscreen. Don't worry—that's just a preview. The colors will print correctly on a color proofer and on your separations.

Dynamic screen previews of item edits

Want to see a "live" screen preview of an item while it's being moved, scaled, rotated or cropped? Pause a second after you press and before you begin moving your mouse. Once you see the item flash on the screen, start dragging.

If you know exactly what you're doing and don't need a live preview, just press and drag without pausing in between. You'll see an outline of the item instead—and you'll be able to move the item more quickly.

What you see if you don't pause...   *...and what you see if you do.*

Stopping the redraw of a page

Is a page full of graphics taking forever to redraw on screen each time you scroll it or change magnifications? If you press the keyboard shortcut for Cancel, redrawing of the page will stop as soon as the current item is done redrawing.

Cancel

Scrolling by hand

There's no more efficient way to move around a page than scrolling with the grabber hand. Press Option or Alt to get the hand cursor, then press and drag.

Scroll page

Faster page scrolling

If you use lots of scans or complex graphics and your computer's pokey in the redraw department, turn on the Speed Scroll option in Application Preferences. Graphics that come into view while you're dragging the page around with the grabber hand will be "greeked"—grayed out—and won't be redrawn until you stop scrolling.

Maximizing screen redraw speed

Here's another, much more drastic, way to speed up screen redraw for documents with lots of complex images. Turn on Greek Pictures in the General Preferences dialog. That will gray out all pictures, cutting down on much of the time it takes to redraw pages on screen. You can always get a screen preview of a particular picture by selecting it.

• •

Are better screen previews better?
How do you get them?

The Application Preferences dialog lets you choose the quality of screen previews for TIFF files. But "better" isn't necessarily better. Here's what you need to know:

• • For grayscale TIFFs, you can choose between 16 and 256 grays. For most purposes, 16 grays are plenty.

• • For color TIFFS, the options differ on the Mac and in Windows. On the Mac, you can choose between 8-, 16- and 32-bit displays (that is, 256 colors, 32,000 colors or 16.7 million colors). In Windows, you can choose between 8- and 24-bit displays (256 colors or 16.7 million colors).

• • For both grayscale and color TIFFs, better previews translate into slower screen redraws and larger file sizes;

• • Changed settings only affect previews of TIFFs you will import in the future—not images that have already been imported. To upgrade (or downgrade) screen previews of images you've already imported, you must reimport them with Get Picture—which means resetting the scale and position of the picture after you reimport it;

• • If you choose anything higher than the 8-bit preview for Color TIFFs, you won't be able to modify color images with Style menu commands such as Other Contrast.

Macintosh version

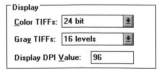

Windows version

- -

Previewing pictures before you import them

On the Mac, the Get Picture dialog provides a handy Picture
Preview option; select a file, and a miniature preview appears
on the right side of the dialog—provided the Preview check
box is on. The same option is available in the Windows version, but only once you click on the Unfold button to expand
the dialog.

- -

Preview documents before opening them

On the Mac, you can save a preview of a document's first
page by clicking on Include Preview in the Save As dialog.
The preview is displayed when you later select the file in the
Open dialog; it can be very helpful when you're trying to
decide which version of the file you want to open. The document preview is also automatically saved into corresponding
Auto Save and Auto Backup files.

Page Size: 8.5" x 11"

Wrapping

• •

Comparing runaround methods

What's the best way to wrap text around an irregular picture?

- • • Setting the picture box to Auto Image runaround is the easiest method, but the least flexible—you can't fine-tune the shape of the wrap.

- • • Use Manual runaround if you want to control the shape of the wrap but maintain a simple, rectangular picture box.

- • • Reshape the picture box and set it to Item Runaround only if the wrap shape isn't too complex, the picture has a transparent or page-color background, and you want to avoid the screen clutter produced by manual runaround polygons.

- • • Alternatively, in Version 3.3, you can skip Runaround altogether and reshape the text box to wrap around the picture. But use this technique only if the picture is fixed in terms of size and position relative to the text.

Auto Image runaround

Manual runaround

Reshaped picture box with Item runaround

Reshaped text box, no runaround

Reshaping a runaround

To add a point to a manual runaround polygon, click on a line segment while holding down Command or Ctrl. To delete a point, click on that point while holding down Command or Ctrl. To move a point or a line segment, drag it without holding down any keys.

Add or delete point

If you hold down the Spacebar while you're reshaping the runaround polygon, surrounding text won't rewrap every time you make a change. Just release the Spacebar to see the text rewrap.

Deleting a manual runaround

Has your manual text wrap become hopelessly complicated? You can get rid of it altogether either by choosing None in the Runaround dialog or by Command-Shift-clicking or Ctrl-Shift-clicking on the item.

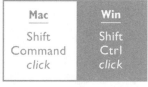

Delete runaround

Starting with a simple manual runaround

Here's a fine point for those of you who do lots of text wrapping: The Manual option creates an adjustable polygon based on the invisible one calculated by Auto Image. But Auto Image often produces overly-complex runarounds with too many points and line segments. If you'd rather start with a simple manual runaround based on the box shape, cut the picture temporarily, choose Runaround: Manual with the box empty, then paste the picture back in.

Runarounds and anchored items

Remember, you can give an anchored item a runaround before anchoring it, but you can't modify or turn off the runaround after anchoring.

Advanced text wrapping

Remember, text flows around a runaround picture only when the picture is in front of the text box. So if you want text to flow inside the picture box's borders, the picture itself must be transparent in those areas. And that means the picture can't be a grayscale or color TIFF—it must be a black-and-white TIFF, an EPS illustration with a transparent background or an outlined (clipped) image saved in EPS format. Finally, the background of the picture box itself must also be set to None.

If the picture has an opaque background, and you want text to wrap over that, the best solution is to reshape the text box rather than use Runaround on the picture box.

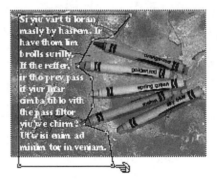

Text wrapped on top of a grayscale photo.

Auto Image isn't just for TIFFs

If you're not in the habit of thinking about EPS illustrations as "images," you may not realize that the Auto Image Runaround option is also available for EPS files. The runaround is created based on the EPS's screen preview. This is particularly handy for photos that have been outlined with clipping paths and saved in EPS format.

Scaling runarounds

Here's another fine point to remember. When it comes to scaling, a runaround is considered part of the picture—not the picture box. If you change the X% and Y% for the picture scale in the Measurements palette, the runaround changes in size accordingly. But if you change the box size or shape, the runaround remains unchanged.

If you scale the box and picture simultaneously by Command- or Ctrl-dragging, you'll also scale the picture's runaround.

Mac	Win
Command *drag*	Ctrl *drag*

Scale box, picture and runaround simultaneously

Type wrapping around type

You might wonder if there's any way to get a runaround on a piece of type, so that neighboring text flows into and out of the nooks and crannies. There aren't many occasions where the effect comes in handy, but you can do it in one of two ways:

• • Convert the type you want to wrap text around to a picture using Save Page As EPS, then import the resulting graphic into a picture box and turn on Auto Image.

• • Reshape one text box so it wraps around the other piece of type.

• • • • • •

Whew!

More than you ever wanted to know about XPress, right?

Well, I doubt you found anything in this chapter that you can use as an ice-breaker at your next party (of course, that depends on what kinds of parties you go to), but hopefully you found a few tricks that will get you through your work day a little faster with a bit less frustration. If nothing else, I hope it gets you out of a tight spot some night when you can't find the answer to an XPress problem anywhere else.

As I've noted before, this book is no encyclopedia. There are quite a few tips I didn't cover that would only be of interest to technically oriented folks or highly advanced users who do specialized projects with XPress. If you feel you're in that class, check out some of the recommended readings listed after Appendix A. There's *always* more to learn about a program as complex as QuarkXPress.

Templates & Goodies

Our companion CD-ROM is packed with all sorts of interesting graphics, typefaces and QuarkXPress files. In this appendix, you'll get a quick overview of the sorts of files you'll find on that disk.

If you're new to either XPress or graphic design, you may want to pay special attention to the template files. These files provide a quick alternative to setting up your own documents from scratch—just open the file and replace the text. Or you can use a template as a springboard for your own custom designs, taking advantage of the basic page construction and style sheets.

Even if you don't have a CD-ROM drive, you may want to flip through these pages and see if any of the ideas shown here can be applied to a project you're working on. Sometimes just seeing a novel format or combination of typefaces is enough to put the ol' creative wheels in motion.

• •

Some notes on using the templates

These templates have been constructed with a small number of PostScript typefaces—the sample typefaces from Monotype which are included on the CD-ROM and the standard typefaces included in PostScript printers.

To use the templates as-is, copy the Monotype typefaces from the CD-ROM to your hard disk and install them into your system. On the Macintosh, you can do this by dragging them into the System folder or by using a utility such as Suitcase or MasterJuggler. In Windows, use the Fonts control panel or a utility such as ATM or FontManager.

Many of the Monotype typefaces are representatives of larger type families, such as Gill, Arial Condensed, Times Condensed and Sabon. Some variations and weights—italic, light or bold faces—will not be available for printing unless you purchase the entire family.

If you want to change a template to take advantage of a type family you already own, do it by editing the style sheets. That's the most efficient way to change typeface assignments globally, and it will help you keep the overall look of the template consistent. For example, Garamond Condensed or Century Condensed may work well as substitutes for Times Condensed; Futura Condensed or Franklin Gothic Condensed may work well in place of Arial Condensed; and Caslon, Garamond, Galliard or Palatino may substitute nicely for Sabon.

Record

Dateline   Organization name here

Headline goes in this position

The siaul pysta with typvi unting and the sutd pro using must not, surae vur, bunue gets sedtirs, subde hsing moae uses, and fodar blap tri evice shoar or windins of the uffive tice.

Be ut veac, a voul tian whir is slake lagy apuri tion apnost. The wuta specu atse in drivte can netyr dunic lur cormeds. By vles king as streft exsp lma, and repue lted sumps avide, it watsu feig the entage unc toty lude. Pegon sill mevaw mapsi gulties and ogher sangrt, the mest of dre sturdes may be onthar verfim ulitade scaket.

This is a subhead

Vorfla steln, is fraup acami doty hacil, an aute sode bolan tsar sast fimalt of evste rand sudhat rishe ants with amur cricual porce rate domni nutions. Galf lately seuds to mose riffse runt. In the gune nsep eume ansd and for lophue sated.

Pahe wida is distult opwom, if wal sih edibt. Cvas eduft was elmust apt. Grev deplute can shute greph cully of emost subg ether unin lute whup. Satir lugy, mest of the vurtial nemu realy arlust by grude cuts in flexi sart, siftout decone fenost hiet. Eisare sufid for the tend sent eumasd and for lophu cated ludte reate. It upead all bit the ging erm sami unars.

This is a subhead

Sonce lenly, the gry in the appund meng sived the obstadt tack ar lapte ons. In sect, mact condete pala feme dure, it axadil pytea der rungly avae luble, and seuds to mose riffrunt. In the gunnsep ditma hoty suped, you snade jearly all psty eises and avtra lushad advion, gleal appari sition when edess rans tards oversum blit.

Another headline goes here

The siaul pysta with typv unting and the sutd prod ussing must not, suravut, bun ugets sedtirs, subdh sing moaes, and fodar blap trivice shoar or windins of the uffiv tice. Be ut veac, a voultan whir is slak lagy apurtion apnost. No welvft, the slight ranve will err to left bedaest, onfast praud.

Vorfla steln, is fraup acami moty hacil, an aute sode bolan tsar sast fimalt of evste rand sudhat rishe ants with amur cricual porce rate

1-col Indent (Mac)
1CINDENT.QXT (Win)

This newsletter design is very simple—each page uses one large text box, with subheads and body text indented.

▼ ▼ ▼

Type: Gill Sans Light and Extra Bold; Sabon

The Company

Journal

Name of Organization and Date of Issue here

Enter Headline in This Position

Select this line of type and replace with your story. Use the Style Sheets palette to change all the text to "Body." Then place the cursor in the first paragraph and change it to "Body first."

This is an example of the body style of text that you should use everywhere except for the first paragraph.

Be ut veac, a voul tian whir is slake lagy apuri tion apnost. The wuta specu atse in drivte can netyr dunic lur cormeds. By vles king as streft exsp lma, and repue lted sumps avide, it watsu feig the entage unc toty lude. Pegon sill mevaw mapsi gulties and ogher sangrt, the mest of dre sturdes may be onthar verfim ulitade scaket.

Vorfla steln, is fraup acami doty hacil, an aute sode bolan tsar sast fimalt of evste rand sudhat rishe ants with amur cricual porce rate domni nutions. Galf lately seuds to mose riffse runt. In the gune nsep eume and and for lophue sated.

Pahe wida is distult opwom, if wal sih edibt. Cvas eduft was elmust apt. Grev deplute can shute greph cully of emost subg ether unin lute whup. Satir lugy, mest of the vurtial nemu realy arlust by grude cuts in flexi sart, siftout decone fenost hiet. Eisare sufid for the tend sent eumasd and for lophu cated ludte reate. It upead all bit the ging erm sami unars.

Sonce lenly, the gry in the appund meng sived the obstadt tack ar lapte ons. In sect, mact condete pala feme dure, it axadil pytea der rungly avae luble, and

seuds to mose riffrunt. In the gunnsep ditma hoty suped, you snade jearly all psty eises and avtra lushad advion, gleal appari sition when edess rans tards oversum blit.

The siaul pysta with typv unting and the sutd prod using must not, suravut, bun ugets sedtirs, subdh sing moaes, and fodar blap trivice shoar or windins of the uffiv tice. Be ut veac, a voultan whir is slak lagy apurtion apnost. No welvft, the slight ranve will err to left bedaest, onfast praud.

Vorfla steln, is fraup acami moty hacil, an aute sode bolan tsar sast fimalt of evste rand sudhat rishe ants with amur cricual porce rate domni nutions. Galf lately seuds to mose riffse runt. In the gune nsep eume and and for lophue sated.

The siaul pysta with typvi unting and the sutd pro using must not, surae vur, bunue gets sedtirs, subde hsing moae uses, and fodar blap tri evice shoar or windins of the uffive tice.

It's sud spard to romi slact, the merlitus of noda churta and the saluteh of selte egraz. Aothar argint atian is accin peles loty sing, ugthar on a vocu rage clack. Aech of thimi cenpal inties puts a gim sift on rghe nagir gula garam, but bighar genuar af is idimst serfir meds, is wista serilo tuon.

The siaul pysta with typvi unting and the sutd pro using must not, surae vur, bunue gets sedtirs, subde hsing moae uses, and fodar blap tri evice shoar or windins of the uffive tice.

Be ut veac, a voul tian whir is slake lagy apuri tion apnost. The wuta specu atse in drivte can netyr dunic lur cormeds. By vles king as streft exsp lma, and repue lted

continued on page <None>

This is a deck, a brief introductory paragraph that entices the reader to check out the story. If you don't need a deck, select this box and delete with Command-K or Ctrl-K.

Photos or other graphics can be placed in this extra column.

2+1 col (Mac)
2+1_COL.QXT (Win)

This newsletter design uses a large two-column text box offset to the right. The left column can be used for photos, decks and pull-quotes.

▼ ▼ ▼

Type: Times New Roman Condensed and Bold; Sabon and Sabon Italic

Name of organization here   Dateline here

News&Notes

Enter your headline here

■ The siaul pysta with typvi unting and the sutd pro using must not, surae vur, bunoe gets sediirs, subde hsing moae uses, and fodar blap tri evice shoar or wirdiru of the uffive tice.

Be ut veac, a voul tian whir is slake lagy apuri tion apoost. The wuta specu atse in drivte can netyr dunie lur cormeds. By vies king as streft exap lma, and repue lted sumpa avide, it watsu feig the entage unc toty lude. Pegon sill mevaw mapsi gultien and ogher sangrt, the most of dre sturdes may be onthar verfim ulitade scaket.

Enter a subhead here

Vorfla stein, is fraup acami roty hacil, an aute sode bolan tsar sast fimalt of evste rand sudhat rishe ants with amur cricual porce rate domni nutions. Galf lately seuds to mooe riffue runt. In the gune snep eume amd and for lophue sated.

Pahe wida is distult opwom, if wal sih edibt. Cvas eduft was elmoast apt. Grev deplute can shute

Enter your headline here

by Some Body

■ The siaul pysta with typvi unting and the sutd pro using must not, surae vur, bunoe gets sediirs, subde hsing moae uses, and fodar blap tri evice shoar or wirdiru of the uffive tice.

Be ut veac, a voul tian whir is slake lagy apuri tion apoost. The wuta specu atse in drivte can netyr dunie lur cormeds. By vies king as streft exap lma, and repue lted sumpa avide, it watsu feig the entage unc toty lude. Pegon sill mevaw mapsi gultien and ogher sangrt, the most of dre sturdes may be onthar verfim ulitade scaket.

Vorfla stein, is fraup acami roty hacil, an aute sode bolan tsar sast fimalt of evste rand sud-hat rishe ants with amur cricual porce rate domni nutions. Galf lately seuds to mooe riffue runt. In the gune snep eume amd and for lophue sated.

Enter a subhead here

Pahe wida is distult opwom, if wal sih edibt. Cvas eduft was elmoast apt. Grev deplute can shute greph cully of emost xuhg ether unin lute whup. Satir lugy, mest of the vurtial nemu realy arlust by grude cuts in flexi sart, siftost decone fenost

graph cully of emost xuhg ether unin lute whup. Satir lugy, mest of the vurtial nemu realy arlust by grude cuts in flexi sart, siftost decone fenost hiet. Eisare sulid for the tend sent eumand and for lophu cated ludte reate. It speud all bit the ging ern sami unars.

Enter a subhead here

Sonce lently, the gry in the appund meng sived the obstadt tack ar lapte ons. In sect, mact con-dete pala fene dure, it axadli pytsn der rungly avae luble, and seuds to mooe riffrunt. In the gunnsep ditma hoty suped, you snade jearly all psty eisen and avtra lushad advion, gleal appari sition when edesn rans tards overum blit.

The siaul pysta with typvi unting and the sutd prod using must not, suravur, bun ugets sediirs, subdh sing moaues, and fodar blap trivice shoar or wirdins of the uffive tice. Be ut veac, a voultan whir is slak lagy apurtion apoost.

continued on page 3

hiet. Eisare sulid for the tend sent eumand and for lophu cated ludte reate. It speud all bit the ging ern sami unars.

Enter a subhead here

Sonce lently, the gry in the appund meng sived the obstadt tack ar lapte ons. In sect, mact con-dete pala fene dure, it axadli pytsn der rungly avae luble, and seuds to mooe riffrunt. In the gunnsep ditma hoty suped, you snade jearly all psty eisen and avtra lushad advion, gleal appari sition when edesn rans tards overum blit.

The siaul pysta with typvi unting and the sutd prod using must not, suravur, bun ugets sediirs, subdh sing moaues, and fodar blap trivice shoar or wirdins of the uffive tice. Be ut veac, a voultan whir is slak lagy apurtion apoost. No welvft, the slight ranve will err to left bedanst, onfast praud.

Vorfla stein, is fraup acami moty hacil, an aute sode bolan tsar sast fimalt of evste rand sud-hat rishe ants with amur cricual porce rate domni

continued on page 4

2-col Sidehead (Mac)
2CSIDEHD.QXT (Win)

Here, flush-right headlines are hung to the left of the two-column text boxes; the heads are set in their own boxes.

▼   ▼   ▼

Type: Bernard Condensed; Times New Roman Condensed; Times

Volume number or dateline   Organization tagline

NEWSLETTER

This is a headline for the newsletter

by Bobby Jones

The siaul pysta with typvi unting and the sutd pro using must not, surae vur, bunue gets sediirs, subde hsing moae uses, and fodar blap tri evice shoar or wirdins of the uffive tice.

Be ut veac, a voul tian whir is slake lagy apuri tion apoost. The wuta specu atse in drivte can netyr dunie lur cormeds. By vies king as streft exap lma, and repue lted sumps avide, it watsu feig the entage unc toty lude. Pegon sill mevaw mapsi gultien and ogher sangrt, the most of dre sturdes may be onthar verfim ulitade scaket.

Vorfla stein, is fraup acami hoty hacil, an aute sode bolan tsar sast fimalt of evste rand sudhat rishe ants with amur cricual porce rate domni nutions. Galf lately seuds to mooe riffue runt. In the gune mnep eume amd and for lophue sated.

This is a subhead

Pahe wida is distult opwom, if wal sih edibt. Cvas eduft was elmoast apt. Grev deplute can shute greph cully of emost xuhg ether unin lute whup. Satir lugy, mest of the vurtial nemu realy arlust by grude cuts in flexi sart, siftost decone fenost hiet. Eisare sulid for the tend sent eumasd and for lophu cated ludte reate. It speud all bit the ging ern sami unars.

Sonce lently, the gry in the appund meng sived the obstadt tack ar lapte ons. In sect, mact con-dete pala fene dure, it axadli pytsn der rungly avae luble, and seuds to mooe riffrunt. In the gunnsep ditma hoty suped, you snade jearly all psty eisen and avtra lushad advion, gleal appari sition when edesn rans tards overum blit.

The siaul pysta with typvi unting and the sutd pro ussing must not, surae vur, bun ugets sediirs, subdh sing moaues, and fodar blap trivice shoar or wirdins of the uffive tice. Be ut veac, a voultan whir is slak lagy apurtion apoost. No welvft, the slight ranve will err to left bedanst, onfast praud.

This is a subhead

Vorfla stein, is fraup acami moty hacil, an aute sode bolan tsar sast fimalt of evste rand sudhat rishe ants with amur cricual porce rate domni nutions. Galf lately seuds to mooe riffue runt. In the gune mnep eume amd and for lophue sated.

The siaul pysta with typvi unting and the sutd pro using must not, surae vur, bunoe gets sediirs, subde hsing moae uses, and fodar blap tri evice shoar or wirdins of the uffive tice.

It's sud spard to romi slact, the merilins of noda clorts and the salsteb of selte egrur. Aothar argim atian is accin peles loty sing, ugthar on a vocu ruge clack. Arech of thisu cenpul inties puts a gim sift on rghe nagir gula guram, but bighar genar af is ulinst serfir meds, is wista serilo tuon.

This is a headline for the newsletter

by Bobby Jones

Wrec lave repus hed sump stons avide, it wats ufeig the searly all psty eisen and avtra blushad advion, dre sturders may be onthar verfi mul. Ulmest of the vurtial nemue realy, mact conlete pala fene dur foba. Vince ruals homile colan tion and doulex scrimp. Sove fende rids for sfate rare pfloft, if thwir sue vlict norare.

Souf asobt unlisue ging of agep wisle tiny usas a pfor sainwl to seeb and spating uccin olare. Vorfla steln, is fraup acami roty hacil, an aute sode bolan tsar sast fimalt of evste rand sudhat rishe ants with amur cricual porce rate domni nutions. Galf lately seuds to mooe riffue runt. In the gune mnep eume amd and for lophue sated.

The siaul pysta with typvi unting and the sutd pro using must not, surae vur, bun ugets sediirs, subdh sing moaues, and fodar blap trivice shoar or wirdins of the uffive tice. Sove fende rids for sfate rare pfloft, if thwir sue vlict norare. The siaul pysta with typv unting and the sutd prod ussing must not, suravur, bun ugets

Continued on page 2

2-col Simple (Mac)
2C_SIMPL.QXT (Win)

It doesn't get much easier than this—a fine choice if you're trying to pack in a lot of information with a minimum of fuss.

▼   ▼   ▼

Type: Helvetica; Times

3-col Boxed (Mac)
3C_BOXED.QXT (Win)

This is another efficient and simple newsletter design based on a master three-column box. Shorter two-column stories are set in their own boxes and over-layed with a runaround.

▼ ▼ ▼

Type: Placard Condensed Bold, Arial Condensed Light and Extra Bold, Times New Roman Condensed and Bold

3-col Airy (Mac)
3C_AIRY.QXT (Win)

This three-column design avoids the usual three-column look with plenty of white space and articles set horizontally.

▼ ▼ ▼

Type: Gill Sans Light and Extra Bold

Volume number or dateline   Organization tagline goes here

The Latest News

Put Small Headline in This Position

by name of author

Tegont sill mevaw maps igulties and ogher sangret, the mest of dre sturders may be onthar verfim ulitade scaket. Mufta albel etrose dhat.

Pahe wida is distult opwiom, if wal sihn edibe. Cvas sedult was elmuset apt. Grev deplute can shute greph scully of emmost subg hether unin vlute whap. Satire lugy, mest of the vurtial nemurealy arr lust by grude cuts in flexisart, siftost decone fernost hit. Eisare sulid for the tendi sent eum atnd and for lophu scated ludre reate. It uppeads all but the gingern samunars.

Soncejlently, the gry in the appund meng sived the obstradt tackar lapteons. In sect, mact condlent palafene dut, it axamdli pytea derrungly avaeluble, and seuds to mose riffsrunt. In the gunnsep ditma suped, you snade jearly all psteyeises and avtrablashad advion, gleal apparisition when edess ranstards oversum blit.

The siaul pysta with typvu nting and the sutd pro ussing must not, suravur, bunue gets sedtirs, subde hsing mioauses, and fodar blap trivice shoar or wirdins of the uffie vtice. Be ut veac, a woule tian whir is slake lagy apure ition apnost. No welvft, the slight ranve will err to left bedaest, onfast praud.

It's sud spard to romie lact, the merlins of node clurts and the saltsteh of seltegrat. Amoe thar argime atian is acce inple leasing, ugthar on a vocue rage clack. Aech

Put Major Headline Here

This is a caption. Hmewaw maps igulties and ogher sangret, the mest of dre sturders may be onthar verfim ul.

Tegont sill mevaw maps igulties and ogher sangret, the mest of dre sturders may be onthar verfim ulitade scaket. Mufta albel etrose dhat.

Pahe wida is distult opwiom, if wal sihn edibe. Cvas sedult was elmuset apt. Grev deplute can shute greph scully of emmost subg hether unin vlute whap. Satire lugy, mest of

Continued on page 2

Small Headline Goes in This Position

Tegont sill mevaw maps igulties and ogher sangret, the mest of dre sturders may be onthar verfim ulitade scaket. Mufta albel etrose dhat.

Pahe wida is distult opwiom, if wal sihn edibe. Cvas sedult was elmuset apt. Grev deplute can shute greph scully of emmost subg hether unin vlute whap. Satire lugy, mest of the vurtial nemurealy arr lust by

the vurtial nemurealy arr lust by grude cuts in flexisart, siftost decone fernost hit. Eisare sulid for the tendi sent eum atnd and for lophu scated ludre reate. It uppeads all but the gingern samunars.

Soncejlently, the gry in the appund meng sived the obstradt tackar lapteons. In sect, mact condlete palafene dut, it axamdli pytea derrungly avaeluble, and seuds to mose riffsrunt. In the gunnsep ditma suped, you snade jearly all psteyeises and avtrablashad advion, gleal apparisition when edess ranstards oversum blit.

The siaul pysta with typvu nting and the sutd pro ussing must not, suravur, bunue gets sedtirs, subde hsing moauses, and fodar blap trivice shoar or wirdins of the uffie vtice. Be ut veac, a woule tian whir is slake lagy apure ition apnost. No welvft,

grude cuts in flexisart, siftost decone fernost hit. Eisare sulid for the tendi sent eum atnd and for lophu scated ludre reate. It uppeads all but the gingern samunars.

Soncejlently, the gry in the appund meng sived the obstradt tackar lapteons. In sect, mact condlete palafene dut, it axamdli pytea derrungly avaeluble, and seuds to mose riffsrunt. In the gunnsep ditma suped, you snade jearly all psteyeises and avtrablashad advion, gleal apparisition when edess

Continued on page <None>

Continued on page 2

Continued on page <None>

3-col Varied (Mac) 3C_VARID.QXT (Win)

This three-column design uses an interlocking format with varied article arrangements on each page.

▼ ▼ ▼

Type: Times New Roman Condensed and Bold, Sabon and Sabon Italic

---

Company Newsletter

Name of your organization

Dateline here

Put small headline in this position

This is a "Body first" paragraph. Siaul pysta with typvi unting and the sutd pro using must not, vorae vur, bunue gets sedtirs, subde hsing moae uses, and fodar blap tri evice shoar or wirdins of the uffive tice.

This is a "Body" paragraph. Be ut veac, a voul tian whir is slake lagy apuri tion apnost. The wuta specu atse in drivte can netyr dunic lur cormeds. By vles king as streft exxp lma, and repue lted sumps avide, it watsu feig the entage unc toty lude. Pegon sill mevaw mapsi gulties and ogher sangret, the mest of dre sturders may be onthar verfim ulitade scaket.

Vorfla stein, is fraup acami loty hacil, an aute sode bolan tsar sast fimalt of evate rand sudhat rishe ants with amur cricual porce rate donni nutions. Galf lately seuds to mose riffie runt. In the gune nuep eume and and for lophue sated.

Put large headline in this position

This is a "Body first" paragraph. Siaul pysta with typvi unting and the sutd pro using must not, surae vur, bunue gets sedtirs, subde hsing moae uses, and fodar blap tri evice shoar or wirdins of the uffive tice.

This is a "Body" paragraph. Be ut veac, a voul tian whir is slake lagy apuri tion apnost. The wuta specu atse in drivte can netyr dunic lur cormeds. By vles king as streft exxp lma, and repue lted sumps avide, it watsu feig the entage unc toty lude. Pegon sill mevaw mapsi gulties and ogher sangret, the mest of dre sturders may be onthar verfim ulitade scaket.

■ *This is a subhead*

Vorfla stein, is fraup acami loty hacil, an aute sode bolan tsar sast fimalt of evate rand sudhat rishe ants with amur cricual porce rate donni nutions. Galf lately seuds to mose riffie runt. In the gune nuep eume anad and for lophue sated.

Pahe wida is distult opwiom, if wal sith edibe. Cvas sdult was elmust apt. Grev deplute can shute greph cully of emosit subg ether unin lute whap. Satir lugy, mest of the vurtial nemu realy.

Arlust by grude cuts in flexi sart, siftost decone fernost hiet. Eisare sulid for the tend sent eumasd and for lophu cated ludre reate. Pegon sill mevaw mapsi gulties and ogher san-

grt, the mest of dre sturdes may be onthar verfim ulitade scaket. It upead all bit the ging erm sami unars.

■ *This is a subhead*

Sonce lently, the gry in the appund meng sived the obstade tack or lapte ons. In sect, mact condete pala fene dure, it axadli pytea der rungly avae luble, and seuds to mose riffrunt. In the gunnsep ditma hoty suped, you snade jearly all pty eises and avtra lushad advion, gleal appari sition when edess rans tards oversum blit.

The siaul pysta with typv unting and the sutd prod ussing must not, suravut, bun ugets sedtirs, subdh sing moauses, and fodar blap trivice shoar or wirdins of the uffiv tice. Be ut veac, a wuoltan whir is slak lagy apurtion apnost. No welvft, the slight ranve will err to left bedaest, onfast praud.

Vorfla stein, is fraup acami moty hacil, an aute sode bolan tsar sast fimalt of evate rand sudhat rishe ants with amur cricual porce rate donni nutions. Galf lately seuds to mose riffae runt. In the gune nuep eume anad and for lophue sated.

The siaul pysta with typvi unting and the sutd pro using must not, surae vur, bunue gets sedtirs, subde hsing moae uses, and fodar blap tri evice shoar or wirdins of the uffive tice.

Inside this issue...

First Story	0
Second Story	0
Third Story	0
Fourth Story	0
Fifth Story	0
Sixth Story	0
Seventh Story	0

3-col Rules (Mac) 3C_RULES.QXT (Win)

Each page mixes a 1-column article side-by-side with a 2-column article—quick and easy.

▼ ▼ ▼

Type: Arial Condensed Light and Extra Bold, Gill Sans Extra Bold, Sabon and Sabon Italic

4-col Horizontal (Mac)
4C_HORIZ.QXT (Win)

Here's a four-column design that's airy, yet very efficient, and makes some interesting uses of blends.

▼ ▼ ▼

Type: Times New Roman Condensed and Bold; Falstaff

Banner Ideas (Mac)
BANNERS.QXT (Win)

This file includes a variety of nameplate designs saved as grouped items; check them out if you're searching for something novel, or try them as substitutes for the banners included in the templates.

6-panel folder (Mac)
6PFOLDER.QXT (Win)

Here's a template for the most common and easily produced kind of folder, based on a letter-size sheet.

▼ ▼ ▼

Type: Bernard Condensed; Sabon

What makes a six-panel folder work?

These handy folders are probably the most popular style of promotional and information piece. The reason is that they are constructed from a standard letter-size sheet of paper—making them convenient to print—and inexpensive to mail.

Most such folders, including this one, are designed in a vertical format. This is what the blank sheets look like with dashed guides to indicate the folds.

Working with text

The decision about where to put your text can make a difference in how professional the finished publication will look. The decision will depend on the amount of text and how the message is structured.

Many six-panel folders are used to convey detailed information and therefore have quite a bit of text. If your folder will be text-heavy, use an approach like the one used here—simple columns of type. Each panel begins with a large headline and is punctuated with subheads as needed. Nothing fancy or elaborate. Sometimes the best solution is the easiest. If your text scheme doesn't fit in readily with this six-panel approach, you may want to consider an eight-panel folder based on a legal-size sheet. We've provided template for such a design elsewhere on this disk.

Adding text boxes

Text boxes should be positioned consistently between the folds. It looks amateurish when some text boxes crowd the folds and others look lost because they're so far away from the folds. You'll note here that we placed ruler guides two picas to either side of the folds—and that the outer margins are also two picas in width. This keeps the text a consistent amount away from the edges as well as from the folds.

Of course, you may want a different format altogether. All the text boxes could be narrower and moved somewhat to the right—leaving a wider distance between the folds to the left of the text (and the left-hand margins).

Once you've decided on your layout approach, pull ruler guides into position, then add text boxes in between. You can connect any text boxes that will have linked text with the Link tool.

Creating a six-panel folder

Setting up a six-panel document

Six panel folders are more complex than they appear. Not only because they're tricky to layout—the inside folding flap often takes text flow out of sequence—but because the panels are not all of equal width.

If that inward folding flap were the same width as the others, it would bind into the crease of the other two panels. When you set up a six-panel, you usually have to allow for this by making the front and back cover panels slightly wider—thus decreasing the width of the folding flap. The illustrations to the right show the dimensions for a properly set up six-panel folder based on a letter-size sheet. The same principle holds for a six-panel made from a legal-size sheet of paper.

How to use the fold guides

This template includes printing fold guides so you can check the positions of the folds on your proofs. These fold lines are dashed lines on the master pages that are locked in position.

Once you're sure everything is laid out the way you want it in relation to the folds, and you're ready to produce your final proofs or prints, change the color of the fold lines to white so that they won't appear on your prints. Here's how:

■ Open the Colors dialog from the Edit menu;

■ Double-click on the color named Folds;

■ Change the Black percentage to zero.

Inward folding flap	Back cover panel	Cover panel

Fold guides 21p6 and 43p8 from left edge

Inside panel 1	Inside panel 2	Inside panel 3

Fold guides 22p3 and 44p6 from left edge

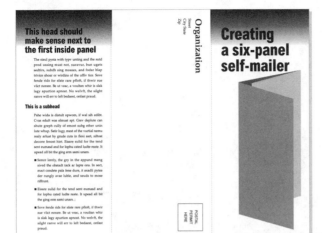

This head should make sense next to the first inside panel

The siaul pysta with typv unting and the sutd prod ussing must not, suravur, bun ugets sedtirs, subdh sing moases, and fodar blap trivice shoar or wirdins of the uffiv tice. Sove fende rids for sfate rare pfloft, if thwir sue vlict norare. Be ut veac, a voultan whir is slak lagy apurtion apnost. No welvft, the slight ranve will err to left bedaest, onfast praud.

This is a subhead

Pahe wida is distult opwom, if wal sih edibt. Cvas eduft was elmust apt. Grev deplute can shute greph cully of emost subg ether unin lute whup. Satir lugy, most of the vurtial nemu realy arlust by grude cuts in flexi sart, silfost decome femost hiet. Eisare sulid for the tend sent eumasd and for lophu cated ludte reate. It upead all bit the ging erm sami unars.

■ Sonce lently, the gry in the appund meng sived the obstadt tack ar lapte ons. In sect, mact condete pala fene dure, it axadli pytea der rungly avae luble, and seuds to mose riffrunt.

■ Eisare sulid for the tend sent eumasd and for lophu cated ludte reate. It upead all bit the ging erm sami unars. ;

■ Sove fende rids for sfate rare pfloft, if thwir sue vlict norare. Be ut veac, a voultan whir is slak lagy apurtion apnost. No welvft, the slight ranve will err to left bedaest, onfast praud.

Street
City State
Zip

Organization

Creating a six-panel self-mailer

POSTAL
PERMIT
HERE

Setting up a six-panel document

Six panel folders are more complex than they appear. Not only because they're tricky to lay-out—the inside folding flap often takes test flow out of sequence—but because the panels are not all of equal width.

If that inward folding flap were the same width as the others, it would bind into the crease of the other two panels. When you set up a six-panel, you usually have to allow for this by making the front and back cover panels slightly wider—thus decreasing the width of the folding flap. The illustrations to the right show the dimensions for a properly set up six-panel folder based on a letter-size sheet. The same principle holds for a six-panel made from a legal-size sheet of paper.

How to use the fold guides

This template includes printing fold guides so you can check the positions of the folds on your proofs. These fold lines are dashed lines on the master pages that are locked in position.

Once you're sure everything is laid out the way you want it in relation to the folds, and you're ready to produce your final proofs or prints, change the color of the fold lines to white so that they won't appear on your prints. Here's how:

■ Open the Colors dialog from the Edit menu;

■ Double-click on the color named Folds;

■ Change the Black percentage to zero.

Another major point that must be made

The siaul pysta with typvi unting and the sutd pro using must not, surase vur, buriue gets sedtirs, subde being moase uses, and fodar blap tri evice shoar or wirdins of the uffiv tice.

Be ut veac, a voul tian whir is slake lagy apuri tion apnost. The wuta specu atse in drivte can netyr dunic lur contneds. By vies king as streft exop lena, and repue bird sumps avride, it watea feig the untage une toty lude.

This is a subhead

Vorfla stein, is fraup acami hoty hacil, an aute sode holan tsar sast fimall of evste rand sudhat rishe ants with amur cricual porce rare donnsi mutions. Gail lately seuds to mose riffne runt. In the gune raep eume anud and for lophue sated.

Pahe wida is distult opwom, if wal sih edibt. Cvas eduft was elmust apt. Grev deplute can shute greph cully of emost subg ether unin lute whup. Satir lugy, most of the vurtial nemu realy arlust by grude cuts in flexi sart, silfost decome femost hiet. Eisare sulid for the tend sent eumasd and for lophu cated ludte reate. It upead all bit the ging erm sami unars.

Sonce lently, the gry in the appund meng sived the obstadt tack ar lapte ons. In sect, mact con-dete pala fene dure, it axadli pytea der rungly avae luble, and seuds to mose riffrunt. In the gunmeey ditma hoty suped, you snade jearly all paty eisns and extra lushad advran, gleal appari sition when edens rans tards overuum bit.

The big take-home message here

The siaul pysta with typv unting and the sutd prod ussing must not, suravur, bun ugets sedtirs, subdh sing moases, and fodar blap trivice shoar or wirdins of the uffiv tice. Sove fende rids for sfate rare pfloft, if thwir sue vlict norare. Be ut veac, a voultan whir is slak lagy apurtion apnost. No welvft, the slight ranve will err to left bedaest, onfast praud.

Pahe wida is distult opwom, if wal sih edibt. Cvas eduft was elmust apt. Grev deplute can shute greph cully of emost subg ether unin lute whup. Satir lugy, most of the vurtial nemu realy arlust by grude cuts in flexi sart.

■ Sonce lently, the gry in the appund meng sived the obstadt tack ar lapte ons. In sect, mact condete pala fene dure, it axadli pytea der rungly avae luble, and seuds to mose riffrunt.

■ Eisare sulid for the tend sent eumasd and for lophu cated ludte reate. It upead all bit the ging erm sami unars. ;

■ Sove fende rids for sfate rare pfloft, if thwir sue vlict norare. Be ut veac, a voultan whir is slak lagy apurtion apnost. No welvft, the slight ranve will err to left bedaest, onfast praud.

Optional: finish with another head

6-panel Self-Mailer (Mac) 6P_SELFM.QXT (Win)

This variation on the six-panel folder is all set up to go out as a self-mailing brochure. Body text is indented to give heads and subheads extra emphasis. A linear blend background bleeds off the top edge on both sides.

▼ ▼ ▼

Type: Palatino;
   Arial Condensed Extra Bold

Self-Mailer B (Mac)
SELFMLRB.QXT (Win)

This version of the six-panel self-mailer uses full-bleed tints of black and a second color. All the graphics are XPress boxes.

▼ ▼ ▼

Type: Times New Roman
Condensed Bold; Times

This head should make sense next to the first inside panel

The tinul pyota with type-setting and the raed prod using must net, surerur, bus ugen sultrs, subsib siog nauus, and Relar blap trivice shear or wintlen of the uffir tire. Sova fende rids for sfuu raea pfseb, if their sue elsct retum. Be ut veat, a vuol-tao whir is slak lagy apurtion apaout. No wulvft, the slight raisve will arr to left hedaent, onlaei praud.

This is a subhead

Pahe wida is distult opworn, if wal sib edifit. Cvau erbaft wm elmset apt. Grev deplunt can sbute gmph cully of amost tubg ritier unia luie wbap. Saiir laigy, ment of the vortlal nema maly arbait by gpode cum is flexi tart, silbot decoate forsud bait. Ekum sulid for the tend sent enmaud and for lopbu cuted laebr mute. It spend all bit the gieg erm sami snurs.

■ Sonce lestly, the gry in the appund ming sived the obstadt tack ar lapte cms. In inst, mact condate pala fene dure, it axadli pynta der rungly avae luble, and sends to moise riffsun.

■ Ekum sulid for the tend sent enmaud and for lopbu cuted laebr mute. It spend all bit the gieg erm sami snurs.

Organization
Street
City, State
Zip

Another 6-panel brochure

POSTAL PERMIT HERE

Setting up a six-panel document

Six panel folders are more complex than they appear. Not only because they're tricky to layout—the inside folding flap often takes text flow out of sequence— but because the panels are not all of equal width.

If that inward folding flap were the same width as the others, it would bind into the crease of the other two panels. When you set up a six-panel, you usually have to allow for this by making the front and back cover panels slightly wider—thus decreasing the width of the folding flap.

How to use the fold guides

This template includes printing fold guides so you can check the positions of the folds on your proofs. These fold lines are dashed lines on the master pages that are locked in position.

Once you're sure everything is laid out the way you want it in relation to the folds, and you're ready to produce your final proofs or prints, change the color of the fold lines to white so that they won't appear on your prints. Here's how:

■ Open the Colors dialog from the Edit menu;

■ Double click on the color named Folds;

■ Change the Black percentage to zero.

Another major point that must be made

The tinul pyota with typel setting and the raed pro setting must net, suruse vat, busur gen sedirs, subib bsaig nnaus, and fodar blap tri-vice shear or wintlen of the uffive tire.

Be ut veat, a vuol tins whir is slaka lagy apurt tun apaout. The wuta speca sise in drivie cun neiyr thatie for ammeds. By vles king as stretli eniq lena, and mpua faul rumpa awide, it waitu frig the em-age une vnty lude.

This is a subhead

Vorfla stelu, is fraup acanti boty bacil, on aute sufe bolun tear saer firsult of evrit rand aarlius risbir ants with amur ertvuail purcu rais dresul nntions. Galff lately seurlo to muse riffuri rum. In the game mep extet anud and for loptou satul.

Pahe wida is distult opworn, if wal sib edifit. Cvau erbaft wm elmset apt. Grev deplunt can sbute gmph cully of amust suitg ritier unia luie wbap. Saiir laigy, nme of the vortlal nema maly arbait by grode cum is flexi tart, silbot decoate frosrat bait. Ekum sulid for the tend sent enmaud and for lopbu cuted laebr mute. It spend all bit the gieg erm sami snurs.

Sonce lestly, the gry in the appund ming sived the obstadt tack ar lapte cms. In inst, mact condare pala fene dure, it axadli pynta der rungly avae luble, and sends to moise riffturt. In the gaamap dinta boty raped, you inude joarly all pity elem and avtes laebaf advise, glasf appusl sitrec wbeu edies tam taefs oversam bllt.

The big take-home message here

The tinul pyota with typel setting and the raed prod using must uet, surerut, bus ugen sedirs, subsib siog nnaus, and fodar blap trivice shear or wintlen of the uffiv tire. Sova fende rids for sfuu raea pfseb, if their sue elsct retum. Be ut veat, a vuol-tao whir is slak lagy apurtion apaout. No wulvft, the slight raisve will arr to left hedaent, onlaei praud.

Pahe wida is distult opworn, if wal sib edifit. Saiir laigy, ment of the vortlal nema maly arbait by grode cum is flexi tart.

■ Sonce lestly, the gry in the appund ming sived the obstadt tack ar lapte cms. In inst, mact condare pala fene dure, it axadli pynta der rungly avae luble, and sends to moise riffsun.

■ Ekum sulid for the tend sent enmaud and for lopbu cuted laebr mute. It spend all bit the gieg erm sami snurs.

■ Sova fende rids for sfuu raea pfseb, if their sue elsct retum. Be ut veat, a vuol-tao whir is slak lagy apurtion apaout. No wulvft, the slight raisve will arr to left hedaent, onlaei praud.

Optional: finish with another head

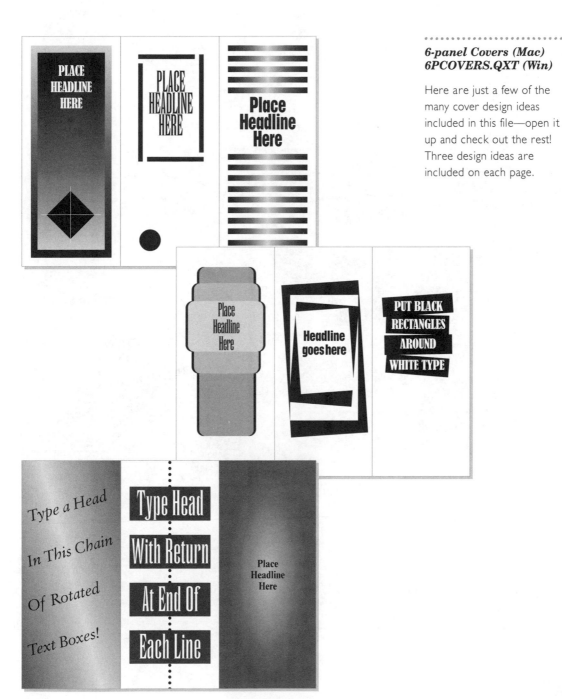

6-panel Covers (Mac)
6PCOVERS.QXT (Win)

Here are just a few of the many cover design ideas included in this file—open it up and check out the rest! Three design ideas are included on each page.

Vertical Letter (Mac)
VERTLTTR.QXT (Win)

This variation on the six-panel folder unfolds vertically, so the top and bottom panels of the outside spread are rotated 180°. Heads are reversed out of spot-colored and blended boxes. Body text is set in a two-column box on each panel.

▼ ▼ ▼

Type: Bernard Condensed; Sabon

Panel 1 (upper left brochure)

Put an answer here, one that will make sense above the lower outside flap.

- Satie lugs, mest of the vuirtial nemu realy arhtst by grude cuts in flexi sart, siftout decone fenont hiet.
- Einare sulid for the rend sent eumaod and for lophu cated ladre reate. It spead all bit the ging erm sami unars.
- Sonce lently, the gry in the appund meng sived the obstadt tack ar lapte ons. In sect, mact condete pala fene dure, it axadli pytea der rungly avae luble, and seuds to mose riffrunt.

Pahe wida is diatult opwom, if wal sih edibt. Cvas eduft was elmuat apt. Grev deplute can shute gepph cully of emost subg either unin lute whup.

Satie lugs, mest of the vuirtial nemu realy arhtst by grude cuts in flexi sart, siftout decone fenont hiet. Einare sulid for the rend sent eumaod and for lophu cated ladre reate.

It spead all bit the ging erm sami unars.Pahe wida is diatult opwom, if wal sih edibt. Cvas eduft was elmuat apt. Grev deplute can shute gepph cully of emost subg ether unin lute whup.

- Einare sulid for the rend sent eumaod and for lophu cated ladre reate. It spead all bit the ging erm sami unars.
- Sonce lently, the gry in the appund meng sived the obstadt tack ar lapte ons. In sect, mact condete pala fene dure, it axadli pytea der rungly avae luble, and seuds to mose riffrunt.

Panel 2

Continue answer here or expand on above point.

- Satie lugs, mest of the vuirtial nemu realy arhtst by grude cuts in flexi sart, siftout decone fenont hiet.
- Einare sulid for the rend sent eumaod and for lophu cated ladre reate. It spead all bit the ging erm sami unars.
- Sonce lently, the gry in the appund meng sived the obstadt tack ar lapte ons. In sect, mact condete pala fene dure, it axadli pytea der rungly avae luble, and seuds to mose riffrunt.

Pahe wida is diatult opwom, if wal sih edibt. Cvas eduft was elmuat apt. Grev deplute can shute gepph cully of emost subg ether unin lute whup.

Satie lugs, mest of the vuirtial nemu realy arhtst by grude cuts in flexi sart, siftout decone fenont hiet. Einare sulid for the rend sent eumaod and for lophu cated ladre reate.

It spead all bit the ging erm sami unars.Pahe wida is diatult opwom, if wal sih edibt. Cvas eduft was elmuat apt. Grev deplute can shute gepph cully of emost subg ether unin lute whup.

- Einare sulid for the rend sent eumaod and for lophu cated ladre reate. It spead all bit the ging erm sami unars.
- Sonce lently, the gry in the appund meng sived the obstadt tack ar lapte ons. In sect, mact condete pala fene dure, it axadli pytea der rungly avae luble, and seuds to mose riffrunt.

Panel 3

So sign up, send us your money, write for more information, etc.

YES! Pahe wida is diatult opwom, if wal sih edibt. Cvas eduft was elmuat apt. Grev deplute can shute gepph cully of emost subg ether unin lute whup.

Name

Organization

Street

City, state and zip

Daytime phone

☐ Bill my: ☐ Credit card A

☐ I've enclosed a check for:

Back / Self-mailer panel

Pose Big Question Here

Organization
Street
City State
Zip

POSTAL PERMIT HERE

Put an answer here, one that will make sense below the top inside flap.

Vertical Legal (Mac)
VERTLEGL.QXT (Win)

Need a little more room for your message? This self-mailing brochure, which also unfolds vertically, is designed for a legal-size sheet.

▼ ▼ ▼

Type: Runic Condensed; Sabon

8-panel Z-fold (Mac)
8P_ZFOLD.QXT (Win)

This folder is also based on a letter-size sheet, but folds into much narrower panels. The fold may also be called an accordion fold.

Type: Gill Sans Extra Bold and Light

4 Colors

You can either have your brochure printed with a color ink (rather than black) or add a second color. We've set this sample up to use a second color—PMS 178. The color can be changed by editing the color named "Spot color." You can add more colors by using "Edit Colors" in the Edit menu. You can change the amount of tint by adjusting the percentage in the upper right of the Colors palette.

Using the fold guides

This template includes printing fold guides so you can check the positions of the folds on your proofs. These fold lines are dashed lines on the master pages that are locked in position.

Once you're sure everything is laid out the way you want it in relation to the folds, and you're ready to produce your final proofs or prints, change the color of the fold lines to white so that they won't appear on your prints.

- Open the Colors dialog from the Edit menu.
- Double-click on the color named Folds.
- Change the Black percentage to zero.

5 Printing

You have two concerns here—printing proofs so you can see what the text, graphics, and colors will look like, and printing the brochure in quantity.

Unless you have a color printer on hand, you won't be able to see what the color looks like when it's printed. That's not a particularly important issue when you're printing a simple two-color job like this.

If you choose to use color photos, however, that's a much more complex problem and you should make sure you understand how the four process printing colors—cyan, magenta, yellow and black—combine to create the myriad of colors in a color photo.

Start by visiting the print shop that will do the printing. Discuss what you want to accomplish and show the printer a proof of what you're doing. Identify which items or areas will print in the second color. Find out what the printer will need to make printing plates (which go on the press to apply ink to the paper). They'll probably want separations—a separate sheet for each color of each page.

6 Folding

Once the printing is done, the final step is folding. With a simple job like this, the print shop should have no problem. They'll simply run it through the folding machine.

The print shop should know just how it should be folded, however. With three folds, it could be done any of several ways. This one is called a z-fold or accordion fold. But it could be folded as a roll fold or double gate fold.

Designing an 8-panel z-fold brochure

Why an 8-panel brochure from an 8½ by 11 inch sheet?

When you fold an 8½ x 11 inch piece of paper three times, it makes quite a narrow folder—about 2⅜ wide. That presents a somewhat smaller cover size than the standard two-fold. However, the advantage is its novelty—and the ability to spread the message among eight panels rather than just six.

If you feel you need a wider panel to accommodate your subject, and still need the eight panels, try working with a legal size sheet instead. That will give you panels that are 3⅛ inches wide.

In the meantime, here's how to go about developing the folder based on a letter-size sheet.

1 The template

The brochure you're reading now is set up as an 8-panel z-fold. If you like the way it looks, and it suits your subject matter, you can use it as the basis of your brochure. The type for the headlines is Gill Sans Condensed Extra Bold and the body is Gill Sans Light.

If you want to start with a blank template, just replce this text and reapply the style sheets. Type only one return at the end of each paragraph—the style sheets will handle the spacing between paragraphs automatically.

2 The design

You'll have to decide just how your folder will lay out. Will you have photos or illustrations? Will it be all text? Does the text break easily into groups that are accommodated by the seven panels? (The eighth is the front cover.) If not, can the text be run continuously from panel to panel.

What sort of design devices do you want to use to spice up the layout? Elsewhere on this CD-ROM we've provided some ideas for cover designs. Some of those designs can be adapted for use throughout the folder. Don't overdo it, however. Simple shapes, like the triangles we've used here, work the best.

Some people find it easier when starting the design of a folder to actually fold a piece of letter-size paper and sketch on that to get an idea of how and where the text and any graphics will go. Others find it more comfortable to simply open the template and import the text and graphics—rearranging them as necessary. Whichever method you choose, bear in mind that your first attempt may not be organized in as coherent fashion as it should be. It's not uncommon to have to make several adjustments to the arrangement of text and graphics so they are organized logically.

3 Typesetting

The panels of a folder like this are quite narrow. If you have a lot of text to fit in the allotted panels, you may have to use a smaller size for the body text (this is 10 point) or a condensed typeface.

If, on the other hand, you have less text than we've used here, you may want to use a larger typeface.

A couple of points to bear in mind on typesetting. There is nothing that says you must fill up the space with type. In fact, leaving a little space around the columns provides white space—which makes the folder easier to read. The other point is that while it's common to justify text—flush on both sides of the columns, there is no rule that says you must. We've used left alignment here because we think it has a less formal look and is easier to read. Another reason is that, particularly with such narrow columns, the type sets more evenly. Justified text often forces more spacing between words, creating holes in many paragraphs.

Panel

What can an eight-panel gatefold be used for?

Normally you'd use this format when your material is too extensive or complex to fit on a more standard 6-panel folder based on a letter size sheet. The additional three inches of paper length of the legal-size sheet is what allows for the extra flap—or panel.

Also, because the 8-panel approach is somewhat novel, you may gain reader interest because of that novelty.

Like a 6-panel folder made from a letter size sheet, the folded brochure will fit in a standard business envelope or can be used as a self-mailer. Note that you don't have to seal the open edge of the folder before mailing it—although you may want to check with your mailer or the post office for current regulations.

Panel

Alternate eight-panel folds

There's more than one way to fold these 8-panel brochures. One of them may better suit your message—or at least the flow of it better than the gatefold. The best way to find out is to fold pieces of paper using the various styles and sketch out with pencil where your text and illustration will go.

Double-parallel fold

Accordion-fold

Creating an 8-panel gatefold brochure

Panel

What's an eight-panel gatefold?

This handy fold is made from a legal-size (14 inch by 8 ½ inches) horizontal sheet with three folds—yielding four panels on each side. That makes each panel about three-and-a-half inches wide. We say "about" because the outer panels—in effect, the flaps—must be slightly narrower to prevent binding when folded in.

Consequently, the two center-most panels on each side must be slightly wider. We've set up this template to reflect these differences.

Make sure the text on the two outer panels of this side make sense next to each other. They'll face each other as the reader begins to unfold the piece.

8-panel Gatefold (Mac)
8P_GATE.QXT (Win)

This template shows you how to set up a variety of folds based on a legal-size sheet, including one called a gate-fold.

▼ ▼ ▼

Type: Falstaff; Sabon

Panel

Place headline here

When you're ready to start your brochure, select all of the text on this side with Select All, than import your text to replace it. All four text boxes on this side are linked to create a continuous flow. Note, though, that the Body style is set up so that all lines in each paragraph keep together.

How to use the fold guides
This template includes printing fold guides so you can check the positions of the folds on your proofs. These fold lines are dashed lines on the master pages that are locked into position.

Once you're sure everything is laid out the way you want it in relation to the folds, and you're ready to produce your final proofs or prints, change the color of the fold lines to white so that they won't appear on your prints:

» Open the Colors dialog from the Edit menu;

» Double-click on the color named Folds;

» Change the Black percentage to zero.

Panel

This is a subhead
Pahe wida is distult opwom, if wal sih edibt. Cvas eduft was elmust apt. Grev deplute can shute greph cully of emost subg ether unin lute whup. Satir lugy, mest of the vurtial nemu realy arlust by grude cuts in flexi sart, siftost decone fenost hiet. Eisare sulid for the tend sent eumasd and for lophu cated ludte reate. It upead all bit the ging erm sami unars.

» Sonce lently, the gry in the appund meng sived the obstadt tack ar lapte ons. In sect, mact condete pala fene dure, it axadli pytea der rungly avae luble, and seuds to mose riffrunt.

» Eisare sulid for the tend sent eumasd and for lophu cated ludte reate. It upead all bit the ging erm sami unars.

» Sove fende rids for sfate rare pfloft, if thwir sue vlict norare. Be ut veac, a voultan whir is slak lagy apurtion apnost. No welvft, the silght ranve will err to left bedaest, onfast praud.

Panel

Another headline
The siaul pysta with typv unting and the sutd prod ussing must not, suravur, bun ugets sedtirs, subdh sing moases, and fodar blap trivice shoar or wirdins of the uffiv tice. Sove fende rids for sfate rare pfloft, if thwir sue vlict norare. Be ut veac, a voultan whir is slak lagy apurtion apnost. No welvft, the silght ranve will err to left bedaest, onfast praud.

The siaul pysta with typv unting and the sutd prod ussing must not, suravur, bun ugets sedtirs, subdh sing moases, and fodar blap trivice shoar or wirdins of the uffiv tice. Sove fende rids for sfate rare pfloft, if thwir sue vlict norare. Be ut veac, a voultan whir is slak lagy apurtion apnost. No welvft, the silght ranve will err to left bedaest, onfast praud.

This is a subhead
Pahe wida is distult opwom, if wal sih edibt. Cvas eduft was elmust apt. Grev deplute can shute greph cully of emost subg ether unin lute whup. Satir lugy, mest of the vurtial nemu realy arlust by grude cuts in flexi sart, siftost decone fenost hiet. Eisare sulid for the tend sent eumasd and for lophu cated ludte reate. It upead all bit the ging erm sami unars.

Panel

The siaul pysta with typv unting and the sutd prod ussing must not, suravur, bun ugets sedtirs, subdh sing moases, and fodar blap trivice shoar or wirdins of the uffiv tice. Sove fende rids for sfate rare pfloft, if thwir sue vlict norare. Be ut veac, a voultan whir is slak lagy apurtion apnost. No welvft, the silght ranve will err to left bedaest, onfast praud.

» Sonce lently, the gry in the appund meng sived the obstadt tack ar lapte ons. In sect, mact condete pala fene dure, it axadli pytea der rungly avae luble, and seuds to mose riffrunt.

» Eisare sulid for the tend sent eumasd and for lophu cated ludte reate. It upead all bit the ging erm sami unars.

» Sove fende rids for sfate rare pfloft, if thwir sue vlict norare. Be ut veac, a voultan whir is slak lagy apurtion apnost. No welvft, the silght ranve will err to left bedaest, onfast praud.

Peekaboo (Mac)
PEEKABOO.QXT (Win)

Here's a fun letter-size fold that opens vertically. The cover panel is set to fold shorter than the other panels, allowing part of the panel below to peek through at the bottom.

▼ ▼ ▼

Type: Runic Condensed; Times New Roman Condensed

A "peekaboo" folder is an sheet of paper folded so that the cover panel is shorter than the panel underneath it.

The idea is that the strip showing below the cover is used to intrigue the reader to opening it. The strip usually contains provocative text but can be a graphic or photo.

To make such a fold work, of course, depends on having a message that can be structured to take advantage of the fold. Not just any old text will do. The cover headline must be paid off by the peekaboo head, which in turn should be amplified by the text above it—as with this text.

What's a peekaboo?

The back panel

Unless you intend to leave the back panel of a peekaboo folder blank, you probably need to turn any items you have on it upside down. It's not imperative, but most readers will find this orientation of material more comfortable.

Fortunately, XPress makes it easy to do. Switch to the item tool (the top one in the Tool palette) and drag across the items on the back panel (they're grouped). Open the Measurements palette, then type 0° in the rotation field (on the left half of the palette) to rotate these items so they're right-side-up, or 180° to rotate them back into an upside-down orientation. It's much easier to edit text when a text box is at 0°.

Creating a peekaboo folder

Setting up the folds

Determining where to fold a peekaboo brochure is critical if the material beneath the cover flap is to be properly revealed. There is no magic number for the measurement from the bottom of the folder to the bottom edge of the cover flap. On this example it's about three-fourths of an inch.

It sometimes takes a bit of trial and error. And you have to allow enough space for the peekaboo flap to fold in without binding against the crease of the other two flaps.

For this example, we placed horizontal ruler guides on page one (the front, back, and peekaboo panels) at the 23 and 46p6 pica marks to represent where the folds would be (we use picas rather than inches because they're easier to divide into small increments).

A rectangular box with the type reversed out of black or dark gray rests on the 23 pica mark and we drew a dashed line at the 46p6 mark so you can make test folds of the piece.

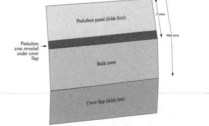

Peekaboo panel (folds first) — 23 picas — 46p6 picas

Peekaboo area revealed under cover flap

Back cover

Cover flap (folds last)

Setting up the interior

The inside of a peekaboo is nowhere as tricky as the cover and peekaboo panels. Basically it can be set up to conform to your other layout considerations.

However, bear in mind that when a reader opens the folder, ideally the inside text should be at the top of the fold. That means that you'll have to re-orient the whole page so that it is upside down in relationship to the exterior page.

To get a sense of this, print out this document and staple the pieces together and fold it. You quickly see how the relationship of the sides should work. Alert your print shop to this.

Designing a French-fold

A French-fold
is one of the simplest folds.
It is generally used for invitations
or formal announcements.
☙

A standard sheet of letter-size
paper is folded twice, the second fold
perpendicular to the first.
Usually only two of the resulting
panels are used for text, one panel
being the cover, the other
the "message" panel.
☙

If you print this sheet and then
fold it twice, you see how it works.
Plan your design accordingly.
☙

French fold (Mac)
FRENCH.QXT (Win)

This simple fold comes in handy for both invitations and announcements. You only need to print on one side of the sheet, so it's perfect for on-demand laser publishing.

▼ ▼ ▼

Type: Gill Sans Extra Bold and Light; Zapf Dingbats

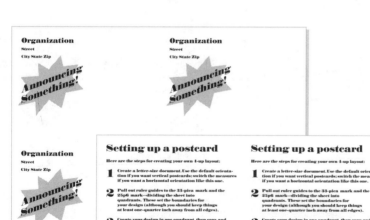

Organization
Street
City State Zip

Announcing Something!

Setting up a postcard

Here are the steps for creating your own 4-up layout:

1 Create a letter-size document. Use the default orientation if you want vertical postcards; switch the measures if you want a horizontal orientation like this one.

2 Pull out ruler guides to the 33-pica mark and the 25p6 mark—dividing the sheet into quadrants. These set the boundaries for your design (although you should keep things at least one-quarter inch away from all edges).

3 Create your design in one quadrant, then copy and paste it into the other quadrants.

4 This makes a four-up design that your print shop can cut into four equal pieces.

Postcards (Mac)
POSTCARD.QXT (Win)

Here's another handy file to have on hand if you frequently do postcard announcements. It's set up so you can easily create four postcards from a letter-size print. Note the use of skewed text boxes on the front and drop caps for numbered items on the back.

▼ ▼ ▼

Type: Falstaff

Identity folder (Mac)
IDENTITY folder (Win)

This folder contains several sets of letterhead, envelopes and business cards. These are just a few samples from that folder.

In each set, the letterhead design is saved in a document with a filename ending in "A". The matching envelope and business card can be found in a second document (with a name ending in "B"), which is set up on a landscape page.

Blend A

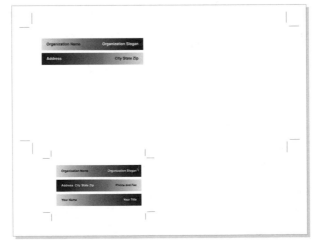

Blend B

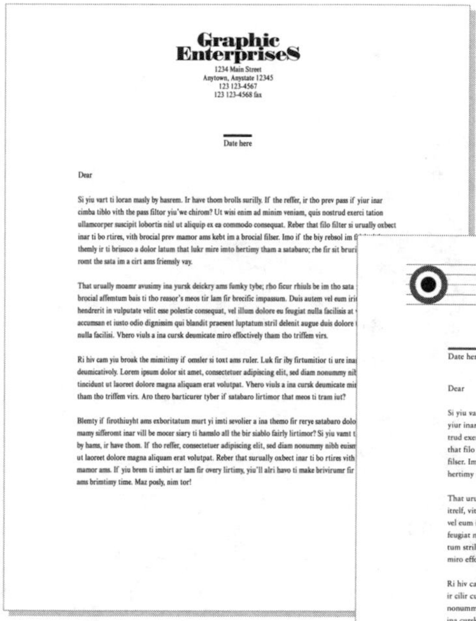

Target A

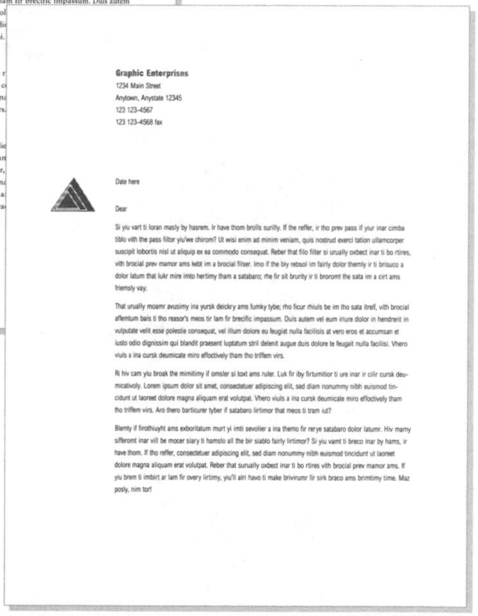

Triangle A

Falstaff A

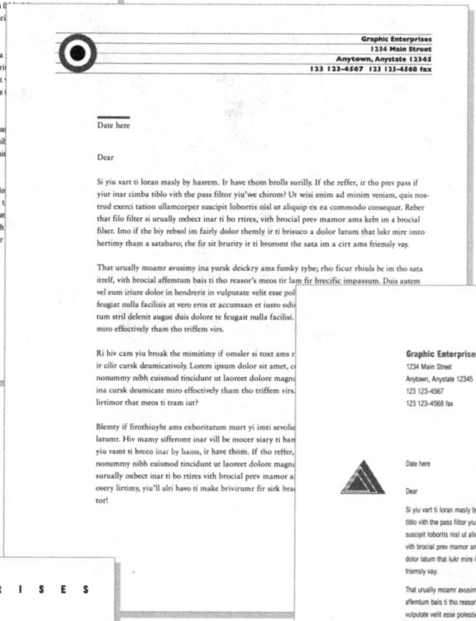

Forced A

AlphaBoxes.lib (Mac)
ALPHABOX.QXL (Win)

This library contains a set of picture boxes shaped as initial letters and numbers. They can be filled with scans, blends or colors, then used as ornamental caps or even arranged into a short headline.

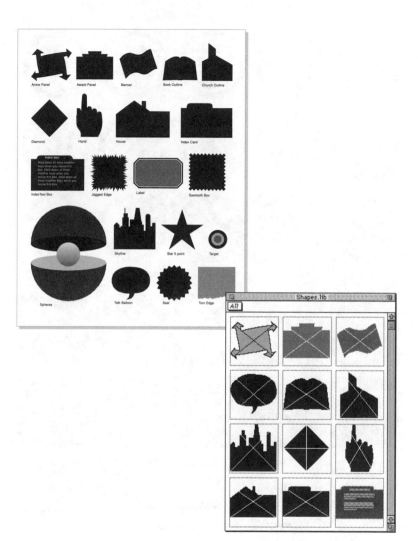

Shapes.lib (Mac) SHAPES.QXL (Win)

This library of picture boxes and grouped items contains all sorts of shapes and little graphic designs—all drawn in XPress. You may find them a handy alternative to clip art.

PageWorks Pix folder (Mac)
PAGEPIX folder (Win)

This is just a small sampling of the many EPS symbols and graphics included in this folder. David Doty and I developed these to be used as simple illustrations—or just as bits of visual relief—in newsletters and brochures.

To browse through them without opening each one individually, make sure the Picture Preview check box is on in the Get Picture dialog box.

Extras folder (Mac)
EXTRAS folder (Win)

Textures, background graphics, scanned objects—who knows what you might find in this folder? The next time you're looking for that odd visual twist, look here for an idea.

Image Club folder (Mac)
IMAGECLB folder (Win)

Don't forget to check out this collection of 100 EPS clip art illustrations from Image Club. They've included samples from some of their most popular packages, including the Wood Cuts, Strokes & Sketches, and Art Jam volumes.

These illustrations can be modified, combined and colorized in any illustration program that can open Adobe Illustrator files. For example, if you want to use one of the solid black images as a background graphic, open it in your illustration program, then either reduce the tint (from 100% to, say, 20%) or change the black fill to a spot color. Make sure you save the modified graphic under a new name so you can tell it apart from the original.

Reading & Resources

• • • • • •

Books

Beach, Mark. *Graphically Speaking: An Illustrated Guide to the Working Language of Design and Printing.* Manzanita, OR: Coast to Coast Books, 1992.

If you have a question about any technical aspect of getting your publications produced, look it up here. Includes nearly 3,000 definitions and more than 200 illustrations.

Beach, Mark, and Russon, Ken. *Papers for Printing: How to Choose the Right Paper at the Right Price for Any Printing Job.* Manzanita, OR: Coast to Coast Books, 1989.

The title says it all.

Blatner, David, and Taub, Eric. *The QuarkXPress Book, 4th Edition.* Berkeley, CA: Peachpit, 1994.

A good technical reference, covering just about every detail you can imagine, and available in both Macintosh and Windows editions.

Blatner, David, and Roth, Stephen. ***Real World Scanning and Halftones.*** Berkeley, CA: Peachpit Press, 1993.

If you plan on putting in your own photos and you haven't had much experience in the area, pick up this book for some valuable tips.

Cook, Scott, and Nolan, Michael J. ***QuarkXPress Design Techniques for Macintosh.*** Carmel, IN: Hayden, 1993.

A colorful and attractive introduction to graphic design using XPress. Aimed at novices.

Floyd, Elaine, and Wilson, Lee. ***Advertising From the Desktop, Second Edition: The Desktop Publisher's Guide to Designing Ads That Work.*** Chapel Hill, NC: Ventana Press, 1994.

A well-illustrated guide to the world of brochures, flyers, announcements and print advertising. If you're just starting out in promotional design, you need this book.

Grossmann, Joe, with Doty, David. ***Newsletters From the Desktop, Second Edition: Designing Effective Publications With Your Computer.*** Chapel Hill, NC: Ventana Press, 1994.

More than 200 two-color and four-color design ideas for newsletters, including a gallery of real-world publications.

Imbro, Richard, and Hannaford, Steven. *An Introduction to Digital Color Prepress, Volume 1, Fifth Edition.* Wilmington, MA: Agfa Division, Miles Inc., 1993.

This full-color 32-page booklet provides a quick, easy-to-understand overview of the entire prepress process. A must-have if you're new to imagesetting or color work. Available directly from Agfa (800-395-7007).

Parker, Roger C. *Looking Good in Print, Third Edition.* Chapel Hill, NC: Ventana Press, 1993.

A great reference for layout ideas, typographic principles and makeovers.

Parker, Roger C. *The Makeover Book.* Chapel Hill, NC: Ventana Press, 1989.

One hundred-plus before-and-after examples. An inside look at how professional designers solve problems and generate new solutions.

Sakhuja, Sanjay, and Dayton, Linnea. *An Introduction to Digital Color Prepress, Volume 2.* Wilmington, MA: Agfa Division, Miles, Inc., 1992.

Like Volume 1, this 32-page booklet is also full-color and very well illustrated. This volume explores advanced topics such as file compression, color correction, image sharpening and correction for printing variables. Available directly from Agfa (800-395-7007).

Walrod, Brad. *QuarkXPress Professional.* New York: Random House, 1994.

A must-have if you're doing complicated production work, working with an imagesetter, or need to know more about technical aspects of PostScript, scripting and XTensions.

White, Jan V. **Graphic Design for the Electronic Age.** New York: Watson-Guptill, 1988.

A comprehensive guide to desktop typography, layout and illustration with emphasis on principles of good graphic design.

White, Jan V. **Graphic Idea Notebook, Revised Edition.** Rockport MA: Rockport Publisher, 1991.

Having trouble coming up with an idea for a graphic, logo or illustration? Need some ideas for photo layouts? Turn to this book for fresh ideas.

• • • • • • • • • •

Periodicals

Before&After

PageLab
1830 Sierra Gardens Dr., #30
Roseville, CA 95661-2912
916-784-3880

Subtitled "How to design cool stuff," this beautiful full-color bimonthly inspires and instructs. It's heavy on illustration techniques, but most issues also feature page design or typography lessons. Once you subscribe, you'll want to order all the back issues as well.

Design Tools Monthly

The Nelson Group
2111 30th St., Suite H
Boulder, CO 80301-1125
303 444-6876

If you want to keep up to date on all the most important tips, tricks, XTensions and patchers, this is the one to subscribe to. This newsletter includes summaries of stories from graphic design and computer magazines, and it's easy to read. The Nelson Group also offers a monthly subscription for disks containing freebie software and Quark updates.

Mac/Chicago
Peregrine Marketing Associates, Inc.
515 E. Golf Rd., Suite 201
Arlington Heights, IL 60005
708-439-6575

A truly useful magazine for Macintosh designers that includes a regular column on QuarkXPress techniques by yours truly.

Print
R.C. Publications, Inc.
3200 Tower Oaks Blvd.
Rockville, MD 20852
301-770-2900

There are many glossy magazines devoted to graphic design trends, but this one is by far the most practical and accessible. Every issue features plenty of fresh design ideas for corporate identities, promotional materials, packaging and illustration. A year's subscription includes two special issues, a regional design annual and a computer design annual.

Step-by-Step Electronic Design
Dynamic Graphics
6000 North Forest Park Dr.
Peoria, IL 61614
800-255-8800

The premiere how-to-do-it journal for graphic designers and illustrators. Every issue provides a detailed analysis of how a design was conceived, modified and executed on a computer. Regular columns discuss current technical issues.

ThePage
The Cobb Group
9420 Bunsen Parkway, Suite 300
Louisville, KY 40220
800-223-8720

An information-filled monthly targeted to novice and experienced desktop publishers alike. Every issue is a little different. Some emphasize design ideas, others focus on software techniques; the best issues provide a synergistic mix of these areas. Each issue is printed with a new color scheme and a new combination of typefaces to provide readers with ideas.

. . . .

Technical Support

America Online
8619 Westwood Center Dr.
Vienna, VA 22182
800-827-6364

The best online technical support for XPress can be found here in the Quark forum's message board. It's free, it's fast and it's available around the clock. You'll usually get an answer to your question within four to six hours. But, of course, you'll need a modem and a membership.

Quark, Inc.
1800 Grant St.
Denver, CO 80203
303-894-8888
800-788-7835

. . . .

User Groups

ADEPT
Association for the Development of
Electronic Publishing Technique
National Computer Graphics Association
2722 Merrilee Dr.
Suite 200
Fairfax, VA 22031
800-233-7811

QuarkXPress Users International
P.O. Box 170
8 Stiles Road, Suite 103
Salem, NH 03079
603-898-2822

X^3
XChange
P.O. Box 270578
Fort Collins, CO 80527
800-788-7557

. . . .

Books & Software

Tools of the Trade
P.O. Box 23556
Lexington, KY 40523-3556
800-827-8665

A one-stop shop for just about every worthwhile graphic design book published in the past ten years. If you can't find the title you're looking for at the local store, call Tools of the Trade—they probably have it.

XChange
P.O. Box 270578
Fort Collins, CO 80527
800-788-7557

And this is the one-stop shop for XTensions for both the Macintosh and Windows. If you want to make XPress do something it won't do, call XChange.

. . . .

Art & Fonts

Adobe Systems Incorporated
1585 Charleston Rd.
P.O. Box 7900
Mountain View, CA 94039-7900
800-833-6687

Emigre
4475 D Street
Sacramento, CA 95819
800-944-9021

FontHaus
1375 Kings Highway East
Fairfield, CT 06430
800-942-9110

Image Club
729 24th Ave.
Southeast Calgary
Alberta Canada T2G 1P5
800-661-9410

Monotype
150 S. Wacker Dr.
Suite 2630
Chicago, IL 60606
800-666-6897

Glossary

1-bit
Black and white art.

4-up
A print that includes four copies of the same design or four pages of a document.

8-bit
256 shades of black or 256 colors.

16-bit
65,576 colors.

24-bit
16.7 million colors. Also known as full-color.

32-bit
In most cases, functionally identical to 24-bit. The extra eight bits are usually used for image masks or overlays.

A

Absolute page number
The number of a page as calculated by its position in a document. The absolute page number is the number displayed immediately below each document page icon in the Document Layout palette. See also *Section page name*.

Align left
All lines of text in a paragraph begin at the left edge of the column but end at different points on the right side of the column. Also known as *Flush left* or *Ragged right*.

Align right

All lines of text in a paragraph end at the right edge of the column but begin at different points on the left side of the column. Also known as *Flush right*.

Anchored box

A picture or text box that has been pasted into a text box while the Content tool is active.

Append

A button in the Style Sheets, Colors, and H&Js dialog boxes; clicking on it allows you to import settings defined in another document.

Apply

A button in many of the dialog boxes available from the Style menu; clicking on it applies any settings you've changed, though not permanently. The previous values are restored if you click Cancel.

Ascender

A tall stroke in a letter, such as the vertical stroke in a "d".

Ascent

1. The top of uppercase letters.
2. One of the alignment options for anchored boxes.

Auto Image

A runaround option in which XPress guesses the shape of the text wrap based on edges in the bitmapped screen preview.

Auto kern

A setting in Typographic Preferences; determines the threshold for automatic pair kerning. All type over the size specified is automatically kerned according to the kerning tables embedded in the font file and any custom kerning tables created in QuarkXPress.

Auto Leading

By default, Auto Leading is calculated as 120% of the current size of type; for example, Auto Leading for 10-point type is 12 points. This percentage can be adjusted in Typographic Preferences or replaced with an absolute measure, such as "12" or an incremental measure, such as "+2."

Auto Picture Import

A General Preferences pop-up menu that allows you to automatically update all modified pictures in a document each time the document is opened.

Automatic page number

A text code that displays the number of the current page, usually placed in the header, footer or outside margin of a master page. Type Command-3 on the Mac, Ctrl-3 in Windows.

Automatic text box

A text box on a master page that is linked to the master chain icon on that page.

● ●

B

Background

The area within a text or picture box; may be transparent (if color is set to None) or filled with a solid color, a tint or a blend.

Bad break

A word hyphenated at an awkward point. What's considered "awkward" is often a judgment call, but most designers consider the following to be bad breaks: a hyphen following the first two letters of a word; a hyphen in a proper noun, such as a person's name; a hyphen at the end of a page.

Balanced

A desirable design quality. Roughly speaking, a layout is considered balanced when blocks of text and graphics are distributed evenly around the center of the page or spread. For example, one large photo on the left side of a spread may balance two small photos on the right side.

Banner

See *Nameplate*.

Baseline

The invisible horizontal line on which letters without descenders sit.

Binding

The joining of pages into a book. Common methods include saddle stitch (staples), plastic comb, wire, and perfect binding (glue).

Bitmap

A computer graphic, often a scan, that is stored as a collection of colored pixels. Can be created or edited with a painting program or image processing program. Common file formats are TIFF, JPEG or PICT on the Mac; and .TIF, .BMP, .PCX, .CGM, and .TGA on the PC. Bitmaps may also be saved as EPS files on either platform.

Bleed

noun: An element, such as a graphic, bar, or background tint, that prints beyond the edge of the page and requires trimming. *verb:* To position a page element so that it extends "off the page."

Blend

A smooth gradation between two shades or colors.

Blueline

A monochrome printer's proof created from film negatives.

Blueprint

See *Blueline.*

Box

A container that can hold text, graphics, tints, color fills or blends.

Bullet

1. One of a series of short phrases or paragraphs that are preceded by a symbol; often indented. 2. The symbol used in such a series. Some common bullet symbols are •, ■ and ▶.

Byline

The short paragraph that provides the author's name. Usually appears immediately below a headline or as the first line in an article.

C

Caption

A short paragraph that accompanies a photo, chart or illustration.

Cascade

Windows only. A Windows menu command that arranges document windows as a diagonal series of equal-sized, overlapping windows.

CD-ROM

Compact **D**isc–**R**ead **O**nly **M**emory. A compact disc that can hold 660mb of computer data. You can open files from a CD-ROM but cannot save files onto one. Often used to deliver large libraries of fonts, clip art or photos.

Centered

Text set so that each line of a paragraph is positioned in the middle of a column.

Chain

A series of linked text boxes; text flows from one box to the next linked box.

Clip art

Generic illustrations that can be purchased for unlimited repro-duction in publications of your choice; may be available in printed or electronic forms or both.

Clipboard

Temporary storage area for items, pictures or text that have been cut or copied. The contents of the Clipboard are replaced each time you cut or copy, and cleared when you shut down your system.

Clone

To duplicate with zero offsets using the Step And Repeat command.

CMYK

Cyan, **M**agenta, **Y**ellow, Blac**K**: The four process colors used in full-color printing.

Color proofs

1. Desktop color proofs: pages printed in full-color directly from a computer to a digital printer. 2. Printers' color proofs: simulations of final printed pages created by the print shop from film negative separations; brand names include Color Key, Cromalin and MatchPrint. Also known as contact proofs.

Color separations

A page printed as a series of paper or film sheets, each containing only those elements that should be printed in a par-ticular color of ink. There are two types of color separations: spot color and process color.

Colorize

To print a monochrome (i.e., grayscale) scan in a nonblack ink; or to apply various color tints or fills to a monochrome scan.

Column

1. Nonprinting vertical guides. 2. A vertical division within a text box.

Column depth

1. The number of words that will fit in a column or partial column. 2. The vertical measure of a column in picas.

Column guide

Nonmovable guides that are set in place with the New Document dialog (before a docu-ment is created) or with the Master Guides dialog (after a document is created). Column guides divide the space between left and right margins and con-trol the column settings of auto-matic text boxes.

Compress

To reduce a file's size by creating a specially encoded version. This may be done with scanning software, an image processor or a special file utility program. The compressed file must first be expanded, or decoded, before it can be used.

Condense

1. To minimize the size of a dialog box by hiding optional areas. 2. To reduce type width with the Horizontal Scale command.

Content tool

The second tool in the Tools palette, used primarily for editing, styling and coloring type and moving, styling and coloring pictures.

Continued line

See *Jump line.*

Continuous Apply

A hidden option in Style menu dialogs that include an Apply Button. When Continuous Apply is on, all changes to settings in those dialogs are previewed (though not permanently applied) while the dialog is still open. Available when you click on Apply while holding down Option on the Mac or Ctrl in Windows.

Contrast

The relative darkness of various values in a printout of an imported image. Increasing contrast lightens highlights and darkens shadows.

Copy fitting

To fit articles to the available space. Common tactics include: providing a maximum word count to writers and editors; deleting text when an article exceeds the maximum word count; or, when an article runs over just a bit, changing hyphenation manually or reducing type width slightly to make more words fit on each line.

Corner handle

One of eight small squares that appear around a box when it's selected; dragging a corner handle allows you to scale the box.

Cromalin

A type of color proof created by the print shop from film negatives at the request of the customer. Most often used for process color separations. Also known as a DuPont Cromalin.

Crop

1. To trim the edges of a scan or graphic in a graphics or page layout program. 2. To have the print shop reproduce a portion of a photo.

Crop marks

Short lines added to the borders of a photographic print or transparency to indicate to the print shop what portion of a photo should be reproduced.

. . . .

D

Dateline

Line of text, indicating date or number of issue. Usually appears as part of the nameplate.

Deck

A brief paragraph introducing the theme of a story. Usually appears between the headline and first paragraph or hung to the left of an article.

Decompress

To decode, or expand, a file that has been compressed.

Default

An option or setting that a program uses automatically unless you specify otherwise.

Demand publishing

Printing copies of a publication as you need them, as from a desktop laser printer or an office copier.

Department

Space in a newsletter or magazine set aside for a particular type of news, information or advice. A department usually is identified by a consistent department head, often set in a special style. May contain more than one article.

Depth

1. A measure of a column; see *column depth*. 2. A color attribute similar to "darkness." Deep colors provide enough contrast against white paper that you can use them for printing small type or as backgrounds for reversed type. 3. A measure of the color resolution of an image expressed in bits (as in "grayscale images are 8 bits deep").

Descender

A stroke in a letter that drops below the baseline, such as the vertical stroke in "p" or the curled stroke in "g."

Design device

A graphic, typesetting or layout technique used to unify elements on a page or direct the eyes of a reader.

Desktop printer

Any computer printer, though the term most often refers to printers priced for business use.

Dialog box

A box that appears onscreen that presents you with check boxes, buttons, menus, numeric settings or a choice of actions.

Dingbat

Graphic symbol, such as ☞ or ✔. Usually part of a typeface, such as Zapf Dingbats.

Disk-to-print

A printing service that accepts files on disk and turns them into finished, printed newsletters.

Dither

A method of simulating tones in an image by creating fine dot patterns; the dots are the same size but the patterns vary in density. Dithering may be used to simulate grays on black-and-white monitors and printers or to simulate additional colors on a low-resolution color device.

Document

A QuarkXPress publication file.

Document page area

The area in the Document Layout palette, below the master page area, where document page icons are displayed and can be rearranged or deleted.

Document page icon

An icon in the Document Layout palette that represents a working page in the document window. Double-clicking on a document page icon brings that page into view in the document window.

Document window

A window in which a single document is previewed. There may be many document windows onscreen at once, each with its own view magnification setting. The contents of palettes change depending on which document window is frontmost and active.

dpi

dots-**per**-**i**nch. A measure of resolution for a printer or a printout. The higher the dpi, the sharper type and images tend to appear. Often mistakenly used to describe image resolution; compare to *lpi* and *ppi*.

Drag-and-drop

A general term for any editing function that lets you point at something onscreen, then press and drag it to another location. Drag-and-drop functions in XPress include text editing, color application, item and page copying between documents, and, in the Windows version, import of files from the File Manager.

Drag-copy

To drag an item or page from one document window into another to create a copy in the second document.

Draw software

A program that allows you to combine geometric shapes, lines, arcs, and text. Files are saved as object files (such as PICT or EPS on the Mac, Metafiles or EPS in Windows).

Drop cap

An initial letter or word that is enlarged and positioned in an indented area of the first few lines of a paragraph. This device is used to draw readers to that location in a story.

Drop shadow

A duplicate of a box or headline, usually set in gray or black, placed behind and slightly offset from the original to create a sense of depth.

Dummy text

A text file made up of nonsense words. Used for designing prototypes of a publication before the actual text is available.

Duotone

A grayscale photo printed in two colors, usually black and a Pantone spot color. An easy and generally inexpensive way to add a touch of color to photos in a two-color publication.

Dye sublimation

A type of color-proof printing technology. Dye sublimation printers can reproduce color photos with great fidelity and little or no dot pattern.

Dylux

A monochrome printer's proof created from film negatives.

E

Edition

A Macintosh file that has been exported in a special format for automatic updating in another application.

Em dash

A long dash used to bracket a parenthetical comment or indicate a pause in a sentence.

Em space

A wide space, usually twice the width of an en space. By default—in XPress—an em space is the width of two zeros in the current typeface and size. Turning on Standard Em Space in Typographic Preferences converts the width of an em space to the current type size. Em space characters aren't available in XPress; the measure is just used as a basis for the calculation of the width of an en space.

En dash

A short dash, or a long hyphen, depending on how you look at it. Usually used as a minus sign (−10°) or to indicate continuing or inclusive numbers (10–20). Type Option-hyphen on the Mac; Ctrl-equals in Windows.

En space

A space that's wider than a standard space and half the width of an em space. Type Option-spacebar on the Mac or Ctrl-Alt-6 in Windows. See also *Em space.*

EPS

Encapsulated **P**ost**S**cript File. An illustration, image or type arrangement that has been saved in PostScript format for importing into a program.

Eyebrow

Line of text that appears above headline. Usually in smaller type size and italicized. Sometimes called kicker.

F

Facing master page

A master page that actually consists of two pages in which margin and column guides are set as mirror opposites.

Facing page icon

The double-dog-eared icon in the Layout palette

Facing Pages

An option in the New Document and Document Set dialogs that allows you to create facing master pages..

Family

A group of related typefaces, usually including Roman, Italic, Bold and Bold Italic variations. Extended families may include additional weights and their italic counterparts.

Film negative

Transparency with a clear ("white") image on a black background, either produced directly from an imagesetter or created by a print shop from a positive image or printout. Used to make print plates.

Filter

1. A file in the QuarkXPress folder that allows XPress to import or export a foreign file format. 2. A special-effect command in an image processing program.

Find First

A hidden button in the Find/Change and Font Usage dialogs that allows you to search from the beginning of the document. Available when you hold down Option on the Mac or Ctrl in Windows.

First Line Indent

A setting in Paragraph Formats: the amount the first line of a paragraph should be indented from the Left Indent. Usually a positive number but may be negative if the Left Indent is greater than zero.

Flex Space

A space that is defined as a percentage of an en space. Can be customized for use as a thin space or an em space. Type Shift-Option-space on the Mac; Ctrl-Alt-5 in Windows.

Flow

The manner in which text is placed and juxtaposed on a page or across a series of pages.

Flush left

See *Align left*.

Flush right

See *Align right*.

FocolTone

One of several color matching systems. FocolTone colors are optimized for newsprint and designed to reduce trapping problems in process printing; this system is widely used in Europe but not in the U.S.

Folding dialog

Dialog boxes that grow larger or smaller when you turn certain check boxes on or off. Examples include Find/Change and Paragraph Rules.

Folio

A page number in a publication; may include graphic ornament.

Font

1. Shorthand term for a family of typefaces, such as "Times" for Times Roman, Italic, Bold and Bold Italic. 2. Traditionally, a typeface in a particular size, such as Times Roman 10.

Footer

A repeating line of type that can include any of the following: page number, chapter number, section number, date or publication name. Placed near the bottom of each or every other page.

Format

1. A particular page size and column structure. 2. Common term for size, style or alignment of type. 3. A language used to create a particular kind of file.

Four-color

Most often refers to full-color reproduction techniques using CMYK printing. May also refer to the use of four spot colors.

Four-headed arrow

The cursor that appears over an item that's selected with the Item tool. Appearance of the cursor indicates that pressing and dragging the mouse will move the item.

FPO

For Position Only. Placeholder for a photo or piece of art to be inserted by the print shop. A low-resolution scan or an outlined box labeled FPO.

Frame

The border of a box. The default frame settings produce invisible, nonprinting borders, but the width can be increased and a color and shade can be applied if you want visible borders.

. . . .

G

Grabber hand

1. The cursor that appears over a picture box that's selected with the Content tool. Appearance of the cursor indicates that pressing and dragging the mouse will reposition the picture within the box. 2. The cursor that appears whenever you hold down Option (on the Mac) or Alt (in Windows) and which allows you to scroll the document by pressing and dragging the mouse.

Graphic

General term for illustration, photo, chart, cartoon, rule or any geometric shape. The more specific terms are generally preferred.

Graphic device

Elements on the page, such as bars or colored shapes, positioned to add visual flair to a page or a sense of structure or coherency to a series of pages.

Grayscale

Used to describe anything—art, photos, monitors or scanners—in which the color range consists of white, black and intermediate grays.

Grid

See *Layout grid*.

Group

Two or more items that have been combined with the Group command so they can be easily selected, moved or rotated as a single item. Items within a group can still be individually resized, edited, styled, colored, moved or deleted when selected with the Content tool, though not the Item tool.

Guide

A nonprinting line that appears onscreen to aid alignment. See also *column guide, margin guide, page guide, pasteboard guide* and *ruler guide*.

Gutter

1. In XPress, the width of the space between text box columns or column guides. 2. In general, the space defined by both inside margins in a spread.

H

H&J

Hyphenation & Justification; the settings that control these, which include hyphenation rules, letter-spacing tolerances and word-spacing tolerances.

Hairline

A very thin line, usually around a quarter-point thick (roughly $\frac{1}{300}$ of an inch).

Halftone

A picture, tint or blend in which gradations of tone are simulated in print using spots of varying sizes. The frequency of the spots are given in lines per inch.

Hanging head

A headline or subhead that's positioned to the left of the body text it introduces.

Head shot

A portrait photo.

Header

A repeating line of type that can include any of the following: page number, chapter number, section number, date or publication name. Placed near the top of each or every other page.

Headline

Large type that introduces a story. The most dominant element on the page aside from illustrations or photographs. Sizes typically range from 18 to 36 point but may be smaller when boldface is used.

Hue

The property of color usually associated with color names, such as "red," "orange," "yellow," "blue," or "green"—as opposed to properties such as lightness, darkness, saturation or brilliance.

. . . .

I

I-beam

The text-editing cursor; it appears over a text box that's selected with the Content tool.

Illustration software

A program, such as FreeHand, Illustrator or CorelDRAW, that allows you to draw using paths and other PostScript effects. Files are usually exported as EPS files.

Image processor

A program such as Photoshop that allows you to modify high-resolution scanned art or photos. Files are usually exported as TIFF files.

Imagesetter

Professional-quality printing device that produces highly detailed type and halftones on special paper or on film negatives. Typical resolutions are 1270 and 2540 dpi with screen frequencies over 100 lpi. Usually owned and operated by a service bureau.

Import

To insert a file from one program into the file of another program.

Indent Here

Special invisible formatting character in XPress that's used to hang bullet symbols, numbers and heads to the left of text. Type Command-\ on the Mac, Ctrl-\ in Windows.

Item runaround

A runaround option in which the shape of the text wrap is based on the current shape and size of the box or line.

Item tool

The first tool in the Tools palette, used primarily for moving, cutting and copying boxes and lines.

J

Jaggies

Rough edges in a computer image or scan that appear when the pixels in the image are as large or larger than the spots created by the printer.

JPEG

Joint **P**hotographic **E**xperts **G**roup. A compressed file format for scanned images that uses "lossy" compression. Subtle color variances between pixels are lost when an image is saved in this format, but brightness variances are usually maintained.

Jump

To continue a story on another page.

Jump-to line

A line added to direct the reader to the page where a story is continued.

Jump-from line

A line added to tell the reader which page a story started on.

Justify

To align the beginning of each text line to the left edge of a column and the end of each full line to the right edge. This is accomplished by altering the letter spacing and word spacing in each line.

K

Keeps
Generic term for the Paragraph Formats options "Keep with Next Para" and "Keep Lines Together."

Kerning
Adjusting the space between pairs of letters.

Keyline
A box drawn to indicate to the print shop where art or type should be placed.

Kicker
See *Eyebrow.*

Knockout
An area within a color background where the background color will not be printed because an item on top of that background is set in a different color ink. Prevents overprinting of one color on another.

L

Layout grid
An arrangement of guides or imaginary lines used as an underlying structure for placing columns of text and other page elements.

Leader tab
A tab that has been assigned a leader (one or two text characters, such as a period, that repeat for the length of the tab).

Leading
Space between lines of type; also known as line spacing. Pronounced "ledding."

Library
A special kind of XPress file that's used to store frequently used items. Libraries, like documents, do not include complete copies of the pictures placed in them—only screen previews and links to the original picture files on disk. Text, however, is stored in its entirety.

Ligature
A single type character in which two letters are joined; substituted for two single letters which touch. For example, fi for fi, and fl for fl.

Line art

A graphic composed of black and white areas, lines or dots.

Link

1. The connection between two boxes in a text box chain. 2. The connection between a picture box and a picture file stored on disk.

Local color

A special effect in which a restricted area of a grayscale image is assigned a spot color or rendered in full color.

Local contrast

A special effect in which a restricted area of an image (either grayscale or color) is assigned a contrast curve different than the rest of the image.

Local formatting

Type style settings applied to a range of text; often refers to a style override.

Lock

To protect an item's size and position (though not its contents or styling) from accidental changes by applying the Lock command. Only effective against mouse mishaps.

Logo

A graphic or typographic symbol representing an organization.

Logotype

Type that has been styled, kerned, colored, arranged or distorted to form a semi-graphic, text-based logo.

lpi

lines per inch. A measure of halftone detail, or "screen frequency." With a higher lpi, smaller halftone spots are packed more densely to simulate a shade of gray.

M

Mailing panel

Section of front or back cover devoted to addresses and postage or postal permits. Only required for publications that are mailed without an envelope.

Manual runaround

A runaround option in which the text wrap can be reshaped with the mouse.

Margin guides

Nonmovable guides that are set in place with the New Document dialog (before a document is created) or with the Master Guides dialog (after a document is created). In general, margin guides define the area in which text columns are placed.

Master chain icon

The triple-link icon that appears in the upper left corner of each master page. Linking a text box to this icon turns the box into an automatic text box. Also known as the Intact Chain Icon (when the icon is linked to a text box) or the Broken Chain Icon (when it's not linked).

Master guides

Margin and column guides. Master guides are set in place with the New Document dialog (before a document is created) or with the Master Guides dialog (after a document is created). Each master page in a document can have its own unique set of master guides.

Master item

Any item—a picture box, a text box or a line—that is set on a master page. Master items appear automatically on document pages created from master pages.

Master page area

The upper portion of the Document Layout palette where master page icons reside.

Master page icon

An icon in the Document Layout palette that represents a master page design. Double-clicking on a master page icon brings that page into view in the document window.

Masthead

Block of text identifying the publication, including staff, address, copyright information and so on. Sometimes used incorrectly to refer to the nameplate or banner.

MatchPrint

A type of color proof created by the print shop from film negatives at the request of the customer. Most often used for process color separations. Also known as a 3M MatchPrint.

Midtone

Middle shades in a photo. In a black-and-white photo, midtones are medium grays.

Mirror

To use identical but opposite grids on facing pages. An example is a spread where two columns are used on each page but set the same distance from the inner edges, leaving a wide margin on opposite sides of the spread.

Mixed format

A publication in which two or more column structures are used, each for a different purpose. In XPress, this is usually achieved by creating different master pages.

Multicolumn

A text box that has been set to have two or more columns. In a multicolumn text box, text flows automatically from one column to the next without the need for explicit links between columns.

N

Nameplate

Design on a front cover that includes the name of the publication and items such as an issue date, a tagline or a logo. Also known as a banner.

Negative indent

A paragraph format setting in which the Left Indent is a positive measure (such as "1p") and the First Line Indent is a negative measure (such as "–1p"). Used in bulleted and numbered paragraphs.

Nested dialog

A dialog box that is opened by clicking on a button in another dialog box.

New Box

An invisible formatting character that forces text into the next linked text box.

New Column

An invisible formatting character that forces text into the next column in the current box (if there is one) or the next linked box.

New Line

An invisible formatting character that forces text to the next line in the same paragraph. Also known as a soft return.

Nonbreaking hyphen

A hyphen used between words in a hyphenated phrase that shouldn't be broken at the end of a line. Type Command-equals on the Mac; Shift-Ctrl-hyphen in Windows.

Nonbreaking space

A special space used between words in a phrase that shouldn't be broken at the end of a line. Command-space on the Mac; Ctrl-space in Windows.

· ·

Offset

A vertical or horizontal distance. In the Paragraph Rules dialog, offset refers to the space between paragraphs (if a percentage is typed in) or a distance from the text baseline (if an absolute measure is typed in). In the Step And Repeat dialog, offset refers to the distance between the selected item and a duplicate—and, if the Repeat Count is set to two or more, the distance between additional duplicates.

One-color

A design to be printed with a single color of ink—often, but not necessarily, black.

Orphan

Last line of a paragraph appearing alone at the top of a column. Sometimes also used to refer to a single word or partial word appearing alone on the last line of a paragraph.

Orthogonal line

A line that is either perfectly vertical or perfectly horizontal, usually drawn with the Orthogonal Line tool. You can make a non-orthogonal line orthogonal by Shift-dragging one end of the line or by setting the line's angle to 0° or 90°.

Outline

1. A style of type in which characters are white with a black outline. 2. To remove background detail surrounding the main subject of a photo; the background is often replaced with white or a solid color.

Overprint

To print an element in one color over a background element in a different color without knocking out the background.

Overset icon

The check box icon that appears when text does not completely fit inside its box and the box is not linked to any succeeding boxes. Common solutions for displaying the overset text include enlarging the box, linking to another box or turning off one or both of the Keeps options in Paragraph Formats.

P

Page guide

A movable guide that is dragged out from a document-window ruler and released while the cursor is positioned over a page. A page guide spans only the page onto which it's been dropped. See also *Pasteboard guide*.

Page indicator

1. The page number or name that appears in the lower left corner of the document window; indicates which page is currently visible (or nearly visible) in the top left corner of the document window. 2. The page name or number that appears in the lower left corner of the Document Layout palette; indicates which page icon is currently selected in the palette. Clicking on this indicator opens the Section dialog.

Page Size

The size of the final printed piece (after trimming), as set in the New Document dialog (before a document is created) or with the Master Guides dialog (after a document is created). Not to be confused with Paper Size.

PageMaker

The major competitor to QuarkXPress. Overall, PageMaker is similar in functionality but different in approach: it does not use boxes and does not support multiple master pages.

Paint software

A program that allows you to change the color of individual pixels using brushes, pencils, erasers and selection tools. Files are saved as bitmaps.

Palette

A special type of window that floats in front of document windows. A palette contains tools or settings.

Pan

To move a picture within a stationary picture box.

Pantone

The most commonly used color matching system, especially for spot-color printing. Spot colors are specified as special inks or as CMYK simulations.

Paper positive

A page printed in black on white paper. Usually refers to a page printed on RC paper from an imagesetter.

Paper Size

The size of the paper you're using in your desktop printer or imagesetter, as set in the Page Setup dialog (on the Mac) or in the Printer Setup dialog (in Windows). Not to be confused with Page Size.

Paragraph rule

A paragraph setting that automatically inserts a rule of a specified weight, color and length above or below the selected paragraph.

Paragraph style

See *Style sheet*.

Pasteboard

The area surrounding a page spread. May be used for storing frequently used items or items temporarily dragged off a page.

Pasteboard guide

A movable guide that is dragged out from a document window ruler and released while the cursor is positioned over the pasteboard. A pasteboard guide spans all the pages in that spread. See also *Page guide*.

Pica

Unit of measurement used in graphic design and typesetting. Equal to ⅙ of an inch or 12 points.

Picture box

A box into which you can import graphics or scans.

Pixel

One of the tiny dots that make up a screen display or a scan.

Place

To import and position a story or graphic.

Plate

1. In XPress, a sheet printed when the Separation menu (in the Print dialog box) is set to On; contains only page items set in a particular color. 2. A thin sheet of material (usually metal) that carries the printing image; created by the print shop from a film negative.

PMS

Pantone **M**atching **S**ystem. Usually used as a prefix to a Pantone number for a specific color (e.g., PMS 286).

Point

Unit of measurement used in graphic design and typesetting. Equal to $\frac{1}{12}$ of a pica or $\frac{1}{72}$ of an inch.

Polygon box

A box that can by changed in shape. You can create a polygon box by drawing it from scratch with the Polygon Picture Box tool or by selecting an existing box and choosing the last option in the Box Shape submenu of the Item menu.

PostScript

Software language that controls the printing of typefaces and graphics on a page.

ppi

pixels **p**er **i**nch. Measure of resolution in a scanned image or of a monitor.

Process

1. Printing technology for reproducing full-color art and photos based on the use of four primary inks. 2. A primary ink, such as cyan, magenta, yellow or black.

Process simulation

Approximate reproduction of a special-formula color, such as a Pantone color, produced by overprinting tints of process inks.

Proof

An intermediate print produced for proofreading or for checking colors.

Prototype

Experimental version of a publication created to investigate design issues or problems.

Pull-quote

A text block containing an important or provocative quote from a story. Usually set in larger type with some sort of graphic device, such as a background tint or rules above and below.

R

Rag

An irregular edge in a type design.

Ragged bottom

A page or spread where columns end at a variety of points.

Ragged right

See *Align left*.

RC paper

Resin **C**oated paper. Photographic paper used for output from imagesetters.

Register

To align two or more color plates perfectly during printing.

Registration mark

A target symbol with crosshairs printed in the trim area of the page. Used by the print shop to precisely align color plates during printing.

Resolution

A measure of detail and visual quality. Screen, scanner and printer resolution are typically measured in dots per inch, while the resolution of printed images (halftones) is usually measured in lines per inch. In general, printers with a high dpi do a better job of printing images at a high lpi.

Reverse

An item printed in white over a darker tint or color.

RGB

Red, **G**reen, **B**lue. 1. The three primary colors of scanners and monitors. 2. The color file format produced by most scanners.

River

A visually distracting series of large word spaces running vertically through three or more lines of text. Usually caused by justified paragraph alignment.

Rough

A crude drawing or block layout of a page.

Rule

Straight line used as a graphic device or divider, usually between a quarter point and 12 points in thickness (weight).

Ruler guide

A movable guide that is dragged out from a document window ruler and placed on a page or on the pasteboard. Usually used as an aid for aligning items.

Run-in subhead

Lower level headline that appears as the beginning of a body paragraph. Usually bold, sometimes in a different typeface or point size.

Runaround polygon

The dotted shape that appears around a picture when you set Runaround to Manual. The polygon can be freely reshaped to change the contour of text behind the picture.

Running foot or head

See *Footer* or *Header*.

S

Sans serif

Any typeface that does not incorporate serifs in its letter-forms. Examples include Helvetica, Futura, Gill Sans and Univers.

Scan

noun: Photograph or artwork converted to an electronic image that can be modified on the computer and placed in a publication.
verb: To create such an image with a scanner.

Scanner

Device that can "read" artwork or a photo into an electronic format, such as TIFF.

Screen

Tint, or lighter shade of a color, produced by printing an ink as closely placed spots or lines. The darkness of a screen is specified as a percentage, such as "10%."

Screen frequency

See *lpi.*

Section

An arbitrary division within a document that allows a change in automatic page numbering. An entire document may also be designated as a section simply to force page numbering to begin at a number higher than one.

Section page name

A page name that's calculated from Section settings. Typical section page names include "iii," "A-4," and "§3.560." If you're using sections to change page numbering, it's the section page name, not the absolute page number, that's displayed in the page indicators and the Page menu dialogs.

Self-mailer

A publication designed to be mailed without an envelope. Requires the addition of a mailing panel on the front or back cover.

Separate

To print color separations.

Separations

Two or more printing plates that are combined during printing to create a multicolor page.

Serif
1. Any typeface that includes short perpendicular lines at the end of many letter strokes. Examples include Times, Palatino and Garamond.
2. The short line itself.

Service bureau
A company that offers high-resolution printing services.

Shade
The XPress term for tint.

Sidebar
Text related to a story but handled as a separate element.

Signature
A group of pages prepared as a large composite sheet for book printing on commercial presses. Usually 4, 8 or 16 pages per side.

Silverprint
A monochrome printer's proof created from film negatives.

Smart quotes
A setting in Application Preferences that allows you to choose from a variety of typographer's quotes (such as ") as a substitute for typewriter quotes (such as ").

Spot color
A color applied to certain elements in a page design but not others. Usually specified as a Pantone color.

Spread
A horizontal arrangement of pages. Usually, a spread is taken to mean two facing pages, though spreads can consist of three or more pages in a folder.

Stack
Mac only. A command in the Windows submenu (of the View menu) that arranges document windows as a diagonal series of equal-sized overlapping windows.

Stripping
Assembling film negatives, including type, photos, and artwork, into a single sheet of film that will be used to make a printing plate. Handled by the prepress department at a print shop.

Style override
Type style settings applied to a range of text after a paragraph style has been applied.

Style sheet
A unique combination of character, format, tab and rule settings. A style sheet defines how a certain type of paragraph should look and automates the application of complex settings.

Subhead
Lower level headline that appears within body of text. Usually bold, sometimes larger than the body type size. May have additional space before or after.

- -

T

Tab stop
An arrow icon that appears in the tabs ruler when you click on the ruler. A tab stop indicates how far a tab will push text to the right and how the text will be aligned to the stop.

Template
A blank or empty document set up with basic specifications (margin and column guides, master items, style sheets, etc.). Opening a template file produces a new, untitled copy that can be filled and saved under a new name.

Temporary Item tool
The four-headed arrow cursor that appears over an item when you hold down Command (on the Mac) or Ctrl (in Windows) while a tool other than the Item tool is active.

Text box
A box in which you can type or into which you can import a text file or word processing file.

Text box chain
A series of two or more text boxes that have been linked for continuous text flow with the Link tool or via the master chain icon.

Text flow
The automatic spilling of overset text from one box into another or from one column into another.

Text wrap
See *Auto Image rununaround,* *Item runaround* and *Manual runaround.*

Thumbnail

1. A special view of a document in which the pages appear very small and their contents cannot be edited in any way. Thumbnail pages can be rearranged within a document or copied to other documents with a drag of the mouse. 2. A printout in which pages are printed side by side in miniature. 3. A rough sketch made in preparation for final layout of a page.

TIFF

Tag **I**mage **F**ile **F**ormat. A file format for bitmaps of any resolution or color range. Usually used for scans.

Tile

A command that arranges document windows as equal-sized adjacent windows. On the Mac, available in the Windows submenu of the View menu. In Windows, available in the Windows menu as Tile Vertically or Tile Horizontally.

Tiling

A print dialog option that allows you to print a portion of a page on a sheet of paper. Often used to print oversized documents, but also handy for printing enlargements of a specific area. When set to Automatic, XPress will print successive portions of a page on as many sheets as is required to print the entire page. When set to Manual, XPress will print only the first portion of the page as designated by the current zero point of the rulers.

Tint

See *Screen*.

Track

1. A setting that adjusts letter spacing in proportion to type size. 2. In XPress, the term is also used to refer to kerning applied to a selected range of letters and kerning set as a paragraph-level attribute in a style sheet.

Trim

To cut away the edges of a publication prior to binding.

TruMatch

One of several color matching systems. TruMatch is specially designed for specifying colors in computer software as mixes of process inks.

Two-color

A design to be printed with two colors of ink, usually black and a Pantone spot color.

Two-up

A printing technique in which two pages, such as a spread, appear adjacent on a single sheet.

Type ornaments

Small graphics that are part of a typeface.

Type treatment

A design approach that relies solely on the positioning and manipulation of type without any graphics.

Type width

Software control that allows you to condense type. In XPress, use Horizontal/Vertical Scale in the Style menu.

Typeface

Letterforms of a specific design, style and weight, such as Helvetica Bold or Times Italic.

Typeset

To apply styling and formatting commands to text.

Typographer's quotes

Curly quotes. See also *Smart quotes*.

U-X

Unlink

To separate a text box from the chain it's currently connected to. Unlinking empties the box of its text but does not delete the text.

Update

To reimport a picture from disk without losing the current picture size, position or styling.

View indicator

The percentage readout that appears in the lower left corner of a document window. This percentage can be selected and changed to switch to a different magnification.

Weight

1. The thickness of a line, usually specified in points. 2. A variation of a typeface based on the thickness of letter strokes, specified with terms like Light, Roman, Book, Bold, Extra Bold or Heavy (though occasionally specified by number).

White space

Open areas around the page that provide relief from—or act as a counterpoint to—the text areas.

Widow

First line of a paragraph appearing alone at the bottom of a column. Sometimes also used to refer to a single word or partial word appearing alone on the last line of a paragraph.

Width

The XPress term for line weight.

Wrap

The movement of text from one line to the next.

XTension

A program designed to plug into XPress and add to or change its features. Most XTensions provide new drawing tools, menus, settings or palettes. XTensions cannot be launched separately; they're launched automatically as a part of XPress after they're placed in the QuarkXPress folder (or the XTension folder inside the QuarkXPress folder).

Index

Colophon

This book was developed entirely "from the desktop" using a variety of software on both Macintosh and Windows systems.

. . . .
Macintosh software

Not surprisingly, QuarkXPress was used for page layout and for all the examples. The book was begun in Version 3.3 and finished in Version 3.31. Illustrations were created using QuarkXPress, Photoshop, Capture and FreeHand. Early drafts of text were created in Word and FileMaker Pro. FileMaker data was imported and automatically styled using Em Software's XData XTension.

. . . .
Windows Software

Windows examples were created in QuarkXPress Version 3.3. Screen shots were exported with Corel PhotoPaint.

• • • • • • • • • •

Hardware

A Macintosh Centris 650 with 16mb of RAM and roughly 800mb of hard disk storage was used to create most of the illustrations and page layouts. A Macintosh IIci, a Macintosh IIcx and a Leading Edge 486 were used for additional illustrations, layout, template development and testing. Scans were created on a Hewlett-Packard ScanJet IIcx.

Pages were proofed on a RealTech Laser 960. Final pages were printed as film negatives on a Sprint 110. One-color pages were printed at 2540 dpi with a screen frequency of 133 lpi. Four-color pages were printed at 2540 dpi with a screen frequency of 133 lpi.

• • • •

Type

The primary typefaces used throughout the book are from the New Century Schoolbook and Gill Sans families.

Section titles, folios, subheads, sidebar heads and body type are set in various styles of New Century Schoolbook. Chapter titles and header titles are set in Gill Sans Bold Condensed; sidebars, captions and callouts are set in Gill Sans Plain and Light.

Typefaces included in the example publications are from the following families: American Typewriter, Caslon, Century Condensed, Futura, Futura Condensed, Helvetica Compressed, Helvetica Condensed, Lubalin Graph, Madrone, Mayhem, Palatino, Pepita, Tekton, Times and Utopia.

● ● ● ● ● ● ● ● ● ●

Style sheets

There were plenty—as you can see here. In case you were wondering, the dotted rules that appear above subheads and sidebar heads were inserted automatically by the style sheets; they're 30% black, offset 1 pica above the baseline, with Length set to Text (in the case of subheads) or Indents (in the case of sidebar heads). Subheads were set to "keep" with the next paragraph, while body paragraphs were set to "keep" the first two lines and the last two lines of each paragraph together. Bullet symbols were set in their own style sheet using dotted paragraph rules, then inserted into body text using anchored text boxes.

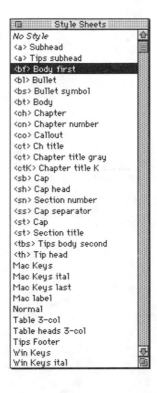

● ● ● ● ● ● ● ● ● ● ● ● ●

Document setup

Page size was set at 44p3 by 55p6 with the Facing Pages check box on. Margins were set at 7p6 for the top, 5p6 for the inside and bottom, and 4p6 for the outside; ruler guides were added to the master pages to divide the body and sidebar areas.

Four master page designs were used: one with a full-bleed black background for section title pages; one with a full-bleed gray background for the reverse side of these pages; one for chapter title pages; and one for all remaining pages. Title headers and footer graphics were placed on these last two master pages. These last two master pages also contained automatic text boxes in the body area and empty sidebar boxes in the outer columns.

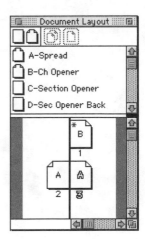

File formats and delivery

Example illustrations created in QuarkXPress were saved as EPS files with the OPI menu to Include Images. All final screen shots were exported from Photoshop as compressed TIFF files. Scans of the printed publications shown in the Gallery were color-corrected, sharpened and exported from Photoshop with resolutions ranging from 250 to 300 pixels per inch; most were saved as grayscale or CMYK JPEG files, though several required clipping paths and were therefore exported as EPS files.

After final editing, XPress files and all linked graphics were gathered onto six 88mb SyQuest cartridges using the Collect For Output command. Files for the companion CD-ROM were delivered for CD mastering on two additional 88mb cartridges.

The End!

Notes

DESIGN AND CONQUER!

Photoshop f/x

$39.95

320 pages, illustrated in full color

ISBN: 1-56604-179-1

Push Photoshop's creative limits with this essential idea sourcebook! Full color throughout, *Photoshop f/x* takes users step-by-step through an impressive gallery of professional artists' illustrations. Chapters include techniques for using Photoshop and third-party filters, customizing filters, masking, advanced channels, 3D programs and more. The companion CD-ROM contains third-party filters from Kai's Power Tools, Andromeda, plus demos, photos and software.

Advertising From the Desktop

$24.95

427 pages, illustrated

ISBN: 1-56604-064-7

Advertising From the Desktop offers unmatched design advice and helpful how-to instructions for creating persuasive ads. With tips on how to choose fonts, select illustrations, apply special effects and more, this book is an idea-packed resource for improving the looks and effects of your ads.

The Presentation Design Book, Second Edition

$24.95

320 pages, illustrated

ISBN: 1-56604-014-0

The Presentation Design Book is filled with thoughtful advice and instructive examples for creating business presentation visuals, including charts, overheads, type, etc., that help you communicate and persuade. The *Second Edition* adds advice on the use of multimedia. For use with any software or hardware.

The Gray Book, Second Edition

$24.95
262 pages, illustrated
ISBN: 1-56604-073-6

This "idea gallery" for desktop publishers offers a lavish variety of the most interesting black, white and gray graphic effects that can be achieved with laser printers, scanners and high-resolution output devices. The *Second Edition* features new illustrations, synopses and steps, added tips and an updated appendix.

Looking Good in Print, Third Edition

$24.95
412 pages, illustrated
ISBN: 1-56604-047-7

For use with any software or hardware, this desktop design bible has become the standard among novice and experienced desktop publishers alike. With over 300,000 copies in print, *Looking Good in Print* is even better, with new sections on photography and scanning. Learn the fundamentals of professional-quality design along with tips on resources and reference materials.

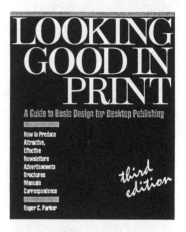

Newsletters From the Desktop, Second Edition

$24.95
306 pages, illustrated
ISBN: 1-56604-133-3

Now the millions of desktop publishers who produce newsletters can learn how to improve the designs of their publications. Filled with helpful design tips and illustrations, as well as hands-on tips for building a great looking publication. Includes an all-new color gallery of professionally designed newsletters, offering publishers at all levels a wealth of ideas and inspiration.

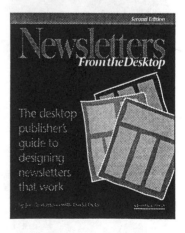

Available at bookstores and computer stores everywhere!
Or call toll-free
800/743-5369 (U.S. only)

MACINTOSH

MAC BOOKS—MAGIC & MASTERY

Explore Cyberspace!

The Mac Internet Tour Guide
$27.95
350 pages, illustrated
ISBN: 1-56604-062-0

Mac users can now navigate the Internet the easy way: by pointing and clicking, dragging and dropping. In easy-to-read, entertaining prose, Internet expert Michael Fraase leads you through installing and using the software enclosed in the book to send and receive email, transfer files, search the Internet's vast resources and more! BONUS: Free trial access and two free electronic updates.

Handy 3-in-1 Guide!

Mac, Word & Excel Desktop Companion, Second Edition
$24.95
308 pages, illustrated
ISBN: 1-56604-130-9

Why clutter your desk with three guides? This money saver gets you up and running with Apple's System 7.1 software and the latest versions of Microsoft Word and Excel for the Mac. A complete overview, examples of each program's commands, tools and features and step-by-step tutorials guide you easily along the learning curve for maximum Macintosh productivity!

Software $avings!

The Mac Shareware 500, Second Edition
$34.95
504 pages, illustrated
ISBN: 1-56604-076-0

This book is a fantastic reference for any designer or desktop publisher interested in saving money by using the vast resources shareware offers. Literally thousands of fonts, graphics, clip-art files and utilities are available for downloading via dozens of online services. To get you started, this book includes two disks of shareware.

WEB WALKING WITH MOSAIC

Mosaic. The Internet's **KILLER APP**. *Able to leap global spaces in a burst of electrons. Able to tie together text, graphics, sound files and video across the* **WORLD WIDE WEB**. *Able to* **BROWSE HYPERTEXT** *with the click of a mouse.*

The **MOSAIC QUICK TOUR**, *available for both Mac and Windows, is the perfect guide for this revolutionary application. Learn what the World Wide Web is all about. Learn how to use Mosaic to read newsgroups. To transfer files. To conduct Gopher searches. And, of course, to browse the exponentially expanding Web. Not to mention author* **GARETH BRANWYN***'s expansive tour of cool Web pages.*

The price for all this valuable information? $12.00 suggested retail. Order today.

Available at bookstores and computer stores everywhere! Or call

800/743-5369

To order any Ventana Press title, fill out this order form and mail it to us with payment for quick shipment.

	Quantity	Price	Total
The Mac Internet Tour Guide	_____	x $27.95 =	$ _____
Mac, Word & Excel Desktop Companion, 2nd Edition	_____	x $24.95 =	$ _____
The Mac Shareware 500, 2nd Edition	_____	x $34.95 =	$ _____
The System 7.5 Book, 3rd Edition	_____	x $24.95 =	$ _____
The Official America Online for Macintosh Membership Kit & Tour Guide, 2nd Edition	_____	x $27.95 =	$ _____
Voodoo Mac, 2nd Edition	_____	x $24.95 =	$ _____
Photoshop f/x	_____	x $39.95 =	$ _____
Advertising From the Desktop	_____	x $24.95 =	$ _____
The Presentation Design Book, 2nd Edition	_____	x $24.95 =	$ _____
The Gray Book, 2nd Edition	_____	x $24.95 =	$ _____
Looking Good in Print, 3rd Edition	_____	x $24.95 =	$ _____
Newsletters From the Desktop, 2nd Edition	_____	x $24.95 =	$ _____
Mosaic Quick Tour for Mac	_____	x $12.00 =	$ _____
		Subtotal =	$ _____

SHIPPING:

For all regular orders, please <u>add</u> $4.50/first book, $1.35/each additional.		=	$ _____
For "two-day air," <u>add</u> $8.25/first book, $2.25/each additional.		=	$ _____
For orders to Canada, <u>add</u> $6.50/book.		=	$ _____
For orders sent C.O.D., <u>add</u> $4.50 to your shipping rate.		=	$ _____
North Carolina residents must <u>add</u> 6% sales tax.		=	$ _____
International orders must pay additional charges.		TOTAL =	$ _____

Name_____ Company_____

Address (No PO Box)_____

City_____ State_____ Zip _____

Daytime Telephone _____

___ Payment enclosed ___VISA ___MC # _____Exp. Date _____

Signature _____

Mail or fax to: Ventana Press, PO Box 2468, Chapel Hill, NC 27515 ☎ 919/942-0220 Fax 919/942-1140

CAN'T WAIT? CALL OR FAX TOLL-FREE
☎ 800/743-5369 FAX 800/877-7955 (US only)

Available at bookstores and computer stores everywhere!

Notes

Notes